D1732911

CONVERGING THEMES IN PSYCHOTHERAPY

Marvin R. Goldfried received his B.A. from Brooklyn College in 1957, and his Ph.D. from State University of New York at Buffalo in 1961. After holding teaching positions at Buffalo and the University of Rochester, he moved to the State University of New York at Stony Brook, where he currently is Professor of Psychology and Psychiatry. He has also been a visiting professor Bar-Ilan University in Israel and at the University of California at Berkeley. He is a Diplomate in Clinical Psychology of the American Board of Professional Psychology, a Fellow in the American Psychological Association, and a member of the Association for the Advancement of Behavior Therapy. He has served as an editorial consultant to numerous professional journals, and has published in the areas of assessment and therapy. His previous coauthored books include *Rorschach Handbook of Clinical and Research Applications*, *Behavior Change Through Self-Control*, and *Clinical Behavior Therapy*. He also maintains a limited private practice in the New York City area.

Contributors

Franz Alexander, M.D.

Stephen A. Appelbaum, Ph.D.

Lee Birk, M.D.

John Paul Brady, M.D.

Ann W. Brinkley-Birk, Ph.D.

Gerald C. Davison, Ph.D.

Paul A. Dewald, M.D.

John Dollard, Ph.D.

Gerard Egan, Ph.D.

James Fadiman, Ph.D.

Jerome D. Frank, M.D., Ph.D.

Sol L. Garfield, Ph.D.

Merton M. Gill, M.D.

Arnold P. Goldstein, Ph.D.

Roy R. Grinker, Sr., M.D.

Irwin Hoffman, Ph.D.

Walter Kempler, M.D.

Richard Kurtz, Ph.D.

Ted Landsman, Ph.D.

Arnold A. Lazarus, Ph.D.

Judd Marmor, M.D.

Abraham H. Maslow, Ph.D.

Neal E. Miller, Ph.D.

Wendy Padawer, B.A.

Morris B. Parloff, Ph.D.

Paul J. Poppen, Ph.D.

Victor Raimy, Ph.D.

David F. Ricks, Ph.D.

Saul Rosenzweig, Ph.D.

Julian B. Rotter, Ph.D.

Anthony Ryle, D.M., F.R.C. Psych.

Irwin G. Sarason, Ph.D.

Hans H. Strupp, Ph.D.

Paul L. Wachtel, Ph.D.

Abraham Wandersman, Ph.D.

CONVERGING THEMES IN PSYCHOTHERAPY

Trends in Psychodynamic, Humanistic, and Behavioral Practice

Marvin R. Goldfried, Ph.D., Editor

Foreword by Hans H. Strupp, Ph.D.

CALIFORNIA SCHOOL OF PROFESSIONAL PSYCHOLOGY LOS ANGELES

SPRINGER PUBLISHING COMPANY
New York

To those clinicians and researchers
who are destined to advance the field

Springer Publishing Company, Inc.
200 Park Avenue South
New York, New York 10003

82 83 84 85 86 / 10 9 8 7 6 5 4 3 2 1

Library of Congress Cataloging in Publication Data

Main entry under title:

Converging themes in psychotherapy.

  Includes bibliographies and indexes.
  1. Psychotherapy. 2. Psychoanalysis. 3. Behavior
therapy. 4. Humanistic psychology. I. Goldfried,
Marvin R. [DNLM: 1. Psychotherapy—Methods. WM 420
C766]
RC480.C65   616.89'14   82-688
ISBN 0-8261-3620-6   AACR2
ISBN 0-8261-3621-4 (pbk.)

Printed in the United States of America

Contents

Foreword

Dr. Marvin Goldfried has shown impressive dedication to the goal of achieving some form of rapprochement or consensus among competing forms of psychotherapy. Being in sympathy with his efforts, and having supported them in a modest way, I appreciate his invitation to write a foreword to what I consider an ambitious and forward-looking enterprise.

As a participant observer of developments in psychotherapy over the past three decades, I have been impressed by a progressive erosion of the barriers that once separated divergent theoretical orientations and "schools." Much evidence in support of this observation could be cited, but none is perhaps more convincing than the decline of acrimonious debates and open hostility, both within and across theoretical orientations. I attribute this phenomenon less to a change in human nature than to a gradual maturation of the fields, or, more specifically, of its enlightened exponents. To be sure, the scene continues to be riddled with sects and cults; however, we also have a number of thoughtful clinicians, theoreticians, and researchers whose commitment is to the understanding of clinical phenomena rather than to the propagation of a faith. Goldfried and likeminded colleagues exemplify the searching and restless spirit of those who are dissatisfied with the status quo of knowledge in our field and are eager to extend its frontiers. Entrenched theories never allow this to happen; only dispassionate observation of the phenomena, critical analyses, and ingenuity can lead to better theories. Thus, Goldfried and the members of an emerging "network" seek to develop the *scientific* aspects of psychotherapy. Can one "kick the Zeitgeist," as Joseph Matarazzo once put it? No one can be sure, but the chances are increased if we can create an open forum instead of retreating to "institutes." History has shown that psychotherapy is peculiarly vulnerable to the latter, typically with disastrous results.

From a personal perspective, two basic questions have been in the forefront of my interest over the years. The first relates to the basic problem of what constitutes psychotherapeutic change; the second, to how the therapeutic change is brought about. The two questions are obviously intertwined, and both are of vital interest to therapists and researchers alike.

Since psychotherapy is concerned with psychological processes, there

are obviously many different ways in which these processes can be conceptualized. It is also clear that, in all forms of psychotherapy, the patient
learns something, and the accumulating evidence strongly suggests that
there are common elements in therapeutic learning. Conversely, it does
not appear to be true that different forms of psychotherapy produce sharply
divergent results, although the routes by which therapeutic results are
achieved may give the appearance of being discrepant. Thus, it makes
eminently good sense to focus attention on psychological processes that
give rise to personality and behavior change that the patient, the therapist,
and society at large characterize as "therapeutic." The goal of science is
always to understand the phenomena of nature, not to promote the relative
virtues of name brands, unless it can be shown that the effective ingredients of one brand are measurably superior to another. Since the search for
"special" ingredients has proven rather unproductive, we are confronted
with the strong possibility that the preponderant weight of therapeutic
change is borne by psychological forces that are shared by the various
therapeutic approaches despite the fact that different languages and concepts are being used.

This is not to suggest that all therapists are doing "the same thing,"
that clinical skills are irrelevant, that outcomes are indistinguishable, or
that one particular therapeutic approach may not be preferable to another
under particular circumstances. For example, very different—and perhaps
irreconcilable—strategies may be called for in getting someone to stop
smoking versus helping a person overcome a lifelong pattern of dependency rooted in childhood deprivations. What I am suggesting is: (1) Whenever a therapeutic interaction produces measurable therapeutic change,
the patient (client) has undergone a learning experience; that is, some form
of "inner change" has occurred; (2) The character of the relationship between the two participants, their interaction, has somehow played a part.
This follows if we view psychotherapy as a form of interpersonal learning,
as I think we should.

While it may sound trite, this highlights the fact that there is a
"teacher," a "student," and a learning process having a particular "outcome." I believe that we have made a certain amount of progress in coming
to grips with the pertinent factors whose understanding must be refined in
the future. There has also been a greater appreciation that the answers are
not likely to be found in the "techniques" favored by a given "theoretical
orientation," but rather that therapeutic change is embedded in the matrix
of the *transactions* between a particular patient (client) and a particular
therapist.

Unfortunately, the field has not yet developed very powerful methodologies to deal with complex interpersonal processes as well as the intrapsychic changes to which they give rise. Progress has also been greatly

hampered, as this volume documents, by idiosyncratic languages that may or may not refer to the same processes. Goldfried and his colleagues are embarked on a concerted effort to determine how these gaps can be bridged, which will prove to be a difficult task.

To give but a few hints of the prevailing confusion: There is as yet very little consensus on what constitutes "improvement" in psychotherapy, or, in fact, what a particular "treatment" is designed to "improve." How can we measure change, and what is the meaning of change? Can we equate one person's "well-being" with that of another? What is meant by "symptom change" as opposed to "characterological change"? How long must a particular change endure before it qualifies as "therapeutic"? Who is the final arbiter of therapeutic change—the patient, a clinical observer, a significant other, or an insurance company? Problems become more complex when we address the question of what therapists "do," how they do it, or what particular activities produce "mutative" changes.

A great sign of progress is represented by the shifting attention to studies of what therapists do as opposed to what they say they do. To this end, sound and videotape records of therapeutic interviews are a great advance over condensed progress notes or the traditional case history. However, there may be a great hiatus between an external observer's evaluations of the therapist's "activity" and the patient's *experience* of that activity. In short, we cannot capture the process of change, and usually we can judge it only after it has occurred. There are probably various avenues for producing the same kind of change, and what may "work" in a particular instance may depend to a very significant extent upon the peculiar constellation of patient, therapist, and manner in which their "personalities" interact.

I continue to believe that psychotherapy can become a science—at least up to a point—although there will always remain many imponderables. To further these efforts, the field will need all the help it can get. Since the best minds are not likely to be found in any one theoretical camp, and since it is reasonable to assume that different approaches may enrich each other, the scientific community can only profit from efforts by its best representatives to seek a clearer understanding of what each is about. This book may be only a modest beginning, but I am convinced that it is an important step in the right direction. Thus, I wish it Godspeed!

Hans H. Strupp
Nashville, Tennessee

Preface

The prospect of integrating varying approaches to psychotherapy has intrigued mental health workers for some time. Only since the mid-1970's, however, has the issue of rapprochement begun to develop into a clearly delineated "area of interest." Previously, it was more of a latent than a dominant theme. Indeed, the task of conducting a literature search for this book was somewhat difficult because the topic of rapprochement rarely has been indexed in bibliographic sources. Nonetheless, the hope of finding some consensus in the psychotherapy field can be traced back some fifty years, and it has been fascinating to observe how the expression of this goal has tended to reemerge periodically since then.

The argument has been advanced by serveral writers that with increased experience, therapists tend to function more similarly in clinical practice. That such commonalities do exist sheds light on some significant therapeutic principles of change as these common factors have managed to emerge in spite of biases inherent in each of the varying theoretical orientations. To conclude that "we all do the same thing," however, and then complacently return to our therapeutic practice as usual, will probably do little to advance the field.

As a professional who is identified primarily with behavior therapy, I have become acutely aware of the strengths as well as the limitations of the intervention procedures associated with this orientation. In reading the psychodynamic and humanistic literature, and in my conversations with colleagues who work within these frameworks, it has become evident that professionals from other orientations are going through a period of self-examination also. I think that we have reached the point in the development of the field of psychotherapy where intellectual and professional honesty demand that each of us, regardless of orientation, acknowledge what we can and cannot do successfully. And in making this acknowledgment, we also should entertain the possibility that our areas of weakness might be complemented by another orientation's area of strength.

This book, which addresses itself to these issues, is intended to have broad appeal. The material included in this volume cuts across professional affiliations and is relevant to psychiatry, psychology, counseling, and social work. It advocates no single theoretical orientation, and consequently has relevance to psychodynamic, humanistic, and behavioral points of view. And it deals with topics that are of concern to both the clinician and researcher.

I would like to take this opportunity to express my gratitude to numerous colleagues and friends for encouraging me to pursue the work reflected in this book. Specific appreciation goes to those who offered their comments and feedback on the introductory chapter, including Allen Bergin, Jerome Frank, Sol Garfield, Anita Powers Goldfried, Sheldon Korchin, Clive Robins, and Paul Wachtel. I thank Isabelle Belman for her very competent secretarial and editorial efforts in putting together this volume, and to Cory Newman for his work on compiling the index. Work on the book was greatly facilitated by National Institute of Mental Health Grant #24327. I owe a debt to my clients who, because they were not familiar with the literature and consequently did not always respond the way they were "supposed to," taught me to entertain options I had not considered originally. And finally, a very special appreciation goes to my wife, Anita, and sons, Dan and Mike, for just being themselves.

Part I
A Perspective
on Rapprochement

Although the topic of rapprochement across varying theoretical orientations has been considered off and on over the past 50 years, it is only recently that this issue has started to develop into what may be called an "area of interest." The chapter by Goldfried and Padawer, prepared especially for this volume, documents the growing attitude among professionals that no one orientation can adequately guide therapists in their clinical work. Goldfried and Padawer trace some of the early concerns with rapprochement and describe what appear to be common elements that cut across different orientations as well as the unique contributions that each may have to make. In considering the issue of the relationship between research and practice, the argument is put forth that it is the actual clinical functioning of the experienced therapist that should be the point of departure in our future clinical research efforts. Goldfried and Padawer also maintain that work in the area of rapprochement requires not only the development of a common and neutral language system for communication but also a professional network to help support further efforts in this general area. Many of the themes developed within this introductory chapter are documented throughout the remainder of the book by the writings of leading clinicians and researchers in the field of psychotherapy.

Chapter 1

Current Status and Future Directions in Psychotherapy

Marvin R. Goldfried and Wendy Padawer

It has been observed that there currently exist more than 130 different approaches to psychotherapy (Parloff, 1979). Certainly, one may argue that diversity is good; we should let "a thousand flowers bloom," as this reflects the field's healthy growth and development. While there may be a certain amount of truth to this argument, there nonetheless comes a time when one needs to question where fruitful diversity ends and where chaos begins. We believe that point has now arrived.

Within the past decade or so, the field of psychotherapy has been characterized by considerable soul-searching, whereby the paradigms within which therapists have typically functioned have been undergoing considerable strain (e.g., Appelbaum, 1975, 1979; Bergin, 1971; Bergin & Strupp, 1972; Birk & Brinkley-Birk, 1974; Brady, 1968; Brown, 1978; Burton, 1976; Dewald, 1976; Egan, 1975; Feather & Rhoads, 1972; Ferster, 1974; Ford & Kendall, 1979; Frank, 1976; Garfield, 1980; Garfield & Kurtz, 1976; Goldfried, 1980; Goldfried & Davison, 1976; Goldstein, 1976; Grinker, 1976; Gurman, 1981; Horwitz, 1976; Landsman, 1974; Lazarus, 1977; Lewis, 1972; Liberman, 1972; London, 1972; Marmor, 1971; Marmor & Woods, 1980; Martin, 1972; Prochaska, 1979; Raimy, 1975, 1976; Rhoads, 1981; Ricks, Wandersman, & Poppen, 1976; Segraves & Smith, 1976; Silverman, 1974; Strupp, 1976a, 1979; Wachtel, 1975, 1977; Wolf, 1966; Woody, 1971). In essence, what practicing clinicians are beginning to recognize is that their particular theoretical frame of reference is not always congruent with their clinical observations. There is an increasing tendency to look toward common factors that cut across all schools of thought, as well as a growing willingness to incorporate procedures into one's clinical armamentarium that may come from other therapeutic orientations.

The field of psychotherapy has evolved over the past 100 years to a state of enormous complexity. We are referring not only to the actual process of therapy itself but also to the many factions that currently exist within the field. There are varying theoretical orientations, different professional disciplines, and applied versus research considerations. As shown in Figure 1.1, this diversity provides us with 18 separate and at times antagonistic factions. In actuality, this figure is somewhat oversimplified in that there are numerous subschools within each orientation, variations in the format of the intervention (e.g., individual, group, family), and various other professions (e.g., nurse practitioners, clergy) that are involved in the practice of psychotherapy. Moreover, one may add still other dimensions to this illustration, such as level of experience and the setting (e.g., clinic, hospital, private practice) within which one functions professionally. It certainly would be a most difficult task to discuss each and every one of those dimensions that prevent us from achieving a more unified approach to the

Figure 1.1. Graphic Depiction of Factions in Psychotherapy

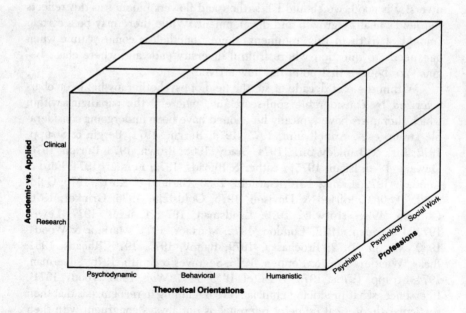

practice of psychotherapy. Although we fully acknowledge that professional rivalries very much characterize the status of the field, we have decided not to deal with this issue in this chapter, as we believe that our efforts can be more fruitfully placed on the other two demensions—namely, theoretical orientation and academic versus applied settings.

We begin the chapter with a description of some of the early attempts at rapprochement across theoretical orientations, after which we suggest that the field may currently be more receptive to serious efforts in that direction than it ever has been before. This receptivity is reflected in the paradigm strain that currently seems to exist within psychodynamic, behavioral, and humanistic approaches to therapy. More and more therapists from each orientation are beginning to question the adequacy of their particular approach. While we acknowledge that it may be difficult to find agreement among the psychotherapies at a theoretical level—at least at present—there nonetheless are possibilities for finding commonalities at a lower level of abstraction, namely the clinical strategy or principle of change. In addition to considering potential points of overlap, we also discuss the need to focus on the unique contributions of any given orientation, particularly those that may serve to enhance our therapeutic effectiveness. Relevant issues in the area of research in psychotherapy are discussed, and a case is made for keeping our research efforts closely tied to what goes on in actual clinical practice. It is in the observation of what clinicians *actually do* that we are likely to arrive at common and unique factors in therapeutic change. For any serious attempts to be made in delineating points of overlap and unique contributions across orientations, however, a common language is needed. Although it is possible to begin such efforts by making use of the vernacular, it has independently been suggested by individuals from varying orientations that a real potential exists in the use of concepts from experimental cognitive psychology in discussing the psychotherapy process. We end the chapter with a discussion of the social system that appears to be supporting some of the current factions in psychotherapy and possible ways in which such existing barriers may be overcome.

Early Stirrings

In analyzing the development of any field, it is often fascinating to trace the historical origins of contemporary thinking. As in the case of almost any kind of historical analysis, however, one is never sure of the impact that certain earlier events have had on later thought and behavior. Quite often, innovative concepts and findings are initially ignored or rejected completely, only to be assimilated into the mainstream at a later time (Barber,

1961). We are particularly fascinated with the possibility that the ultimate impact of an idea often has more to do with the mere fact that a topic has appeared in the literature than with the specific nature of the idea itself. Whether one agrees with the idea or not, it calls the field's attention to an issue. In a sense, the introduction of new ideas may have a consciousness-raising function, as it sensitizes us to otherwise neglected areas of thought. In the field of psychotherapy, many notions have continued to live on over the years, whereas others have failed to pass the test of time. Still other areas of concern disappear after their introduction, only to re-emerge at a later time when the zeitgeist becomes more hospitable. The entire issue of developing a rapprochement across different therapeutic orientations appears to fit into this last category.

In one of the early steps in the direction of rapprochement, Thomas French presented a paper at the meeting of the American Psychiatric Association in 1932 dealing with the relationship between psychoanalysis and Pavlovian conditioning. This presentation was published in the following year (French, 1933), together with the reactions of several of the members of the audience. Taking these two lines of inquiry, which represented "almost opposite poles of scientific approach" and which focused on very different kinds of material (impulses and drives versus simple reflexes), French attempted to draw a number of conceptual links between these two disciplines. In his long and detailed treatise, parallels were made between the Pavlovian notions of inhibition and extinction and the psychoanalytic concept of repression. He compared differentiation (discrimination training) to sublimation, suggesting that acceptable and unacceptable manifestations of impulsive tendencies were differentiated through the learning process. French also noted that what psychoanalysts referred to as an individual's more general adjustment to reality may very well reflect learning processes based on conditioning principles.

Given this conceptual leap, and certainly the time at which it was introduced, it should come as little surprise to learn that French received mixed reactions from his audience which, for the most part, was skeptical. Having had personal familiarity with both the psychoanalytic and Pavlovian movements, Adolf Meyer began by questioning:

> I have asked myself, Why is it that we have not made more of the verbalization which has shown us this morning the convergence of kindred efforts to get at truth and at fact? Why have those tendencies not taken more shape with us than they actually have? [In French, 1933, pp. 1200–1201].

Meyer goes on to suggest that the phenomena dealt with by therapists are indeed most complex, and, moreover,

It is important to get to simple terms and to simple investigations, but . . . we deal with facts that we want to cultivate side by side and that we do not want to substitute for each other too quickly. Let them be stimulations, each set of facts in its own way, and thus enjoy the convergencies which show in such discussions as we have had this morning [p. 1201].

The response by A. Myerson was not nearly as understanding, as he confessed:

I was tempted to call for a bell-boy and ask him to page John B. Watson, Ivan Pavlov, and Sigmund Freud, while Dr. French was reading his paper. I think Pavlov would have exploded; and what would have happened to Watson is scandalous to contemplate, since the whole of his behavioristic school is founded on the conditioned reflex . . . . Freud . . . would be scandalized by such a rapprochement made by one of his pupils, reading a paper of this kind [In French, 1933, p. 1201].

On the other hand, there were those who were far more receptive. Gregory Zilboorg commented:

I do not believe that these two lines of investigation could be passed over very lightly. . . . There is here an attempt to point out, regardless of structure and gross pathology, that while dealing with extremely complex functional units both in the physiological laboratory and in the clinic, we can yet reduce them to comparatively simple phenomena [In French, 1933, pp. 1198–1199].

In response to these various reactions, French offered the following rebuttal:

I think that the comments on my paper can be classified into two groups. The first set of comments take it for granted that it is a priori impossible to make any really useful correlation between two types of scientific approach that are so fundamentally different as those of Pavlov and Freud; in other words, that, whatever interest may attach to them, analogies such as I have been bringing forward, can only be regarded as amusing play. I am attempting, however, quite seriously, to make a detailed comparison of the work of the two schools and hope that there will be some who will be willing to examine my evidence in detail instead of rejecting it in advance as an attempt to solve the impossible.

Turning to the second group of comments, I agree most heartily with Dr. Zilboorg's suggestion that these analogies should have further experimental confirmation. The usefulness of such a correlation as I have been attempting this morning can be none other than that of stimulating further experimental and clinical work in both fields in order to check up the correlations between them [French, 1933, p. 1202].

    In the following year, Kubie (1934) extended French's thinking by
analyzing the relationship that the conditioned reflex had to psychoanalytic
technique. Kubie noted that Pavlov had dealt with the distinction between
conscious and unconscious phenomena and suggested that the association
between events that were not in an individual's awareness probably took
place under a state of inhibition. Kubie further observed that certain psychoanalytic methods—such as the passive role of the analyst and the encouragement of spontaneous free association—may be serving to remove
those external inhibitions that then allow the patient's learned associations
to emerge into conscious awareness.

    In a brief but most interesting paper, Rosenzweig (1936) outlined what
he viewed as common factors cutting across all forms of psychotherapy. He
questioned the validity of any specific theoretical explanations for why a
given approach to therapy might work, suggesting that the effectiveness of
diverse therapeutic interventions might have more to do with factors that are
common to the different approaches. The three common factors he
outlined—which have continually re-emerged in the writings of others—
were as follows: (1) The therapist's personality plays an important role in
influencing the patient/client, regardless of the particular orientation one
may embrace. Acknowledging that it is difficult to define the characteristics
of good therapists with any degree of precision, Rosenzweig nonetheless
suggested that their stimulating and inspiring qualities may have some sort
of catalytic effect. (2) The interpretations offered by therapists produce
change, but not because of the inherent correctness of these interpretations.
Rather, argued Rosenzweig, it is the therapist's presentation of an alternative, plausible view of the problem that distressed individuals may use to
replace what previously may have been a state of confusion. (3) Although
different psychological explanations of the patient's/client's problem may
point to different aspects of their psychological functioning, human behavior
is so multifaceted that a change in any one area of functioning can often have
a synergistic effect on other areas of functioning. Consequently, suggested
Rosenzweig, the change process may be implemented from any one of a
number of different starting points.

    In addition to enumerating these common factors, Rosenzweig did
acknowledge that it may ultimately turn out that some theories of personality may be shown to be more adequate than others, and that certain kinds
of therapeutic interventions may prove to be more effective than others for
certain kinds of psychological problems. Rosenzweig's objective in this
paper, however, was to point to the commonalities, at least as he was able
to determine them at that time.

    In tracing the history of rapprochement across therapeutic orienta-
tions, it is, of course, fitting to point to the influence of Dollard and
Miller's important work *Personality and Psychotherapy*, which is still in

print since its original publication in 1950. Dedicated to "Freud and Pavlov and their students," this classic presents a detailed translation of psychoanalytic thinking in learning-theory terms. Going well beyond the writings of French and of Kubie, Dollard and Miller outlined in great detail how such psychoanalytic concepts as repression, anxiety, regression, displacement, conflict, and the like may be understood from within a learning framework, and how various psychoanalytic techniques may assist patients in learning new ways of functioning. In discussing the important role of the therapist in bringing about change, they pointed to factors that may very well cut across all therapeutic orientations. Thus, they maintained that therapists' ability to support an individual's attempt at changing comes from their expressed interest, empathy, and open approval of such efforts. Dollard and Miller further suggested that the therapist's role is that of a model, demonstrating to clients/patients that heretofore upsetting topics can be thought about, discussed, and handled in a calmer way.

As an aside, we might note that behavior therapists have frequently argued that the work of Dollard and Miller has had little impact on the development of behavioral procedures, as the authors merely translated existing psychoanalytic concepts and techniques into learning terms. However, the very fact that so many behavior therapists have noted that the impact of this book was negligible also suggests that it was widely read. Even if one found little merit in Dollard and Miller's work, it nonetheless may very well have served the kind of consciousness-raising function we alluded to earlier, calling the field's attention to the issue of rapprochement. A careful reading of the book, however, uncovers what appear to be the roots of many contemporary behavioral techniques, such as the use of modeling procedures, reciprocal inhibition, hierarchically arranged tasks and the reinforcement of gradual approximations toward a goal, the reinforcing characteristics of the therapist, the use of masturbation in the treatment of orgasmic dysfunctions, the utility of problem-solving methods, and the importance of analyzing the reinforcing characteristic of the patient's/client's environment.[1]

Some 30 years after French delivered his address on Pavlov and psychoanalytic theory to the Annual Meeting of the American Psychiatric Association, Franz Alexander stood before the same organization and presented his views on what learning theory had to contribute to the dynamics of psychotherapy (Alexander, 1963). As a therapist dedicated to innovation

---

[1]In this regard, Rotter's *Social Learning and Clinical Psychology*, published in 1954, similarly had "minimal" impact on behavior therapy, despite the fact that Rotter wrote about the importance of standards for self-reinforcement, stressed the need to reinforce adaptive alternative behaviors, described problem-solving techniques, dealt with expectations and cognitions, stressed the importance of self-monitoring, and in general indicated that it was important for the science of psychotherapy to extrapolate from laboratory-derived principles of psychology to the clinical situation.

throughout much of his career, he deplored the absence of change in certain psychoanalytic circles, arguing that "no medical practitioner could treat patients with the same methods he learned 50 years ago without being considered antiquated" (p. 440). He argued for greater flexibility in the use of psychotherapeutic techniques, including the recognition that "corrective emotional experiences" could produce therapeutic change without extensive reconstruction of a patient's past history. His own research, involving a detailed analysis of tape recordings made of psychoanalytic sessions, provided more objective observations of what transpired during the therapeutic interaction. Echoing what Rosenzweig had suggested earlier, Alexander saw much that went on therapeutically that was not readily explained in terms of psychoanalytic theory. In fact, he came to a somewhat startling conclusion:

> In studying this transactional material I came to the conviction that the therapeutic process can best be understood in terms of learning theory. Particularly the principle of reward and punishment and also the influence of repetitive experiences can be clearly recognized [p. 446].

He went on to suggest:

> Learning theory appears to be at present the most satisfactory framework for the evaluation of observational data and for making valid generalizations. As it continually happens at certain phases of thought development in all fields of science, different independent approaches merge and become integrated with each other. At present, we are witnessing the beginnings of a most promising integration of psychoanalytic theory with learning theory, which may lead to unpredictable advances in the theory and practice of the psychotherapies [p. 448].

Before concluding this discussion of some of the historical roots of rapprochement, we might make note of Carl Rogers' (1963) comments on this issue. Acknowledging that there is wide diversity across different schools of thought, and that one indeed may conclude that "the field of psychotherapy is in a mess," Rogers nonetheless maintained that the "intellectual chains" that bound therapists to their own particular orientations were beginning to wear thin, and that this represented a healthy trend within the field. His reference was to *all* educational and training facilities—be they psychoanalytic institutes or university departments specializing in client-centered therapy—that exposed their students to only one way of looking at the therapeutic process. Rogers went on to say: "I am well aware that such narrow institutions may continue to function for a long time, but I believe their day of vital influence on thoughtful individuals is past" [p. 13].

While this has certainly not been a comprehensive or exhaustive historical analysis of trends toward rapprochement, it nonetheless captures the flavor of what has been in the wind, off and on, for a number of years. These issues are again upon us in a stronger and more pervasive way, as will be seen in the sections that follow.

On Paradigm Strain

In describing how scientific revolutions occur, Kuhn (1970) has indicated that the abandonment of any given paradigm is usually preceeded by a period of "crisis," which is characterized by the proliferation of different orientations, the open expression of discontent about the current state of affairs, as well as the willingness to "try anything." As suggested earlier, the field of psychotherapy currently appears to be undergoing such a crisis.

In a survey of clinical psychologists within the United States, Garfield and Kurtz (1976) have found a very strong trend in the direction of greater eclecticism, in that approximately 55 percent of the respondents depicted their theoretical orientation as one that drew from several different sources. A somewhat more recent survey by Kelly, Goldberg, Fiske, and Kilkowski (1978) placed the figure at 58 percent. Perhaps one of the most dramatic shifts that has occurred over the years has been the decrease in the number of therapists who adhere solely to a psychoanalytic orientation. Thus, Garfield and Kurtz found only 19 percent of clinicians indicating that their orientation was purely psychoanalytic, a decrease from the 41 percent found in a survey that had been conducted some 13 years earlier. When asked to select the two theoretical orientations that best described their eclectic outlook, the most frequent viewpoints reported by the respondents were either psychoanalytic and learning theory or neo-Freudian and learning theory orientations (Garfield & Kurtz, 1977). And the single most frequent reason for using more than one orientation was primarily pragmatic in nature, suggesting that clinicians end up by choosing methods that they have found to work.

In commenting on the "malaise" that characterizes psychoanalytic psychotherapy, Strupp (1976a) has pointed to the tendency of psychoanalysis to use essentially the same approach to all patients, thereby limiting its potential effectiveness. Inasmuch as psychoanalytic therapy retains close ties with organized psychoanalysis, it too has suffered from the tendency to remain insulated from new developments in the behavioral sciences. Younger therapists, observes Strupp, are considerably more skeptical of this general approach to therapy and show a greater willingness to incorporate newer methods into their practice. While acknowledging the importance of the earlier insights provided by psychoanalysis, Strupp goes on to argue that some of these notions are obsolete and need to be replaced by procedures that are found to be empirically effective—regardless of the theoretical source. Agreeing with Strupp's position, Grinker (1976) also indicates that he has observed that once the office doors are closed, much goes on within the psychoanalytic hour that clearly departs from orthodox analysis. Despite what one reads in the literature, says Grinker, most analysts dilute the pure gold of psychoanalysis with whatever nonanalytic copper is indicated by the case at hand. And in the preface to their book *The Interface Between the Psychodynamic and Behavorial Therapies,* Marmor and Woods (1980) argue that, in light of the complexities of human functioning, "no one theory or discipline is likely, in the foreseeable future, to explain, much less predict, all of the complexities of human behavior" (p. xi).

Similar trends have been occurring in behavior therapy as well. After spending a period of time observing Joseph Wolpe and Arnold Lazarus doing clinical work, Klein, Dittman, Parloff, and Gill (1969) reported that there were numerous aspects of the actual treatment strategies that went beyond what was typically described in the behavioral literature, such as the important use of the therapeutic relationship and relevance of clinical judgment. As observed by Klein et al., "much of what they did was what any clinician does in dealing with patients, and they did it by second nature, so to speak" (p. 264). A growing acknowledgment by behavior therapists themselves of this phenomenon can be seen in the comment by Goldfried and Davison (1976):

> While the definition of behavior therapy as deriving its techniques from the well-established body of knowledge in psychology sounds reasonable, it often does not occur that way in clinical practice. We have found instances where "insights" occur to us in the midst of clinical sessions, prompting us to react in specific ways that paid off handsomely in the therapeutic progress of our clients. . . . In accordance with most common definitions of behavior therapy, this might be viewed as heresy. Perhaps in some way it is. Nonetheless our contact with reality is relatively veridical, and what we have observed under such instances is not terribly unique. If, in fact, some of these phenomena are reliable, even if they are not easily derived from basic principles of psychology, should we ignore them because we call ourselves behavior therapists? [p. 16].

Arnold Lazarus, one of the leading figures in the early development of behavior therapy, has more recently published an article entitled "Has Behavior Therapy Outlived Its Usefulness?" (Lazarus, 1977). On the basis of his extensive clinical experience and repeated observations of what tends to work in both the short and long run, Lazarus concludes that the traditional conceptualization of behavior therapy is far too limited to handle everything one sees in clinical practice. Considering Lazarus' instrumental role in the development of behavior therapy as a separate orientation, it is particularly significant that he voices his opposition to the "advancement of any delimited school of thought," including behavior therapy. Compare this with Rogers' comments on the topic, quoted earlier, on page 10. London (1972) has similarly argued that now that the ideological phase of the behavior movement is over ("the borders are secure now" and "the settlers are thriving"), it is time for behavior therapists to look more dispassionately at what actually works in clinical practice and even to consider what other orientations may have to offer.

Within the humanistic approach to therapy, signs of paradigm strain are evident as well. Landsman (1974) has argued that cross-fertilization with behavior therapy would benefit humanistic therapists, noting that:

> If humanists are truly confident that they have much to offer then they ought to welcome what is being offered by the responsible behaviorists—attention to specifics, to details, careful quantification, modesty in claims, demonstrable results [(p. 15].

Although operating within a basically humanistic view of the personal growth process, Egan (1975) has maintained that certain behavioral procedures may be useful when the therapist is ready to collaborate with the client in "working out specific action programs." Ricks, Wandersman, and Poppen (1976) have similarly called for a 'creative synthesis" of humanism and behaviorism, suggesting that "the field of therapy would be diminished without humanists such as Jourard, and it would be equally diminished without behaviorists such as Wolpe" (p. 386). And as a response to Lazarus' (1977) call for rapprochement across various therapeutic orientations, the editor of the *Journal of Humanistic Psychology* (Greening, 1978) has urged the readers of the journal to be open to such attempts.

This is but a brief sampling of the integrative course that the field of psychotherapy seems to be taking. A more detailed analysis of this trend will be provided in everything else that we have to say from here on in. But before concluding this section, we might relate one brief anecdote. This is one used by Garfield (1980), who has illustrated the need to look for the essential ingredients in therapeutic change with an apt essay by Charles Lamb, "A Dissertation on Roast Pig." As the story goes, the practice of eating roasted, as opposed to raw, pig, was accidentally discovered in ancient China when a fire occurred in a swineherder's cottage. Realizing that the taste of the pig was greatly improved by this method, the swineherder, as well as many of the villagers, proceeded to build and subsequently burn down numerous other cottages. It took some time, and many burnt houses, until it was finally realized that this delicacy could be prepared by more parsimonious methods.

Common Ingredients in Psychotherapy

The field of psychotherapy has most typically been characterized by the differences, rather than the similarities that may exist among various approaches. The end result of this greater emphasis on uniqueness is that prospective clients/patients must choose from over 130 distinct approaches to therapeutic intervention (Parloff, 1976). Jerome Frank (1976) has suggested that "features which are shared by all therapists have been relatively neglected, since little glory derives from showing that the particular method one has mastered with so much effort may be indistinguishable from other methods in its effects" (p. 74). Moreover, numerous political, economic, and social factors exist to encourage the tendency to emphasize the uniqueness of any given therapeutic orientation, a point we shall return to later on in this chapter.

It has been argued that the philosophical and theoretical differences among the therapies are so basic that no attempts at rapprochement are possible. This, however, may be a totally inappropriate level of analysis at which to look for commonalities. If any search for elements across therapeutic orientations is to be successful, one needs to focus on an optimal level of abstraction (Goldfried, 1980). At a level of abstraction most removed from what may be directly observed within any given session, we have the *theoretical framework* that has been derived to explain why the particular set of intervention procedures is likely to work. At the lowest level of abstraction, we have the specific *therapeutic techniques* themselves, be they relaxation training, free association, reflection of feeling, role reversal, or any other procedure. It is our contention that points of comparison at a theoretical level are unlikely to reveal similarities, especially since little theoretical consensus exists *within* any given orientation, be it psychoanalytic, behavioral, or humanistic. By looking for similarities at the lowest level of abstraction—therapeutic techniques—any similarities that may be derived are likely to be relatively trivial. It is at a level of abstraction between these two extremes where there exists the most promising potential in the search for commonality, as this intermediate level is more likely to reveal the basic *principles* or *strategies* associated with the therapeutic change process. As suggested elsewhere, *"To the extent that clinicians of varying orientations are able to arrive at a common set of strategies, it is likely that what emerges will consist of robust phenomena, as they have managed to survive the distortions imposed by the therapists' varying theoretical biases"* (Goldfried, 1980, p. 996). In essence, such strategies function as clinical heuristics that implicitly guide our efforts during the course of therapy.

In considering the levels of abstraction at which to view the therapeutic interaction, it is particularly relevant to make passing reference to the work by Rosch and her associates on categorizing events and objects (Rosch, Mervis, Gray, Johnson, & Boyes-Braem, 1976). The results of their research indicate that categories that are either too abstract (e.g., "furniture") or too specific (e.g., "kitchen chair") are not nearly as useful for categorizing objects as is a classification that is somewhere between these two extremes (e.g., "chair"). This middle level of categorical abstraction has been found to allow individuals to better sort objects that share common features and at the same time to differentiate those objects not having these features. Essentially the same conclusion has been reached by Cantor and Mischel (1979) in their recent work on classifying personality types.

A review of the available literature dealing with points of commonality across different therapeutic approaches reveals a number of similarities that have been described at this intermediate level of abstraction. We shall briefly touch on some of these, such as the culturally induced expectations that therapy can be helpful, the participation in a therapeutic relationship, the possibility of obtaining an external perspective on one's problems, the encouragement of corrective experiences, and the opportunity to repeatedly test reality.

Expectation That Therapy Will Help

It has been suggested by several writers in the field (e.g., Frank, 1961, 1976; Garfield, 1974; Marmor, 1976; Patterson, 1967; Prochaska, 1979) that the very societal definition of the therapeutic enterprise carries with it the expectation that the patient/client will be helped. In his classic work *Persuasion and Healing*, Jerome Frank (1961) has carefully documented how therapeutic intervention carries with it placebo characteristics that are likely to enhance an individual's positive expectations for improvement. When individuals present themselves for psychotherapy, they are typically in a demoralized state. It is the offering of hope that something can be done, argues Frank, that represents a common denominator underlying different therapeutic schools, and indeed such other forms of healing as the placebo effect in medical treatment, religious cures, and the changes associated with healing in primitive societies. There are obvious limits to the kinds of benefits that faith can instill, however, and therapeutic change often requires other factors as well.

Therapeutic Relationship

In addition to engendering the expectation that psychotherapy holds some promise of alleviating one's personal distress, it has been suggested that all therapeutic orientations involve an interpersonal relationship that in itself is believed to provide a vehicle for change (Applebaum, 1978; Brady, et al; 1980; Frank, 1961, 1976; Garfield, 1980; Horwitz, 1974; Luborsky, Singer,

& Luborsky, 1975; Marmor, 1976; Patterson, 1967; Prochaska, 1979; Sloane, 1969; Strupp, 1973a, 1976b). This relationship has been characterized as one whereby a warm, understanding, and nurturing therapist wins the trust and respect of the patient or client. This in itself is believed to have a beneficial effect, as it is relatively rare for people to experience interactions with others in our society who are willing to listen sympathetically. But the therapeutic relationship can offer even more than this, in that it provides an important context within which change may occur. In the most general sense, Strupp (1973a) likens the therapeutic interaction to a parent–child relationship, a phenomenon that Freud had called "after-education." Although the change process may focus directly on the interaction between client/patient and therapist, the therapeutic relationship also can serve as a source of influence for clients or patients to function differently in their relations with others. And while the therapist may serve as a significant other during the process of encouraging individuals to feel, think, and behave differently, the primary objective is to have them reach a point of greater autonomy and self-mastery.

Obtaining an External Perspective on Oneself and the World

When individuals enter therapy, they frequently do so with a somewhat distorted view of themselves and the world. Goldfried and Robins (in press) have suggested somewhat waggishly that such distortions are biological in origin: the very fact that people's eyes are situated within their head limits their view of themselves. As a way of correcting this limited outlook, it has been suggested that all forms of therapy share a common clinical strategy of providing patients/clients with an alternate way of looking at themselves, their behavior, and the world around them (Appelbaum, 1978; Brady et al., 1980; Frank, 1961, 1976; Garfield, 1974; Goldfried, 1980; Luborsky et al., 1975; Marmor, 1976; Prochaska, 1979; Raimy, 1975; Rice, 1974; Rosenzweig, 1936; Sloane, 1969; Staub, 1972; Wexler, 1974). An essential ingredient in offering clients or patients a different perspective involves some sort of direct feedback. This more general strategy of direct feedback may be implemented with a wide variety of therapeutic techniques, such as reflection, clarification, confrontation, interpretation, client's/patient's self-observation, or bibliotherapy. All are directed, however, at correcting clients'/patients' subjective views of their functioning. In addition to offering feedback, varying theoretical rationales and explanations are typically provided. Such explanations give individuals a different framework by which they can better understand their personal distress, one that clearly implies that change is possible.

Corrective Experiences

Regardless of their theoretical orientation, therapists have typically acknowledged that a central component of therapeutic change entails the individual's involvement in new, corrective experiences (Alexander, 1963; Alexander & French, 1946; Appelbaum, 1978; Brady et al., 1980; Frank, 1976; Goldfried, 1980; Grinker, 1976; Horwitz, 1974; Korchin, 1976; Marmor, 1976; Prochaska, 1979; Raimy, 1975; Rotter, 1954; Strupp, 1976b; Thoresen & Coates, 1978). Alexander and French (1946) coined the phrase "corrective emotional experience" to refer to the process of having patients behave in ways that they may have avoided in the past, and the accompanying realization that the consequences they feared do not, in fact, occur. Coming from a very different theoretical orientation Rogers (1961) has also dealt with what appears to be a very similar change process. In discussing how the therapy relationship can produce change, Rogers offers a client's own personal observations: "I can even tell him just how I'm feeling toward him at any given moment and instead of this killing the relationship, as I used to fear, it seems to deepen it. Do you suppose I could be my feelings with other people too? Perhaps that wouldn't be too dangerous either" (p. 68).

When asked to respond to the question, "What is the role played by new experiences provided to the patient/client in facilitating change?", a number of therapists from different orientations suggested that this aspect of the therapeutic process was "critical," "essential," "crucial," and "basic" (Brady et al., 1980). Within psychodynamic and humanistic frameworks, these corrective experiences typically were seen to occur within the patient–therapist relationship. More behaviorally oriented therapists tended to emphasize the corrective experiences that occur in the client's relationship with people outside of the consultation session, although it is not inconsistent with this viewpoint to focus on within-session changes as well. According to these respondents, such corrective experiences, regardless of the context in which they originated, have the effect of changing the patients' or clients' views of themselves and others.

Continued Reality Testing

Very closely aligned to both the notions of an external perspective and corrective experiences is the therapeutic need for ongoing reality testing, whereby patients/clients continually observe how their distorted views of themselves and others are manifested in their daily life experiences, and whereby they repeatedly attempt to correct these distortions and behavior patterns (Dewald, 1971; Frank, 1976; Marmor, 1976; Raimy, 1975; Rice, 1980; Wachtel, 1977). Although different orientations may vary with regard to the content of the distortions that are the focus of therapy, the explanation for their origins, and the amount of structure and direction offered in assisting the patient or client to change, there appears to be a striking similarity across orientations in the reality-testing process itself.

In describing the "working through" process, Dewald (1971) presents the case of a shy and sexually anxious young man who, while able to bring himself to ask a woman out for a date, nonetheless had some unpleasant experiences. Dewald suggests that under such instances the psychoanalytically oriented therapist should not focus on the problem but rather "support the effort it required to make the attempt to change" (p. 249). In all likelihood, a behavior therapist would respond strategically to such an individual in much the same way, so as to encourage successive approximations toward a therapeutic goal. Similarly, in her chapter on the "Tyranny of the Should," Horney (1950) has suggested a general strategy for changing a patient's distorted outlook on things that appears to be most consistent with a cognitive behavior therapy viewpoint. Noting that a general awareness of certain unrealistic thoughts does little to undermine a person's upset, Horney observed: "What counts is the individual becoming aware of *specific* ways in which these factors operate within him and how in *concrete detail* they manifest themselves in his *particular* life . . ." (p. 342). Certainly, the more recent work by Beck (1976) has addressed itself to this very issue.

It is particularly interesting to note that in the same year that certain cognitive restructuring procedures were described in the behavior therapy literature (Goldfried, Decenteceo, & Weinberg, 1974), Bieber (1974) outlined a remarkably similar therapeutic strategy to be used within a psychoanalytic context. And in a more recent convention presentation, Rice (1980) described a similar working through strategy that she developed from a client-centered point of view. All three independently derived procedures outline how one may assist clients/patients in their ongoing efforts to overcome their distorted views of current life situations.

Although we have described what appear to be common therapeutic elements cutting across different orientations, it should be kept in mind that these observations are based on what therapists "say they do," not what they "actually do." Just as we all have observed that our patients and clients do not always have a totally correct view of their actions, so should we anticipate that we, their therapists, may similarly not be faithful observers of our own therapeutic activities. In the final analysis, what is clearly needed is a more direct empirical test of what similarities actually exist across different orientations. In any attempt to achieve a consensus on the active ingredients for therapeutic change, it is also important to bear in mind that few therapists strictly adhere to a particular therapeutic orientation in actual practice (cf. Grinker, 1976; Hunt, 1971; Klein et al., 1969; Strupp, 1978a). In many respects, therapists may very well become "shaped" by their patients or clients during the course of their professional careers, gradually learning to use those procedures and strategies that they have experienced as being successful. Stated in somewhat different terms, Wachtel (1977) has suggested that there exists a therapeutic "underground," reflecting an unofficial consensus of what experienced clinicians know to be true. Inasmuch as many of these factors are not associated with any particular school, one rarely sees them described in the literature.

When questioned by Bergin and Strupp (1972) about future directions in psychotherapy, Neal Miller predicted that as behavior therapy started to deal with more complicated types of problems, and as psychoanalytically oriented therapy began to emphasize ego mechanisms and the working through process, both schools of thought would be likely to converge in some interesting ways. Strupp (1978a) has more recently suggested that such convergence is already taking place. Wachtel (1977) has made a very good case for the integration of psychodynamic and behavioral therapies in working with patients/clients on an individual basis. In the field of sex therapy (Kaplan, 1974, 1979), behavioral and psychodynamic procedures have been integrated to enable the clinician to deal with the wide variety of sexual dysfunctions likely to be seen within the clinical setting. In the area of marriage and family therapy, Gurman (1981) has suggested that behavioral and nonbehavioral approaches might be integrated in certain fruitful ways, as the former offers a good methodology for producing change, whereas the latter provides us with information needed to understand marital and family processes. Some of the ways in which different therapeutic orientations may complement each other are considered next.

Therapists Look at Other Approaches

In discussing the possibility of integrating psychoanalytic and behavior therapy, the argument has been put forth that these are basically incompatible systems by virtue of their differing theoretical assumptions and philosophical world views (Messer & Winokur, 1980). We find it difficult to disagree. Indeed, as suggested earlier, we maintain that any attempt at integration at this highest level of abstraction is doomed to failure. At the same time, it has been our observation that there are a growing number of therapists who acknowledge that their preferred paradigm is incomplete and that some sort of integration is required at the pragmatic/clinical level. Even in their strong opposition to the prospect of an integration between behavior therapy and psychoanalytic therapy, Messer and Winokur nonetheless do acknowledge that such pragmatic eclecticism may be possible, as do others who have written on this issue (e.g., Franks, 1978; Lazarus, 1967, 1971; Marmor, 1969; Murray, 1976). Garfield and Kurtz's (1976) survey of practicing therapists who preferred an eclectic approach indicated that their reasons for such integration were clinical rather than theoretical. Marmor and Woods (1980) have speculated that therapeutic failures that occur within a behavioral orientation may very well be due to the relative lack of attention that the clinician has paid to the patient's or client's cognitive distortions and/or emotional reactions to the therapist. Conversely, they argue that the clinical failures of psychodynamic therapists in working with phobias, compulsions, and various sexual dysfunctions might be reduced if they made use of the behavior-therapy procedures that have been found to be successful in alleviating such problems.

Inasmuch as the social systems that surround the field of psychotherapy are typically organized according to schools of thought, there is the unfortunate tendency to stereotype therapists who align themselves with another viewpoint. Thus, we often hear categorical statements that behavior therapists "do" this, that psychodynamic therapists "do" another thing, and that humanists "do" still something else. And while it may be true that certain emphases characterize different schools of thought, it is misleading to assume that experienced clinicians do not borrow from other orientations. In discussing the inherent limitations associated with either a psychodynamic or a behavioral orientation, London (1964) has observed:

> There is a quiet blending of techniques by artful therapists of either school; a blending that takes account of the fact that people are considerably simpler than the Insight schools give them credit for, but that they are also more complicated than the Action therapists would like to believe [p. 39].

Ricks et al. (1976), in considering the potential integration of humanistic and behavioral approaches to therapy, similarly suggest:

> So long as we stay out of the day to day work of psychotherapy, in the quiet of the study or library, it is easy to think of psychotherapists as exponents of competing thoughts. When we actually participate in psychotherapy, or observe its complexities, it loses this specious simplicity [p. 401].

There have been a number of clinical cases in the literature involving an integration of behavior therapy and psychodynamic therapy. In certain instances, this has involved concurrent treatment by therapists representing the two orientations (e.g., Levay, Weissberg, & Blaustein, 1976; Segraves & Smith, 1976; Woody, 1973). We even know of one case in which an analyst actually sat in on the therapy sessions that his patient was having with a behavior therapist (Fay, 1981). In other cases, the integration has been accomplished by means of behavioral and psychodynamic procedures that were employed by a given therapist (e.g., Birk & Brinkley-Birk, 1974;

Brady, 1968; Feather & Rhoads, 1972; Kaplan, 1974; Lambley, 1976; Wachtel, 1977).

Dewald's (1971) well-known book on psychodynamic psychotherapy is, in actuality, two books in one: One involves insight-oriented therapy, where the goal is basic personality change. The other describes supportive therapy, the object of which is symptom relief and "overt behavioral change." Interestingly enough, but certainly not surprisingly, we find that the supportive therapy as outlined from within this psychodynamic framework contains numerous procedures used by behavior therapists. As suggested by Dewald, "In the supportive situation, the therapist actively uses suggestion, reinforcement, approval, disapproval, or whatever interventions are appropriate to produce the desired behavioral change" (p. 177). In reporting the results of the Menninger Foundation Psychotherapy Research Project that unexpectedly found supportive therapy to yield positive and lasting improvement in patients, Horwitz (1974, 1976) suggested that a rethinking of therapeutic change from within a psychodynamic framework was in order. Wachtel (1977) has gone on to make a detailed and scholarly account of the clinical changes that need to be made and has provided a conceptual framework for making such an integration. In particular accord with the findings of the Menninger study, Wachtel discusses how "active intervention" methods may be compatibly viewed from within a psychodynamic framework.

As behavior therapists have begun to gain experience in dealing with a wide variety of clinical cases, their emphasis has become more cognitive in nature (Beck, 1976; Goldfried & Davison, 1976; Lazarus, 1971; Mahoney, 1974; Meichenbaum, 1977). In recent developments in the area of "cognitive-behavior therapy," there has also been the acknowledgment that it may not always be possible for individuals to provide accurate introspective information on their cognitive processes, as they may not be immediately available to conscious awareness (Beck, 1976; Goldfried, 1979; Mahoney, 1980; Meichenbaum, 1980). In light of these trends, as well as those occurring from within the psychodynamic frame of reference, Strupp (1978a) has raised the question of whether or not psychoanalytic therapists are beginning to practice cognitive behavior therapy, or whether behavior therapists may be becoming more psychodynamic. We recognize that when the issue is presented in this way, there are likely to be strong objections from therapists within each orientation, but primarily because they are being identified with another school of thought. However, if we focus on what *we do* and not *who we are,* perhaps it might be easier to acknowledge this trend and to better appreciate what other approaches might have to offer.

In arguing for the important contributions that different therapeutic orientations may have to an effective, multidimensional therapeutic intervention, Bergin (1982) has observed that it would be unrealistic for us to look for a single set of principles to explain the working of the human body.

As he points out, the principles of fluid mechanics that determine the manner in which the heart operates differ greatly from those electrochemical principles that govern the transmission of impulses through neurons. Despite these different operational mechanisms, however, these separate systems work in a coordinated fashion within the body. Just as separate laser beams are needed to achieve a three-dimensional holograph, suggests Hunt (1976), so are different therapeutic vantage points needed to achieve a comprehensive intervention approach. Arguing for an integrated approach to therapeutic intervention, Birk and Brinkley-Birk (1974) have similarly made the case for a synergistic model of human functioning to take into account the interplay between emotional, cognitive, and behavioral change. It is our contention that each of the three major approaches to therapy—psychodynamic, behavioral, and humanistic—has something important to offer the practicing therapist.

It has been suggested that a unique contribution of *psychodynamic therapy* involves its emphasis on understanding the idiosyncratic meaning that patients or clients apply to various events and individuals, the hidden agendas that pervade their interpersonal relationships, and the specific maladaptive interpersonal patterns in their lives (e.g., Bergin, 1982; Hunt, 1971; Marks & Gelder, 1966; Wachtel, 1975, 1977). Another aspect of psychodynamic therapy that is potentially useful to therapists of other orientations is the observation that the patient's/client's reaction to the therapist can offer a sample of problematic reactions to others and that such reactions may be changed by focusing on what goes on within the therapeutic relationship. Related to this is the suggestion that the therapists need to be mindful of how their own personal biases may at times interfere with therapeutic progress.

A unique feature of *behavior therapy* has to do with its detailed and systematic therapeutic guidelines, particularly those that encourage clients or patients to act in ways that can provide them with the corrective experiences that they need for change (cf. Bergin, 1981; Franks, 1978; Garfield, 1980; Landsman, 1974; Liberman, 1972; Marks & Gelder, 1966; Rhoads, 1981; Shapiro, 1978; Thoresen, 1973; Wachtel, 1975, 1977). Behavior therapy has also underscored the importance of attending to environmental factors that may be influencing a person's functioning in the current life situation. Two final contributions of the behavioral approach have been its emphasis on applying basic research findings to the clinical context and its development of clinical research methods to study the effectiveness of our therapeutic interventions.

A number of writers have pointed to some of the unique contributions that can come from a *humanistic orientation* to intervention (e.g., Appelbaum, 1975, 1976; Bergin, 1982; Goldstein, 1976; Liberman, 1972; Ricks et al., 1976; Shapiro, 1978). Beginning with the pioneering work of Carl

Rogers, an increasingly greater emphasis has been placed on the importance of an accepting, caring, and understanding therapist in the change
process. Advocates of varying theoretical orientations have acknowledged
that this aspect of the therapist's relationship to clients or patients can
provide an essential interpersonal environment within which they can explore various possibilities of change. Humanistic therapists have also underscored the importance of assisting individuals in becoming more accurately aware of their emotional states, often with the aid of ingenious
exercises. Recognizing that overt behavior change was insufficient in working with couples, behavior therapists (e.g., Gottman, Notarius, Gonso, &
Markman, 1976; Jacobson & Margolin, 1979; O'Leary & Turkewitz, 1978)
involved in marital therapy have been making use of communication training methods that have their foundation within a more humanistic orientation (e.g., Gordon, 1970).

Although it is one thing to acknowledge what unique contributions
may be made from each of the separate orientations, it is quite another
matter to define one's orientation as being "eclectic." It is indeed unfortunate that this term, as currently used, conjures up an image of a therapist
who has difficulty in making a commitment to an accepted and coherent
viewpoint and whose professional identity tends to fall somewhere "between the cracks." Conceptual frameworks of a transtheoretical nature have
been suggested by several writers in an attempt to integrate what appears
to be the best of different orientations (e.g., Dimond, Havens, & Jones,
1978; Lazarus, 1976; Prochaska, 1979), but none of these appears to have
provided us with a paradigm that can be readily accepted by most therapists. Part of this reluctance stems from political, economic, and social factors, which will be discussed later in this chapter. In the final analysis,
however, any integrated approach to therapy must await actual empirical
evidence on the therapeutic efficacy of certain principles of change. As
concluded by a psychoanalyst interested in achieving a better integration of
gestalt and psychoanalytic interventions:

> If any of us are to benefit from the ideas and experiences of others, then the
> whole has to be defined . . . as knowledge. Only knowledge can unite dispar-
> ate schools, techniques, and views of man and change. Only knowledge is
> boundaryless and infinite [Appelbaum, 1979, p. 501].

A Look at Psychotherapy Outcome Research

Diverging points of view and varying schools ultimately need to be replaced by an empirical account of therapeutic effectiveness. And while it
certainly goes well beyond the scope of this chapter to detail the findings of

research in psychotherapy—which have been thoroughly reviewed else-where (Garfield & Bergin, 1978)—it nonetheless is appropriate to touch upon a few issues that are relevant to the topic of converging themes in the practice of psychotherapy.

In an attempt to tie together the results of separate psychotherapy outcome studies, Smith and Glass (1977) and Smith, Glass, and Miller (1980) conducted a "meta-analysis" of several hundred previously published research reports. Using a novel statistical approach to determine "effect size," reflecting the differences obtained between treated and untreated patients/clients, Smith and her associates were able to pool the results of studies so as to look at the influence of such variables as nature of therapy procedure, experience of therapist, type of client, areas of improvement, and so forth. On the basis of their analyses, one of the more interesting conclusions they draw is that the average patient or client who has under-gone therapy was better off than 80 percent of untreated controls, espe-cially in regard to the alleviation of fear and anxiety. Although Smith and her co-workers have provided us with a novel approach to combining the findings of several outcome studies, it should be kept in mind that their conclusions are only as good as the specific studies on which they were based. Inasmuch as they included "analogue" outcome studies in their analysis, where the intervention was very brief and where the therapists had only minimal clinical experience, we are reluctant to accept their conclusions as clearly depicting the efficacy of psychotherapy as it is prac-ticed in the "real world." Nonetheless, they have provided us with a valu-able method of integrating and evaluating research findings, and a more valid test of their methods awaits outcome research reflecting improved clinical sophistication and research methodologies.

This is not to say that we know nothing about the effectiveness of our intervention procedures. Although the President's Commission on Mental Health (1978) has indicated that there continue to exist large gaps in knowledge, it nonetheless concluded that some progress has been made in the development of procedures for the treatment of certain clinical prob-lems, such as fears, phobias, compulsive rituals, and nonpsychotic forms of depression. Jerome Frank (1979), who has been an advocate of the primary importance of "nonspecific" factors for therapeutic change, has echoed this recent progress in the field. Coming from an individual of his stature, who has long maintained that change resulted from the general nature of the therapeutic interaction itself, this acknowledgment should be taken as a very definite indication that the field has truly begun to advance in recent years.

It is no secret that practicing clinicians are often reluctant to alter what they do as a function of reported research findings. There are probably several reasons to account for this phenomenon, not the least of which is the fact that our therapy-outcome research does not always mirror clinical reality. Speaking as individuals who have been directly involved in therapy research, and at the same time as practicing therapists who have worked with clients/patients in a clinical setting, we must confess to being guilty of schizophrenic behavior. Our concerns for methodological rigor in the research context have at times led us to use treatment procedures that bore only a general semblance to what we would do clinically. So as to enhance the ecological validity of our psychotherapy research, Frank (1979) and Strupp (1978b) have argued that future outcome research should make more realistic attempts to tailormake the intervention procedure to the particular case at hand.

There are certainly legitimate reasons for practicing therapists to question the relevance of available outcome research. However, it has been documented that clinicians often approach the research literature with definite biases and tend to be more critical of research methodology when the reported results indicate therapy has not been shown to be effective (Cohen, 1979). Biases also stem from one's theoretical outlook, as demonstrated in a controlled study in which it was found that psychodynamically oriented clinicians were more critical of research findings indicating the superiority of behavior therapy than they were of findings that supported the greater effectiveness of psychodynamic therapy (Cohen & Suchy, 1979). There were also trends suggesting that behavior therapists were biased against findings demonstrating the superiority of psychodynamic therapy, but these failed to reach statistical significance, perhaps because of the smaller number of subjects involved in this group.

Clinicians are not the only ones who selectively attend to findings; Mahoney (1976) has provided a detailed and vivid analysis of how research in psychology in general hardly supports the contention that the scientist is a logical, dispassionate, altruistic, and apolitical being. An investigation by Mahoney revealed that judged adequacy of a study being considered for publication was often a function of the reviewer's bias, and not the study itself. It may come as little surprise to learn that Mahoney experienced considerable difficulty in getting this study published. And lest one think that such biases occur only in the case of the behavioral sciences, Polanyi (1946) has amply documented how empirical findings in the "hard" sciences are typically viewed by scientists subjectively and are used accordingly to either confirm or refute their preferred viewpoints. In other words, scientists tend to operate within their own personal working assumptions ("faith") of how things really are, and if they are clever enough, they can readily explain away any contradictory results. Only after the weight of evidence consistently contradicts their particular viewpoint do they concede that they were wrong.

In an attempt to accumulate research evidence on the efficacy of psychotherapy, we have continually been confronted with the issue of how to measure change (Frank, 1979; Rogers, 1963; Strupp, 1978b; Waskow & Parloff, 1975). In many respects, outcome measures represent the Achilles heel of psychotherapy research. Unlike other applied fields, where changes can be more readily discerned and agreed upon, the field of psychotherapy has done relatively little to achieve a consensus on the goals of therapeutic intervention and the methods by which such goals may be measured. Grappling with the conceptual and methodological considerations involved in measuring change would probably require far more time and energy than would the study of intervention procedures themselves. Indeed, perhaps this is the reason that the issue of outcome measures has been so sorely neglected. Nonetheless, in order for us to accumulate and draw conclusions from the findings obtained by various psychotherapy studies, it is apparent that we eventually need to have a standard assessment battery that is acceptable to therapists of varying persuasions. Such an assessment battery clearly needs to deal with the various "systems" associated with psychological functioning, entailing subjective, overt behavioral, and physiological indices of change.

As a result of a series of interviews conducted with psychotherapy researchers throughout the nation, Bergin and Strupp (1970) concluded that large-scale collaborative research efforts were simply not feasible. Approximately a decade later, however, Parloff (1979) argued that the field was now at a point of methodological sophistication where we are indeed ready to embark on such research programs. Initiated by the National Institute of Mental Health, the first of such large-scale, multi-institutional collaborative studies is currently underway, comparing the relative effectiveness of different approaches to the treatment of depression. In order to conduct such a study, it has been necessary to establish some consensus among various researchers as to what would constitute a successful outcome in the treatment of depression. This in itself is a huge step forward and is likely to mark a turning point in psychotherapy research. It may also very well have an important impact on training in psychotherapy, as this collaborative study has made use of carefully delineated therapy guidelines, as well as procedures for rating the effectiveness of any given therapist in implementing the treatment procedures.

In a sweeping overview of the current status in psychotherapy research and practice, Strupp (1978b) has emphasized the strong impetus that insurance companies and governmental policymakers are likely to provide for sharpening our views of effective therapeutic practice. Indeed, he predicts: "Perhaps it is not entirely utopian to envisage the creation of an analogue to the Food and Drug Administration to protect the public from worthless or potentially damaging therapies. The mood of the times certainly points in that direction" (p. 20). In an enlightening, indeed sobering, account of the effect that this growing demand for accountability is likely to have on the field of psychotherapy, Parloff (1979) points out to all mental health professionals that governmental policymakers are beginning to read our literature. Acknowledging the need to demonstrate the effectiveness of the services we deliver to the public, Parloff underscores the crucial need for some sort of consensus on the effectiveness of various therapeutic procedures. Unless the field can come up with such a consensus, it may be done for us by outside agencies.

Given the fact that psychotherapy has existed for close to 100 years now, it is certainly appropriate for us to ask the question of whether or not it works. As stated, however, such a question is unanswerable and requires a more detailed and comprehensive set of subquestions before any conclusion can be made about the state of the field as a whole. We can no longer pit one therapy against another with regard to general effectiveness, and more of our research needs to focus on the specificity of treatment for particular instances, as well as the often neglected but nonetheless real question of cost-effectiveness. The time has also come when our research has to be conducted on what actually goes on clinically, particularly as it is currently practiced in a wide variety of settings. Clearly, this requires a closer and more collaborative arrangement between those who actually conduct therapy and those who study its effectiveness.

The Interplay of Practice and Research

Although the field has given much lip-service to the important interplay between clinical practice and research in psychotherapy, most of us know that this interrelationship is more often the exception than the rule. As depicted at the outset of this chapter in Figure 1.1, the field of psychotherapy is also divided on the basis of whether one functions in a clinical or a research context. The question that we need to consider here is whether or not this clinical–research rift is inherent to the field or whether there exists any potential for providing a meaningful integration of these two activities. In addressing ourselves to this complex issue, it might be fruitful (1) to discuss some of the possible reasons for the tension that often exists between clinicians and researchers, (2) to touch on the question of whether or not psychotherapy is an art or a science, and then (3) to consider the possibility that clinical practice may provide us with a useful starting point for our research activities.

Rift Between Clinicians and Researchers

For the most part, clinicians and researchers have a long history of mutual intolerance, if not outright impatience (Strupp, 1968). In much of the research literature in psychotherapy—either explicitly or implicitly—there is the pervasive message that practicing clinicians are naive and fuzzy-minded when it comes to evaluating the efficacy of their interventions. Their observations that something "works clinically" or is "clinically useful" is often put down by researchers as being self-deluding. The only path to truth, argues the researcher, lies in controlled experimentation. Because of the compromises that need to be made in order to do clinical research, however, the clinician can write off these research efforts as being inappropriate or trivial. Instead, practicing clinicians typically make judgments about the efficacy of their procedures on the basis of their own personal experiences, not empirical findings (Strupp, 1968).

There are various underlying factors that may very well contribute to the conflict between the roles of clinician and researcher. Some of these include:

1. It may be that two basically different types of individuals are involved in these two enterprises, with the clinician being a "warmer" and more interpersonally oriented person and the researcher tending to be more aloof and task oriented. This stereotyping can at times be most extreme, as in the case of one clinician who has concluded that research in psychotherapy is possible only if one views the entire enterprise "in the mechanical way that is so fashionable among many of our colleagues who are too frightened and too inept to establish an interpersonal relationship of a therapeutic variety with a patient" (Lehrer, 1981, p. 42). While practice and research may attract different types, the differences between clinician and researcher are probably not as extreme as some would maintain (cf. Goldstein, 1968).

2. Although many clinicians are creative, insightful, and talented enough to conduct research, they may deliberately have chosen not to do so for personal reasons. The highly competitive and at times impersonal system that so very much characterizes academic and research settings may simply represent too much of a price to pay.

3. Anyone who has been directly involved in clinical work knows that it requires a certain amount of tolerance for ambiguity, to say nothing of the ability to tolerate interpersonal stress. Many researchers readily acknowledge that they are unwilling or unable to function in this professional context.

4. The clinician may feel threatened by the researcher because of the ever-present possibility that any data obtained will not confirm the efficacy of the intervention methods used by practitioners (cf. Garfield, 1980). In other words, clinicians may not feel too good about researchers looking over their shoulders, making demands for accountability.

5. Practitioners may feel uncomfortable about the prospects of being involved in research, as these may represent areas of expertise for which

they had either discomfort or disdain during their earlier training (e.g., statistics, experimental design). While these were the kinds of activities that clinicians may have been expected to engage in during their graduate or professional training, practitioners may have viewed these as unpleasant hurdles they had to overcome in order to reach their professional status.

6. Even though an individual's professional and personal disposition may allow him or her to function competently within both a clinical and a research role, the realities are such that it is most difficult to be a scientist-professional in the real world. For the most part, the professional world is simply not set up to provide the necessary encouragement for clinical and research activities within the same individual. It is an uphill struggle even for the most dedicated therapist to do clinical work in an academic setting and for the clinician to do research in a service context. This is indeed unfortunate, as it has been historically observed that innovations in applied fields are often made by "role hybrids" who have their feet planted both in applied and research camps (Ben-David, 1964).

7. Clinicians and researchers approach the process of psychotherapy from very different vantage points. The clinician is more of an active participant, whereas the researcher tends to view the phenomenon of psychotherapy as more of an external observer. Although neither one is the "correct" vantage point, this distinction nonetheless makes for difficult communication between the two. It has been our observation that even when individuals are actively involved in both clinical work and research, it is almost as if these are isolated parts of their being, and many will readily admit that they often trust their personal experiences more than the findings of their own research.

Psychotherapy: Art or Science?

The argument has been put forth by some that it is really a futile task to carry out research on psychotherapy, as the practice of therapy involves more of an art than a science. For example, Matarazzo (1971) has suggested that no two psychotherapists practice the same way, even though they may have been carefully trained within a given school of thought. Matarazzo argues that clinicians are first and foremost human beings, possessing varying degrees of interpersonal skill and sensitivity, and that their efficiency in using various psychotherapeutic techniques is only secondary. Thus, the only really effective way of learning the art of psychotherapy is through an apprenticeship undertaken with a skilled clinician, and even there one cannot guarantee the development of competence. The limitations inherent to the practice of behavior therapy have been noted by Hunt (1971), who suggests that while this orientation provides broad outlines, therapists must rely on their general clinical sensitivities in order to determine what must be done in any given instance.

Although we must wholeheartedly agree with many of the points made about the "nonscientific" aspects associated with the practice of psychotherapy, we believe that the dichotomy between art and science is not totally accurate. To begin with, one can make this distinction only by assuming that scientific activities are relatively straightforward, requiring little in the way of artistry. Researchers who have agonized over the design of any given experiment can well attest to the need for creativity in order to make an experiment work. To quote two respected researchers in the area of social psychology:

> In any experiment, the investigator chooses a procedure which he intuitively feels is an empirical realization of his conceptual variable. All experimental procedures are "contrived" in the sense that they are invented. Indeed, it can be said that the *art of experimentation* rests primarily on the skill of the investigator to judge the procedure which is the most accurate realization of his conceptual variable and has the greatest impact and the most credibility for the subject [Aronson & Carlsmith, 1968, p. 25 (italics added)].

All one need do is to substitute certain key words (e.g., "clinical intervention" for "experiment," "clinician" for "investigator," "client" or "patient" for "subject"), and the very close parallel between research and practice becomes more evident.

Although there is the tendency to refer to the practice of psychotherapy as an "art," its applied and functional aspects would indicate that it is more accurate to conceptualize it as a "craft" (cf. Colby, 1962). In order to be a skillful craftsperson, such as a potter, one needs to have certain technical knowledge and skills as to how to work with one's material. However, one must also possess a natural talent for this kind of activity. While potters may be able to gain some invaluable information from the available textbooks describing the technical aspects of the craft, their eventual proficiency depends on the extent to which their native ability can be enhanced by this technical knowledge, together with an extensive apprenticeship under a more experienced tutor. And although a certain amount of subjective judgment is required, it nonetheless is possible to evaluate the eventual product of one's craft. It is our firm belief that the field of psychotherapy will have come of age when it has developed a pool of therapeutic principles and techniques that, in the hands of an experienced, sensitive, and interpersonally skilled clinician, may be used to reach certain therapeutic goals. The extent to which these goals have been achieved, as well as the processes involved in achieving them, comprises the empirical study of the craft.

Clinical Practice as a Starting Point

It is our contention that there exists a very definite potential for greater interplay between practice and research. But before considering this potential, it might be helpful to comment briefly on the more general issue of how research advances are made.

In looking at scientific inquiry from a sociological vantage point, the distinction has been made between those who are "problem finders" and those who are "problem solvers" (Wilkes, 1979). The problem finders are most relevant within science prior to the development of an agreed-upon paradigm. Their primary function is to identify relevant research questions that are most likely to advance the field. Once these basic issues have been delineated, the task of problem solvers becomes that of investigating the empirical status of those phenomena noted by the front-line observers.

In discussing research in psychotherapy with Bergin and Strupp (1972), Neal Miller has emphasized that research should begin with a "discovery phase," only after which the "confirmatory phase" can be pursued. The general goal is to make certain that research efforts are carried out in potentially fruitful, not trivial, areas. Miller notes the following about his own research strategy:

> During the discovery or exploratory phase, I am interested in finding a phenomenon, gaining some understanding of the most significant conditions that affect it, and manipulating those conditions to maximize the phenomenon and minimize the "noise" that obscures it. During this phase I am quite free-wheeling and intuitive—follow hunches, vary procedures, try out wild ideas, and take short-cuts. During it, I usually am not interested in elaborate controls; in fact I have learned to my sorrow that one can waste a lot of time on designing and executing elaborate controls for something that is not there [p. 348].

Bergin and Strupp's (1972) interview with Henry B. Linford, a chemical engineer, also revealed potentially interesting parallels between psychotherapy and chemical engineering—two applied fields. It was noted that in the case of chemical engineering, many discoveries were made by inventors and pragmatists, even though the processes involved were as yet not understood by chemists. Nonetheless, these inventors were able to discover reliable phenomena, and it was only later that the field of chemical engineering developed, reflecting the blending of pragmatism and scientific understanding.

In his fascinating book *The Psychology of Science*, Maslow (1966) similarly suggests that in the case of most psychological problems, we need to begin with our direct observations and experiences, only after which more objective experimental methods are employed. He observes that:

To begin the scientific study of love, for instance, with physicalistic methods would be to be meticulous about something only crudely known, like exploring a continent with a pair of tweezers and magnifying glass. But also to restrict oneself to phenomenological methods is to be content with a lower degree of certainty and reliability than is actually attainable [p. 47].

Going on to argue for empirical evaluation, Maslow also cautions us against unleashed theorizing, pointing out that we need to avoid the development of a tight-knit school of thought that reaches the point of blinding us to certain aspects of observable reality. Finely spun theoretical conceptualizations about the therapy process and the intricacies of human functioning face the danger of developing into a sophisticated form of autism.

The importance of direct, applied experiences can be illustrated by the work of Paracelsus, a controversial figure in 16th century medicine (Ackerknecht, 1968, 1973; Debus, 1966). The first physician to make use of the vernacular in the medical literature, Paracelsus maintained that the available theories that pervaded the university curricula were outdated, and in fact served as an obstacle to medical progress. He argued that there was a need to return to more direct observation and experience, as this would provide the essential foundation on which more effective medical practices could be based. In addition to having observed that medical problems could often be cured by mere suggestion of improvement, Paracelsus is credited with providing the impetus for the ultimate development of the experimental approach to medicine.

In a discussion of current constraints to progress in psychological research, Wachtel (1980) has suggested that the academic community reinforces research productivity more than it does the careful consideration of ideas that need to be investigated. Wachtel suggests that we need to give further encouragement to theoreticians who can come up with testable hypotheses, who can synthesize diverse findings and observations, and who can point to potentially fruitful areas for future investigation.

These observations and suggestions for how scientific advances are made have definite implications for the field of psychotherapy. We maintain that there currently exists a great need for gathering clinical observations from experienced therapists, who, as "problem finders," can offer us a very rich source of hypotheses to pursue in our research on psychotherapy. This is certainly not a novel suggestion, and other workers in the field have similarly pointed to the need for closer interplay between firsthand clinical experience and objective evaluation (e.g., Barlow, 1980; Goldstein, 1968; Klein & Gurman, 1981; Lazarus & Davison, 1971; Schaffer & Lazarus, 1952; Strupp, 1968). It is the experienced and skilled practicing clinician who should be the point of departure in our generalizations.

Birk and Brinkley-Birk (1974) have emphasized the importance of "saving the phenomena," an observation that dates back to the arguments of Greek philosophers who noted that it would be a mistake to overlook phenomena when they failed to conform to our theoretical presuppositions. It perhaps represents a very important phase in the field of psychotherapy for us to admit that our theoretical notions and research findings do not encompass all of clinical reality. If one views the split between clinicians and researchers from outside the entire system, it becomes more evident that both groups are deluding themselves in thinking that they alone will advance the field. Stated more positively, it is perhaps more productive to conclude that both groups very much need each other. The experience and wisdom of the practicing clinician cannot be overlooked. But because these observations are often not clearly articulated, may be unsystematic or at times idiosyncratic, and are typically kept informal, it is less likely that these insights can add to a reliable body of knowledge. The growing methodological sophistication of the researcher, on the other hand, is in need of significant and ecologically valid subject material. Our knowledge about what works in therapy must be rooted in clinical observations, but it must also have empirical verification. For the researcher and clinician to ignore the contributions that each has to make is to perpetuate a system in which no one wins (Goldstein, 1968).

A Common Language for Dialogue

A major obstacle in any attempt at a dialogue or collaboration across different theoretical orientations is language. Unless we use the same concepts, how are we to know whether the similarities and differences we detect are real or an artifact of our different language systems? There are obvious difficulties in comprehending what colleagues from other orientations may be attempting to communicate when they use concepts associated with their approach to therapy. The problem, however, is more than just a difficulty in comprehension. Upon hearing certain terms used by colleagues having orientations other than our own, we often experience a negative emotional reaction, although such feelings may not always be directly expressed. Such affective reactions are frequently accompanied by fleeting questions about the competence of these other therapists and thoughts about their obtuseness in missing certain points that may be obvious to us. In our more rational moments, we may very well respect these same colleagues and may openly acknowledge their professional expertise. Nonetheless, all this can get undercut when we hear such terms as "transference," "reinforcement," or "self-actualization." It is indeed unfortunate that this prevents us from sharing our common clinical observations, experiences, or empirical findings about therapeutic effectiveness.

Despite any commitment we might have to communicate with therapists from other orientations, we are confronted with the dilemma of finding a common language. One possibility that deserves our serious consideration is that we make use of the language system that we all learned
before we became professionals, namely, the vernacular. This is often easier said than done, however, as most of us have become accustomed to
thinking and speaking in terms of our own unique jargon; indeed, we are
often unaware that we are even doing so. In a dialogue between one of us
and Strupp on the possibility of rapprochement between behavioral and
psychodynamic approaches (Goldfried & Strupp, 1980), the issue of the
language barrier was discussed. The irony of it all was that in the process of
suggesting that we use the vernacular as a common language, Goldfried
illustrated the difficulty when he at one point suggested: "We need to
retrieve from storage in our long-term memory the language system we
knew before we became professionals." Only after the statement was made
did the automatic intrusion of jargon become apparent.

There is no doubt that it is difficult and far more cumbersome to
communicate without our well-learned jargon. Nonetheless, we do so at
times, particularly when we are attempting to explain certain phenomena
to intelligent but nonprofessional lay audiences. Brady et al. (1980), in
providing their answers to a series of questions on effective ingredients in
psychotherapy, were in fact able to report their observations without the
use of any technical concepts. What we are suggesting is that the vernacular may serve some interim function to facilitate better communication—as
it did in the case of Paracelsus' contributions to medicine in the 16th
century.

Although the vernacular may provide us with an initial common language, it is ultimately essential that our common language system be more
closely tied to research findings on human functioning. A number of contemporary writers have independently suggested the possibility that a common language may eventually come from the field of experimental cognitive psychology (Goldfried, 1979; Landau & Goldfried, 1981; Ryle, 1978;
Sarason, 1979; Shevrin & Dickman, 1980). We hasten to emphasize that it
is *not* being suggested that cognitive psychology can provide us with a
comprehensive theory that may be used to translate one language system
into another, in the sense that Dollard and Miller (1950) attempted to do
some years ago. Instead, the language from cognitive psychology has been
suggested as offering us a set of relatively neutral concepts, having a minimal theoretical superstructure, and being closely related to the kinds of
phenomena that we all see in our clinical work.

In making his point that experimental cognitive psychology can deal
with the phenomena of psychodynamic and behavioral approaches to therapy, Ryle (1978) illustrates how a number of psychoanalytic constructs may

be described in cognitive terms. As behavior therapy has become more cognitive in its emphasis, argues Ryle, such concepts from cognitive psychology may be applied to this orientation as well. In an interesting discussion of research efforts in the experimental study of unconscious processes as they relate to psychodynamic theories of personality, Shevrin and Dickman (1980) have echoed Sarason's (1979) suggestion that behaviorally oriented researchers and clinicians need to take into account such phenomena. Writing from a psychodynamic viewpoint, Shevrin and Dickman argue that human functioning cannot be fully understood without taking into account conscious processes, and that conscious processes cannot be fully understood in the absence of any considerations of unconscious factors. They go on to point out that much of the basic research and theory in the area of experimental cognitive psychology has caught up with many of the phenomena that have been of interest to psychodynamic therapists and researchers. Having its roots in psychodynamic theory, some of the early research in this general area was carried out in the field of perception during the 1950s (Allport, 1955). In considering the relevance of contemporary cognitive research to clinical work, Shevrin and Dickman note: "The laboratory and the consulting room do seem to be sharing at least a common wall, which in fact may turn out to have a door to it" (1980, p. 432). Behavior therapists, who have long acknowledged the need to extrapolate from experimental findings to the clinical setting, should certainly be able to resonate to this notion even if the phenomena being studied by experimental cognitive psychologists have a strong psychodynamic flavor.

Although the cognitive emphasis in behavior therapy began with the assumption that people engaged in "internal dialogues" that mediate their emotional reactions and behavior patterns, there has been a more recent acknowledgment that individuals at times may lack the ability to provide accurate introspective information on their cognitive processes (Arnkoff, 1980; Beck, 1976; Goldfried, 1979; Mahoney, 1980; Meichenbaum, 1980). Rather than assuming that people always deliberately "tell themselves" certain things in given situations, it has been suggested that such cognitive processes might more accurately be described as involving *implicit meaning structures* that mediate an individual's interaction with the world. This shift in conceptualization is particularly noteworthy, particularly since the very essence of psychoanalytic therapy has been said to involve the study of idiosyncractic meanings (e.g., Rycroft, 1970; Schafer, 1976). More recent conceptualizations of psychotherapy conducted according to client-centered guidelines have described a person's inappropriate reactions as reflecting faulty schemas, leading to the idiosyncratic meanings attributed to various life events (Rice, 1974, 1980; Wexler, 1974).

In their discussion of the current status of learning theory, Bower and Hilgard (1981) have pointed out that the grand, competing theories of the past have given way to concepts (e.g., short-term memory) that allow experimental psychologists to better communicate with each other. Moreover, researchers have been applying such concepts to everyday phenomena. The mazes and nonsense syllables of the past have been replaced by the study of memory for real-life events, factors associated with cognitive distortions, variables that assist or interfere with the comprehension of meaningful material, and knowledge of appropriate actions in social situations.

It is our contention that experimental cognitive psychology is becoming more "relevant" to the concerns of the clinician, and some of its concepts may be used without necessarily ascribing to a more general theoretical framework. The potential utility of cognitive psychology's language system may be illustrated with the concepts of "schema," "scripts," and "meta-cognitions."

The concept of *schema* essentially refers to an individual's cognitive representation of past experiences, particularly as they relate to current functioning. Acting much like a template that people impose upon life events, schemas are believed to assist individuals in attending to and interpreting relevant information in their current life situation and to affect recall of any relevant information from the past. Particularly pertinent to clinical work is the fact that schemas can often lead people to make faulty inferences about themselves and the world in which they live. When information is not presented in a given situation, people have a tendency to fill in the gaps according to their schema most closely associated with such events. In a particularly lucid discussion of how individuals' schemas are related to social information processing, Taylor and Crocker (1980) suggest that the reason people tend to overlook sources of information that may contradict their stereotypic judgments is built into the very nature of the schema itself. That is, the content and structure of a schema provide guidelines for identifying external events that are consistent with it, rendering little meaning to external events that are inconsistent or irrelevant.

Wachtel has made use of the schema concept as a way of understanding the transference phenomenon. According to Piaget, one's schema about the physical world results from personal action and feedback, with both modification of stimulus input (assimilation) and change in schema as a result of environmental feedback (accommodation). One learns fairly early in life that it is indeed difficult to walk through walls. In dealing with interpersonal events, however, the feedback one receives is considerably more ambiguous, which accounts for the persistence of such schemas over time. In addition, individuals often selectively place themselves in situations that are consistent with their schemas. The role of the therapist, suggests Wachtel, is to assist patients in becoming aware of the outdated schemas they have about others, to help sensitize them to the kinds of events that will allow for both the confirmation and disconfirmation of these schemas, and to take care not to become an "accomplice" in unwittingly confirming patients' distorted views of others. Rice (1974, 1980) has similarly suggested that the essence of change in client-centered therapy involves change in the client's inadequate and distorting schemas. She suggests that the built-in tendency to filter out contradictory information and the disrupting effects of emotional arousal on accurate cognitive processing contribute to the maintenance of faulty schemas. The concept of schema has also been used by cognitive behavior therapists (e.g., Beck, 1976; Goldfried & Robins, in press) who have suggested therapeutic procedures for aiding clients in cognitively processing personal experiences that can correct faulty schemas.

Whereas the notion of schema deals with an individual's particular meaning structure about various life events, *scripts* refer to more global patterns of functioning. Specifically, scripts describe those well-learned, and often implicit rules or guidelines for how individuals are likely to deal with various types of situations (Schank & Abelson, 1977). Of particular relevance to clinical phenomena is the fact that individuals differ in their knowledge of which scripts are likely to be appropriate in different social contexts, and also in the personal or implicit scripts that guide their day-to-day interpersonal relations.

As a final illustration of the potential relevance of cognitive psychology, we point to the concept of *metacognition*, which refers to the ability of individuals to monitor their experiences and make self-appraisals (cf. Flavell & Wellman, 1977). Clearly, metacognitive processes have been dealt with by therapists of varying orientations, who have referred to this self-appraisal capacity with such diverse terms as "experiencing versus observing ego," "self-monitoring," "corrective feedback," "witnessing," and "reframing."

In our consideration of the potential use of cognitive psychology as providing us with a common language system, we have offered but a brief sampling to suggest its relevance. A more detailed consideration of the applicability of such concepts to varying therapeutic orientations may be found elsewhere (Landau & Goldfried, 1981; Ryle, 1978; Sarason, 1979). And although some clinicians and researchers may understandably question whether it is worth the time and effort to learn a new set of labels and concepts, we believe that a common language is essential for the future development of the field.

Where Do We Go From Here?

Parsons (1951) has pointed out that one of the dominant characteristics of social systems associated with science is their inherent instability. He observes: "There is always the possibility that someone will make a new discovery. This may be merely a specific addition to knowledge of fact, in which case it will simply be fitted in with the rest in its proper place. But it may be something which necessitates the *reorganization* to a greater or lesser degree of the systematized body of knowledge" (p. 336). Even though a change in thinking and knowledge is the hallmark of any advancing scientific or technical pursuit, the participants themselves are often reluctant to accept such advances (cf. Barber, 1961; Kuhn, 1970; Polanyi, 1946). In the field of psychotherapy, we are all aware of those true believers who tenaciously hold on to their conceptions at all costs. As suggested by Bergson (1935), while the strength of one's faith may be measured by the belief that one can move mountains, it is even more dramatically manifested by an inability to see the mountain that needs to be moved.

As we indicated at the very outset of this chapter, there are a growing number of professionals who are finding it difficult to maintain with any intellectual honesty the belief that any one therapeutic orientation has all the answers. Certainly, this has happened within behavior therapy, the orientation with which we have had most direct and ongoing familiarity. As suggested by a researcher-clinician who entered the ranks of behavior therapy in the mid-1970s (Kendall, 1979), this orientation to clinical intervention appears to have been undergoing some interesting developmental changes. Referring to the earlier period of industry and hard work that behavior therapy needed in order to establish its separate identity, Kendall suggests that the growing tendency to look toward other approaches represents a more advanced stage of growth: "Only after one has established a healthy identity can true intimacy be achieved." Continuing on with this Eriksonian analysis of developments within behavior therapy, Kendall suggests that we should all strive toward a greater sense of generativity, so that our professional activities can have some impact on the future of the field. Quite apart from the accuracy of this developmental analysis, the very fact that a behavior therapist would choose this particular developmental model for conceptualizing growth within the behavioral orientation illustrates that the trend toward rapprochement is clearly upon us.

All indications point to the likelihood that the practice of psychotherapy over the next several decades is likely to undergo some very definite changes. Having said that, however, we hasten to acknowledge that it is far easier to describe and document what currently exists than to predict what will be. This difficulty in predicting the future is vividly illustrated by Bergin and Strupp's (1970) conclusion after interviewing leading clinical researchers throughout the country that, while coordinated/collaborative therapy research was needed, it simply was not feasible in the near future. As a result of developments both within and outside of the field, the National Institute of Mental Health has been able to launch a large-scale collaborative study on the treatment of depression scarcely one decade later.

While the issue of a rapprochement across therapeutic orientations has been discussed by numerous others in the past, and in many ways seems to make good sense, there exist numerous barriers. Grinker (1979), who has written about this very issue, laments: "It seems that we are writing for ourselves with little effect on others." One of the barriers to rapprochement has been documented within the sociology of science, which has described the extraordinarily competitive set of rules by which the scientific community operates (Hagstrom, 1965; Merton, 1969; Reif, 1961). The reward system is such that scientists are encouraged to outdo each other. Although their initial motivation may have involved an honest attempt to advance the field, there is always the danger that the extrinsic rewards of fame and position can subvert such original motives (Merton, 1969). Because originality and novel information are prized most highly, we have witnessed an extraordinary proliferation of different schools of psychotherapy. In comparison to other disciplines, the field of psychotherapy has some other factors that complicate matters still further, such as the obvious financial benefits that may accompany one's following a given therapeutic orientation. And without clear standards for what constitutes therapeutic effectiveness, it is always possible for therapeutic approaches to continue to thrive through a system of social networks and referral systems.

Although we are accustomed to think of psychotherapy as changing and advancing on the basis of work that occurs within the field, sociologists have long recognized that scientific advancements are very strongly affected by outside influences, be they economic, political, or military in nature (Cole & Cole, 1973; Merton, 1938/1970). Few would deny the very dramatic advances that physics and other disciplines made as a result of the cooperative "war effort" made in the early 1940s. Similarly, numerous scientific and technological advances have been made as the result of the Soviet Union's initial demonstration of their aerospace capabilities. The basic point is that once science becomes more directly involved with the needs of society, there is a possibility it will make great leaps forward in growth and influence, moving from what has been called "little science" to "big science" (Price, 1963). There is every reason to believe that with the increased pressures for accountability coming from insurance companies and governmental policymakers—to say nothing of consumer groups—psychotherapy is likely to be in store for some dramatic changes.

It is possible that these external pressures for accountability may mobilize efforts within each of the several professions to convince policymakers that each offers a viable, if not better, treatment service (cf. Parloff, 1979). However, it is unlikely that this course of action will provide us with any "consensus" that deals with the issues at hand, namely, the effectiveness of certain therapeutic interventions. We have said little about the issue of interdisciplinary rivalries in this chapter. Although they are real, we maintain that by putting our energies in that arena we can only dilute efforts that are needed elsewhere.

Like all human beings who at times experience difficulty in maintaining a clear perspective on their lives, there is the constant danger that clinicians and researchers can get caught up in a system that prevents them from recognizing what needs to be done to advance the field. The field of psychotherapy is comprised of numerous professional networks, most of which reflect a particular theoretical outlook. As we have noted elsewhere, "without a specific therapeutic orientation, how would we know what journals to subscribe to or which conventions to attend?" (Goldfried, 1980, p. 996). We are not saying that professional networks within the field are not needed, but rather that the particular kind we now have may not provide enough scope to advance the field much beyond its current point. What we are suggesting is the need for a network of professionals who are interested in taking steps toward the ultimate achievement of some kind of rapprochement and consensus—not only to determine the common elements that may cut across different therapeutic orientations, but also to identify those unique contributions that any particular approach may have to offer. Based on what we have read, our observations at conferences and conventions, and our numerous conversations with colleagues from various therapeutic orientations, we believe that there are many professionals who are most sympathetic to the establishment of such a network. Certainly, there exists a very large number of clinicians and researchers who identify themselves as being "eclectic," even in the face of the negative connotations that are typically associated with that label. There are also those professionals who ascribe to some theoretical orientation but who have recognized and openly acknowledged that other schools have something to offer. While still maintaining their own theoretical identities, they nonetheless are willing to explore potential sources of convergence. Another potential group includes basic researchers, particularly those who are involved in the areas of experimental cognitive psychology and social cognition. Many of the questions these researchers have been investigating in recent years are very closely related to the kinds of phenomena one sees in a clinical setting. Beginning steps to establish this informal network, encompassing all of these various groups, have already begun to take place.

Once a network of individuals interested in exploring points of rapprochement is formed, work in this area might involve ongoing dialogues, symposia, conferences, and relevant research projects. Although past attempts have been made to compare different therapeutic approaches, participants appear to have embarked on such projects with their minds already made up, attempting to get others to come around to their position while knowing at some level that they never would. Somewhere along the way, some efforts need to be made to obtain more direct samples of what other therapists actually do, so as to break down our stereotypes and prejudices that may otherwise blind us to an added perspective that another orientation may offer us. While there will always be those who are not likely to budge—true believers or those who otherwise have too much at stake—it is our hope that a growing number of practitioners and researchers will be willing to put their energies in this general direction.

We are at a very exciting point in the evolution and growth of psychotherapy. It has been approximately 100 years since the practice of psychotherapy began, and during this time we have witnessed considerable confusion along with the accumulation of a body of knowledge. It is only within the past few decades that we have really made some attempt to conduct research addressed to the broad question of whether psychotherapy works, and if so, how it does. As a result of some of our clinical and research efforts, we are starting to make some headway, and we anticipate continued progress in years to come.

Conclusion

Although varying theoretical orientations have clearly been useful in helping us to develop a wide variety of therapeutic procedures, we see a need to make greater use of what actually goes on clinically as a way of generating fruitful research hypotheses. Without such close links between clinician and researcher, we face the danger of our theory and research becoming too far removed from the clinical foundations of our generalizations.

Just as we believe that neither the clinician nor the researcher, working alone, can be successful in advancing the field, so do we maintain that no one theoretical orientation can provide us with all the answers. We need to take a close look at the points of commonality that cut across different orientations, as well as the unique contributions that each has to offer. With growing demands for therapists to be accountable for the efficacy of their procedures, the time may be increasingly ripe for clinicians and researchers of various theoretical persuasions to begin to mobilize collaborative efforts.

References

Ackerknecht, E. H. *A short history of medicine*. New York: Ronald Press, 1968.

Ackerknecht, E. H. *Therapeutics from the primitive to the 20th century*. New York: Hafner Press, 1973.

Alexander, F. The dynamics of psychotherapy in light of learning theory. *American Journal of Psychiatry*, 1963, *120*, 440–448. [Reprinted in this volume.]

Alexander, F., & French, T. M. *Psychoanalytic therapy*. New York: Ronald, 1946.

Aronson, E., & Carlsmith, J. M. Experimentation in social psychology. In G.
    Lindzey & E. Aronson (Eds.), *The handbook of social psychology* (Vol. 2).
    Research Methods. Reading, Mass.: Addison-Wesley, 1968.
Allport, F. H. *Theories of perception and the concept of structure*. New York:
    Wiley, 1955.
Appelbaum, S. A. The idealization of insight. *International Journal of Psychoana-
    lytic Psychotherapy*, 1975, *4*, 272–302.
Appelbaum, S. A. A psychoanalyst looks at Gestalt therapy. In C. Hatcher & P.
    Himmelstein (Eds.), *The handbook of Gestalt therapy*. New York: Jason Aron-
    son, 1976.
Appelbaum, S. A. Pathways to change in psychoanalytic therapy. *Bulletin of the
    Menninger Clinic*, 1978, *42*, 239–251. [Reprinted in this volume].
Appelbaum, S. A. *Out in inner space: A psychoanalyst explores the new therapies*.
    Garden City, N.Y.: Anchor Books, 1979.
Arnkoff, D. B. Future directions for research on cognitive counseling and therapy.
    Paper presented at the meeting of the American Psychological Association,
    Montreal, 1980.
Barber, B. Resistance by scientists to scientific discovery. *Science*, 1961, *134*, 596–
    602.
Barlow, D. H. Behavior therapy: The next decade. *Behavior Therapy*, 1980, *11*,
    315–328.
Beck, A. T. *Cognitive therapy and the emotional disorders*. New York: Interna-
    tional Universities Press, 1976.
Ben-David, J. Scientific growth: A sociological view. *Minerva*, 1964, *2*, 455–476.
Bergin, A. E. The evaluation of therapeutic outcomes. In A.E. Bergin & S.L.
    Garfield (Eds.), *Handbook of psychotherapy and behavior change*. New York:
    Wiley, 1971.
Bergin, A. E. The search for a psychotherapy of value. *Tijdschrist voor Psycho-
    therapie (Journal of Psychotherapy*, Amsterdam), 1982, *8*, in press.
Bergin, A. E., & Strupp, H. H. New directions in psychotherapy research. *Journal
    of Abnormal Psychology*, 1970, *76*, 13–26.
Bergin, A. E., & Strupp, H. H. *Changing frontiers in the science of psychother-
    apy*. Chicago: Aldine-Atherton, 1972.
Bergson, H. L. *The two sources of morality and religion*. New York: Holt, 1935.
Bieber, I. The concept of irrational belief systems as primary elements of psycho-
    pathology. *Journal of the American Academy of Psychoanalysis*, 1974, *2*, 91–100.
Birk, L., & Brinkley-Birk, A. Psychoanalysis and behavior therapy. *American Jour-
    nal of Psychiatry*, 1974, *131*, 499–510. [Reprinted in this volume.]
Bower, G. H., & Hilgard, E. R. *Theories of learning* (5th ed.). Englewood Cliffs,
    N.J.: Prentice-Hall, 1981.
Brady, J. P. Psychotherapy by a combined behavioral and dynamic approach. *Com-
    prehensive Psychiatry*, 1968, *9*, 536–543. [Reprinted in this volume.]
Brady, J. P., Davison, G. C., Dewald, P. A., Egan, G., Fadiman, J., Frank, J. D.,
    Gill, M. M., Hoffman, I., Kempler, W., Lazarus, A. A., Raimy, V., Rotter, J.
    B., & Strupp, H. H. Some views on effective principles of psychotherapy.
    Cognitive Therapy and Research, 1980, *4*, 271–306. [Reprinted in this volume.]

Brown, M. A., Psychodynamics and behavior therapy. *Psychiatric Clinics of North America,* 1978, *1,* 435–448.

Burton, A. (Ed.). *What makes behavior change possible?* New York: Brunner/Mazel, 1976.

Cantor, N., & Mischel, W. Prototypes in person perception. In L. Berkowitz (Ed.), *Advances in experimental social psychology* (Vol. 12). New York: Academic Press, 1979.

Cohen, L. H. Clinical psychologists' judgments of the scientific merit and clinical relevance of psychotherapy outcome research. *Journal of Consulting and Clinical Psychology,* 1979, *47,* 421–423.

Cohen, L. H., & Suchy, K. R. The bias in psychotherapy research evaluation. *Journal of Clinical Psychology,* 1979, *35,* 184–187.

Colby, K. M. Discussion of papers on therapist's contribution. In H.H. Strupp & L. Luborsky (Eds.), *Research in psychotherapy (Vol. 2).* Washington, D. C.: American Psychological Association, 1962.

Cole, J. R., & Cole, S. *Social stratification in science.* Chicago: University of Chicago Press, 1973.

Debus, A. G. *The English Paracelsians.* New York: Franklin Watts, 1966.

Dewald, P. A. *Psychotherapy: A dynamic approach* (2nd ed.). New York: Basic Books, 1971.

Dewald, P. A. Toward a general concept of the therapeutic process. *International Journal of Psychoanalytic Psychotherapy,* 1976, *5,* 283–299.

Dimond, R. E., Havens, R. A., & Jones, A. C. A conceptual framework for the practice of prescriptive eclecticism in psychotherapy. *American Psychologist,* 1978, *33,* 239–248.

Dollard, J., & Miller, N. E. *Personality and psychotherapy.* New York: McGraw-Hill, 1950. [Reprinted in this volume.]

Egan, G. *The skilled helper.* Monterey, Calif.: Brooks/Cole, 1975.

Fay, A. Personal communication. January 8, 1981.

Feather, B. W., & Rhoads, J. M. Psychodynamic behavior therapy: II. Clinical aspects. *Archives of General Psychiatry,* 1972, *26,* 503–511.

Ferster, C. B. The difference between behavioral and conventional psychology. *The Journal of Nervous and Mental Disease,* 1974, *159,* 153–157.

Flavell, J. H., & Wellman, H. M. Meta-memory. In R.V. Kail, Jr., & J.W. Hagen (Eds.), *Perspectives on the development of memory and cognition.* Hillsdale, N.J.: LEA Associates, 1977.

Ford, J. D., & Kendall, P. C. Behavior therapists' professional behaviors: Converging evidence of a gap between theory and practice. *The Behavior Therapist,* 1979, *2,* 37–38.

Frank, J. D. *Persuasion and healing.* Baltimore: Johns Hopkins, 1961. [Reprinted in part in this volume.]

Frank, J. D. Restoration of morale and behavior change. In A. Burton (Ed.), *What makes behavior change possible?* New York: Brunner/Mazel, 1976.

Frank, J. D. The present status of outcome studies. *Journal of Consulting and Clinical Psychology,* 1979, *47,* 310–316. [Reprinted in this volume.]

Franks, C. M. On the importance of conceptual integrity and its mutual advantages to two fundamentally incompatible systems. Paper presented at the Association for the Advancement of Behavior Therapy, Chicago, November, 1978.

French, T. M. Interrelations between psychoanalysis and the experimental work of Pavlov. *American Journal of Psychiatry*, 1933, *89*, 1165–1203.

Garfield, S. L. What are the therapeutic variables in psychotherapy? *Psychotherapy and Psychosomatics*, 1974, *24*, 372–378. [Reprinted in this volume.]

Garfield, S. L. *Psychotherapy: An eclectic approach*. New York: Wiley-Interscience, 1980.

Garfield, S. L., & Bergin, A. E. (Eds.). *Handbook of psychotherapy and behavior change: An empirical analysis* (2nd ed.). New York: Wiley, 1978.

Garfield, S. L., & Kurtz, R. Clinical psychologists in the 1970's. *American Psychologist*, 1976, *31*, 1–9.

Garfield, S. L., & Kurtz, R. A study of eclectic views. *Journal of Consulting and Clinical Psychology*, 1977, *45*, 78–83. [Reprinted in this volume.]

Goldfried, M. R. Anxiety reduction through cognitive-behavioral intervention. In P. C. Kendall & S. D. Hollon (Eds.), *Cognitive-behavioral interventions: Theory, research, and procedures*. New York: Academic Press, 1979. [Reprinted in part in this volume.]

Goldfried, M. R. Toward the delineation of therapeutic change principles. *American Psychologist*, 1980, *35*, 991–999. [Reprinted in this volume.]

Goldfried, M. R., & Davison, G. C. *Clinical behavior therapy*. New York: Holt, Rinehart, and Winston, 1976.

Goldfried, M. R., Decenteceo, E. T., & Weinberg, L. Systematic rational restructuring as a self-control technique. *Behavior Therapy*, 1974, *5*, 247–254.

Goldfried, M. R., & Robins, C. On the facilitation of self-efficacy. *Cognitive Therapy and Research*, in press.

Goldfried, M. R., & Strupp, H. H. Empirical clinical practice: A dialogue on rapprochement. Presented at the meeting of the Association for the Advancement of Behavior Therapy, New York, November, 1980.

Goldstein, A. Appropriate expression training: Humanistic behavior therapy. In A. Wanderman, P. J. Poppen, & D. F. Ricks (Eds.), *Humanism and behaviorism: Dialogue and growth*. Elmsford, N.Y.: Pergamon Press, 1976.

Goldstein, A. P. Psychotherapy research and psychotherapy practice: Independence or equivalence? In S. Lesser (Ed.), *An evaluation of the results of the psychotherapies*. Springfield, Ill.: Charles C. Thomas, 1968. [Reprinted in this volume.]

Gordon, T. *PET: Parent effectiveness training*. New York: Wyden Books, 1970.

Gottman, J., Notarius, C., Gonso, T., & Markman, H. *A couple's guide to communication*. Champaign, Ill.: Research Press, 1976.

Greening, T. C. Commentary. *Journal of Humanistic Psychology*, 1978, *18*, 1–4.

Grinker, R. R., Sr. Discussion of Strupp's Some critical comments on the future of psychoanalytic therapy. *Bulletin of the Menninger Clinic*, 1976, *40*, 247–254. [Reprinted in this volume.]

Grinker, R. R., Sr. Personal communication. February, 1979.

Gurman, A. S. Integrative marital therapy: Toward the development of an interpersonal approach. In S. Budman (Ed.), *Forms of brief therapy*. New York: Guilford Press, 1981.

Hagstrom, W. O. *The scientific community*. Carbondale, Ill.: Southern Illinois University Press, 1965.

Horney, K. *Neurosis and human growth*. New York: Norton, 1950.

Horwitz, L. *Clinical prediction in psychotherapy*. New York: Jason Aronson, 1974.

Horwitz, L. New perspectives for psychoanalytic psychotherapy. *Bulletin of the Menninger Clinic*, 1976, *40*, 263–271.

Hunt, H. F. Behavioral considerations in psychiatric treatment. In J. Masserman (Ed.), *Science and psychoanalysis* (Vol. XVIII). New York: Grune & Stratton, 1971.

Hunt, H. F. Recurrent dilemmas in behavioral therapy. In G. Serban (Ed.), *Psychopathology of human adaptation*. New York: Plenum, 1976.

Jacobson, N. S., & Margolin, G. *Marital therapy: Treatment strategies based on social learning and behavior exchange principles*. New York: Brunner/Mazel, 1979.

Kaplan, H. S. *The new sex therapy*. New York: Brunner/Mazel, 1974.

Kaplan, H. S. *Disorders of desire*. New York: Brunner/Mazel, 1979.

Kelly, E. L., Goldberg, L. R, Fiske, D. W., & Kikowski, J. M. Twenty-five years later: A follow-up study of the graduate students in clinical psychology assessed in the V.A. selection research project. *American Psychologist*, 1978, *33*, 746–755.

Kendall, P. C. Personal communication. October, 1979.

Klein, M., Dittmann, A. T., Parloff, M. B., & Gill, M. M. Behavior therapy: Observations and reflections. *Journal of Consulting and Clinical Psychology*, 1969, *33*, 259–266.

Klein, M. H., & Gurman, A. S. Ritual and reality: Some clinical implications of experimental designs. In L. Rehm (Ed.), *Behavior therapy for depression*. New York: Academic Press, 1981.

Korchin, S. J. *Modern clinical psychology*. New York: Basic Books, 1976.

Kubie, L. S. Relation of the conditioned reflex to psychoanalytic technic. *Archives of Neurology and Psychiatry*, 1934, *32*, 1137–1142.

Kuhn, T. S. *The structure of scientific revolutions* (2nd ed.). Chicago: University of Chicago Press, 1970.

Lambley, P. The use of assertive training and psychodynamic insight in the treatment of migraine headache: A case study. *Journal of Nervous and Mental Disease*, 1976, *163*, 61–64.

Landau, R. J., & Goldfried, M. R. The assessment of schemata: A unifying framework for cognitive, behavioral, and traditional assessment. In P. C. Kendall & S. D. Hollon (Eds.), *Assessment strategies for cognitive-behavioral interventions*. New York: Academic Press, 1981.

Landsman, T. Not an adversity but a welcome diversity. Paper presented at the meeting of the American Psychological Association, New Orleans, August, 1974. [Reprinted in this volume.]

Lazarus, A.A. In support of technical eclecticism. *Psychological Reports*, 1967, *21*, 415–416.

Lazarus, A. A. *Behavior therapy and beyond*. New York: McGraw-Hill, 1971.

Lazarus, A. A. *Multi-modal behavior therapy*. New York: Springer, 1976.

Lazarus, A. A. Has behavior therapy outlived its usefulness? *American Psychologist*, 1977 *32*, 550–554. [Reprinted in this volume.]

Lazarus, A. A., & Davison, G. C. Clinical innovation in research and practice. In A. E. Bergin & S.L. Garfield (Eds.), *Handbook of psychotherapy and behavior change*. New York: Wiley, 1971.

Lehrer, A. Not a science. *APA Monitor*, 1981, *12*, 42.

Levay, A. N., Weissberg, J. H., & Blaustein, A. B. Concurrent sex therapy and psychoanalytic psychotherapy by separate therapists: Effectiveness and implications. *Psychiatry*, 1976, *39*, 355–363.

Lewis, W. C. *Why people change*. New York: Holt, Rinehart & Winston, 1972.

Liberman, R. P. Learning interpersonal skills in groups: Harnessing the behavioristic horse to the humanistic wagon. In P. S. Houts & M. Serber (Eds), *After the turn-on, what?* Campaign, Ill.: Research Press, 1972.

London, P. The end of ideology in behavior modification. *American Psychologist*, 1972 *27*, 913–920.

London, P. *The modes and morals of psychotherapy*. New York: Holt, Rinehart & Winston, 1964.

Luborsky, L., Singer, B., & Luborsky, L. Comparative studies of psychotherapies: Is it true that "Everyone has won and all must have prizes?" *Archives of General Psychiatry*, 1975, *32*, 995–1008.

Mahoney, M. J. *Cognition and behavior modification*. Cambridge, Mass.: Ballinger, 1974.

Mahoney, M. J. *Scientist as subject: The psychological imperative*. Cambridge, Mass.: Ballinger, 1976.

Mahoney, M. J. Psychotherapy and the structure of personal revolutions. In M. J. Mahoney (Ed.), *Psychotherapy process*. New York: Plenum, 1980.

Marks, I. M., & Gelder, M. G. Common ground between behavior therapy and psychodynamic methods. *British Journal of Medical Psychology*, 1966, *39*, 11–23.

Marmor, J. Neurosis and the psychotherapeutic process: Similarities and differences in the behavioral and psychodynamic conceptions. *International Journal of Psychiatry*, 1969, *7*, 514–519.

Marmor, J. Dynamic psychotherapy and behavior therapy: Are they irreconcilable? *Archives of General Psychiatry*, 1971, *24*, 22–28, [Reprinted in this volume.]

Marmor, J. Common operational factors in diverse approaches to behavior change. In A. Burton (Ed.), *What makes behavior change possible?* New York: Brunner/Mazel, 1976.

Marmor, J., & Woods, S. M. *The interface between psychodynamic and behavioral therapies*. New York: Plenum, 1980.

Martin, D. G. *Learning-based client-centered therapy*. Monterey, Calif.: Brooks/Cole, 1972.

Maslow, A. H. *The psychology of science: A reconnaissance*. New York: Harper 1966. [Reprinted in part in this volume.]

Matarazzo, J. D. The practice of psychotherapy is art and not science. In A. R. Mahrer & L. Person (Eds.), *Creative developments in psychotherapy*. Cleveland: Case Western Reserve Press, 1971.

Meichenbaum, D. H. *Cognitive behavior modification*. New York: Plenum, 1977.

Meichenbaum, D. H. Nature of conscious and unconscious processes: Issues in cognitive assessment. Invited address presented at the Meetings of the Eastern Psychological Association, Hartford, Conn., April, 1980.

Merton, R. K. Behavior patterns of scientists. *American scholar*, 1969, *38*, 197–225.

Merton, R. K. *Science, technology, and society in seventeenth-century England*. New York: Harper & Row, 1970. (Originally published, 1938.)

Messer, S. B., & Winokur, M. Some limits to the integration of psychoanalytic and behavior therapy. *American Psychologist*, 1980, *35*, 818–827.

Murray, M. E. A dynamic synthesis of analytic and behavioral approaches to symptoms. *American Journal of Psychotherapy*, 1976, *30*, 561–569.

O'Leary, K. D., & Turkewitz, H. Marital therapy from a behavioral perspective. In T. J. Paolino & B. S. McCrady (Eds.), *Marriage and marital therapy*. New York: Brunner/Mazel, 1978.

Parloff, M. B. Shopping for the right therapy. *Saturday Review*, February 21, 1976, pp. 14–16.

Parloff, M. B. Can psychotherapy research guide the policymaker? A little knowledge may be a dangerous thing. *American Psychologist*, 1979, *3*, 296–306. [Reprinted in this volume.]

Parsons, T. *The social system*. New York: Free Press, 1951.

Patterson, C. H. Divergence and convergence in psychotherapy. *American Journal of Psychotherapy*, 1967, *21*, 4–17.

Polanyi, M. *Science, faith and society*. Chicago: University of Chicago Press, 1946. (Introduction revised 1964).

President's Commission on Mental Health. *Report to the President* (Vol. 4). Washington, D. C.: U. S. Government Printing Office, 1978.

Price, D. J. deS. *Little science, big science*. New York: Columbia University Press, 1963.

Prochaska, J. O. *Systems of psychotherapy: A transtheoretical analysis*. Homewood, Ill.: Dorsey Press, 1979.

Raimy, V. *Misunderstandings of the self*. San Francisco: Jossey-Bass, 1975.

Raimy, V. Changing misconceptions as the therapeutic task. In A. Burton (Ed.), *What makes behavior change possible?* New York: Brunner/Mazel, 1976.

Reif, F. The competitive world of the pure scientist. *Science*, 1961, *134*, 1958–1962.

Rhoads, J. M. The integration of behavior therapy and psychoanalytic theory. *Journal of Psychiatric Treatment and Evaluation*, 1981, *3*, 1–6.

Rice, L. N. The evocative function of the therapist. In D. A. Wexler & L. N. Rice (Eds.), *Innovation in client-centered therapy*. New York: Wiley-Interscience, 1974.

Rice, L. N. The context of recurring events during psychotherapy: A task analysis of an event from client-centered therapy. Paper presented at the Meetings of the Society for Psychotherapy Research, Asilomar, Calif. 1980.

Ricks, D. F., Wandersman, A., & Poppen, P. J. Humanism and behaviorism: Toward new syntheses. In A. Wandersman, P. J. Poppen, & D. F. Ricks (Eds.), *Humanism and behaviorism: Dialogue and growth*. Elmsford, N.Y.: Pergamon Press, 1976. [Reprinted in this volume.]

Rogers, C. R. *On becoming a person*. Boston: Houghton Mifflin, 1961.

Rogers, C. R. Psychotherapy today or where do we go from here? *American Journal of Psychotherapy*, 1963, *17*, 5–15.

Rosenzweig, S. Some implicit common factors in diverse methods in psychotherapy. *American Journal of Orthopsychiatry*, 1936, *6*, 412–415. [Reprinted in this volume.]

Rosch, E., Mervis, C., Gray, W., Johnson, D., & Boyes-Braem, P. Basic objects in natural categories. *Cognitive Psychology*, 1976, *8*, 382–439.

Rotter, J. B. *Social learning and clinical psychology*. Englewood Cliffs, N.J.: Prentice-Hall, 1954.

Rycroft, C. Causes and meaning. In S. G. M. Lee & M. Hubert (Eds.), *Freud and psychology*. Harmondsworth, Great Britain: Penguin, 1970.

Ryle, A. A common language for the psychotherapies? *British Journal of Psychiatry*, 1978, *132*, 585–594. [Reprinted in this volume.]

Sarason, I. G. Three lacunae of cognitive therapy. *Cognitive therapy and research*, 1979, *3*, 223–235. [Reprinted in this volume.]

Schafer, R. *A new language for psychoanalysis*. New Haven: Yale University Press, 1976.

Schaffer, G. S., & Lazarus, R. S. *Fundamental concepts in clinical psychology*. New York: McGraw, 1952.

Schank, R., & Abelson, R. *Scripts, plans, goals and understanding*. Hillsdale, N.J.: Erlbaum, 1977.

Segraves, R. T., & Smith, R. C. Concurrent psychotherapy and behavior therapy. *Archives of General Psychiatry*, 1976, *33*, 256–263.

Shapiro, D. H., Jr. *Precision nirvana*. Engelwood Cliffs, N.J.: Prentice-Hall, 1978.

Shevrin, H., & Dickman, S. The psychological unconscious: A necessary assumption for all psychological theory? *American Psychologist*, 1980, *35*, 421–434.

Silverman, L. H. Some psychoanalytic considerations of non-psychoanalytic therapies: On the possibility of integrating treatment approaches and related issues. *Psychotherapy: Theory, Research, and Practice*, 1974, *11*, 298–305.

Sloane, R. B. The converging paths of behavior therapy and psychotherapy. *American Journal of Psychiatry*, 1969, *125*, 877–885.

Smith, M. L., & Glass, G. V. Meta-analysis of psychotherapy outcome studies. *American Psycholgist*, 1977, *32*, 752–760.

Smith, M. L., Glass, G. V., & Miller, T. I. *The benefits of psychotherapy*. Baltimore: Johns Hopkins University Press, 1980.

Staub, E. Fantasy, self-preservation and the reinforcing power of groups. In P. S. Houts & M. Serber (Eds.), *After the turn-on, what?* Champaign, Ill.: Research Press, 1972.

Strupp, H. H. Psychotherapists and (or versus?) researchers. *Voices: The Art and Science of Psychotherapy*, 1968, *4*, 28–32.

Strupp, H. H. On the basic ingredients of psychotherapy. *Journal of Consulting and Clinical Psychology*, 1973, *41*, 1–8. (a)

Strupp, H. H. *Psychotherapy: Clinical, research, and theoretical issues*. New York: Jason Aronson, 1973. (b)

Strupp, H. H. Some critical comments on the future of psychoanalytic therapy. *Bulletin of the Menninger Clinic*, 1976, *40*, 238–254. (a) [Reprinted in this volume.]

Strupp, H. H. The nature of the therapeutic influence and its basic ingredients. In A. Burton (Ed.), *What makes behavior change possible?* New York: Brunner/ Mazel, 1976. (b)

Strupp, H. H. Are psychoanalytic therapists beginning to practice cognitive behavior therapy or is behavior therapy turning psychoanalytic? Presented at symposium, Clinical-Cognitive Theories of Psychotherapy, American Psychological Association, Toronto, 1978. (a)

Strupp, H. H. Psychotherapy research and practice: An overview. In S. L. Garfield & A. E. Bergin (Eds.), *Handbook of psychotherapy and behavior change: An empirical analysis* (2nd ed.). New York: Wiley, 1978. (b)

Strupp, H. H. A psychodynamicist looks at modern behavior therapy. *Psychotherapy: Theory, Research and Practice,* 1979, *2,* 124–131.

Taylor, S. E., & Crocker, J. Schematic bases of social information processing. In E. T. Higgins, P. Hermann, & M. P. Zanna (Eds.), *The Ontario Symposium on Personality and Social Psychology* (Vol. I). Hillsdale, N.J.: Lawrence Erlbaum, 1980.

Thoresen, C. E. Behavioral humanism. In C. E. Thoresen (Ed.), *Behavior modification in education.* Chicago: University of Chicago Press, 1973.

Thoresen, C. E., & Coates, T. J. What does it mean to be a behavior therapist? *The Counseling Psychologist,* 1978, *7,* 3–21.

Wachtel, P. L. Behavior therapy and the facilitation of psychoanalytic exploration. *Psychotherapy: Theory, Research and Practice,* 1975, *12,* 68–72. [Reprinted in this volume.]

Wachtel, P. L. *Psychoanalysis and behavior therapy: Toward an integration.* New York: Basic Books, 1977.

Wachtel, P. L. Investigation and its discontent: Some constraints on progress in psychological research. *American Psychologist,* 1980, *35,* 399–408.

Wachtel, P. L. Transference, schema, and assimilation: The relevance of Piaget to the psychoanalytic theory of transference. In Chicago Institute for Psychoanalysis (Eds.), *Annual of Psychoanalysis* (Vol. 8). New York: International Universities Press, 1981.

Waskow, I. E., & Parloff, M. B. (Eds.), *Psychotherapy change measures.* Rockville, Md.: National Institute of Mental Health, 1975.

Wexler, D. A. A cognitive theory of experienceing, self-actualization, and therapeutic process. In D. A. Wexler & L. N. Rice (Eds.), *Innovation in client-centered therapy.* New York: Wiley-Interscience, 1974.

Wilkes, J. M. Cognitive issues arising from study in the sociology of science. Paper presented at the Annual Meeting of the American Psychological Association, New York, September, 1979.

Wolf, E. Learning theory and psychoanalysis. *British Journal of Medical Psychology,* 1966, *39,* 1–10.

Woody, R. H. *Psychobehavioral counseling and therapy: Integrating behavioral and insight techniques.* New York: Appleton-Century-Crofts, 1971.

Woody, R. H. Integrated aversion and psychotherapy: Two sexual deviation case studies. *Journal of Sex Research,* 1973, *9,* 313–324.

Part II
Early Stirrings

As an historical backdrop, the selections that follow represent some of the early writings by prominent therapists who advocated the need to look for common principles of therapeutic change. Although these specific early articles and book selections directly influenced the thinking of later writers, their impact was probably even more pervasive, as they no doubt served a consciousness-raising function by calling the field's attention to the general issue of rapprochement.

Rosenzweig's brief article calls into question the accuracy of any particular theoretical explanation for why a therapeutic intervention might work, suggesting that the actual change process might actually be a reflection of variables that were common to all therapies. Among these factors, suggests Rosenzweig, are the therapist's personal style of interacting with patients/clients, the novel conceptual explanation offered to distressed individuals for why they are having problems, and the synergistic nature of human functioning that allows therapeutic change to begin from any one of a variety of different starting points. The selection from Dollard and Miller's classic work *Personality and Psychotherapy* focuses specifically on the role of the therapeutic relationship as a means of producing change. Dollard and Miller suggest that the therapist's influence on the patient/client comes from such factors as differential approval, the calm and generally permissive attitude conveyed by therapists, and the support they offer to patients/clients to confront their fears. They also consider the several functions that interpretive comments may have. The article by Alexander is based on his extensive clinical career, as well as his research on what actually goes on in psychoanalysis. Among the various topics discussed are the interplay between cognitive and emotional experiences and the way they constitute a far-reaching component of therapeutic change. Alexander, like Rosenzweig, calls into question the adequacy of the traditional psychoanalytic theoretical explanations of the change process that many of his colleagues were taking for granted. The final selection in this section comes from Frank's *Persuasion and Healing,* which provides a comprehensive overview of past and current practices in psychotherapy within our culture, concluding that elements that are common to each of various therapeutic practices deserve more of our attention.

Chapter 2
Some Implicit Common Factors in Diverse Methods of Psychotherapy

Saul Rosenzweig

"At the last the Dodo said, "*Everybody* has won, and *all* must have prizes.""

It has often been remarked upon that no form of psychotherapy is without cures to its credit. Proponents of psychoanalysis, treatment by persuasion, Christian Science, and any number of other psychotherapeutic ideologies[1] can point to notable successes. The implication of this fact is not, however, univocal. The proud proponent, having achieved success in the cases he mentions, implies, even when he does not say it, that his ideology is thus proved true, all others false. More detatched observers, on the other hand, surveying the whole field tend, on logical grounds, to draw a very different conclusion. If such theoretically conflicting procedures, they reason, can lead to success, often even in similar cases, then therapeutic result is not a reliable guide to the validity of theory.

It takes but little reflection to arrive at the roots of the difficulty from the standpoint of logical deduction. Not only is it sound to believe that the

Reprinted by permission of the author, Saul Rosenzweig, and the publisher from the *American Journal of Orthopsychiatry*, 1936, 6, 412–415.

[1]*Specific* techniques, such as hypnotism, fall outside the intended scope of the present brief discussion. Only such forms of psychotherapy as are based upon a general theory of personality are here being examined.

same conclusion cannot follow from opposite premises but when such a contradiction appears, as seems to be true in the present instance, it is justifiable to wonder (1) whether the factors *alleged to be* operating in a given therapy are identical with the factors *that actually are* operating and (2) whether the factors that actually are operating in several different therapies may not have much more in common than have the factors alleged to be operating.

Pursuing this line of inquiry it is soon realized that besides the intentionally utilized methods and their consciously held theoretical foundations, there are inevitably certain *unrecognized factors* in any therapeutic situation—factors that may be even more important than those being purposely employed. It is possible for the procedures consciously utilized by the therapist to have a largely negative value in distracting attention from certain unconscious processes by means of which the therapeutic effect is actually achieved. Thus it might be conceivably argued that psychoanalysis, for example, succeeds, when it does, not so much because of the truth of the psychoanalytic doctrines about genetic development but rather because the analyst, in the practice of his method, quite unwittingly allows the patient to recondition certain inadequate social patterns in terms of the present situation—a phenomenon better explained by Pavlov's than by Freud's theories. Granting for the purpose of argument that this is the case, then the concepts of Freud are far less true by the successful analysis of a patient than are those of Pavlov—and therapeutic result achieved cannot uncritically be used as a test of theory advanced!

While this negative conclusion may be satisfying in some measure, it fails to solve the problem inherent in the fact from which it was derived. What, it is still necessary to ask, accounts for the result that apparently diverse forms of psychotherapy prove successful in similar cases? Or if they are only *apparently* diverse, what do these therapies actually have in common that makes them equally successful?[2] In undertaking to answer these questions, it will be assumed for purposes of exposition that all methods of therapy when competently used are equally successful. This assumption is not well-founded, for certain forms of treatment are very likely better suited than others to certain types of cases. For the present, however, this likelihood, as well as the related problem of determining the criteria for applying one method rather than another to a given patient, will be intentionally disregarded.

In seeking the factors common to diverse methods of psychotherapy the foregoing discussion of implicit procedures should be recalled. Such unverbalized aspects of the therapeutic relationship as were there illus-

[2]It is by no means being overlooked that there is another far more pressing problem which these notes do not consider—how it is that in so many cases all methods of therapy prove equally *unsuccessful*.

trated by the concept of social reconditioning may be equally represented in therapies of quite dissimilar guise. The possibility for catharsis constitutes another example of the same sort. With such potent implicit factors in common, externally different methods of therapy may well have approximately equal success.

Very closely related to such implicit factors is the indefinable effect of the therapist's personality. Though long recognized, this effect still presents an unsolved problem. Even the personal qualities of the good therapist elude description for, while the words *stimulating, inspiring,* and so on suggest themselves, they are far from adequate. For all this, observers seem intuitively to sense the characteristics of the good therapist time and again in particular instances, sometimes being so impressed as almost to believe that the personality of the therapist would be sufficient in itself, apart from everything else, to account for the cure of many a patient by a sort of catalytic effect. Since no one method of therapy has a monopoly on all the good therapists, another potentially common factor is available to help account for the equal success of avowedly different methods.

From the standpoint of the *psychological interpretations* given by therapists of different persuasions, another partial solution of the present problem may be offered. If it is true that mental disorder represents a conflict of disintegrated personality constituents, then the unification of these constituents by some systematic ideology, regardless of what that ideology may be, would seem to be a *sine qua non* for a successful therapeutic result. Whether the therapist talks in terms of psychoanalysis or Christian Science is from this point of view relatively unimportant as compared with the *formal consistency* with which the doctrine employed is adhered to, for by virtue of this consistency the patient receives a schema for achieving some sort and degree of personality organization. The very one-sidedness of an ardently espoused therapeutic doctrine might on these grounds have a favorable effect. Having in common this possibility of providing a systematic basis for reintegration, diverse forms of psychotherapy should tend to be equally successful.

From a somewhat different approach, though still under the general heading of interpretation, another notion contributing to the solution of the problem suggests itself. There are several steps in the argument. In the first place, psychological events are so complex and many-sided in nature that they may be *alternatively formulated* with considerable justification for each alternative. Under these circumstances any interpretation is apt to have a certain amount of truth in it, applying at least from one standpoint or to one aspect of the complex phenomenon being examined. Hence it is often difficult to decide between various interpretations of the same psychological event: they are all relevant, though perhaps to a greater or less degree, and are all therefore worthy of some consideration.

In the second place, personality seems to consist in an *interdependent organization* of various factors, all of them dynamically related.[3] It is impossible to change any significant factor or aspect of this organization without affecting the whole of it, for it is all of a piece. If this description is correct, it follows that in attempting to modify the structure of a personality, it would matter relatively little whether the approach was made from the right or the left, at the top or the bottom, so to speak, since a change in the total organization would follow regardless of the particular significant point at which it was attacked.

If, now, a given method of psychotherapy represents but one alternative formulation of the problem presented, it does not need to be completely adequate from every standpoint and may still be *therapeutically* effective. It needs to have merely enough relevance to impress the personality organization at some significant point and so begin the work of rehabilitation. The interdependence of the personality system will communicate this initial effect to the totality. This line of reasoning would, if true, considerably decrease the therapeutic importance of differences in psychological interpretation and so once more contribute to the explanation of how allegedly diverse methods of psychotherapy prove to have about equal success.[4]

In conclusion it may be said that given a therapist who has an effective personality and who consistently adheres in his treatment to a system of concepts which he has mastered and which is in one significant way or another adapted to the problems of the sick personality, then it is of comparatively little consequence what particular method that therapist uses. It is, of course, still necessary to admit the more elementary consideration that in certain types of mental disturbances certain kinds of therapy are indicated as compared with certain others. Were the problem of psychotherapy being considered in detail here, an attempt would be made to show that the therapist should have a repertoire of methods to be drawn upon as needed for the individual case. It would also be important to discuss the intricate psychodynamics of the relationship between the personality of the patient and that of the therapist in order to determine whether a particular sort of patient would not get along best with a therapist having a particular sort of personality. Even with such additions, however, much room would be left for the foregoing general argument based

[3]The interdependence of the factors is not incompatible with their "disintegration," as may at first glance appear, since factors that are inharmoniously related ("disintegrated") are nevertheless related within the given individual in some measure. The notion of conflict bears out this statement.

[4]The *scientific* adequacy of the theory of personality upon which a method of therapy is based is quite another matter. It is, moreover, not at all implied that a more scientifically adequate theory of personality would not give rise to a more effective method of psychotherapy, now or in the future. The point is simply that complete or absolute truth is by no means necessary for therapeutic success.

upon the following considerations which apply in common to avowedly diverse methods of psychotherapy: (1) the operation of implicit, unverbalized factors, such as catharsis, and the as yet undefined effect of the personality of the good therapist; (2) the formal consistency of the therapeutic ideology as a basis for reintegration; (3) the alternative formulation of psychological events and the interdependence of personality organization as concepts which reduce the effectual importance of mooted differences between one form of psychotherapy and another.

Chapter 3

Techniques of Therapeutic Intervention

John Dollard
and Neal E. Miller

Various techniques of therapeutic intervention have already been mentioned elsewhere during the discussion of other topics (Dollard & Miller, 1950). These will be brought together here in a convenient summary with the focus directly on the problem of how the therapist can influence the patient. It will be seen that the different techniques are not completely separate; there are intermediate blends, and they may be combined with infinite variety.

Suggesting, Urging, Commanding, and Forbidding

The techniques of suggesting, requesting, urging, commanding, and forbidding are commonly used methods of trying to influence another person's everyday social behavior. As has already been pointed out (Dollard & Miller, 1950), because these techniques are so commonly used by the person's friends and associates, any difficulties that will respond to them are usually solved before he is driven to visit a therapist. We have shown that the patient with strong repressions and inhibitions is only thrown into more severe conflict when his motivation to approach the feared goals is

Reprinted by permission of the first author, J. Dollard, and the publisher from *Personality and psychotherapy*. New York: McGraw-Hill, 1950, pp. 393–398.

increased directly by urging him to approach, or indirectly by forbidding his symptoms. These techniques usually do not reduce the avoidance, motivated by fear, which is the cause of the neurotic's conflict. Even where they are of some benefit, they often do not help to free the patient to use his own higher mental processes. Therefore, Freudian therapy and its various derivatives use these techniques much less frequently than they are encountered in normal social life.

There are a few special places where these techniques are used. The therapist commands free association; he urges the patient to say everything that comes into his mind and forbids holding anything back. Before the formal sessions begin, the therapist generally places a taboo on making any drastic decision of an irreversible nature during the course of the treatment. This tends to protect the patient from things that he might be driven to do when his conflicts are heightened by the negative therapeutic effect and to give him a chance to correct exaggerated first attempts at new problem solutions. It also takes the burden off the therapist; he does not have to disapprove specific major decisions but can always relax the taboo if he is convinced that this is in the best interests of the patient. In this connection Alexander and French (1946, pp. 37–41) emphasize that it is often a necessity of the cure that the patient make such decisions when he is ready for them and not wait for any routine date such as "end of therapy."

When the therapist judges that avoidance has been weakened enough so that approach to the goal is possible, he may request the temporary abstinence from a symptom that is too drive-reducing. For example, he may request a patient to try abstaining from a drug or to try going into a phobic situation.

Reward and Punishment, Disapproval and Approval

As has already been emphasized, the therapist does not control the important primary rewards and punishments in the patient's life; he usually does not even control the most important learned rewards and punishments. The exceptions to this are in the Armed Forces and in mental institutions, but even here the potential control usually is not used. Our moral codes and humanitarian customs set strict limits to the creation and use of strong drives to modify a patient's behavior. Thus hunger, pain, and fatigue may not be used in unconventional ways or degrees.

Approval and disapproval have strong learned reward and punishment value. They may be expressed either directly and openly, or indirectly and subtly. In ordinary social life they are commonly used methods of influencing another person's behavior.

Most neurotics have met with a preponderance of disapproval. The effects of disapproval are likely to generalize and heighten the fears responsible for repression and inhibition. Therefore, the therapist is careful about expressing disapproval. In cases where there is a real danger that the patient will do himself irreparable harm, the therapist must point this out and thus by implication disapprove the behavior. If the therapist fails to predict real dangers, the patient will lose confidence in him.

The therapist uses approval to reward good effort on the part of the patient. He does not lose its specific value by dispensing it randomly. He makes the patient work for approval but shows that he realizes how hard therapeutic work can be. Finally, he knows that the ultimate goal is for the patient to become able to win the approval of his own social group, outside the therapeutic situation.

Permissiveness: Failing to Criticize or Show Alarm as a Powerful Intervention

When the patient has said something that frightens him, the therapist's calm, accepting manner can be a striking contrast to the type of social response that has reinforced the patient's fears. Under the right circumstances, merely saying nothing can therefore be a powerful intervention that reduces fear and is a condition for its extinction. We believe that this is a necessary condition for "catharsis," and that, by contrast, no relief is secured by expressing a suppressed feeling of emotion if the other person shows signs of strong disapproval. It is permissive also, when the patient asks about topics that are usually shied away from or discussed with embarrassment, for a therapist to give him calmly and objectively the information he wants. It is important for the therapist to be a good model. Since he has a great deal of prestige, his calmness, courage, and reasonableness are imitated by the patient, who thus tends to become somewhat calmer, more courageous, and more reasonable. Because it reduces the fear motivating repression and inhibition, the therapist's permissiveness is an effective form of intervention.

Sympathetic Interest and Understanding

Warm, sympathetic interest and understanding are powerful rewards, particularly for those who are usually misunderstood and who have worn out the sympathy and interest of their friends. This is further heightened by the social prestige of the therapist. It rewards the patient for coming to therapy and continuing to try. Specific signs of interest may also reinforce specific types of behavior. Questions can serve as a sign of interest and reinforce talking about the general topic that elicited the question. Repeating or "reflecting back" (Rogers, 1942) what the patient has said is also a sign of interest and has the same effect. Since the therapist does not repeat everything that the patient says, the effect is bound to be differential. The patient will learn to talk about the topics that are reflected back instead of those that are ignored. In this connection the reader will remember Greenspoon's (1950) experiment on the reinforcing effect of saying "mmm-hmm."

Reassurance

Reassurance is a common way of reducing fear. By reducing fear, it can serve as a strong reward. The patient's friends usually have tried to reassure him, but this has not been entirely effective or else he would not have been forced to come to the therapist. The therapist is able to use this technique somewhat better than the friends because he is freer from anxiety himself and has more prestige. He will not have much better luck than the friends, however, with blanket reassurance. In order to succeed when they have failed, he must be better able to locate the important sources of fear and thus to give the right kind of reassurance exactly when and where it is most needed. Reassurance must be used to reduce fear so that new thoughts and acts can occur, and then to reward those new thoughts and actions. If it is used merely to make the patient feel better, it will only teach the patient to come for more reassurance.

Manifold Functions of Questions

As we have said previously, questions can serve as a sign of interest and hence can reward talking about the topics eliciting the question. On the other hand, as we have stated before, probing cross-questioning tends to evoke anxiety and thus cause the patient to stop sooner and allow more margin of safety the next time.

Suitable questions can help to focus attention, stimulate thought, cause the patient to discover incongruities and see obscured relationships. The therapist often finds the Socratic method useful. For example, after the patient has reproached himself harshly, the therapist may ask: "Is your attitude toward this typical of other members of your crowd?" At another time he may ask: "Hasn't something like that happened before?"

An advantage of a skillful question over a direct assertion is that it forces the patient to respond by thinking and seeing relationships for himself. Thus he is less likely to learn to listen and more likely to learn to think. The ultimate goal, of course, is for the patient to ask the right questions for himself.

Functions of an Interpretation

Interpretations may have a number of different functions which are not neccessarily mutually exclusive. An interpretation often implies permission or nonpunishment. The presumption is that what the therapist says he will permit the patient to say. When the therapist gives an interpretation (*e.g.*, "Perhaps you are angry with me.") in a calm tone of voice, he in effect says: "I already know and I am not shocked or angry at you for having those thoughts or feelings."

Another function of an interpretation is to label a drive, emotion, or type of behavior. It should be noted that a connection can be formed between the cues of the drive or emotion and the response of the label only when they are both present simultaneously. The beginning therapist often makes the mistake of thinking of an interpretation after the episode is over and telling the patient about it the next day. This is usually ineffective because the patient is not being stimulated by the drive or emotion at that time. In those rare cases where the therapist believes that the labeling is very important and that the appropriate situation may not occur again for a long time, our type of analysis suggests the theoretical possibility of asking the patient to remember and report as exactly as possible all the details of what he was saying at that time. If he is able to supply enough cues, he may elicit the proper emotions again so that they will be present to be labeled.

Without a label, the patient can respond only directly and unconsciously to the drive or emotion; with a label he can initiate an intervening series of cue-producing responses or, in other words, use his higher mental processes. Labeling a drive, a goal, or a means to an end may also help to define the problem and suggest a course of action.

On the other hand, interpretations may be used to block a course of action by attaching an anxiety-arousing label to it. Thus if the therapist interprets a certain pattern of behavior as "homosexual drinking," he attaches a label to it that tends to arouse anxiety and motivates the patient to avoid it. Similarly, by convincing the patient of the unacceptable, and hence previously unconscious, gains from a symptom the therapist pits the patient's conscience and guilt squarely against the symptom. In another case, one may ask the person who is continually psychoanalyzing one's behavior in social situations: "Am I getting all this valuable information free?" This calls attention to the person's hostile motivation and tends to stop him.

Finally, by predicting the patient's action or the consequence of his action, an interpretation can aid foresight and put the patient on his guard. For example, Mrs. A told the therapist that if a man "tried to take advantage of her," she would probably faint. The therapist pointed out that fainting is exactly what would allow him to take advantage of her. Then the therapist went on to present her with other evidence for her unconscious wish to have someone take advantage of her. This type of interpretation supplied labels which helped to put her on her guard. As a result she stopped getting into dangerous situations.

References

Alexander, F. & French, T. M. *Psychoanalytic therapy*. New York: Ronald, 1946.

Dollard, J., & Miller, N. E. *Personality and psychotherapy*. New York: McGraw-Hill, 1950.

Greenspoon, J. The effect of verbal and mechanical stimuli on verbal behavior. Personal Communication, 1950.

Rogers, C. R. *Counseling and psychotherapy*. Boston: Houghton Mifflin, 1942.

Chapter 4

The Dynamics of Psychotherapy in the Light of Learning Theory[1]

Franz Alexander

Most of what we know about the basic dynamic principles of psychotherapy is derived from the psychoanalytic process.

One of the striking facts in this field is that the intricate procedure of psychoanalytic treatment underwent so few changes since its guiding principles were formulated by Freud between 1912 and 1915 (Freud, 1912/1924a, 1912/1924b, 1913/1924, 1914/1924, 1915/1924). Meanwhile substantial developments took place in theoretical knowledge, particularly in ego psychology. Moreover, in all other fields of medicine, treatments underwent radical changes resulting from a steadily improving understanding of human physiology and pathology. No medical practitioner could treat patients with the same methods he learned 50 years ago without being considered antiquated. In contrast, during the same period the standard psychoanalytic treatment method as it is taught today in psychoanalytic institutes remained practically unchanged.

It is not easy to account for this conservatism. Is it due to the perfection of the standard procedure which because of its excellence does not require reevaluation and improvement, or does it have some other cultural rather than scientific reasons?

Reprinted by permission of the publisher from *American Journal of Psychiatry*, 1963, *120*, 440–448. Copyright 1963 by the American Psychiatric Association.

[1]Read at the 119th annual meeting of the American Psychiatric Association, St. Louis, Mo., May 6–10, 1963.

Among several factors one is outstanding: to be a reformer of psychoanalytic treatment was never a popular role. the need for unity among the pioneer psychoanalysts, who were universally rejected by outsiders, is one of the deep cultural roots of this stress on conformity. The majority of those who had critical views became "dissenters" either voluntarily or by excommunication. Some of these became known as neo-Freudians. Some of the critics, however, remained in the psychoanalytic fold.

(Some analysts jocularly expressed the view that the stress on conformity was a defense against the analyst's unconscious identification with Freud, each wanting to become himself a latter-day Freud and founder of a new school. Conformity was a defense against too many prima donnas.) Another important factor is the bewildering complexity of the psychodynamic processes occurring during treatment. It appears that the insecurity which this intricate field necessarily provokes creates a defensive dogmatism which gives its followers a pseudosecurity. Almost all statements concerning technique could be legitimately only highly tentative. "Tolerance of uncertainty" is generally low in human beings. A dogmatic reassertion of some traditionally accepted views—seeking for a kind of consensus—is a common defense against uncertainty.

In spite of all this, there seems to be little doubt that the essential psychodynamic principles on which psychoanalytic treatment rests have solid observational foundations. These constitute the areas of agreement among psychoanalysts of different theoretical persuasion. Briefly, they consist in the following observations and evaluations:

1. During treatment unconscious (repressed) material becomes conscious. This increases the action radius of the conscious ego: the ego becomes cognizant of unconscious impulses and thus is able to coordinate (integrate) the latter with the rest of conscious content.
2. The mobilization of unconscious material is achieved mainly by two basic therapeutic factors: interpretation of material emerging during free association and the patient's emotional interpersonal experiences in the therapeutic situation (transference). The therapist's relatively objective, nonevaluative, impersonal attitude is the principal factor in mobilizing unconscious material.
3. The patient shows resistance against recognizing unconscious content. Overcoming his resistance is one of the primary technical problems of the treatment.
4. It is only natural that the neurotic patient will sooner or later direct his typical neurotic attitude toward his therapist. He develops a transference which is the repetition of interpersonal attitudes, mostly the feelings of the child to his parents. This process is favored by the therapist encouraging the patient to be himself as much

as he can during the interviews. The therapist's objective nonevaluative attitude is the main factor, not only in mobilizing unconscious material during the process of free association, but also in facilitating the manifestation of transference. The original neurosis of the patient, which is based on his childhood experiences, is thus transformed in an artificial "transference neurosis" which is a less intensive repetition of the patient's "infantile neurosis." the resolution of these revived feelings and behavior patterns—the resolution of the transference neurosis—becomes the aim of the treatment.

There is little disagreement concerning these fundamentals of the treatment. Controversies, which occur sporadically, pertain primarily to the technical means by which the transference neurosis can be resolved. The optimal intensity of the transference neurosis is one of the points of contention.

This is not the place to account in detail the various therapeutic suggestions which arose in recent years. Most of these modifications consisted in particular emphases given to certain aspects of the treatment. There are those who stressed interpretation of resistance (Willheim Reich, Helmuth Kaiser), while others focused on the interpretation of repressed content. Fenichel stated that resistance cannot be analyzed without making the patient understand what he is resisting (Fenichel, 1945).

It is most difficult to evaluate all these modifications because it is generally suspected that authors' accounts about their theoretical views do not precisely reflect what they are actually doing while treating patients. The reason for this discrepancy lies in the fact that the therapist is a "participant observer" who is called upon constantly to make decisions on the spot. The actual interactional process between therapist and patient is much more complex than the theoretical accounts about it. In general there were two main trends: (1) Emphasis on cognitive insight as a means of breaking up the neurotic patterns. (2) Emphasis upon the emotional experiences the patient undergoes during treatment. These are not mutually exclusive, yet most controversies centered around emphasis on the one or the other factor: cognitive versus experiential.

While mostly the similarity between the transference attitude and the original pathogenic childhood situation has been stressed, I emphasized the therapeutic significance of the difference between the old family conflicts and the actual doctor–patient relationship. This difference is what allows "corrective emotional experience" to occur, which I consider as the central therapeutic factor both in psychoanalysis proper and also in analytically oriented psychotherapy. The new settlement of an old unresolved conflict in the transference situation becomes possible, not only because the intensity of the transference conflict is less than that of the original conflict, but also because the therapist's actual response to the patient's emotional expressions is quite different from the original treatment of the child by the parents. The fact that the therapist's reaction differs from that of the parent, to whose behavior the child adjusted himself as well as he could with his own neurotic reactions, makes it necessary for the patient to abandon and correct these old emotional patterns. After all, this is precisely one of the ego's basic functions—adjustment to the existing external conditions. As soon as the old neurotic patterns are revived and brought into the realm of consciousness, the ego has the opportunity to readjust them to the changed external and internal conditions. This is the essence of the corrective influence of those series of experiences which occur during treatment (Alexander, 1956, 1958). As will be seen, however, the emotional detachment of the therapist turned out under observational scrutiny to be less complete than this idealized model postulates.

Since the difference between the patient–therapist and the original child–parent relationship appeared to me a cardinal therapeutic agent, I made technical suggestions derived from these considerations. The therapist in order to increase the effectiveness of the corrective emotional experiences should attempt to create an interpersonal climate which is suited to highlight the discrepancy between the patient's transference attitude and the actual situation as it exists between patient and therapist. For example, if the original childhood situation which the patient repeats in the transference was between a strict punitive father and a frightened son, the therapist should behave in a calculatedly permissive manner. If the father had a doting all-forgiving attitude toward his son, the therapist should take a more impersonal and reserved attitude. This suggestion was criticized by some authors, that these consciously and purposefully adopted attitudes are artificial and will be recognized as such by the patient. I maintained, however, that the therapist's objective emotionally not participating attitude is itself artificial inasmuch as it does not exist between human beings in actual life. Neither is it as complete as has been assumed. This controversy will have to wait to be decided by further experiences of practitioners.

I made still other controversial technical suggestions aimed at intensifying the emotional experiences of the patient. One of them was changing the number of interviews in appropriate phases of the treatment in order to make the patient more vividly conscious of his dependency needs by frustrating them.

Another of my suggestions pertains to the ever-puzzling question of termination of treatment. The traditional belief is that the longer an analysis lasts the greater is the probability of recovery. Experienced analysts more and more came to doubt the validity of this generalization. If anything, this is the exception; very long treatments lasting over many years do not seem to be the most successful ones. On the other hand, many so-called transference cures after very brief contact have been observed to be lasting. A clear correlation between duration of treatment and its results has not been established. There are no reliable criteria for the proper time of termination. Improvements observed during treatment often prove to be conditioned by the fact that the patient is still being treated. The patient's own inclination to terminate or to continue the treatment is not always a reliable indication. The complexity of the whole procedure and our inability to estimate precisely the proper time of termination induced me to employ the method of experimental temporary interruptions, a method which in my experience is the most satisfactory procedure. At the same time it often reduces the total number of interviews. The technique of tentative temporary interruptions is based on trusting the natural recuperative powers of the human personality, which are largely underestimated by many psychoanalysts. There is an almost general trend toward "overtreatment." A universal regressive trend in human beings has been generally recognized by psychoanalysts. Under sufficient stress every one tends to regress to the helpless state of infancy and seek help from others. The psychoanalytic treatment situation caters to this regressive attitude. As Freud stated, treatments often reach a point where the patient's will to be cured is outweighed by his wish to be treated.

In order to counteract this trend a continuous pressure on the patient is needed to make him ready to take over his own management as soon as possible. During temporary interruptions patients often discover that they can live without their analyst. When they return, the still not worked out emotional problems come clearly to the forefront.[2]

Furthermore, I called attention to Freud's distinction between two forms of regression. He first described regression to a period of ego-development in which the patient was still happy, in which he functioned well. Later he described regressions to traumatic experiences, which he explained as attempts to master subsequently an overwhelming situation of the past. During psychoanalytic treatment both kinds of regression occur. Regressions to pretraumatic or preconflictual periods—although they offer excellent research opportunity for the study of personality development— are therapeutically not valuable. Often we find that the patient regresses in his free associations to preconflictual early infantile material as a maneuver to evade the essential pathogenic conflicts. This material appears as "deep material" and both patient and therapist in mutual self-deception spend a great deal of time and effort to analyze this essentially evasive material. The recent trend to look always for very early emotional conflicts between mother and infant as the most common source of neurotic disturbances is

---

[2]This type of "fractioned analysis," which was practiced in the early days of the Outpatient Clinic of the Berlin Institute, is an empirical experimental way to find the correct time for termination.

the result of overlooking this frequent regressive evasion of later essential pathogenic conflicts. Serious disturbances of the early symbiotic mother–child relation occur only with exceptionally disturbed mothers. The most common conflicts begin when the child has already a distinct feeling of being a person (ego-awareness) and relates to his human environment, to his parents and siblings, as to individual persons. The oedipus complex and sibling rivalry are accordingly the common early sources of neurotic patterns. There are many exceptions, of course, where the personality growth is disturbed in very early infancy.

Another issue which gained attention in the post-Freudian era is the therapist's neglect of the actual present life situation in favor of preoccupation with the patient's past history. This is based on the tenet that the present life circumstances are merely precipitating factors, mobilizing the patient's infantile neurosis. In general, of course, the present is always determined by the past. Freud in a rather early writing proposed the theory of complementary etiology. A person with severe ego defects acquired in the past will react to slight stress situations in his present life with severe reactions; a person with a relatively healthy past history will require more severe blows of life to regress into a neurotic state (Freud, 1933). Some modern authors like French, Rado, myself, and others feel that there is an unwarranted neglect of the actual life circumstances (Alexander & French, 1946; Rado, 1922–1956/1956, 1956–1961/1962). The patient comes to the therapist when he is at the end of his rope, is entangled in emotional problems which have reached a point when he feels he needs help. These authors feel that the therapist never should allow the patient to forget that he came to resolve his present problem. The understanding of the past should always be subordinated to the problems of the present. Therapy is not the same as genetic research. Freud's early emphasis upon the reconstruction of past history was the result of his primary interest in research. At first he felt he must know the nature of the disease he proposed to cure. The interest in past history at the expense of the present is the residue of the historical period when research in personality dynamics of necessity was a prerequisite to develop a rational treatment method.

These controversial issues will have to wait for the verdict of history. Their significance cannot yet be evaluated with finality. One may state, however, that there is a growing inclination to question the universal validity of some habitual practices handed down by tradition over several generations of psychoanalysts. There is a trend toward greater flexibility in technique, attempting to adjust the technical details to the individual nature of the patient and his problems. This principle of flexibility was explicitly stressed by Edith Weigert, Thomas French, myself, and still others.

While there is considerable controversy concerning frequency of interviews, interruptions, termination, and the mutual relation between intellectual and emotional factors in treatment, there seems to be a universal consensus about the significance of the therapist's individual personality for the results of the treatment. This interest first manifested itself in several contributions dealing with the therapist's own emotional involvement in the patient—"the countertransference phenomenon." Freud first used the expression *countertransference* in 1910. It took, however, about 30 years before the therapist's unconscious, spontaneous reactions toward the patient were explored as to their significance for the course of the treatment. The reasons for this neglect were both theoretical and practical. Originally Freud conceived the analyst's role in the treatment as a blank screen who carefully keeps his incognito and upon whom the patient can project any role, that of the image of his father (father transference), of mother (mother transference), or of any significant person in his past. In this way the patient can reexperience the important interpersonal events of his past undisturbed by the specific personality of the therapist. The phenomenon called "countertransference," however, contradicts sharply the "blank screen" theory.

It is now generally recognized that in reality the analyst does not remain a blank screen, an uninvolved intellect, but is perceived by the patient as a concrete person. There is, however, a great deal of difference among present-day authors in the evaluation of the significance of the therapist's personality in general and his countertransference reactions in particular.

Some authors consider countertransference as an undesirable impurity just as the patient's emotional involvement with his therapist (transference) originally was considered as an undesirable complication. The ideal model of the treatment was that the patient should freely associate and thus reveal himself without controlling the train of his ideas, and should consider the therapist only as an expert who is trying to help him. Later, as is well known, the patient's emotional involvement turned out to be the dynamic axis of the treatment. So far as the therapist's involvement is concerned, it is considered by most authors as an unwanted impurity. The therapist should have only one reaction to the patient, the wish to understand him and give him an opportunity for readjustment through the insight offered to him by the therapist's interpretations. The latter should function as a pure intellect without being disturbed by any personal and subjective reactions to the patient.

The prevailing view is that the analyst's own emotional reactions should be considered as disturbing factors of the treatment.

Some authors, among them Edith Weiger, Frieda Fromm-Reichmann, Heimann, Benedek, and Salzman, however, mention certain assets of the countertransference; they point out that the analyst's understanding of his countertransference attitudes may give him a particularly valuable tool for understanding the patient's transference reactions (Benedek, 1953; Fromm-Reichmann, 1957; Heimann, 1950; Weigert, 1954). As to the therapeutic significance of the countertransference, there is a great deal of disagreement. While Balint and Balint consider this impurity as negligible for the therapeutic process (Balint & Balint, 1939), Benedek states in her paper on countertransference that the therapist's personality is the most important agent of the therapeutic process (Benedek, 1953). There is, however, general agreement that a too intensive emotional involvement on the therapist's part is a seriously disturbing factor. Glover speaks of the "analyst's toilet" which he learns in his own personal analysis, which should free him from unwanted emotional participation in the treatment. This is, indeed, the most important objective of the training analysis; it helps him to know how to control and possibly even to change his spontaneous countertransference reactions.

I believe that the countertransference may be helpful or harmful. It is helpful when it differs from that parental attitude toward the child which contributed to the patient's emotional difficulties. The patient's neurotic attitudes developed not in a vacuum but as reactions to parental attitudes. If the therapist's reactions are different from these parental attitudes, the patient's emotional involvement with the therapist is not realistic. This challenges the patient to alter his reaction patterns. If, however, the specific countertransference of the therapist happens to be similar to the parental attitudes toward the child, the patient's neurotic reaction patterns will persist and an interminable analysis may result. There is no incentive for the patient to change his feelings. I recommended therefore that the therapist should be keenly aware of his own spontaneous—no matter how slight—feelings to the patient and should try to replace them by an interpersonal climate which is suited to correct the original neurotic patterns.

One of the most systematic revisions of the standard psychoanalytic procedure was undertaken by Sandor Rado, published in several writings, beginning in 1948 (Rado, 1956). His critical evaluation of psychoanalytic treatment and his suggested modifications deserve particular attention because for many years Rado has been known as one of the most thorough students of Freud's writings.

As years went on, Rado became more and more dissatisfied with the prevailing practice of psychoanalysis and proposed his adaptational technique based on his "adaptational psychodynamics." As it is the case with many innovators, some of Rado's formulations consist in new terminology. Some of his new emphases, however, are highly significant. He is most concerned, as I am, with those features of the standard technique of psychoanalysis which foster regression without supplying a counterforce toward the patient's progression, that is to say, to his successful adaptation to the actual life situation. He raises the crucial question: Is the patient's understanding of his past development sufficient to induce a change in him? "To overcome repressions and thus be able to recall the past is one thing; to learn from it and be able to act on the new knowledge, another" (Rado, 1962).

Rado recommends, as a means to promote the goal of therapy, raising the patient from his earlier childlike adaptations to an appropriate adult level—"to hold the patient as much as possible at the adult level of cooperation with the physician." The patient following his regressive trend "parentifies" the therapist, but the therapist should conteract this trend and not allow himself to be pushed by the patient into the parent role. Rado critizes orthodox psychoanalytic treatment as furthering the regressive urge of the patient by emphasizing the "punitive parentifying" transference (the patient's dependence upon the parentalized image of the therapist) (Rado, 1962). Rado points out that losing self-confidence is the main reason for the patient to build up the therapist into a powerful parent figure. Rado's main principle, therefore, is to "bolster up the patient's self-confidence on realistic grounds." He stresses the importance of dealing with the patient's actual present life conditions in all possible detail. Interpretations must always embrace the conscious as well as unconscious motivations. In concordance with mine and French's similar emphasis (Alexander & French, 1946), Rado succinctly states: "Even when the biographical material on hand reaches far into the past, interpretation must always begin and end with the patient's present life performance, his present adaptive task. The significance of this rule cannot be overstated."

Rado considers his adaptational technique but a further development of the current psychoanalytic technique, not something basically contradictory to it. It should be pointed out that while criticizing the standard psychoanalytic procedure, Rado in reality criticizes current practice, but not theory. According to accepted theory, the patient's dependent—in Rado's term—"parentifying" transference should be resolved. The patient during treatment learns to understand his own motivations; this enables him to take over his own management. He assimilates the therapist's interpretations and gradually he can dispense with the therapist, from whom he has received all he needs. The therapeutic process thus recapitulates the process of emotional maturation; the child learns from the parents, incorporates their attitude, and eventually will no longer need them for guidance. Rado's point becomes relevant when one points out that the current procedure does not always achieve this goal, and, I may add, it unneccessarily prolongs the procedure. The reason for this is that the exploration of the past became an aim in itself, indeed the goal of the treatment. The past should be subordinated to a total grasp of the present life situation and serve as the basis for future adaptive accomplishments.

At this point my emphasis is pertinent, that it is imperative for the therapist to correctly estimate the time when his guidance becomes not only unneccessary but detrimental, inasmuch as it unneccessarily fosters the very dependency of the patient on the therapist which the latter tries to combat. I stated that deeds are stronger than words; the treatment should be interrupted at the right time in order to give the patient the experience that he can now function on his own and thus gain that self-confidence which Rado tries to instill into the patient by "positive interpretations." No matter, however, what technical devices they emphasize, the goal of these reformers is the same: to minimize the danger implicit in the psychotherapeutic situation, namely, encouraging undue regression and evasion of the current adaptive tasks. It is quite true that regression is necessary in order to give the patient opportunity to reexperience his early maladaptive patterns and grapple with them anew to find other more appropriate levels of feeling and behavior. The key to successful psychoanalytic therapy is, however, not to allow regression in the transference to become an aim in itself. It is necessary to control it.

In view of these controversies the need for a careful study of the therapeutic process became more and more recognized. Different research centers initiated programs from grants given by the Ford Foundation to study the therapeutic process. At the Mount Sinai Hospital in Los Angeles under my direction, we undertook a study of the therapeutic process, in which a number of psychoanalysts observed the therapeutic interaction between therapist and patient in several treatment cases. All interviews were sound recorded and both the participant observer—that is the therapist—and the nonparticipant observers recorded their evaluation of the process immediately after each interview. Our assumption was that the therapist being an active participant in the interactional process is not capable of recognizing and describing his own involvements with the same objectivity as those who observe him. His attention is necessarily focused on patient's material and being himself involved in this complex interaction cannot fully appreciate his own part in it. This expectation was fully borne out by our study.

As was expected, the processing of the voluminous data thus collected proved to be a prolonged affair which will require several years of collaborative work. Yet even at the present stage of processing, several important conclusions emerge. The most important of these is the fact that the traditional descriptions of the therapeutic process do not adequately reflect the immensely complex interaction between therapist and patient. The patient's reactions cannot be described fully as transference reactions. The patient reacts to the therapist as to a concrete person and not only as a representative of parental figures. The therapist's reactions also far exceed what is usually called countertransference. They include in addition to this, interventions based on conscious deliberations and also his spontaneous idiosyncratic attitudes. Moreover, the therapist's own values are conveyed to the patient even if he consistently tries to protect his incognito. The patient reacts to the therapist's overt but also to his nonverbal hidden intentions and the therapist reacts to the patient's reaction to him. It is a truly transactional process.

In studying this transactional material I came to the conviction that the therapeutic process can be best understood in the terms of learning theory. Particularly the principle of reward and punishment and also the influence of repetitive experiences can be clearly recognized. Learning is defined as a change resulting from previous experiences. In every learning process, one can distinguish two components. First the motivational factor, namely, the subjective needs which activate the learning process, and second, certain performances by which a new behavioral pattern suitable to fill the motivational need is actually acquired. In most general terms unfulfilled needs no matter what their nature may be—hunger for food, hunger for love, curiosity, the urge for mastery—initiate groping trial and error efforts which cease when an adequate behavioral response is found. Adequate responses lead to need satisfaction, which is the reward for the effort. Rewarding responses are repeated until they become automatic and their repetition no longer requires effort and further experimentation. This is identical with the feedback mechanisms described in cybernetics. Every change of the total situation requires learning new adequate responses. Old learned patterns which were adequate in a previous situation must be unlearned. They are impediments to acquiring new adequate patterns.

I am not particularly concerned at this point with the controversy between the more mechanistic concepts of the older behaviorist theory and the newer Gestalt theory of learning. The controversy pertains to the nature of the process by which satisfactory behavior patterns are acquired. This controversy can be reduced to two suppositions. The older Thorndike and Pavlov models operate with the principle of contiguity or connectionism. Whenever a behavioral pattern becomes associated with both a specific motivating need and need satisfaction, the organism will automatically repeat the satisfactory performance whenever the same need arises. This view considers the organism as a passive receptor of external and internal stimuli, which become associated by contiguity. The organism's own active organizing function is neglected. The finding of the satisfactory pattern, according to the classical theory, takes place through blind trial and error.

In contrast, the Gestalt theoretical model operates with the supposition that the trials by which the organism finds satisfactory behavioral responses are not blind but are aided by cognitive processes. They are intelligent trials which are guided by certain generalizations arrived at with the aid of the memory of previous experiences. They imply an active organization of previous experiences. This organizational act amounts to a cognitive grasp of the total situation. I am not concerned at this juncture with the seemingly essential difference between the connectionistic and Gestalt theories of learning. Probably both types of learning exist. The infant learns without much help from previous experiences. In this learning, blind trials and errors must of necessity prevail. Common basis in all learning, whether it takes place through blind trials and errors or by intelligent trials, is the forging of a connection between three variables: a specific motivating impulse, a specific behavioral response, and a gratifying experience, which is the reward.

Accepting Freud's definition of thinking as a substitute for acting, that is to say, as acting in fantasy, the reward principle can be well applied to intellectual solutions of problems. Groping trials and errors in thought—whether blind or guided by cognitive processes—lead eventually to a solution which clicks. Finding a solution which satisfies all the observations without contradictions is accompanied by a feeling of satisfaction. After a solution is found—occasionally it may be found accidentally—the problem-solving urge, as everyone knows who has tried to solve a mathematical equation or a chess puzzle, ceases and a feeling of satisfaction ensues. The tension state which prevails as long as the problem is not solved yields to a feeling of rest and fulfillment. This is the reward for the effort, whether it consists of blind or intelligent trials. The principle of reward can be applied, not only to a rat learning to run a maze, but to the most complex thought processes as well. The therapeutic process can be well described in these terms of learning theory. The specific problem in therapy consists in finding an adequate interpersonal relation between therapist and patient. Initially this is distorted because the patient applies to this specific human interaction feeling-patterns and behavior-patterns which were formed in the patient's past and do not apply either to the actual therapeutic situation or to his actual life situation. During treatment the patient unlearns the old patterns and learns new ones. This complex process of relearning follows the same principles as the more simple relearning process hitherto studied by experimental psychologists. It contains cognitive elements as well as learning from actual interpersonal experiences which occur during the therapeutic interaction. These two components are intricately interwoven. They were described in psychoanalytic literature with the undefined, rather vague term "emotional insight." The word "emotional" refers to the interpersonal experiences, the word "insight" refers to the cognitive element. The expression does not mean more than the recognition of the presence of both components. The psychological process to which the term refers is not yet spelled out in detail. Our present observational study is focused on a better understanding of this complex psychological phenomenon—emotional insight—which appears to us as the central factor in every learning process including psychoanalytic treatment. Every intellectual grasp, even when it concerns entirely nonutilitarian preoccupations, such as playful puzzle-solving efforts, is motivated by some kind of urge for mastery and is accompanied with tension resolution as its reward. In psychotherapy the reward consists in less conflictful, more harmonious interpersonal relations, which the patient achieves first by adequately relating to his therapist, then to his environment, and eventually to his own ego ideal. At first he tries to gain the therapist's approval by living up to the supreme therapeutic principle—to the basic rule of frank self-expression. At the same time he tries to gain acceptance by living up to the therapist's expectations of him, which he senses in spite of the therapist's overt non-evaluating attitude. And finally, he tries to live up to his own genuine values, to his cherished image of himself. Far-reaching discrepancy between the therapist's and the patient's values is a common source of therapeutic impasse.

This gradually evolving dynamic process can be followed and described step by step in studies made by nonparticipant observers. Current studies give encouragement and hope that we shall eventually be able to understand more adequately this intricate interpersonal process and to account for therapeutic successes and failures. As in every field of science, general assumptions gradually yield to more specific ones which are obtained by meticulous, controlled observations. The history of sciences teaches us that new and more adequate technical devices of observation and reasoning are responsible for advancements. In the field of psychotherapy the long over-due observation of the therapeutic process by nonparticipant observers is turning out to be the required methodological tool. This in itself, however, is not sufficient. The evaluation of the rich and new observational material calls for new theoretical perspectives. Learning theory appears to be at present the most satisfactory framework for the evaluation of observational data and for making valid generalizations. As it continuously happens at certain phases of thought development in all fields of science, different independent approaches merge and become integrated with each other. At present, we are witnessing the beginnings of a most promising integration of psychoanalytic theory with learning theory, which may lead to unpredictable advances in the theory and practice of the psychotherapies.

References

Alexander, F. *Psychoanalysis and psychotherapy*. New York: W. W. Norton & Company, 1956.

Alexander, F. Unexplored areas in psychoanalytic theory and treatment. *Behavioral Science*, 1958, *3*, 293–316.

Alexander, F., & French, T. M. *Psychoanalytic therapy. Principles and application*. New York: Ronald Press, 1946.

Balint, A., & Balint, M. On transference and counter transference. *International Journal of Psychoanalysis*, 1939, *20*, 223–230.

Benedek, T. Dynamics of the countertransference. *Bulletin of the Menninger Clinic*, 1953, *17*, 201–208.

Fenichel, O. *The psychoanalytic theory of neurosis*. New York: W. W. Norton, 1945.

Freud, S. The dynamics of the transference (1912). *Collected papers* (Vol. II). London: Hogarth Press, 1924. (a)

Freud, S. Recommendations for physicians on the psychoanalytic method of treatment (1912). *Collected papers* (Vol. II). London: Hogarth Press, 1924. (b)

Freud, S. Further recommendations in the technique of psychoanalysis on beginning the treatment. The question of the first communications. The dynamics of the cure (1913). *Collected papers* (Vol. II). London: Hogarth Press, 1924.

Freud, S. Further recommendations in the technique of psychoanalysis, recollection, repetition, and working through (1914). *Collected papers* (Vol. II). London: Hogarth Press, 1924.

Freud, S. Further recommendations in the technique of psychoanalysis, observations on transference-love (1915). *Collected papers* (Vol. II). London: Hogarth Press, 1924.

Freud, S. *New introductory lectures on psychoanalysis*. New York: W. W. Norton, 1933.

Fromm-Reichmann, F. *Principles of intensive psychotherapy*. London: Allen & Unwin, 1957.

Heimann, P. On countertransference. *International Journal of Psychoanalysis*, 1950, *31*, 81–84.

Rado, S. Psychoanalysis of behavior: *Collected papers* (Vol. I). (1922–1956). New York: Grune & Stratton, 1956.

Rado, S. Psychoanalysis of behavior. *Collected papers* (Vol. II) (1956–1961). New York: Grune & Stratton, 1962.

Weigert, E. The importance of flexibility in psychoanalytic technique. *Journal of the American Psychoanalytic Association*, 1954, *2*, 702–710.

Chapter 5

Psychotherapy in America Today

Jerome D. Frank

Throughout his life every person is influenced by the behavior of others towards him. His relationships with his fellows shape his own behavior, attitudes, values, self-image, and world view and also affect his sense of well-being. It is customary to classify different forms of personal influence in accordance with their settings and the role of the influencing figure. Thus we say that a person is brought up by his parents in the family, educated by his teachers in school, and led by his officers in battle, for example.

Attempts to enhance a person's feeling of well-being are usually labeled treatment, and every society trains some of its members to apply this form of influence. Treatment always involves a personal relationship between healer and sufferer. Certain types of therapy rely primarily on the healer's ability to mobilize healing forces in the sufferer by psychological means. These forms of treatment may be generically termed psychotherapy.

Although psychotherapeutic methods have existed since time immemorial and a vast amount of accumulated experience supports a belief in their value, some of the most elementary questions about them remain unanswered. Research has not yet yielded sufficient information to permit description of the different methods in generally acceptable terms, specification of the conditions for which different methods are most suitable, or comparison of their results. These difficulties spring largely from persisting lack of precise knowledge concerning the nature of psychotherapeutic principles.

Reprinted by permission of the author, Jerome D. Frank, and the publisher from *Persuasion and healing: A comparative study of psychotherapy* (1st ed.), Baltimore: Johns Hopkins Press, 1961, pp. 1–17.

The purpose of *Persuasion and Healing* (Frank, 1961) has been to review data from various sources that may help to identify and clarify the active ingredients of various forms of psychotherapy in our own and other cultures by searching for their common features. If these features can be found, they will presumably include the active components since they would otherwise be unlikely to reappear under so many guises and circumstances. In embarking on this review, it seems appropriate to begin with a definition of psychotherapy, followed by a brief consideration of its historical roots and its place in America today, and a brief consideration of the problems involved in the evaluation of the relative efficacy of its different forms.

What Is Psychotherapy?

Since practically all forms of personal influence may affect a person's sense of well-being, the definition of psychotherapy must of necessity be somewhat arbitrary. We shall consider as psychotherapy only those types of influence characterized by the following features:

1. A trained, socially sanctioned healer, whose healing powers are accepted by the sufferer and by his social group or an important segment of it.
2. A sufferer who seeks relief from the healer.
3. A circumscribed, more or less structured series of contacts between the healer and the sufferer, through which the healer, often with the aid of a group, tries to produce certain changes in the sufferer's emotional state, attitudes, and behavior. All concerned believe these changes will help him. Although physical and chemical adjuncts may be used, the healing influence is primarily exercised by words, acts, and rituals in which sufferer, healer, and—if there is one—group, participate jointly.

These three features are common not only to all forms of psychotherapy as the term is generally used, but also to methods of primitive healing, religious conversion, and even so-called brain-washing, all of which involve systematic, time-limited contacts between a person in distress and someone who tries to reduce the distress by producing changes in the sufferer's feelings, attitudes, and behavior. By this definition, the administration of an inert medicine by a doctor to a patient is also a form of psychotherapy, since its effectiveness depends on its symbolization of the physician's healing function, which produces favorable changes in the patient's feelings and attitudes. Our search for the active ingredients of psychotherapy, then, will require exploration of these activities, as well as a consideration of experimental studies of the transmission of influence.

Historical Roots of Psychotherapy

Since at least part of the efficacy of psychotherapeutic methods lies in the shared belief of the participants that these methods will work, the predominant method would be expected to differ in different societies and in different historical epochs. This is, in fact, the case. Modern psychotherapies are rooted in two historical traditions of healing—the religio-magical and the naturalistic, or scientific. The former, originating before recorded history, regards certain forms of suffering or of alienation from one's fellows as caused by some sort of supernatural or magical intervention, such as loss of one's soul, possession by an evil spirit, or a sorcerer's curse. Treatment consists in suitable rites conducted by a healer who combines the roles of priest and physician. These rites typically require the active participation of the sufferer and members of his family or social group and are highly charged emotionally. If successful, they undo the supernaturally or magically caused damage, thereby restoring the victim's health and reestablishing or strengthening his ties with his group. As we shall see, the religio-magical tradition is still influential, even in secularized Western society, and many of its principles have been incorporated into naturalistic forms of psychotherapy.

The earliest surviving account of these principles is in the writings attributed to the Greek physician Hippocrates in the fifth century B.C. He viewed mental illness, like all other forms of illness, as a phenomenon that could be studied and treated scientifically. Though largely eclipsed in the Middle Ages, this view has come into increasing prominence since the early nineteenth century and is the dominant one today in the Western world.

Like the religio-magical view, the naturalistic view originally did not clearly distinguish mental illness from other forms of illness, and treatment for both was essentially similar. The emergence of psychotherapy as a distinctive form of healing probably began with the dramatic demonstration by Anton Mesmer, in the late eighteenth century, that he could cause the symptoms of certain patients to disappear by putting them into a trance. Though his particular theories and methods were soon discredited, mesmerism was the precursor of hypnotism, which rapidly became recognized as a method of psychotherapy. Through the use of hypnosis, Sigmund Freud and Joseph Breuer discovered, towards the end of the nineteenth century, that many symptoms of their patients seemed to be symbolic attempts to express and resolve chronic conflicts that had their roots in upsetting experiences of early life. This led Freud to develop a form of treatment based on minute exploration of patients' personal histories, with emotional reliving of childhood experiences in the treatment setting. From the information thus gained he formed a theory of human nature and mental illness known as psychoanalysis, which supplied a rationale for his psychotherapy. During the same period the Russian physiologist I. P. Pavlov demonstrated by experiments with conditioned reflexes that dogs could be made "neurotic" by exposing them to insoluble conflicts, and this led to a "conditioned reflex" theory of mental illness and treatment.

In recent years American experimental psychologists have developed various theories of learning based on experiments with animals and humans. Some of these concepts seem applicable to mental illnesses conceived as disorders of the learning process. Thus most current naturalistic theories of mental illness and its treatment represent various combinations and modifications of ideas derived from Freud, Pavlov, and experimental studies of learning.[1] Fortunately these three conceptual schemes are not incompatible, despite differences in terminology. They supply a scientifically respectable rationale for contemporary naturalistic methods of psychotherapy. In America, which accords high prestige to science, this probably contributes to their efficacy.

Cultural Aspects of Mental Illness and Psychotherapy

As the preceding discussion implies, the definition of mental illness depends heavily on the attitudes and values of the society or group in which it occurs.[2] For example, the same symptoms that in the Middle Ages were viewed as evidence of demoniacal possession to be treated by exorcism are now regarded as signs of mental illness to be treated by a psychiatrist. In World War II Russian soldiers were never classified as having psychoneuroses, which can only mean that the Russian army did not recognize this condition. Presumably soldiers with complaints that we would term psychoneurotic were regarded either as malingerers subject to disciplinary action or medically ill and therefore treated by regular physicians. In the American army, by contrast, many commonplace reactions to the stresses

[1] A good summary of psychoanalytic theory is Brenner (1954); of conditioned reflex theory, Pavlov (1941); and of learning theories, Hilgard (1948).
[2] For an excellent, concise statement of the interplay of social and personal factors in the causes, manifestations, and treatment of mental illness, see Claussen (1959). Freedman and Hollingshead (1957) present interesting data demonstrating that the diagnosis of psychoneurosis is the result of an interaction process involving the patient, the physician, and the social group.

of military life were initially regarded as signs of psychoneurotic illness, warranting discharge from the service. Today many of these same soldiers would be promptly returned to duty.

Similarly, whether or not a person is sent to a mental hospital for treatment depends at least as much on the attitudes of those around him as on his symptoms. Many actively hallucinating persons function in the community because their families, neighbors, and employers are willing to put up with their eccentricities, while other persons, especially among the elderly, wind up in the hospital largely because the family want to rid themselves of responsibility for their care (Claussen & Yarrow, 1955).

Contemporary America has gone far in the direction of regarding socially deviant behavior as illness, which requires treatment rather than punishment. This is probably partially attributable to the strong humanitarian trend in American society and the high value it places on the welfare of the individual.

Probably more significant, however, is the recognition that certain criminals, alcoholics, and sex deviates, for example, appear to be attempting to cope with the same types of conflicts and other stresses as other persons who are regarded as mentally ill, but their efforts take the form of deviant behavior rather than symptom formation.

An interesting, if somewhat unfortunate, consequence of the fact that social attitudes play such a big role in the definition of mental illness is that mental health education may be a two-edged sword. By teaching people to regard certain types of distress or behavioral oddities as illnesses rather than as normal reactions to life's stresses, harmless eccentricities, or moral weaknesses, it may cause alarm and increase the demand for psychotherapy. This may explain the curious fact that the use of psychotherapy tends to keep pace with its availability. The greater the number of treatment facilities and the more widely they are known, the larger the number of persons seeking their services. Psychotherapy is the only form of treatment which, at least to some extent, appears to create the illness it treats. It can never suffer the unfortunate fate of Victor Borge's physician uncle who became despondent on realizing that he had discovered a cure for which there was no disease.

Cultural values influence not only the definition of mental illness but also the nature of its treatment. Psychotherapies in societies or groups with a primarily religious world view are based on religio-magical theories, and healing rituals merge with religious rites. The scientific world view of Western societies is reflected in the tendency to regard psychotherapy as a form of medical treatment, based on scientific understanding of human nature. Furthermore, naturalistic psychotherapies tend to express the dominant values of their cultures. Thus, methods of psychotherapy in Germany and the USSR[3] tend to reflect the authoritarian values of these societies. In the United States, permissive, democratic therapies have a higher prestige, consistent with the high value placed on individual freedom and responsibility.[4]

Within a given society, the dominant type of treatment depends in part on the class position and group affiliation of the recipient. In America, religio-magical forms of healing are practiced by certain religious groups. Lower-class patients, who view treatment as something the doctor does to one, are more likely to receive directive treatment, often accompanied by physical measures of medication. Middle- and upper-class patients, who put a high value on self-knowledge and self-direction, are more likely to receive permissive forms of treatment stressing insight.[5]

In mid-twentieth-century America, mental illness has not fully shaken off its demonological aura, as evidenced by the stigma still attached to it. In the minds of many it implies moral weakness. The insane still tend to elicit a kind of fascinated horror, reflected in their being shunted off to isolated hospitals on the one hand and being objects of morbid curiosity on the other, as shown by the popularity of novels, plays, and films about them. Nevertheless, all forms of suffering or troublesome behavior that involve emotional or psychological factors are viewed as treatable by psychotherapy. This is reflected in the great variety of recipients and purveyors of psychotherapy and its settings. To reduce this chaotic scene to some sort of order, we shall describe it first from the standpoint of those receiving psychotherapy and then from the standpoint of those offering it.

Who Receives Psychotherapy?

The many thousands of Americans who undergo some form of psychotherapy cover an extraordinarily broad range. At one extreme are some who are best characterized as mental hypochondriacs, searching for someone to lift the normal burdens of living from their shoulders. At the other are persons who are severely ill with disturbances of thinking, feeling, and behavior. They constitute the populations of our mental hospitals. In between is a vast group of persons suffering from chronic emotional stress produced by faulty patterns of living.

The most clearly definable recipients of psychotherapy are persons

---

[3]For an account of contemporary German and Russian psychotherapy, see Winkler (1956) and Guilyarovsky (1958), respectively.
[4]This issue is interestingly discussed by Skinner (1956) and C. R. Rogers (1956).
[5]Hollingshead and Redlich (1958) thoroughly document this point.

who are regarded by themselves or others as patients. Candidates for psychotherapy are distinguished from those who do not receive this type of treatment by the presence of a recognizable emotional or psychological component in their illnesses. The difficulty here is the word "recognizable." As the contributions of unhealthy emotional states to all forms of illness and disability are becoming increasingly recognized, psychotherapeutic principles are being incorporated into all forms of medical healing. It is possible, however, to distinguish four classes of patients for whom psychotherapy constitutes the entire treatment or a major part of it.

The first class comprises the hospitalized insane, patients who are so disturbed that they cannot carry out the ordinary tasks of life and need to be protected. The bulk of these are senile and schizophrenic patients. Both can be helped by psychotherapy, but it can do more for the latter, because their adaptive capacity has not been irreversibly reduced by brain damage. The second class of psychiatric patients consists of neurotics, whose distress seems clearly related to chronic emotional strain and often involves some disturbance of bodily functioning. Akin to these is the third group, patients with so-called "psychosomatic" illnesses such as asthma, peptic ulcer, and certain skin diseases, in whom definite and chronic disorders of bodily organs seem related to emotional tension. The fourth group of patients in whose treatment psychotherapy should play a prominent part are the chronically ill. This category cuts across the other three and also includes those with chronic disease or disability that was initially unrelated to psychological causes, such as loss of a limb, epilepsy, rheumatic heart disease, and so on. Since the emotional stresses created by chronic disease probably contribute more to the distress and disability of these patients than their bodily damage, increasing use of psychotherapeutic principles is being made in rehabilitation methods.

No one questions that psychotics, psychoneurotics, the psychosomatically ill, and the chronically ill are suitable candidates for psychotherapy, but from this point on confusion reigns. The difficulty is that many emotional stresses result in misbehavior, which comes into conflict with the standards and values of society, so that its moral and medical aspects are inseparable. Alcoholics, drug addicts, and sexual deviates are clearly sick in the sense that they are caught up in behavior patterns they cannot control, but they also offend against social standards, which brings them to the attention of the legal authorities. Their deviant behavior often seems attributable to emotional difficulties related to disturbing childhood experiences, such as parental mistreatment or neglect, broken homes, and lack of adequate socialization, suggesting that they might respond to psychotherapy. Modern criminology is increasingly emphasizing the use of psychotherapeutic principles in the rehabilitation of offenders, but much work remains to be done to determine which approach is most suitable for different types of criminals.[6] Current views distinguish the socialized criminal, who represents the values of his own deviant group and is a well-integrated member of it, from the so-called sociopath or psychopath, who cannot get along with anyone and is always in trouble. The proper handling of offenders is a knotty problem requiring cooperation of the healing, legal, and corrective professions.

A large and heterogeneous group of people who may receive psychotherapy may be termed "misfits." Their distress results from failure to cope satisfactorily with their environments, yet they are not severely enough out of step to be considered either ill or criminal. The failure to adjust may be temporary or permanent, and sometimes the chief fault lies in the environment, sometimes in the patient. Misfits include those who seek help or are brought to it because of difficulties on the job, at home, or, in the younger age groups, at school. They include tired business executives, married couples on the verge of divorce, unruly or emotionally disturbed children and their parents, and the like. In this category may also be included members of the intelligentsia or middle and upper classes who have leisure to worry about themselves and who look to psychotherapy to solve their general state of dissatisfaction, malaise, spiritual unrest, or feeling that they are not living life to the full.

Finally, mention must be made of psychotherapists in training who are required to undergo psychotherapy as part of their training program. Although these are in no sense patients and represent a very small proportion of persons receiving psychotherapy, they are of some importance in the total scene because their psychotherapy occupies a large proportion of the time of some of the most able and experienced psychotherapists, at the expense of the patients who might receive their services.

Who Conducts Psychotherapy?

The variety of practitioners of psychotherapy in one form or another is almost as great as the range of persons they seek to help. Psychotherapists in the naturalistic tradition include a relatively small group specifically trained for this art, and a much larger number of professionals who practice psychotherapy without labeling it as such in connection with their healing or advisory activities. The largest group of professionals trained to conduct psychotherapy are psychiatrists, numbering about ten thousand. Their

---

[6]See, for example, the work of Rood (1958) with sex offenders.

ranks are supplemented by well over four thousand clinical psychologists and five thousand social workers.[7]

Psychologists enter the field of psychotherapy through the scientific study of human thinking and behavior, and they supply most of the sophisticated researchers in this field. In clinical settings such as hospitals and psychiatric clinics they carry out diagnostic tests and do therapy under the more or less nominal supervision of psychiatrists. The major institutional settings in which they work independently are schools and universities. Increasing numbers, especially in the larger cities, are going into independent private practice as both diagnosticians and therapists.

Psychiatric social workers are specialists within the helping profession of social work. Like clinical psychologists, they are members of treatment teams in hospitals and clinics under psychiatric supervision, but they also operate independently in social agencies, family agencies, marriage counseling centers, and so on, and as private practitioners.

Psychotherapy in one guise or another forms part of the practice of many other professional groups. An indeterminate number of America's approximately 215,000 nonpsychiatric physicians[8] use psychotherapy with many of their patients, often without recognizing it as such. To them must be added osteopaths and healers on the fringes of medicine such as chiropractors, naturopaths, and others. The effectiveness of these latter, especially with emotionally disturbed persons, probably rests primarily on their intuitive use of psychotherapeutic principles.[9]

In addition to the healers more or less linked to medicine, a wide variety of counselors and guides may use psychotherapeutic principles with their clientele. These include marriage counselors, rehabilitation and vocational counselors, parole officers, group workers, clergymen, and others.

Members of different disciplines tend to describe their activities in different terms. For example, medical and quasimedical healers treat patients, psychiatric social workers do case work with clients, clergymen offer pastoral counseling, and group workers do group work. For obvious reasons, each discipline tends to emphasize the special features of its ap-

[7]The figure for psychiatrists represents approximately the membership of the American Psychiatric Association in 1959. Figures for clinical psychologists and psychiatric social workers were obtained from the Health Manpower Chart Book (1955).

[8]This figure was also obtained from the Health Manpower Chart Book (1955).

[9]Healing cults are astonishingly popular. A survey (Reed, 1932) found some 36,000 sectarian medical practitioners, exclusive of esoteric and local cults, which equaled almost one-fourth of the total number of medical practitioners at that time, to whom people paid at least $125,000,000 annually. One physician found that 43 percent of his private patients and 26 percent of his clinic patients had patronized a cult during the three months preceding their visits to him. Although one reason for the continuing popularity of these cults is that most persons recover from acute illnesses regardless of what is done or not done to them, it seems likely that the adherents of cults also derive more specific benefits, such as increased peace of mind and sense of well-being.

proach, leading to a greater appearance of difference than may actually exist. In all likelihood their similarities far outweigh their differences.

The distinction between different healers and advisers lies less in what they do than in the persons with whom they do it, and this, in turn, depends largely on the settings in which they work. Certain settings sharply limit the kinds of persons who seek or receive psychotherapeutic help. Thus the bulk of the population of mental hospitals consists of the insane; those using the services of social agencies tend to be persons struggling with economic, social, marital, or parental problems. The school psychologist inevitably deals with children with school problems, the prison psychologist or psychiatrist with offenders, and so on.

The private office of the independent practitioner, however, sets no such limits on the kind of person who comes to him. A person may wind up in different hands depending on the referral channel he happens to pick, or the way in which he defines his problems. The very same patient might be treated by a psychiatrist, a psychologist, a psychiatric social worker, or even a clergyman, depending on where his feet carry him. As a result, the relationships among the different professions that conduct psychotherapy are in a state of flux. Clergymen and psychiatrists have formally recognized their field of common concern by forming the Academy of Religion and Mental Health. Jurisdictional problems are most acute in the larger cities where, in response to the increasing demand for psychotherapy, psychologists and psychiatric social workers have gone into independent private practice in direct competition with psychiatrists, resulting in attempts by the various groups involved to settle the issue by legislation.

This review of psychotherapeutic practitioners would be seriously incomplete without mention of the thousands of religious healers who are members of established sects such as Christian Science and New Thought, and, on their fringes, cultists of all sorts whose claim to healing powers rests solely on their own assertions. Though there is no way of counting these last, they must treat vast numbers of troubled people indistinguishable from those receiving more recognized forms of psychotherapy (Steiner, 1945).

What Are the Effects of Psychotherapy?

The ever-increasing investment of time, effort, and money in psychotherapy and its steadily increasing popularity imply that both its recipients and its practitioners are convinced that it does some good. Patients must believe it to be helpful or they would not seek it in increasing numbers, and every psychotherapist has seen permanent and striking improvement in a patient following some occurrence in psychotherapy. To date, however, although proponents of every method present persuasive accounts of their successes and vast amounts have been spent on research in psychotherapy,[10] convincing objective demonstration that one form of psychotherapy produces better results than another is lacking.

Statistical studies of psychotherapy consistently report that about two-thirds of neurotic patients and 40 percent of schizophrenic patients are improved immediately after treatment, regardless of the type of psychotherapy they have received, and the same improvement rate has been found for patients who have not received any treatment that was deliberately psychotherapeutic. Thus about 70 percent of neurotic patients who received only custodial care in state hospitals are released, and the same percentage of patients with neurotically based disabilities treated by insurance doctors have returned to work at the end of two years.[11] Similarly, the few follow-up studies that exist fail to show differences in long-term improvement from different types of treatment.[12] Indeed, with hospitalized psychotics, although certain procedures such as electroconvulsive therapy seem able to accelerate improvement of certain illnesses, no procedure has been shown to produce five-year improvement rates better than those occurring under routine hospital care (Zubin, 1959).

The question of the relative effectiveness of different forms of psychotherapy is also puzzling when viewed from the standpoint of the amount or duration of therapeutic contact. Within wide limits, these seem to depend largely on the therapist's notion of how much treatment is necessary, rather than on the patient's condition. With respect to amount of contact, an eminent psychiatrist has pointed out that when psychoanalysis was transplanted from Europe to America, the frequency of sessions soon dropped from six times a week to five, then to three times a week or even less. There is no reason to think that this reduction depended on differences in the severity of illness between European and American patients, and the writer suggests that it was probably a reflection of the increasing demands on the therapists' time created by the growing number of patients seeking help. Yet "in actual duration of treatment, in terms of months or years, the

---

[10]In 1958 the United States Public Health Service alone spent about two million dollars for research in psychotherapy.

[11]Good reviews and discussions of improvement data are found in Appel, Lhamon, Myers, and Harvey (1953), Teuber and Powers (1953), and Eysenck (1952). Recently Wolpe (1958) and Ellis (1957) have claimed that their methods produce an improvement rate of over 90 percent in neurotics, and Whitehorn and Betz (1954) have found that certain physicians obtain an improvement rate of about 80 percent with groups of hospitalized schizophrenics, but these results have not yet been duplicated by others.

[12]Characteristic follow-up studies are those of Hastings (1958) and Levitt (1957). See also chapter 11 in Frank (1961).

patient going five times a week takes about as long to be cured as the patient going three times." (Thompson, 1950, p. 235).[13]

Duration of treatment also may be more closely related to the therapist's conception of how long treatment should take than to the patient's condition. Practitioners of long-term therapy find that their patients take a long time to respond; those who believe that they can produce good results in a few weeks report that their patients respond promptly (Conn, 1949, 1953; Ellis, 1957; Wolpe, 1958).[14] There is no evidence that a larger proportion of patients in long-term treatment improve or that improvement resulting from long-term treatment is more enduring than that produced by briefer treatment.

However, psychotherapy has tended to become increasingly prolonged in settings where there are no external obstacles to its continuance. Psychoanalysis that originally lasted a year or two at most now often lasts five to six years. At one university counseling center the average number of sessions increased from six in 1949 to thirty-one in 1954 (Seeman, quoted in Shlien, 1957). It is hard to believe that the lengthening of treatment reflects changes in the severity of patients' or clients' illnesses. More probably it reflects certain changes in the therapist's attitudes produced by increasing experience.[15]

At this point it must be emphasized that the failure to find differences in improvement rate from different forms or amounts of psychotherapy is a sign of ignorance, not knowledge. These negative results may well be due to lack of criteria of improvement that would permit comparison of different forms of treatment.[16] In many reports improvement is left undefined, so that there is no way of knowing precisely what the therapist had in mind, or whether or not he shifted his criterion from one patient to another.

When improvement is defined, the relationship between criteria used

---

[13]Of course, treatment contact cannot be attenuated indefinitely without reducing its effectiveness, but the lower limit of effective contact has yet to be determined. Imber, Frank, Nash, Stone, and Gliedman (1957) present experimental evidence indicating that treatment limited to not more than half an hour every two weeks is less effective in producing certain types of immediate improvement than treatment consisting of an hour once a week. See also chapter 11 in Frank (1961).

[14]It is instructive in this regard to compare two reports of group therapy with peptic ulcer patients, one of which was limited to six weeks (Chappell, Stefano, Rogerson, and Pike, 1936), the other unlimited in time (Fortin & Abse, 1956). Though the studies, unfortunately, are not strictly comparable, both seemed to obtain about the same results. Especially interesting is Shlien's experiment (1957) indicating that, with the identical type of therapy, patients improve more promptly if they know in advance that therapy will last only ten weeks than if no time limit is set.

[15]The role of therapists' attitudes is considered elsewhere (Frank, 1961, chapter 7).

[16]Regardless of theoretical orientation, observers show a high degree of agreement with respect to patients who are greatly improved or apparently cured. Agreement drops sharply, however, with respect to lesser degrees of improvement, suggesting that the criteria underlying these judgments need greater explication than has yet been achieved. Conceptual and methodological questions involved in the evaluation of improvement are discussed in Parloff, Kelman, and Frank (1954) and Frank (1959).

in different studies is usually unclear. Criteria determining the discharge of patients from state hospitals, the resumption of work by patients receiving disability payments, and the diagnosis of "recovered" by a psychoanalyst obviously may have little in common.

The problem of lack of comparability of measures of improvement is most acute in studies that define improvement in terms of a particular theory of psychotherapy. Criteria based on such definitions often can be precisely measured, but their relevance to clinical improvement may be problematical. Moreover, in order to get precise quantitative results, the research must confine itself to special types of patients. One such study, for example, compared changes on certain psychological test scores in a group of outpatients who received eight months of psychotherapy with a matched group who received no treatment over seven months, and found no differences between them (Barron & Leary, 1955). But the experiment had to be confined to persons who were able to do the test, and also were willing to forgo treatment for seven months, so one can draw no general conclusion from the negative findings.

In short, the inability to prove that a phenomenon exists is quite different from proving that it does not exist. The difficulty in demonstrating by statistical or experimental methods that therapy works or that one form is superior to another may lie in our inability to define adequately any of the variables involved. We cannot yet describe patients, therapies, or improvement in terms that permit valid comparison of the effects of different therapies on the same class of patient.

In the present state of ignorance, the most reasonable assumption is that all forms of psychotherapy that persist must do some good, otherwise they would disappear. Furthermore, it is likely that the similarity of improvement rate reported from different forms of psychotherapy results from features common to them all. The improvement rate for each form, then, would be composed of patients who responded to the features it shares with other forms and therefore would have improved with any type of psychotherapy, plus, perhaps, some patients who would have responded favorably only to the particular type of psychotherapy under consideration. If this were so, it would be hard to tease out the unique contributions of different forms of treatment until the features they share—and the attributes of patients that cause them to respond favorably to these features— were better understood.

Summary

This chapter has attempted a general definition of psychotherapy, briefly reviewed its historical roots, and described the types of patients, therapists, and settings characteristic of psychotherapy in America today. It appears that many thousands of troubled people of all sorts seek psychotherapy or have it thrust upon them, and its practitioners are almost as varied as its recipients. Despite this feverish activity, there is little established knowledge about the relative efficacy of various forms, and the therapist's expectations seem to influence the length and amount of treatment required to produce improvement. These observations lead to the tentative conclusion that the features common to all types of psychotherapy probably contribute more to their efficacy than the characteristics that differentiate them.

References

Appel, K. E., Lhamon, W. T., Myers, J. M., & Harvey, W. A. Long term psychotherapy. In Association for Research in Nervous and Mental Disease, *Psychiatric treatment* (Research Publication 31). Baltimore: Williams & Wilkins, 1953.

Barron, F., & Leary, T. F. Changes in psychoneurotic patients with and without psychotherapy. *Journal of Consulting Psychology*, 1955, *19*, 239–245.

Brenner, C. *An elementary textbook of psychoanalysis.* New York: International Universities Press, 1954.

Chappell, M. N., Stefano, J. J., Rogerson, J. S., & Pike, F. H. The value of group psychological procedures in the treatment of peptic ulcer. *American Journal of Digestion Diseases and Nutrition*, 1936, *3*, 813–817.

Claussen, J. A. The sociology of mental illness. In R. K. Merton, L. Broom, & L. S. Cottrell (Eds.), *Sociology Today.* New York: Basic Books, 1959.

Claussen, J. A., & Yarrow, M. R. Paths to the mental hospital. *Journal of Social Issues*, 1955, *11*, 25–32.

Conn, J. H. Brief psychotherapy of the sex offender: A report of a liaison service between a court and a private psychiatrist. *Journal of Clinical Psychopathology*, 1949, *10*, 1–26.

Conn, J. H. Hypnosynthesis III. Hypnotherapy of chronic war neuroses with a discussion of the value of abreaction, regression, and revivication. *Journal of Clinical Experimental Hypnosis*, 1953, *1*, 29–43.

Ellis, A. Outcome of employing three techniques of psychotherapy. *Journal of Clinical Psychology*, 1957, *13*, 344–350.

Eysenck, H. J. The effects of psychotherapy: An evaluation. *Journal of Consulting Psychology*, 1952, *16*, 319–323.

Fortin, J. N., & Abse, D. W. Group psychotherapy with peptic ulcer. *International Journal of Group Psychotherapy*, 1956, *6*, 383–391.

Frank, J. D. Problems of controls in psychotherapy as exemplified by the Psychotherapy Research Project of the Phipps Psychiatric Clinic. In E. A. Rubinstein, & M. B. Parloff (Eds.), *Research in psychotherapy.* Washington: American Psychological Association, 1959.

Frank, J. D. *Persuasion and healing.* Baltimore: Johns Hopkins Press, 1961.

Freedman, L. Z., & Hollingshead, A. B. Neurosis and social class: I. Social interaction. *American Journal of Psychiatry*, 1957, *113*, 769–775.

Guilyarovsky, V. The contemporary situation in Soviet psychiatry. In J. H. Masserman & J. L. Moreno (Eds.), *Progress in psychotherapy* (Vol. 3). New York: Grune & Stratton, 1958.

Hastings, D. W. Follow-up results in psychiatric illness. *American Journal of Psychiatry*, 1958, *114*, 1057–1066.

Health Manpower Chart Book. Washington: U. S. Department of Health, Education and Welfare (Public Service publication No. 511), 1955.

Hilgard, E. R. *Theories of learning*. New York: Appleton-Century-Crofts, 1948.

Hollingshead, A. B., & Redlich, F. C. *Social class and mental illness*. New York: John Wiley, 1958.

Imber, S. D., Frank, J. D., Nash, E. H., Stone, A. R., & Gliedman, L. H. Improvement and amount of therapeutic contact: An alternative to the use of no-treatment controls in psychotherapy. *Journal of Consulting Psychology*, 1957, *21*, 309–315.

Levitt, E. E. The results of psychotherapy with children. *Journal of Consulting Psychology*, 1957, *21*, 189–196.

Parloff, M. B., Kelman, H. C., & Frank, J. D. Comfort, effectiveness and self-awareness as criteria of improvement in psychotherapy. *American Journal of Psychiatry*, 1954, *III*, 343–351.

Pavlov, I. P. Lectures on conditioned reflexes. *Conditioned reflexes and psychiatry* (Vol 2). Translated and edited by W. H. Gantt. New York: International Universities Press, 1941.

Reed, L. S. *The healing cults; a study of secterian medical practice: Its extent, causes and control*. Chicago: University of Chicago Press, 1932.

Rogers, C. R. Part II of: Rogers, C. R., & Skinner, B. F. Some issues concerning the control of human behavior: A symposium. *Science*, 1956, *124*, 1060–1066.

Rood, R. The nonpsychotic offender and the state hospital. *American Journal of Psychiatry*, 1958, *115*, 512–513.

Shlien, J. M. Time-limited psychotherapy: An experimental investigation of practical values and theoretical implications. *Journal of Counseling Psychology*, 1957, *4*, 318–322.

Skinner, B. F. Part I of: Rogers, C. R., & Skinner, B. F. Some issues concerning the control of human behavior: A symposium. *Science*, 1956, *124*, 1057–1060.

Steiner, L. *Where do people take their troubles?* New York: International Universities Press, 1945.

Teuber, H. L., & Powers, E. Evaluating therapy in a delinquency prevention program. In Association for Research in Nervous and Mental Disease, *Psychiatric treatment* (Research publication 31). Baltimore: Williams & Wilkins, 1953.

Thompson, C. *Psychoanalysis: Evolution and development*. New York: Hermitage House, 1950.

Whitehorn, J. C., & Betz, B. J. A study of psychotherapeutic relationships between physicians and schizophrenic patients. *American Journal of Psychiatry*, 1954, *3*, 321–331.

Winkler, W. T. The present status of psychotherapy in Germany. In F. Fromm-Reichmann, & J. L. Moreno (Eds.), *Progress in psychotherapy*. New York: Grune & Stratton, 1956.

Wolpe, J. *Psychotherapy by reciprocal inhibition*. Stanford: Stanford University Press, 1958.

Zubin, J. Role of prognostic indicators in the evaluation of therapy. In J. O. Cole & R. W. Gerard (Eds.), *Psychopharmacology: Problems in evaluation*. Washington: National Academy of Sciences, National Research Council (publication 583), 1959.

Part III
On Paradigm Strain

Focusing on a more contemporary view of psychotherapy, this section illustrates the paradigm strain that currently exists within the field. With increased clinical experience, therapists are finding it ever more difficult to place their day-to-day clinical reality within any one given theoretical context. Indeed, they are becoming more willing to acknowledge openly that their theoretical framework does not provide them with sufficient direction for clinical intervention and are starting to consider the possibility that other approaches might have something to offer. Lazarus, who can be credited with providing some of the important impetus for the development of behavior therapy, has openly acknowledged the limitations of this particular viewpoint. Like Rogers, he maintains that it no longer serves the field well to put our energies into the advancement of any delimited school of thought. Although operating from within a psychoanalytic orientation, Strupp nonetheless has questioned the adequacy of this particular frame of reference. Although he does not deny the contributions that a psychoanalytic point of view has provided to the field, he nonetheless emphasizes that it has failed to keep up with new developments. Grinker's comment on Strupp's article reaffirms this position and suggests that once the consultation door is shut, few analysts will function according to orthodox guidelines. Garfield and Kurtz's survey of practicing therapists provides evidence that eclecticism is indeed on the rise. The reason for such eclecticism, according to the therapists involved, is that the use of procedures from different orientations (typically psychodynamic and learning) are needed in order to deal with the clinical cases at hand. In essence, the realities of the clinical situation make it most difficult for the practicing clinician to function within a clearly delineated therapeutic school.

Chapter 6

Has Behavior Therapy Outlived Its Usefulness?[1]

Arnold A. Lazarus

There is still a tendency to equate *behavior therapy* with *behaviorism*. This creates confusion and beclouds significant clinical concerns. Many researchers and practitioners have challenged the view that *behavior therapists* are *behaviorists*. Locke (1971) has argued that the methods of behavior therapy contradict "every major premise of behaviorism." Indeed, most behavior therapists have extended, if not shed, their behavioristic heritage. They apply methods designed to change images and thoughts, emphasis is placed upon self-management, self-reports are employed for assessment and therapy, and clients' self-attitudes and other covert processes are thoroughly explored (Goldfried & Davison, 1976; O'Leary & Wilson, 1975).

There is a very high degree of diversification among the members of this Association (Franks, 1976b). Yet there does seem to be one central notion to which we would all subscribe. We place great value on meticulous observation, careful testing of hypotheses, and continual self-correction on the basis of empirically derived data. As Franks (1976b) has suggested, "are we not at this stage in our development basically an

[1]This article is based on an invited address delivered at the Tenth Annual Convention of the Association for the Advancement of Behavior Therapy, New York City, December 5, 1976.

I am grateful to Allen Fay, Cyril Franks, Peter Nathan, Terry Wilson, and Rob Woolfolk for their cogent criticisms of the initial draft.

Association for Advancement of the Scientific Study of Human Interaction—in all its ramifications?"

Characteristic of the thinking in behavior therapy in the early stages of its development were such books as Eysenck's (1960) *Behaviour Therapy and the Neuroses* and Ullmann and Krasner's (1965) *Case Studies in Behavior Modification*. These books cover some basic pioneering efforts, but with the advantage of hindsight, we can now see that, outstanding as these writings were in their time, they are now primarily of historical significance. In terms of current thinking, the points of view expressed in these and several other books would be regarded as naive. As Kanfer (1976) points out, "If a practitioner of behavior therapy had decided to take a long leave of absence in 1965, he would be astonished and confused if he returned today." One need only consult the *Annual Review of Behavior Therapy* (Franks & Wilson, 1973) from 1973 through 1976 to realize how far behavior therapy has evolved. Present-day behavior therapy has

> no universally accepted definition, no consensus as to goals, concepts or underlying philosophy, no agreement as to its purview, no monolithic point of view, no overriding strategy or core technique, no single founding father, no general agreement about matters of training, and there is no single profession to which primary allegiance is declared [Lazarus & Wilson. 1976, p. 153].

Generally, to understand the present and to predict the future we must appreciate the past. Yet, as many scholars point out, the first duty of a historian is to be on guard against his or her own sympathies. My sympathies remain firmly committed to "behavioral" principles—if by that we mean due regard for scientific objectivity, extreme caution in the face of conjecture and speculation, a rigorous process of deduction from testable theories, and a fitting indifference toward persuasion and hearsay. But if we reserve the term "behavioral" for those who tread the path of empiricism while avoiding what Franks (1976a) aptly called "the treacherous slops of the notional," many of Jay Haley's writings would be considered "behavioral," even Carl Rogers could be regarded as "behavioral," and Hans Strupp would be accorded a similar fate.

A major point, therefore, is that several "nonbehavioral" researchers have remained true to the canons of scientific methodology and have furnished data that are open to verification or disproof. Their frameworks, rather than stemming from learning principles or social learning theory, may be derived from group process, systems theory, cybernetics, information processing, communications theory, or socioecological sources. With a trenchant distaste for overgeneralization, and a vigilant avoidance of capricious conclusions, these "nonbehavioral" scientists have accumulated clinical notions and therapeutic procedures that we dare not overlook (e.g., Haley, 1976; Malan, 1976; Minuchin, 1974).

The Original Errors

In the 1940s and 1950s, the field of psychotherapy was dominated by psychoanalysis. Even those researchers who clearly recognized that psychodynamic principles and theories were inconsistent and untestable nevertheless embraced basic psychoanalytic tenets (e.g., Dollard & Miller, 1950). It was erroneously assumed that by translating psychoanalytic concepts into the language of conditioning and learning theory, the latter would gain clinical utility, and psychodynamic principles would achieve scientific respectability. As far back as 1933, French published a paper in the *American Journal of Psychiatry* on the "interrelations between psychoanalysis and the experimental work of Pavlov." In 1934, Kubie addressed the relation of the conditioned reflex to psychoanalytic technique, and Shaw (1946) was among the first to provide "a stimulus–response analysis of repression and insight in psychotherapy." These writings did little to advance knowledge and merely demonstrated how readily the concepts from one discipline could be transposed into the terms of another.

During the 1920s, a considerable amount of clinical practice was based upon conditioning and deconditioning procedures. Kretschmer's (1922/1934) text on medical psychology described "systematic habituation therapy" and other "behavioral" techniques. A book on phobic disorders by Williams (1923) viewed "reconditioning" as the foundation of psychotherapy, and Jones (1924) devised several "deconditioning" strategies for overcoming children's fears. Gesell (1938) listed 57 early references to learning and conditioning procedures for overcoming children's clinical problems. But these works failed to rescind the prevailing Freudian zeitgeist and were almost completely eclipsed by it.

It was not until the mid-1950s that a significant number of clinicians developed an enduring interest in the writings of Pavlov, Watson, Hull, Thorndike, Guthrie, Tolman, and Skinner. The die was cast. If psychotherapy was essentially a learning process, why not draw upon the major learning theorists of the day? Thus, through massive extrapolation, Hull's reinforcement theory and Guthrie's contiguity theory were drawn into the domain of psychotherapy. An overzealous adoption of stimulus–response theory led these clinical pioneers to embrace *behaviorism* in the same way, and for many of the same reasons, that Watson eschewed all internal constructs in response to the introspectionists of his day. As London (1972) has pointed out, we have yet to live down this unfortunate choice of ideology.

The terms *behavior therapy* and *behavior therapist* first appeared in print in the *South African Medical Journal* when I applied them to Wolpe's "reciprocal inhibition" framework (Lazarus, 1958). Something had to be done to demonstrate that behavior was often clinically significant in its own right. Most therapists (with the exception of certain hypnotists) remained strongly opposed to "symptomatic treatment." Behavior per se was almost completely ignored in favor of "underlying" dynamics that were viewed as the only respectable domain of intervention. All else was considered mere palliation. Thus, in order to bring behavior back into therapy, we witnessed the birth (or rebirth) of "behavior therapy" and "behavior modification." But less than 20 years later, we seem to be witnessing what Krasner (1976) regards as the premature demise of behavior modification. (The death of behavior modification refers to the *system*, not to the basic principles. Reinforcement and punishment are ubiquitous and exert a continual impact on human conduct. Disputes center around the interpretation, implementation, and application of these fundamental principles.)

Enter Cognitions and Other Covert Processes

The emergence of behavior therapy was presaged by (1) the belief in automatic and autonomic conditioning, (2) the eschewal of most cognitive processes, and (3) constant extrapolation from animal experimentation to human functioning. Over the span of almost three decades, Wolpe (1948, 1958, 1976) has remained dedicated to the proposition that cognitive processes are entirely secondary to subcortical autonomic reconditioning as the *real* basis of emotional and behavioral change. Thus, Wolpe (1976, p. 29) contends that "in the majority of neuroses, conditioned anxiety habits are the sole problem." But our current view is that in humans, conditioning does not occur automatically and is in fact cognitively mediated (Bandura, 1974; Brewer, 1974; Mahoney, 1974). The nonmediational model cannot account for vicarious learning, semantic generalization, and other "exclusively human" functions such as imaginal response patterns and symbolic processes. We need not belabor the fact that the nonmediational model provides an attenuated and truncated view of human functioning. To account for behavior solely in terms of external rewards and punishments overlooks the fact that human beings can be rewarded and punished by their *own thinking*, "even when this thinking is largely divorced from outside reinforcements and penalties" (Ellis, 1962, p. 16). There are compelling data that demonstrate how self-evaluative and self-produced reactions take precedence over external consequences (Bandura, 1973).

While behaviorists (e.g., Rachlin, 1976) remain staunchly opposed to the notion that behavior, however complex, can be influenced by cognitions, the field of behavior therapy has become increasingly "cognitive."

(Radical behaviorists still claim that only environmental events and contingencies can directly influence behavior.) Of course, nearly everyone, apart from ESP enthusiasts, will agree that the only way we can know anything about another person is through his or her *behavior* (verbal and nonverbal responses), but those of us who work extensively and intensively with patients or clients find it necessary to make inferences about "private events" and "covert processes" in addition to observing, quantifying, and modifying overt behaviors. And as one enters the area of "self-talk" and "mediating constructs," the existence of *ambiguity* becomes evident. Behaviorism and stimulus–response learning theory have no way of recognizing ambiguity and various levels of abstraction—let alone dealing with them. To cite a simple clinical example, early behavior therapists regarded phobias as conditioned avoidance responses (Rachman, 1968; Wolpe, 1973) and thereby completely overlooked the fact that phobias can be used as manipulative ploys, as face-saving pretexts, and as symbolic retreats (Lazarus, 1971).

Another important outcome of ambiguity is the widespread influence of paradoxical communications in most areas of human interaction. The clinical use of "paradoxical procedures" (e.g., Watzlawick, Weakland, & Fisch, 1974) offers a range of potentially powerful interventions. These methods, while easily explained in terms of communications theory, are extremely difficult to interpret according to reinforcement theory. No doubt, a determined learning theorist can "explain" virtually anything, on a post hoc basis, in a manner congruent with conditioning and radical behavioristic principles. But from a therapeutic standpoint, a theory is only as useful as the effective repertoire of techniques it successfully generates. I recognize, of course, that the therapeutic emphasis is quite separate from the concerns of the research scientist, for whom clinical techniques are quite secondary to the generality of a theory.

As far back as 40 years ago, a number of theorists considered it necessary to draw on cognitive proceses when accounting for some kinds of conditioning (Razran, 1935; Woodworth, 1938). Zener (1937) even suggested the necessity of a cognitive theory to account for the Pavlovian conditioning of dogs! Brewer's (1974) scholarly review argues persuasively that behavioristic psychology is unable to explain even simple behavior, and that any convincing evidence for operant or classical conditioning in adult humans is nonexistent. The essence of his compelling argument is that in human subjects, conditioning is produced through the operation of higher mental processes—through cognitive mediation. Only a few die-hards would not agree that the stimulus–response "learning theory" basis of behavior therapy is passé and that a distinctly cognitive orientation now prevails.

Whither Behavior Therapy?

None of the foregoing is meant to gainsay the invaluable services that "behavioral" orientations have rendered. The inestimable virtues of quantification, replication, specificity, and objectivity cannot be overstated. By challenging and questioning the heuristic value of disease analogies and various medical models, behavior therapy has placed psychological change and intervention in its proper context—within education rather than medicine. And by adding foresight to hindsight (as in the formula of behavior as a frequent, but not invariable, function of its consequences), we have learned that etiological or antecedent factors alone are grossly limited in accounting for human interaction. Behavior therapy has pinpointed the need to search for current maintaining factors in addition to antecedent events.

Nevertheless, behavior therapy and behavior modification have acquired a bad press. To receive funding, many hospitals and community agencies have had to drop the label *behavior* from their program proposals. In several quarters, the term *behavior modification* is an adrenalin-raiser that evokes unfortunate stereotypes. One grows weary of explaining that behavior therapists do not deny consciousness, that they do not treat people like Pavlovian dogs, that they are not Machiavellian and coercive, that aversion therapy (except in the hands of a lunatic fringe) has always been a minor and relatively insignificant part of our armamentarium, and that we are not ignorant of the part played by mutual trust and other relationship factors among our treatment variables.

When making therapeutic recommendations, however, the degree of diversification among behavior therapists appears to be no less extensive than the differences between behavioral and nonbehavioral practitioners (Loew, Grayson, & Loew, 1975). There are multiple approaches for overcoming human woes, but we require precise knowledge about what is best under specified conditions. All therapists need to be wary of any uncritical acceptance of ideas, while also realizing that their theories and methods must necessarily undergo change. It takes courage to abandon pet notions and favored strategies when the disciplined light of science reveals their shortcomings. I believe that therapists of all persuasions must transcend the constraints of factionalism in which cloistered adherents of rival schools, movements, and systems each cling to their separate illusions or unwisely seek solace in volatile blends or overinclusive amalgams.

I am opposed to the advancement of psychoanalysis, to the advancement of Gestalt therapy, to the advancement of existential therapy, to the advancement of behavior therapy, or to the advancement of any delimited school of thought. I would like to see an advancement in psychological knowledge, an advancement in the understanding of human interaction, in the alleviation of suffering, and in the know-how of therapeutic intervention. As a reflection of my evolving commitment of these developments, my own clinical work has grown from a fairly strict behavioral orientation to a broad-spectrum, behavior therapy approach, with a current emphasis on multifaceted interventions that constitute "multimodal behavior therapy" (Lazarus, 1965, 1971, 1976). Behavioral and interpersonal factors constitute about 28 percent of the variance in multimodal therapy. The other 72 percent of assessment-intervention strategies are devoted to affective, sensory, imaginal, cognitive, and biochemical/neurophysiological considerations.

If behavior therapy, in keeping with the views of this Association (the AABT), is limited to principles and methods derived from research in experimental and social psychology, it can be seen as a small but significant part of a multimodal therapy approach. Within the confines of this delimitative context, behavior therapy can continue to serve a useful function. But no practitioner who wishes to be effective with a broad range of clients can afford to limit himself or herself in this manner. Strictly speaking, behavior therapy, like psychoanalysis, can be defended only as a research tactic. The real world of human suffering and the vicissitudes of psychological growth demand much more than any of us have offered to date.

Summary

Initially, "behavior therapy" connoted a movement whose rallying point was its struggle to bring the scientific method to bear upon psychotherapeutic processes and to treat "symptoms" directly. Today, the term has no clear denotation and tends to be confused with "behaviorism." Those who adhere to the more delimited meanings of "behavior therapy" tend to disregard significant "nonbehavioral" therapeutic developments. They also overlook convincing data demonstrating that in adult humans, conditioning is produced through cognitive mediation. Clinical exigencies demand that a therapist be able to account for events that the behavior therapy model cannot readily explain. Adoption of a more comprehensive (multimodal) framework is required.

References

Bandura, A. *Aggression: A social learning analysis*. Englewood Cliffs, N.J.: Prentice-Hall, 1973.

Bandura, A. Behavior theory and the models of man. *American Psychologist*, 1974, *29*, 859–869.

Brewer, W. F. There is no convincing evidence for operant or classical conditioning in adult humans. In W. B. Weimer & D. S. Palermo (Eds.), *Cognition and the symbolic processes*. New York: Halsted Press, 1974.

Dollard, J., & Miller, N. E. *Personality and psychotherapy*. New York: McGraw-Hill, 1950.

Ellis, A. *Reason and emotion in psychotherapy*. New York: Lyle Stuart, 1962.

Eysenck, H. J. *Behaviour therapy and the neuroses*. Oxford, England: Pergamon Press, 1960.

Franks, C. M. Foreword. In A. A. Lazarus, *Multimodal behavior therapy*. New York: Springer, 1976. (a)

Franks, C. M. Personal communication, November, 1976. (b)

Franks, C. M., & Wilson, G. T. (Eds.). *Annual review of behavior therapy: Theory and practice*. New York: Brunner/Mazel, 1973.

French, T. Interrelations between psychoanalysis and the experimental work of Pavlov. *American Journal of Psychiatry*, 1933, *12*, 1165–1203.

Gesell, A. The conditioned reflex and the psychiatry of infancy. *American Journal of Orthopsychiatry*. 1938, *8*, 19–30.

Goldfried, M. R., & Davison, G. C. *Clinical behavior therapy*. New York: Holt, Rinehart & Winston, 1976.

Haley, J. *Problem solving therapy*. San Francisco: Jossey-Bass, 1976.

Jones, M. C. The elimination of children's fears. *Journal of Experimental Psychology*, 1924, *1*, 382–390.

Kanfer, F. H. The many faces of self-control, or behavior modification changes its focus. Paper presented at the 8th International Banff Conference, Banff, Alberta, Canada, March 1976.

Krasner, L. On the death of behavior modification: Some comments from a mourner. *American Psychologist*, 1976, *31*, 387–388.

Kretschmer, E. *Kretschmer's textbook of medical psychology* (E. B. Strauss, Trans.). London: Oxford University Press, 1934. (Originally published, 1922).

Kubie, L. S. Relation of the conditioned reflex to psychoanalytic technique. *Archives of Neurology and Psychiatry*, 1934, *32*, 1137–1142.

Lazarus, A. A. New methods in psychotherapy: A case study. *South African Medical Journal*, 1958, *32*, 660–664.

Lazarus, A. A. Towards the understanding and effective treatment of alcoholism. *South African Medical Journal*, 1965, *39*, 736–741.

Lazarus, A. A. *Behavior therapy and beyond*. New York: McGraw-Hill, 1971.

Lazarus, A. A. *Multimodal behavior therapy*. New York: Springer, 1976.

Lazarus, A. A., & Wilson, G. T. Behavior modification: Clinical and experimental perspectives. In B. B. Wolman (Ed.), *The therapist's handbook*. New York: Van Nostrand Reinhold, 1976.

Locke, E. A. Is "Behavior therapy" behavioristic? An analysis of Wolpe's psychotherapeutic methods. *Psychological Bulletin*, 1971, *76*, 318–327.

Loew, C. A., Grayson, H., & Loew, G. H. (Eds.) *Three psychotherapies*. New York: Brunner/Mazel, 1975.

London, P. The end of ideology in behavior modification. *American Psychologist*, 1972, *27*, 913–926.

Mahoney, M. J. *Cognition and behavior modification*. Cambridge, Mass.: Ballinger, 1974.

Malan, D. H. *The frontier of brief psychotherapy.* New York: Plenum, 1976.

Minuchin, S. *Families and family therapy.* Cambridge, Mass.: Harvard University Press, 1974.

O'Leary, K. D., & Wilson, G. T. *Behavior therapy: Application and outcome.* Englewood Cliffs, N.J.: Prentice-Hall, 1975.

Rachlin, H. *Introduction to modern behaviorism* (2nd ed.). San Francisco: Freeman, 1976.

Rachman, S. *Phobias: Their nature and control.* Springfield, Ill.: Charles C. Thomas, 1968.

Razran, G. H. S. Conditioned responses: An experimental study and a theoretical analysis. *Archives of Psychology,* 1935, *28,* No. 191.

Shaw, F. A. stimulus–response analysis of repression and insight in psychotherapy. *Psychological Review,* 1946, *53,* 36–42.

Ullmann, L. P., & Krasner, L. *Case studies in behavior modification.* New York: Holt, Rinehart & Winston, 1965.

Watzlawick, P., Weakland, J., & Fisch, R. *Change: Principles of problem formation and problem resolution.* New York: Norton, 1974.

Williams, T. A., *Dreads and besetting fears.* Boston: Little, Brown, 1923.

Wolpe, J. An approach to the problem of neurosis based on the conditioned response. Unpublished M.D. thesis, Witwatersrand Medical School, 1948.

Wolpe, J. *Psychotherapy by reciprocal inhibition.* Stanford, Calif.: Stanford University Press, 1958.

Wolpe, J. *The practice of behavior therapy* (2nd ed.). Elmsford, N.Y.: Pergamon Press, 1973.

Wolpe, J. *Theme and variations: A behavior therapy casebook.* Elmsford, N.Y.: Pergamon Press, 1976.

Woodworth, R. S. *Experimental psychology.* New York: Holt, 1938.

Zener, K. The significance of behavior accompanying conditioned salivary secretion for theories of the conditioned reflex. *American Journal of Psychology,* 1937, *50,* 384–403.

Chapter 7

Some Critical Comments on the Future of Psychoanalytic Therapy

Hans H. Strupp (with a discussion by Roy R. Grinker, Sr.)[1]

My remarks will concern the current status and the future of psychoanalytic therapy, a topic on which I have commented over the years (Strupp, 1960, 1968, 1971, 1972, 1973). In this presentation I must strive to be succinct, and therein lies the danger of being misunderstood. Let me therefore try to put my critical remarks in perspective by emphasizing my abiding admiration for and commitment to the insights into the nature of man that psychoanalysis has given us as well as the utility of basic techniques which have evolved within the psychoanalytic framework for alleviating neurotic suffering and misery. In competent hands these represent the best the field has been able to develop. Indeed, it is precisely because of my abiding admiration for Freud's genius and the potentialities of psychoanalysis as a science and as a set of therapeutic techniques that I voice my concern for the embattled position of psychoanalytic therapy today.

Once in the forefront of revolutionary change, psychoanalytic therapy is with increasing monotony described as antiquated, passé, and even defunct. Psychoanalytic theory is seen as based on formulations and working assump-

Reprinted by permission of the author, Hans H. Strupp, the discussant, Roy R. Grinker, Sr., and the publisher from *Bulletin of the Menninger Clinic*, 1976, *40*, 238–254.

[1]Presented to the American Psychological Association, September 2, 1975, Chicago, Illinois, as part of a symposium entitled "A Critical Assessment of Psychoanalytic Therapy."

tions in dire need of massive overhaul; the therapeutic effectiveness of analytic therapy is being seriously questioned; its applicability to the vast problems of contemporary society doubted; and psychoanalysis, as a branch of the behavioral sciences appears, to be approaching its nadir. Many students are no longer "turned on" by what psychoanalysis has to offer; granting agencies have become critical of research proposals emanating from within the psychoanalytic framework; universities have turned their attention to more "exciting" developments both within psychology and in the neighboring sciences; and the general public has become deeply disillusioned.

The zeitgeist I am sketching is less apparent in places like New York, Chicago, Boston, and Philadelphia; it is also obscured by the "business-as-usual" attitude prevailing in hospitals, clinics, university-based departments of psychiatry, and specialized training institutes that remain committed to the psychoanalytic tradition. Furthermore, the influence of psychoanalytic teachings on the professional work of thousands of practicing therapists remains impressive, particularly in the United States. To appreciate more fully what is happening in the field today one must observe the burgeoning literature on behavior therapy, the enormous proliferation of techniques (many of which have gained currency by garish appeals of their originators to the general public), the insatiable hunger of a wide spectrum of the populace for books relating to "therapy," the encounter group and human potential movements, and the religious zeal with which "discoveries" like meditation, biofeedback, Zen, etc., are greeted. In the din surrounding these contemporary developments, psychoanalytic psychotherapy is all but being drowned out.

In the spirit that diagnosis bears some relationship to treatment, let me enumerate factors that, in my judgment, have significantly contributed to the malaise from which psychoanalytic psychotherapy is currently suffering:

1. Psychoanalytic psychotherapy has failed to make explicit to the public and the scientific community its precise nature, goals, outcomes, applicability, and limitations. To cite a few examples: (a) While few therapists practice orthodox analysis today and various theoretical and technical developments have occurred, the image evoked by the term "psychoanalytic psychotherapy"—not only among college sophomores and readers of *The New Yorker*—is that of a patient reclining on the couch, presumably engaged in free association for interminable periods of time. In other words, the image of analytic therapy became frozen decades ago. (b) Practicing therapists are notoriously vague in their thinking as well as their operations concerning specific goals in treatment and how these goals might be reached through specific technical operations. (c) Therapists continue to have foggy notions of what constitutes a good therapeutic outcome and how therapeutic change is to be assessed. (d) While there is a growing tendency to combine psychoanalytic psychotherapy with other treatment modalities

(e.g., in the area of sexual dysfunctions), many practitioners remain committed to the traditional open-ended, exploratory approach in which analysis of the transference reigns supreme. No doubt, there are clear indications for this approach, but the circumstances in which it is fruitful and how it is related to outcome need to be carefully spelled out. In my view, this tendency to apply one aproach to all comers has been one of the great failings of psychoanalysis and accounts in large measure for its problems. It is like prescribing aspirin for all ailments.

2. Because of its close alliance with organized psychoanalysis, psychoanalytic therapy has been insufficiently open to influences from and contact with developments in the behavioral sciences. The "closed shop" mentality still pervading psychoanalytic training institutes has had numerous untoward implications: (a) Training of therapists practicing psychoanalytic psychotherapy, while often quite thorough, has been extremely restricted and one-sided. (b) Innovations, questioning of time-honored practices, and vigorous experimentation have been discouraged; conversely, there has been a tendency to elevate the writings of Freud and those of other pioneers to a status of Gospel truth, when instead they should be regarded as working hypotheses, subject to refinement and even radical change. (c) For many years collaborative relationships between analytic therapists and researchers have been discouraged or thwarted by the analytic establishment. As a result, the field has largely failed to profit from the growing research sophistication in psychology and the behavioral sciences. Instead, the convenient fiction was adopted that each treatment case was a "research" case, that "validation" could be carried out by the clinical method, and that the practicing therapist was the best person to do research. In short, many practitioners of psychoanalytic psychotherapy still have a deficient understanding of the nature of scientific research and what can be expected from scientific investigations.

3. In general, the role and function of theory, particularly their relationship to technique, have been poorly understood, and relatively few concerted efforts have been made to elucidate attendant problems. This statement is not meant to deny the advances in theory such as the growing emphasis on ego psychology, but it is not clear to what extent these changes in theoretical formulations have brought about significant modifications in therapeutic technique. In general, insufficient attention has been paid to empirical data.

Let me raise some crucial questions: How is it possible that in a field like modern psychotherapy, which will soon reach its first centennial, questions continue to be raised whether it has *any* therapeutic utility? How is it possible for controversy to persist on what constitutes a satisfactory outcome, the relative usefulness of one set of techniques over another, the relative importance of the therapist's personality in comparison to the techniques he employs, the selection of suitable patients for a particular form of therapy, the conditions that impede or alternatively potentiate the success of a given form of treatment, the factors responsible for the absence of therapeutic change or the occurrence of deterioration? Questions and doubts are being raised not only by an uninformed public—who might be forgiven for its ignorance—but by experts within the field. What has happened is a polarization between a sizable and influential group of practitioners, who are obviously ego-involved because the practice of psychotherapy has evolved into a prestigious and extraordinarily lucrative occupation, and a growing group of skeptics, many of whom are not necessarily hostile to analytic psychotherapy but who remain unconvinced in the absence of powerful demonstrations that the factors to which psychotherapy attributes its effectiveness are indeed the ones to which success should be credited when it occurs. We hear a great deal about placebo effects—a force to be reckoned with in any healing method, nonspecific factors operating in any "good" human relationship—and we are brought face-to-face with the extremely uncomfortable finding that all psychotherapeutic methods, regardless of their theoretical underpinnings, have approximately the same rates of success and failure.

The answer to these questions is that psychotherapy has not done its homework, or in Engel's (1968) blunt phrase, psychoanalysts "haven't delivered the goods." But what is it that we have not done? What have we failed to deliver? We must be more specific. Put simply, if psychotherapy of whatever variety is a treatment modality, that is, if it is to ameliorate a problem in living or psychopathology however defined, it is incumbent upon those who advance such claims to specify: (1) the nature of the problem or problems it is supposed to help; (2) the conditions under which it is helpful; (3) the kinds of changes or improvements that may reasonably be expected; (4) the operations necessary to bring about the change; and (5)—perhaps somewhat further down the road—the advancement of reasonable theoretical formulations to explain its modus operandi. Each of these requirements entails careful definition of variables, the description of measurement or assessment operations, and the ruling out of alternatives, e.g., the possibility that the observed changes are "spontaneous," that is, due to extraneous factors unrelated to the treatment under investigation. Toward the end of his career, Freud said in cavalier fashion that the problem of therapeutic action in psychoanalysis was well understood, and he added that he was not in need of "statistics" to demonstrate what, to him, were established facts. Many clinicians continue to subscribe to this comforting belief, and any one of us who has practiced psychotherapy has certainly witnessed therapeutic change in a fair number of our patients. However, we have failed to convince the larger scientific community, legislators who hold the purse strings, as well as the general public of the uniqueness of our contribution or the efficacy of our treatment efforts.

A major source of the difficulty resides in the multiple meanings of the word *psychoanalysis* itself. Traditionally, distinctions have been made between psychoanalysis as a theory of personality and human development, as a *Weltanschauung*, as a technique for investigating the structure and function of the human mind, as a set of theories for analyzing social, cultural, and anthropological phenomena, and as a treatment modality for bringing about therapeutic change in feelings, cognitions, and behaviors seen as maladaptive or pathological. While psychoanalysis, emerging from the original work of Breuer and Freud, staked its early claims on being a treatment modality, and while Freud never lost interest in this aspect of his work, he assigned it a relatively minor role in the future of psychoanalysis. It is also noteworthy—although frequently overlooked—that he rather stringently delineated the range of applicability of the psychoanalytic technique by which he meant essentially classical analysis. Yet, over the years Freud's conservatism in this area gave way to what came to be known as the "widening scope of psychoanalysis" (Stone, 1954). As I noted earlier (Strupp, 1968):

> Yet, a broadening of applications gradually occurred, encompassing the treatment of psychoses, character disorders, perversions, behavior disorders in childhood and adolescence, borderline states, psychosomatic conditions, and numerous others. Furthermore, with the rise of "the affluent society" in America, there is scarcely a human problem which has not been brought to or treated by psychoanalysis, which thus has become the panacea for all human ills. This lack of discrimination may have been partly a function of the great social pressure for psychotherapeutic services, which has been mounting steadily, but therapists as a group must share some of the blame for undertaking tasks that often lay beyond their technical means [p. 320].

In short, by failing strictly to define limits to itself and the public, the therapeutic community has either permitted itself to be maneuvered into a position of omnipotence or it has tacitly accepted the magical expectations that have always been part of the human condition, particularly in times of crises or when confronted with seemingly insoluble problems. The field has failed to go unequivocally on record as saying:

> *This much we can do, and given particular circumstances we can demonstrate that we can do it well. In fact, under proper conditions, there is no treatment modality that can equal our efforts in terms of elegance, radical change, humaneness, and permanence. We are not faith healers, miracle workers, or evangelists, but neither are we charlatans or opportunists. There are hosts of*

human problems we can do little about. Do not look to us for revolutionary social change; do not expect us to change an imperfect world where poverty, technology, racial discrimination, pollution, and man's inhumanity to man have created a plethora of problems that we deplore but do not have the power to change. Our techniques are appropriate for a relatively select clientele. Unfortunately, such variables as intelligence, education, psychological-mindedness, an "intact ego," and other considerations which may be seen as elitist play a part in our selection. Our techniques are arduous, time-consuming, and expensive, which is regrettable, but we cannot escape it. Above all, we have no monopoly on The Truth. We know a number of things about neurotic suffering and how to alleviate it. We have certain theories and certain hypotheses that guide our work. They are not immutable, they are the best we have, but they are subject to change as our knowledge advances. We maintain an open mind about alternate approaches, and we continue to explore, question, experiment. We are continually examining our own operations, and we support serious research by others bent upon such efforts. In particular, we are attempting to modify our techniques to bring them in line with changing social conditions and advancing knowledge. We are also seeking ways and means to adapt our techniques to patient populations that may appear to be or have traditionally been regarded as unreachable or refractory. We take pride in our work, and like everyone else we expect to get paid for it. But do not look to us for utopias, "pop" psychological solutions, unmitigated bliss, or for the solution of man's existential dilemmas. We are professionals, not gurus. And we resist strenuously any effort to attribute to us powers we do not possess, nor do we capitalize on such attributions.

Although in the din of the therapeutic marketplace it is easy to lose sight of more positive developments, it would be wise to keep the following in mind:

1. A vast storehouse of clinical knowledge exists, amassed over the years, that forms the underpinnings of modern psychotherapy and, at least in part, guides its operations. While there are great gaps in our knowledge, an impressive theoretical and clinical literature has contributed materially to the therapist's understanding of the forces he is confronting in his therapeutic work. Much of this knowledge is far from exact, but it has a great deal of relevance to the therapist's grasp of the problems he is called upon to treat.

2. While systematic research has been relatively sparse, it is far from nonexistent. Indeed, in recent years research efforts have been intensified, and the level of sophistication, both in clinical sensitivity and scientific rigor, has grown enormously. (To appreciate these developments one must look in places other than the traditional psychoanalytic journals, which continue to be preoccupied with clarifying esoteric theoretical issues, often far removed from empirical data.)

3. We have moved away from such simplistic formulations as "Does psychotherapy do any good?" and instead have made strides in clarifying major issues (Bergin & Strupp, 1972). Furthermore, a number of beachheads have been created via systematic research that mitigate to a considerable extent the bleak picture of the past. Under particular circumstances we can be much more certain that psychotherapy is far more than a placebo (Bergin, 1971; Meltzoff & Kornreich, 1970) or the purchase of friendship. Serious collaboration between clinicians and researchers in certain areas (e.g., in the treatment of depressions) and systematic comparisons between treatment modalities under reasonably specified conditions have been carried out [Sloane, Staples, Cristol, Yorkston, & Whipple, 1975; Di Loreto, 1971].

4. The younger generation of practicing therapists is less committed to orthodoxy and is less overawed by authoritarian pronouncements on therapeutic issues. Concomitantly, they exhibit a greater willingness to experiment with new techniques that promise results and that require greater tolerance for ambiguity and greater open-mindedness on all issues. A greater emphasis on pragmatism is leading to the development of practical, less expensive, less time-consuming techniques. Therapeutic goals have become less ambitious, and the ideal of the "perfectly analyzed" patient has receded into the background. Brief or time-limited psychotherapy has begun to attract notable interest. The model of one-to-one intensive psychotherapy carried out over a period of years is no longer considered the "ideal" treatment modality. Greater attention is being paid to lower-class, lower-income, and other patient populations that traditionally have been considered refractory to therapeutic effort. The limitations of what psychotherapy can accomplish are gradually becoming better appreciated.

What does the future hold in store for psychoanalytic psychotherapy? In general terms, there can be little doubt that it is here to stay. In fact, it is my impression that as exaggerated claims by competing approaches are subjected to critical analysis (e.g., the sober comparison between psychoanalytic therapy and behavior therapy by Sloane et al., 1975), the status of psychoanalytic psychotherapy is strenghtened. Secondly, there remains a powerful force of practitioners who carry forward the tradition and who continue to be committed to its basic utility. Nevertheless, the entire field of psychotherapy remains beset with innumerable fads, conceptual unclarity, muddy theories, and grossly unwarranted claims for the effectiveness of simplistic techniques. All these factors have conspired to impede progress and to retard dispassionate examination of basic scientific issues. A dire need exists for separating the wheat from the chaff, for pruning, thus taking full advantage of earlier insights which in terms of sophistication often surpass contemporary formulations. We need also to discard obsolete theoretical notions that have questionable empirical relevance. Withal, a serious return to empirical data is imperative.

A distinction should be made between the tasks that must be undertaken to enhance the field's scientific respectability and the social forces
that will shape its destiny. On the former subject, the issues have been
clearly delineated [Fiske, Hunt, Luborsky, Orne, Parloff, Reiser, & Tuma,
1970; Bergin & Strupp, 1972]. Remaining obstacles are primarily strategic
and practical, and there is no reason for questioning the field's ability to
overcome them. Serious research of high quality is going forward; and
contrary to the pessimistic climate of the 1960s, there is a renewed air of
rigor, hope, and commitment on the part of a relatively small cadre of
investigators.[2] I concur with Shakow's (1965) observation:

> A scientific area belongs ultimately to its investigators, not to its practitioners.
> No field can maintain its vitality, in fact its viability, without such a group. One
> of the most cogent criticisms that can be made of psychoanalysis at the present
> time is that it has neglected this indispensable rule for growth [p. 355fn].

It is encouraging that over the years the prestige of the investigator has
grown, and he no longer plays second fiddle to the practicing clinician and
theoretician.

The foregoing prescription notwithstanding, a field like psychotherapy,
which is so deeply anchored in man's strivings for happiness, self-realization, and a place in a pluralistic society, is continually influenced by forces
other than scientific considerations. Significant advances in the area have
traditionally not come from scientific investigators but from clinicians who
have been deeply committed to the alleviation of human suffering and the
search for techniques that have optimal practical utility. Breuer and
Freud's early work is a case in point, as are the contributions of Wolpe,
Rogers, Ellis, Perls, and many others. But in the final analysis it is the
scientific investigator who keeps the field honest and who refines and
distills the principles on which responsible practice must ultimately rest.[3]

In summary, I view the future of psychoanalytic therapy as the quest
for principles and operations that stand the test of scientific rigor. As I
stated in 1968:

> . . . by working toward realistic goals, and by abandoning grandiose aspira-
> tions, analytic therapy seems to be assured of its value as a potent weapon in

---

[2]See the proceedings of the flourishing Society for Psychotherapy Research.
[3]Some authors have questioned whether future advances can come from within the psychoanalytic framework. Eissler (1969) concludes that " . . . all that can be learned by way of the couch Freud had already
learned" (p. 468) and that " . . . the next phase of progress in psychoanalysis will come about through the
supply of data obtained from outside the psychoanalytic situation proper" (p. 470). If Eissler's statement is
intended to broaden the clinical-therapeutic situation as the context for research, I agree; on the other
hand, I believe that systematic research within the therapeutic process broadly conceived and sharpened by
incisive quantitative and qualitative analyses of the transactions still has a bright future.

man's continued fight against neurotic suffering and misery. We may be sure that the future will not be utopia, but neither need there be cause for despair [pp. 336–337].

DISCUSSION
Roy R. Grinker, Sr.

Strupp has spent most of his academic life investigating the rationale and effectiveness of various forms of psychotherapy, a field few investigators have the temerity to approach. He has applied scientific concepts and techniques to areas dominated by repetitive, anecdotal statements that have given satisfaction to the few but have created skepticism in the many. In this presentation, Strupp begins with paeans of praise for Freud and psychoanalysis, followed by critical statements indicating the need for overhauling the field; yet Strupp remains optimistic to the end. The old cliché comes to mind: "With such friends, who needs enemies?" However, I should state at the outset as an analyst within the organization (by no means an envious outsider), student, teacher, and investigator, I thoroughly agree with Strupp's ambivalence and have so written repeatedly.

Beginning residents do not feel as they did in the 1940s and 1950s that psychoanalytic training is necessary to become a "first-class citizen of psychiatry," nor do universities favor psychoanalysts as chairmen of their departments. The emphasis has turned to psychopharmacology—the current bandwagon which likely will experience only brief dominance even though it now seems a better form of treatment for most patients. Those who see no decrease in patients for analysis are the training analysts who have a captive patient load of students; at the same time, the list of analysts in Chicago seeking patients includes experienced analysts with good reputations; they all do more psychotherapy than classical analysis. The number of proliferating, competing therapies based on religious zeal, lower cost, less time, and greater temporary satisfaction is increasing. They too have a temporary following, destined for disillusionment (Grinker, 1975). As Strupp indicates, analysts from the various societies and splinter groups quarrel over theory. But in their private offices where they are immune from inspection by umpires or policemen, they do not practice orthodox analysis but throw in what Eissler calls "parameters"—a misuse of a word now used to indicate the violations of so-called psychoanalytic orthodoxy.

Strupp correctly states that analysts and many psychotherapists do not know their goals or at least do not make explicit when the patient will attain the highest possible level of improvement, resulting in the phenomenon of interminable treatment which Alexander tried to combat with his concept of brief psychoanalysis but which is really psychotherapy. However, results are difficult to determine for any therapy. What is good outcome and how long does it last? Wallerstein's (1968) report of the Menninger Foundation's Psychotherapy Research Project indicated that after hard, long, tedious work the results were not conclusive because of the many uncontrollable variables. Grinker and Spiegel (1945), working on war neuroses, correctly predicted that the rate of improvement for patients from the combat zone to the continental United States no matter what the form of treatment would be 60 to 70 percent. One resident at Michael Reese questioned all our therapists as well as their discharged patients from hospital and clinic to find the results of treatment by all mental health disciplines. Surprisingly the patients reported a far better outcome than their therapists expected. The therapists still nursed the illusion of reorganizing character and personality which they could not nor could anyone achieve. The truth of this statement can be found by looking at many distinguished graduate analysts, for they exhibit a wide range of neurotic thinking and behavior. Most practitioners use the rationalization that if the patient does not come back or call, then the result is good.

No substitute has yet been found for long-term follow-up studies to verify diagnosis and to determine treatment effectiveness. Despite devout statements, there is now no average expectable environment to receive the treated patients. The goal of health has to be related to the particular ethnic, social, and situational environment in which the subject works and lives. In addition, the behavioral characteristics of the psychiatric entities are changing. Finally, there is currently less emphasis on conflict theory of the psychoses and more focusing on developmental defects. Holt (1973) in a recent article states, " . . . much of what Freud had to say is more or less false unless read sympathetically—that is, not with the desire to find him right at all costs, but to learn from him" (p. 3), meaning that we should not take Freud's pronouncements too seriously or as Gospel truths.

Psychoanalysts tend to apply their special techniques to all patients, but so do all therapists. Purity of one technique or restricting oneself to a single technique does not last long for most therapists; but this fact they are reluctant to admit for their training has been rigidly one-sided, and innovations are discouraged. As they get older, analysts become freer and more adaptive to the needs of their patients rather than remaining bound to their theories.

Practicing psychoanalysts are poor researchers. Holzman (1973) states that analysts have inadequate clinical experience, poor scientific training, and a narrow concept of research tasks. How then can they do research on

therapy beyond substantiating the illusion that patients collaborate in research and that the therapist's hypotheses (i.e., interpretations) can be
confirmed by the patient's responses? Other factors have muddied the
waters of research. Among them is the tendency of therapists to report
successes but not failures. The data are often selected to conform to the
therapist's theories and eventually the patient complies. There is often a
ruthless decrying of nonpsychoanalytic methods as nothing but suggestion,
abreaction, or clarification (Wallerstein 1966).

The extensive Psychotherapy Research Project conducted at the Menninger Foundation contained a section on prediction as a component of
types of curative processes in psychotherapy. Appelbaum (1975), summarizing a paper presented by Leonard Horwitz, reports,

> At the beginning of the project, predictions were made about the individual
> responses of forty-two people to psychoanalysis and psychoanalytically-
> oriented psychotherapy, and the predictors made explicit the theoretical as-
> sumptions underlying each prediction. For example, the predictors expected
> psychoanalysis to bring about more extensive and more stable changes than
> those from less thorough efforts to modify symptoms and character traits. They
> expected the analysis of a transference neurosis to resolve unconscious con-
> flicts, with resulting structural change in the ego.
>
> For patients in expressive psychotherapy, which the predictors believed
> was similar to psychoanalysis, the prediction was that since interventions other
> than interpretation would be used, regression would be less profound. They
> believed the more "supportive" a psychotherapy, the greater would be its
> reliance upon gratifying the infantile needs of the patient, giving him a correc-
> tive emotional experience, allowing him to improve for the sake of pleasing or
> defying the therapist without interpreting these wishes, facilitating or permit-
> ting the patient to internalize the therapist's ego and superego attitudes. They
> believed change resulting from any of the foregoing mechanisms would reflect
> altered impulse-defense configurations rather than "structural change in the
> ego"; hence, since the person's basic conflicts would not have been uncovered
> and resolved, change would be less stable and extensive than change brought
> about by conflict resolution [p. 384].

The research team came to the conclusion that the strength or weakness of the therapeutic alliance was the crucial element in outcome. Since
both patient and therapist contributed to this alliance, the patient viewed
the therapist as benign and helpful; the therapist gratified the patient to
conform to this conception. Even with no uncovering or interpretation of
the transference several patients maintained stable change for at least two
years. The patients apparently internalized this relationship as "a permanent part of his inner world of object relationships" (p. 386). Horwitz
believes that this internalization comes about not from insight, a thor-

oughly misused, indefinable process term, but is reinforced by an approving environment which requires considerable time.

> Internalization is made up of a number of "part processes" that are the result of a growing working relationship and that act in a reciprocally enhancing manner with the therapeutic relationship, contributing to its development. These interrelated part processes are: (1) the enhancement of self-esteem; (2) the corrective emotional experience; (3) transference cure (i.e., changed behavior in order to impress the therapist); and (4) identification with the therapist's attitudes [p. 386].

He also states that this process does not depend on the therapeutic modality.

It is as essential to determine what is common to all forms of psychotherapy as to determine what is specific for each. The list of both is extensive, so I shall mention only a few. One general commonality is the so-called therapeutic alliance. The patient is motivated to seek help to improve. He has faith that he can be helped. Such faith is strengthened by the therapist's respect and concern for the patient and his realistic expectations for what can be accomplished. Even so the therapist needs auxiliary help. One resident at Michael Reese studied African witch doctors who spend two years in training. They house their patients near their well furnished homes, carry a bag of "instruments," speak in jargon, and charge high fees. The results are as good as any therapist could accomplish. Meltzer (1975) states:

> What is required from the psychiatrist during the inpatient phase of treatment is not the establishment of dominance or an overemphasis on the importance of the doctor–patient relationship, but to be a reliable friend, a sensitive listener, an able counselor, a sage psychopharmacologist, and an effective coordinator of the many other potentially therapeutic elements present in a good clinical setting [p. 135].

Despite the analyst's depreciation of the dilution with copper of the analytic gold, all use the necessary copper. Conditioning, reinforcement, suggestion, behaving warmly are used by most successful therapists. And most settle for symptomatic improvement with less and less denial that this gain is real and in many cases is all that can be accomplished. Learning new behavior does not require so-called "insight" but what Alexander termed "corrective emotional experience" in reality. Deutsch's "sector analysis" and Balint's "focal analysis" correspond to what is really possible. Surely the extensive and variable life situations, the extratherapeutic successes or failures, the therapist's personality, the match between patient and therapist are all important in any form of therapy. Of course, these are not necessarily spontaneous but are accidental, extraneous factors unrelated to treatment per se.

Largely because of the number of uncontrolled variables—even among patients treated, compared with those on waiting lists—few people except Strupp will engage in this type of research. I sincerely feel sorry when I tell my residents that there are no hard data in the field of therapeutic research. I attempt to neutralize this blow to these young psychiatric missionaries by telling them they will build up a series of valid anecdotes based on their personal experiences, but these are specific to them and usually cannot be generalized or transferred. If they treat patients, they may draw on their memory banks to ensure that past successful procedures will be carried out. But the strictness of what and when to say something or the idea that interpretation is only suggestion need not worry them. What is specific for psychoanalytic technique, ignoring the confused body of Freudian theory, is the regressive transference relationship and the interpretation of dreams. But as Glover (1956) stated, " . . . *the greatest hindrance to psycho-analytical progress lies in the unrestricted licence to interpret, which although unavoidable in therapeutic work, gives rise to a degree of fabrication in clinical researchers which tends to vitiate any conclusions arrived at"* (p. 390). Indeed there is grave doubt that the transference can repeat infantile nonverbal childhood experiences.

Strupp finally recommends for psychoanalysis what indeed holds for all psychiatry: These fields need to define strict limits for themselves and for the public in order to counteract the bureaucratic exhortations that they should embark on "primary prevention," attempting to transfer to the frail reed of psychiatry the responsibility for reorganizing society, economics, housing, and poverty by having psychiatrists become social engineers. What we can do Strupp outlines in a credo which should be all therapists' bible. He then expounds his optimistic hopes for the future. In my own 40 years of struggles in this area I have seen little in the way of hope. Repeatedly I read and hear about psychoanalysis as "our science," which means no science. In a taped interview I once heard a distinguished analyst say, "We know all there is to know—now how to apply it?"

Strupp is absolutely correct when he advocates that investigations not be limited to practitioners who are members of a closed shop. To counteract our "inexact knowledge" he advocates more experiments, more empirical data, and a series of specifications or propositions for future research. All these recommendations are highly commendable, but the tasks are difficult, and few competent people seem willing to undertake them. A recent review of the comparative literature on different forms of therapy by Luborsky, Singer, & Luborsky (1975) indicates that statistically "tie scores" predominate. Perhaps Strupp (1968) is closer to reality when he states that "the future will not be utopia, but neither need there be cause for despair."

References

Appelbaum, A. Transactions of the Topeka Psychoanalytic Society. *Bulletin of the Menninger Clinic*, 1975, *39*, 384–390.

Bergin, A. E. The evaluation of therapeutic outcomes. In A. E. Bergin & S. L. Garfield (Eds.), *Handbook of psychotherapy and behavior change: An empirical analysis*. New York: Wiley, 1971.

Bergin, A. E., & Strupp, H. H. *Changing frontiers in the science of psychotherapy*. Chicago: Aldine-Atherton, 1972.

Di Loreto, A. O. *Comparative psychotherapy: An experimental analysis*. Chicago: Aldine-Atherton, 1971.

Eissler, K. R. Irreverent remarks about the present and the future of psychoanalysis. *International Journal of Psychoanalysis*, 1969, *50*, 461–471.

Engel, G. L. Some obstacles to the development of research in psychoanalysis. *Journal of American Psychoanalysis Association*, 1968, *16*, 195–204.

Fiske, D. W., Hunt, H. F., Luborsky, L., Orne, M. T., Parloff, M. B., Reiser, M. F., & Tuma, A. H. Planning of research on effectiveness of psychotherapy. *Archives of General Psychiatry*, 1970, *22*, 22–32.

Glover, E. *Selected papers on psycho-analysis (Vol. 1). On the Early Development of Mind*. New York: International Universities Press, 1956.

Grinker, R. R. *Psychiatry in broad perspective*. New York: Behavioral Publications, 1975.

Grinker, R. R., & Spiegel, J. P. *Men under stress*. Philadelphia: Blakiston, 1945.

Holt, R. R. On reading Freud. In C. L. Rothgeb (Ed.), *Abstracts of the standard edition of the complete psychological works of Sigmund Freud*. New York: Jason Aronson, 1973.

Holzman, P. S. Some difficulties in the way of psychoanalytic research: A survey and a critique. In M. Mayman (Ed.), *Psychoanalytic research: Three approaches to the experimental study of subliminal process*. New York: International Universities Press, 1973.

Luborsky, L., Singer, B., & Luborsky, L. Comparative studies of psychotherapies: Is it true that "Everybody has won and all must have prizes"? *Archives of General Psychiatry*, 1975, *32*, 995–1021.

Meltzer, H. Y. Regression is unnecessary. In J. G. Gunderson & L. R. Mosher (Eds.), *Psychotherapy of schizophrenia*. New York: Jason Aronson, 1975.

Meltzoff, J., & Kornreich, M. *Research in psychotherapy*. New York: Atherton Press, 1970.

Shakow, D. Seventeen years later: Clinical psychology in the light of 1947 committee on training in clinical psychology report. *American Psychologist*, 1965, *20*, 353–362.

Sloane, R. B., Staples, F. R., Cristol, A. H., Yorkston, N. J., & Whipple, K. *Psychotherapy versus behavior therapy*. Cambridge: Harvard University Press, 1975.

Stone, L. The widening scope of indications for psychoanalysis. *Journal of American Psychoanalytic Association*, 1954, *2*, 567–594.

Strupp, H. H. Some comments on the future of research in psychotherapy. *Behavioral Science*, 1960, *5*, 60–71.

Strupp, H. H. Psychoanalytic therapy of the individual. In J. Marmor (Ed.), *Modern psychoanalysis: New directions and perspectives*. New York: Basic Books, 1968.

Strupp, H. H. Some comments on the future of psychoanalysis. *Journal of Contemporary Psychotherapy*, 1971, *3*, 117–120.

Strupp, H. H. Ferment in psychoanalysis and psychotherapy. In B. B. Wolman (Ed.), *Success and failure in psychoanalysis and psychotherapy*. New York: Macmillan, 1972.

Strupp, H. H. Perspectives in psychotherapy. *Current Psychiatric Therapy*, 1973, *13*, 31–37.

Wallerstein, R. S. The current state of psychotherapy: Theory, practice, research. *Journal of American Psychoanalytic Association*, 1966, *14*, 183–225.

Wallerstein, R. S. The psychotherapy research project of the Menninger Foundation: A semifinal view. In J. M. Shlien (Ed.), *Research in psychotherapy: Proceedings of the third conference*. Washington: American Psychological Association, 1968.

Chapter 8

A Study of Eclectic Views

Sol L. Garfield
and Richard Kurtz

In a recent survey of theoretical orientations among a sample of clinical psychologists, it was found that a majority of the sample labeled themselves as eclectics (Garfield & Kurtz, 1974). This was clearly the dominant orientation reported; an increase in adherence to an eclectic viewpoint was reflected as compared with a comparable survey reported some years earlier (Kelly, 1961). In contrast, the number adhering to psychoanalytic and related orientations had decreased from 41 percent in the previous survey to 19 percent in the 1974 survey. Although the latter drop was not totally unexpected, the shift appeared to be primarily toward the eclectic view, rather than to such currently popular orientations as "learning theory" and "humanistic," which increased by only one percentage point each and together accounted for slightly less than 13 percent of the sample. Clearly, a significant shift toward an eclectic view appears to have taken place, with almost 55 percent of those surveyed identifying themselves as eclectics.

Because of this heavy emphasis on an eclectic orientation, it was deemed worthwhile to conduct an additional inquiry concerning this point of view. Most individuals understand that an eclectic does not follow one specific theoretical view but instead draws from more than one orientation. *The American Heritage Dictionary of the English Language* (1971), for example, gives the following definition of the word *eclectic:* "*adj*. 1. Choos-

We would like to acknowledge the assistance of Robert Assael in tabulating the replies received and to thank the 154 psychologists who participated in this study.
Reprinted by permission of the first author, Sol L. Garfield, and the publisher from *Journal of Consulting and Clinical Psychology*, 1977, 45, 78–83.

ing what appears to be the best from diverse sources, systems, or styles. 2. Consisting of that which has been selected from diverse sources, systems, or styles." However, although a general definition is provided, we have little information concerning the views or systems that are selected or the processes by which this is done. Few, if any, studies have been reported in this area, and even textbooks on personality theory have little or nothing to say about eclectic views (Allport, 1961; Bischof, 1970; Gilbert, 1970; Hall & Lindzey, 1970; Maddi, 1968).

Because of the limited information on this topic, and also because the term eclectic does not convey any precise meaning theoretically, we decided to conduct a small inquiry of our own and to mail questionnaires to half of those clinical psychologists who designated themselves as eclectics in our previous survey. Consequently, we devised a brief inquiry form and sent it to every other person who had indicated previously that their theoretical orientation was eclectic.

Method

A one-page form consisting of three items was mailed to 234 members of the Division of Clinical Psychology. Included also was a letter of explanation and a stamped return envelope. The first item simply requested the respondent to "try to define or explain your eclectic theoretical view." Approximately a half page was left blank for this purpose. The second item asked each respondent if he had previously adhered to a specific theoretical orientation and, if so, to indicate what it was. The final item asked the respondents to indicate which two orientations (out of eight listed) were most characteristic of their own eclectic view and which two were least characteristic. The eight most frequent theoretical orientations as indicated by our previous survey were listed.

Results

One hundred and fifty-four individuals completed and returned the inquiry form. Thus, 66 percent of those to whom the forms were sent did comply with our request.

Of the total group of respondents, 71 (46 percent) stated that they had not previously adhered to a particular theoretical viewpoint, whereas 75 (almost 49 percent) said that they had. Of those who had adhered to a specific theoretical orientation previously, the overwhelming majority of those who identified their previous views followed a psychoanalytic orientation. Of the 62 respondents in this category, 40 had adhered to a psychoanalytic orientation. The only other theoretical orientations with more than one adherent were Rogerian, 12; neo-Freudian, 8; learning or behavior theory, 7; and Sullivanian, 3. Thus, the largest shift has been from a psychoanalytic orientation, with a smaller secondary shift away from Rogerian views.

As mentioned previously, the respondents were also asked to select the two theoretical orientations most characteristic of their eclectic views, as well as the two orientations least characteristic of their views. A summation of these responses is given in Table 8.1. As can be noted, considerable variability is evident in the responses of our sample. Learning theory emerged as the most frequent positive orientation, followed by the psychoanalytic and neo-Freudian orientations. The existential and rational-emotive views received the fewest positive responses. Conversely, the rational-emotive, existentialist, and psychoanalytic views received the most negative responses.

The relative preferences indicated in Table 8.1 are interesting. They indicate a relatively positive preference for learning theory and analytic approaches among eclectics but a rather negative preference for rational-emotive views. One can only speculate that the postulates of rational-emotive therapy may not appear particularly congruent with other theoretical views. This seems supported by the data in Table 8.2. Whereas each of the other views appears to be combined with most of the others to some extent, the rational-emotive orientation is combined only with learning theory.

In any event, these responses strongly suggest that the designation "eclectic" covers a wide range of views, some of which are apparently quite the opposite of others. This diversity is apparent also in the actual combinations of theoretical views that the respondents selected as most characteristic of their eclectic orientation. The combination listed in Table 8.2 represent only the most frequent of the 32 combinations listed by the 145

Table 8.1. Positive and Negative Responses to Selected Theoretical Orientations

Orientation	Positive	Negative
Psychoanalytic	46	41
Neo-Freudian	43	21
Sullivanian	24	16
Rogerian	36	25
Learning theory	72	26
Existentialist	17	44
Humanistic	29	16
Rational-emotive	18	57

Table 8.2. Combinations of Theoretical
Orientations Selected by Five or More
Respondents

Orientation	n
Psychoanalytic & learning theory	21
Neo-Freudian & learning theory	16
Neo-Freudian & Rogerian	9
Learning theory & humanistic	8
Rogerian & learning theory	8
Psychoanalytic & Rogerian	7
Sullivanian & learning theory	7
Learning theory & rational-emotive	7
Psychoanalytic & neo-Freudian	6
Rogerian & humanistic	5
Sullivanian & humanistic	5
Psychoanalytic & humanistic	5

respondents who answered this item. However, they do convey something of the diversity of views held by our eclectic sample. For example, although psychoanalytic and learning theory appear to be diametrically opposed, these two orientations are combined or utilized together by 21 of our subjects. Learning theory also appears to be used in combination with neo-Freudian, Rogerian, humanistic, Sullivanian, and rational-emotive viewpoints. The eclectic orientation thus covers a variety of viewpoints and includes individuals whose views are far from identical.

The results presented above clearly indicate that there is no precise theoretical definition of eclectic beyond suggesting that the individual has no commitment to one specific orientation or that he tends to utilize aspects of more than one theoretical view. The findings do not tell us how or why individuals use or integrate different, and often opposing, theoretical viewpoints. It was in terms of obtaining some more meaningful and, hopefully, operational definitions or descriptions by individual clinical psychologists that our study was undertaken. For this reason, our respondents were asked to define or explain their own eclectic views. No further instructions were offered here. Rather, we were interested in getting actual firsthand reports from self-designated eclectics.

It is not a simple matter to categorize the 154 different responses received from our sample or to accurately convey the different communications and nuances of meaning. Nevertheless, this seemed to be the only way to initiate a meaningful attempt at elucidating what an eclectic orientation signified, at least to clinical psychologists. Consequently, we grouped the responses of our respondents according to the main or central idea communicated. Even though these were expressed in various ways, there was a definite similarity in the emphases made by a large number of respondents. (See Table 8.3)

Categories of Response

The largest single category of responses clearly emphasized a central theme. The main idea here was that the eclectic clinical psychologist uses "whatever theory or method seems best for the client." Another way of stating this view is that the eclectic selects procedures according to the client and his problem and not because of adherence to a given theoretical view. Some individuals emphasized that an eclectic orientation provided them with a wide range of therapeutic techniques that could be used with different patients.

Altogether, 72 of our 154 respondents, or 47 percent, gave a response of this type. Some verbatim examples of responses placed in this category are the following:

> By eclectic, I mean whatever frame of reference seems to best fit a particular client. . . . Eclectic does *not* mean for me a hodgepodge of different techniques applied to the same person willy-nilly.

> Sometimes certain formulations and techniques seem "just right" for the client.

> I deplore the propensity of many therapists to fit all patients into one or two favored frameworks. This smacks of indulging the therapist's theoretical preferences at the expense of the patients' abilities to relate to the approach.

> My orientation is that each client is unique and his situation or reason for coming for help is unique, and so I apply whichever orientation helps me understand the dynamics best—or whichever formulation all observations fit into best, plus which treatment seems most appropriate.

Table 8.3. Classification of Responses

Category	f
Use whatever theory or method seems best for the client. Select procedures according to the client and his problem. Pragmatic	72
Basically use and combine two or three theories in therapy	19
Amalgamation of theories or aspects of theories	22
No theory is adequate—some better for some purposes	10
Other	31

Different strokes for different folks. Learning theory to influence behavioral problems. Psychodynamic approach to motivational conflicts. Group process orientation to people with interpersonal difficulties.

Much of working with patients in a counseling or so-called therapeutic situation involves what many of us would not like to admit, trial and error, and if we confine ourselves to the use of methodology from one orientation, confining limitations are imposed immediately in terms of helping the patient. However, if we are skilled enough and oriented broadly enough to be able to draw the best from a number of orientations, then our capacity to help the patient is enhanced.

My view of the eclectic approach is to use the valid elements of several doctrines or theories.

My basic strategy is to use whatever method makes sense and which works.

I found that Rogerian methods worked with one type of patient, Sullivanian with another, rational-emotive with still another. . . . I found I could combine hypnotic methods with my behavior modification techniques.

My eclecticism is more practical than theoretical, i.e., I would not pretend to have effectively blended a variety of conceptions from different theoretical orientations. Rather, I am "eclectic" in applied clinical work in that I will try to bring to bear some aspects of different theories on different aspects of problems presented by a client—whatever fits best or is productive and effective. . . . Essentially, I try to fit a theory and an approach to the individual client, not the client to my theory.

I consider myself as an eclectic in terms of using every and any approach which I feel would be of help to my clients. In view of the concept of individual differences, which I consider one of the few contributions in psychology on which all the returns are practically in, it is theoretically probably nonsense that any one system of therapy is or can be applicable to every problem. However, at the same time, what I choose as viable and useful, and *how* I use what seems useful, I feel depends on a theoretical orientation—one that is open to making use of what fits in other theoretical stances, and the findings in therapeutic approach they engender.

Because all schools of psychotherapy claim successes, and yet all have their failures, the best bet (own experience suggests it) is that different patients (and therapists) need different treatment experiences. The biggest failure has been the verbal "insight therapies" when applied to all problems, all social classes, and to those that don't use language as their main expressions.

It is based primarily on the view that individuality must be respected and therefore individuals require different treatment approaches. . . . Being a clinician almost requires some eclecticism.

Some of those grouped into this category stressed the empirical or pragmatic aspects of their eclecticism. They select "what works best." Some examples are:

> It is difficult to describe my theoretical view because I suppose I am really atheoretical—at least I am no longer interested or supportive of adherence to "big" theory. I am much more persuaded by empirical results and sometimes find a small theory or piece of a big theory helpful to explain and organize a problem. My orientation is pretty pragmatic and technique oriented.

> Combining those aspects of various theories that have held up over time, in different settings, and with a variety of patients.

> Selecting from various schools and theory what seems to work best in the practice of clinical psychology, e.g., psychoanalytic orientation to help understand genetics, developmental process of family structure as related to psychopathology, Rogerian concepts in therapeutic relationships—also learning theory in the modification of behavior on the wards.

> I should hope that "eclecticism" is not confused with "expediency"—although undoubtedly there is a relationship. Working in a clinic, one is faced with a variety of types of patients, and with realistic (as opposed to theoretical) needs of the patient, the community and the center. In my daily work I have to choose, from patient to patient—and from situation to situation—between the luxury of a relatively long interpretive, uncovering type therapy and a briefer, crisis-intervention, supportive type—with everything else in between.

It should, perhaps, be emphasized again that even though all of the respondents who were placed in this category characterized their eclectic views in a similar manner, this does not mean that they would necessarily agree on the operations utilized with a given client or on the rationale behind their selection of procedures. They simply agreed on the general view that different operations and views are required for different clients.

Another group of responses ($n = 19$) appeared to differ in important ways from the two preceding categories. The individuals giving these responses basically indicated an adherence to two, and occasionally three, main theoretical orientations. They considered themselves eclectics because they did not adhere to just one viewpoint. However, they differed from the preceding groups of individuals by adhering mainly to a few specific orientations. Examples include:

> I choose to identify myself as an "Eclectic" because "my" personality theory is Freudian, while the theoretical framework for my therapy work is dependent on the particular issues involved with the particular person with whom I am working. This primarily results in a Rogerian style for the majority of my work, and a Learning Theory style or background for other situations.

It is fundamentally a cognitive social learning theory in which my treatment approach centers on the use of a variety of behavioral techniques to alter contemporary cognitions and overt behavior. I usually formulate clients' problems in a more psychodynamic-interpersonal framework.

I rely heavily on a combination of existential views regarding the nature of man and the human condition plus communication theory as a way of understanding the patients' view of self. . . .

My eclecticism combines constructs from both social learning theory and psychoanalysis. I find that I can understand emotional process best using psychoanalysis and many aspects of molar behavior best by using constructs from social learning theory.

Another category of responses offered by 22 respondents defined the latter's eclecticism in a somewhat different manner and perhaps was closer to some individuals' general notion of what an eclectic is. These psychologists referred to their eclectic views as "amalgamations of theories or aspects of theories" ($n = 12$) or as "a combination of many orientations and facts" ($n = 10$). As contrasted with the first category of responses that emphasized psychotherapeutic techniques and the selection of techniques for particular clients, the current group of responses implied some integrated synthesis of different theoretical orientations. Although it is conceivable that the difference noted here might be less apparent if the actual clinical operations of the individuals were studied closely, nevertheless, the verbal statements of the respondents do reflect some difference. Examples of responses in this category are:

It always seemed to me that any one theoretical view or frame of reference was inadequate by itself to do the job. Thus, I tried to be "eclectic" in the sense of choosing certain principles from two or more theories which, in a sort of *amalgamation* fashion, could explain more (make more clinical sense) about the "case" than one could singly do.

Eclectic means to me, knowing all I can of the leading thinkers and internalizing them in such a way that the product is my own, leaving me the greatest freedom.

It is a mixture of psychoanalytic, neo-analytic, Rogerian, existential theories, plus a heavy reliance on learning theory, particularly as applied to behavioral modification techniques.

My view is eclectic in terms of techniques applied to clinical problems. However, I hew to a theory of my own which, while it builds on a wide variety of predecessors (Lewin, Freud, Hull, Allport, and many others), is a genuinely integrated theoretical system in its own right. Primarily, it builds on data generated by many kinds of investigators. . . . The clinical methods I use are consistent with this theory. They exclude certain techniques such as psycho-analytic interpretation or early-Rogerian nondirectiveness, but they include techniques borrowed from behavior therapy, Ellis, Franke . . . and the con-sensual core of the more traditional psychotherapies.

The categories reviewed thus far account for slightly over 73 percent of the statements offered by our respondents. Most of the remaining re-sponses were either more idiosyncratic and therefore more difficult to cate-gorize or were very general. One group of 10 responses, for example, did not delineate their views very explicitly but had a common unifying theme: "No theory is adequate, and some are better for some purposes than others."

> No theory or set of theories is presently adequate to explain the range of behaviors confronting a clinical psychologist. Each theory suggests particular dimensions of relevance for the fuller description of the complex world of human behavior, but no one—or any combination of them—describes the whole story. Eclecticism is the acknowledgment of the truthfulness and usefulness of mul-tiple perspectives and the present inadequacy of single perspectives.

The implication clearly was that one had to have recourse to more than one theory in order to handle clinical problems effectively.

The remaining 31 responses were more scattered and need not be commented upon in any detail. One, for example, stated that eclectics were the "agnostics of the profession" and were not blind followers of one single approach. Three respondents indicated that even though they drew from many orientations, they really utilized themselves. Two others stressed that being an eclectic meant being open to all views rather than being doctrinaire. One admitted that an eclectic view was really a "hodge-podge." Three individuals indicated that the complexity of the client and his problem necessitated a recourse to more than one approach. Five es-sentially gave no explanation of their views.

Discussion

In attempting to explore more fully the term eclectic we have utilized descriptions offered by clinical psychologists who designated themselves as eclectics. In analyzing their responses, it is clear that there are both certain commonalities and differences in the way this term is interpreted or used by these psychologists. Those who identify themselves as eclectics do not follow any one theoretical orientation and tend to draw either theoretical concepts or clinical techniques from two or more theoretical viewpoints. A common theme expressed was that no present theory was adequate to explain or predict all of the behavior that a clinician observes. Another common emphasis is that in working with individual clients one must select the approach that appears to be more appropriate. Somewhat different from the above was the view offered by several individuals that their approach was an amalgam of several different theoretical orientations and was derived from their own clinical experience.

Essentially then, a common feature of eclecticism is a lack of satisfaction with one orientation. Also evident is the relationship of their views to the respondents' actual therapeutic work with the individuals seeking their help. There is thus an emphasis on pragmatic utility and the relationship of one's views to actual clinical practice. Several emphasized that to adhere to strictly one view was to be doctrinaire; eclecticism allowed greater flexibility. A number stressed that they worked with a variety of clients of varying ages and socioeconomic status and that no one approach was adequate for such a diversity of problems. Again, flexibility was demanded, and one could not simply follow the orientation previously preferred or emphasized in training. It seems apparent also that these individuals were rather satisfied with the eclectic orientations that they had developed on the basis of their own clinical experience.

Finally, it can be noted that even though eclectics have certain features in common, they are not necessarily identical in their views. Some value psychodynamic views more than others, some favor Rogerian and humanistic views, others clearly value learning theory, and various combinations of these are used in apparently different situations by different clinicians. Thus, although an eclectic may utilize a variety of theoretical concepts and therapeutic techniques, we do not know how a particular eclectic will function unless we can appraise what he actually does. This fact, plus the finding that apparently a majority of clinical psychologists view themselves as eclectics, appears to have some definite implications for research in psychotherapy. If one conducts investigations of psychotherapy in terms of specific theoretical orientations, it is obvious that one is studying only a minority of those engaged in psychotherapeutic practice. It is also conceivable that even within a similar orientation, psychotherapists may actually perform differently. Some respondents in the present study also appeared to equate a given theoretical orientation with a specific technique or techniques without necessarily accepting the theoretical rationale underlying these techniques. This may perhaps explain why some individuals apparently can combine or draw from such opposed orientations as psychoanalysis and learning theory. It seems evident, therefore, that studies evaluating psychotherapy will have to pay primary attention to the actual operations and interactions of the participants in psychotherapy. Evaluating "psychotherapy" without such investigation or specification is bound to provide inadequate results.

Summary

The present study reports on the views of 154 clinical psychologists who had designated themselves as eclectics in a previous survey. Both commonalities and differences were found among the respondents' characterizations of their theoretical views, as well as a great diversity of combinations of theoretical views and therapeutic techniques. A common theme was that no current theory was adequate for handling the diversity of clients seen in practice and that clinicians must select the approach that best fits a given client. The findings appear to have some implications for research on psychotherapy.

References

Allport, G. W. *Pattern and growth in personality*. New York: Holt, Rinehart & Winston, 1961.

The American Heritage Dictionary of the English Language. New York: American Heritage, 1971.

Bischof, L. J. *Interpreting personality theories* (2nd ed.). New York: Harper & Row, 1970.

Garfield, S. L., & Kurtz, R. A survey of clinical psychologists: Characteristics, activities, and orientations. *The Clinical Psychologist*, 1974, *28*, 7–10.

Gilbert, G. M. *Personality dynamics: A biosocial approach*. New York: Harper & Row, 1970.

Hall, C. S., & Lindzey, G. *Theories of personality* (2nd ed.). New York: Wiley, 1970.

Kelly, E. L. Clinical psychology—1960. Report of survey findings. *Newsletter: Division of Clinical Psychology of the American Psychological Association*, 1961, *14*, 1–11.

Maddi, S. R. *Personality theories: A comparative analysis*. Homewood, Ill.: Dorsey Press, 1968.

Part IV
Common Ingredients in Psychotherapy

In a sense, this section deals with the current state of the art, containing selections that outline the ingredients that may be common to all therapeutic orientations. Noting that differences are emphasized far more often than commonalities, Garfield highlights what he perceives to be overlapping features of various therapies, including the nature of the therapeutic relationship and the arousal of hope within the patient/client that something can be done. Appelbaum similarly discusses common pathways to change and draws on his experience as a practicing psychoanalyst, the results of the Psychotherapy Research Project of the Menninger Foundation, and also his personal involvement with humanistically oriented therapies. In outlining potential commonalities, Appelbaum grapples with the issue of how insight and action may be interrelated within the change process. The final selection is somewhat unique as articles go, in that its authorship is comprised of prominent therapists from various theoretical orientations (Brady, Davison, Dewald, Egan, Fadiman, Frank, Gill, Hoffman, Kempler, Lazarus, Raimy, Rotter, and Strupp). Each individual was provided with a set of questions regarding the potential effective ingredients in therapy and was asked to respond on the basis of his own personal experiences and observations as a therapist. So as to allow a more ready comparison across answers, each participant made every attempt to respond without the use of any theoretical concepts. Their reactions are reprinted in their entirety.

Chapter 9

What Are the Therapeutic Variables in Psychotherapy?

Sol L. Garfield

For many years there has been evident a controversy concerning the effectiveness of psychotherapy. This controversy became particularly marked after the appearance of Eysenck's (1952) first critical appraisal of the results of psychotherapy, but has more or less continued since that time (Bergin, 1971; Eysenck, 1966). An additional aspect of this problem was the possibility initially pointed out by Truax (1962) and later discussed by Bergin (1963) that psychotherapy produced both positive and negative results which were canceled out in the group analyses. Later research by Rogers and his group also lent some empirical support to this point of view (Rogers, Gendlin, Kiesler, & Truax, 1967; Truax and Carkhuff, 1967).

While such controversies perhaps add a bit of spice to professional life, they clearly do not provide any adequate answers to the problems at hand. Not only must we have systematic studies, but we must ask questions in such a manner that meaningful answers are possible. I submit that the question, "Is psychotherapy effective?" is unanswerable as stated. There are too many variants of psychotherapy to treat it as a unitary process and the processes and procedures which are utilized are many and ofttimes complex. It seems more appropriate at this time to try to examine what are the variables which appear to account for whatever positive changes are presumed to take place

This chapter originally appeared in Proceedings of the Ninth International Congress of Psychotherapy, Oslo, 1973, *Psychotherapy and Psychosomatics*, 24: 372–378 (Karger, Basel 1974). Reprinted with the permission of the author and the publisher.

during psychotherapeutic intervention. In other words, what are the possible variables which are therapeutic in psychotherapy?

Much of the writing in the area of psychotherapy, while listing many procedures, techniques, and processes of psychotherapy, either tends to lack specificity as to what exactly produces change or fails to present evidence in support of whatever assertions are made. Thus, one encounters discussions of catharsis or abreaction, empathy, reassurance, insight, interpretation, transference, confrontation, relationship, cognitive restructuring, and similar variables without any clear picture of how they supposedly produce changes in the client and usually without any supporting empirical data. At the same time, there are a host of different therapeutic approaches with different theoretical premises and procedures but all claiming to be successful. The latter situation has led several workers to question whether the different procedures of the various schools of psychotherapy are in fact the significant variables making for positive outcome in psychotherapy, or whether there are some factors which are common to most psychotherapeutic approaches and which conceivably may be the important variables.

One of the individuals who has called our attention to this problem has been Jerome Frank. In a series of reports and papers with his colleagues, as well as in a book and other writings, Frank has called our attention to what he has termed "non-specific" factors in psychotherapy. One group of such factors appeared to be related to the "clarity of patients' perceptions of their own problems and how psychotherapy may help" (Stone, Imber, & Frank, 1966). In one study, for example, patients showed some improvement even prior to the administration of a placebo (Frank, Gliedman, Imber, Stone, & Nash, 1959) and in a study by Friedman (1963) patients also improved following an evaluation interview.

Other work has tended to lend some support to the importance of patient expectancies in psychotherapy (Goldstein 1962), although conflicting findings have also been reported (Garfield, 1971). Related factors concern the expectations of the therapists with regard to the effectiveness of psychotherapy and the congruence of patient and therapist expectancies concerning psychotherapy. The not infrequent discrepancy between the expectancies of clients and therapists, for example, can be noted in the findings of two studies. In one by Avnet (1965) where therapy was arbitrarily limited to 15 sessions because of insurance payments, therapists recommended further treatment in 94 percent of the cases, but most of the patients did not follow their recommendations. In a study by the author, where therapists were interested in long-term therapy, but where the great majority of patients expected to be "cured" within 10 sessions, half of the patients terminated therapy by the seventh interview (Garfield and Wolpin 1963). Nevertheless, research on this problem also has produced some conflicting results (Garfield, 1971).

Somewhat related to the area of expectancies is the matter of hope which is generated when an individual consults a socially sanctioned healer for help with his difficulties. Frank (1961), in his book *Persuasion and Healing*, has dealt very lucidly with the possible significance of this aspect of treatment. All types of healing, whether they be religious, magical, placebo, or psychotherapy, may depend, at least for part of their success, on "their ability to arouse the patient's expectation of help."

More recently, Frank (1971) has provided us with another formulation concerning the common factors in psychotherapy to which I will refer briefly. Six factors are delineated: (1) an intense confiding relationship with a helping person; (2) a rationale or myth which includes an explanation of the patient's difficulty and a method for relieving it; (3) provision of new information relative to the patient's problems and possible alternative ways of dealing with them; (4) strengthening the patient's expectations of help; (5) provision of success experiences, e.g., insights, progress through an anxiety hierarchy, etc., and (6) facilitation of emotional arousal.

There have been some other workers in this field who have also discussed the importance of common factors in psychotherapy, although these presentations do not appear to have received very wide attention. Heine (1953) reported a study comparing psychoanalytic, nondirective, or client-centered, and Adlerian psychotherapy. One of his principle conclusions was that a factor (or factors) common to all schools studied was the therapeutic aspect responsible for the changes secured. He also recommended that future research should be concerned with the identification and precise description of these common therapeutic factors. Writing in 1957, I also called attention to the possible importance of a number of common features which may operate in most, if not all, psychotherapies such as a sympathetic nonmoralizing healer, the emotional and supporting relationship in therapy, catharsis, and the opportunity to gain some understanding of one's problems (Garfield, 1957). More recently, in a somewhat amusing, but at the same time highly provocative paper, entitled, "What Western Psychotherapists Can Learn from Witchdoctors," Torrey (1972) has also discussed four common features of psychotherapy. Time does not permit any lengthy presentation of his discussion, but the four common components mentioned are essentially ones which have already been mentioned—naming (or explaining) what is wrong, the personal qualities of the therapist, patients' expectations, and the techniques of therapy.

For heuristic reasons, it may be worthwhile to discuss further one possible common factor which has been alluded to and which has intrigued me for some time. Here I have reference to such a phenomenon as insight, understanding, or naming of one's difficulties. While much has been written about insight-oriented psychotherapy and the importance of securing insight, the broader psychological significance of this process has been overlooked by those eager to provide their particular brand of insight. It should appear obvious that the insights provided by Freudians, Sullivanians, Jungians, Adlerians, Rogerians, Behavior Therapists, and Witch Doctors are quite different—yet each brand is apparently therapeutic. The most parsimonious explanation appears to be that the actual naming or explaining of the client's difficulties is reassuring or therapeutic for the client *regardless* of what explanation is given. Torrey (1972) labels this the "Principle of Rumpelstiltskin" whereas Frank (1971) refers to it as a therapeutic rationale or myth. In essence, as I see it, the therapist provides the patient with a belief system which potentially explains his behavior. Such beliefs are obviously culture bound and perhaps even class bound, and would also appear to be interactive with the client's expectancies and the particular role and status of the healer. However, a large number of therapists are seemingly unaware of the possibility of such a phenomenon. They adhere strongly to one system of beliefs, and apparently, secure some personal value or support from such adherence.

While some of the common factors discussed here have received some research documentation, not all have. Thus, while they appear logical and tenable, systematic research into their actual significance in affecting change is needed. On the other hand, Rogers and some of his colleagues (Truax and Carkhuff, 1967), in studying the personal qualities of therapists, have attempted to delineate what they believe are the essential ingredients in psychotherapy. Most recently, three therapeutic or therapist conditions have been specified as the necessary conditions for positive change in psychotherapy, and scales for rating these conditions on tape-recorded therapy sessions have been developed (Traux and Carkhuff, 1967). These conditions have been designated as accurate empathy, warmth, and genuineness or congruence. While Traux and Carkhuff (1967) have marshalled some evidence in support of the hypothesized relationship of these variables to outcome in psychotherapy, some conflicting findings have also been reported. In some studies, the intercorrelations between these scales have been negative, and in some instances, one of the scales has been negatively correlated with measures of outcome—a perplexing finding for a necessary therapeutic condition. Furthermore, in a recent study of these scales with a group of predominantly non-client-centered therapists, the scores on the scales showed no relationlship to a variety of outcome measures (Garfield and Bergin, 1971).

On the basis of what has been reviewed here, there is as yet no clear consensus as to what the essential variables for producing change are, nor has there been sufficient evidence or research to support any particular view. While there is some evidence to support the hypothesis that client expectancies play some role in continuation and outcome in psychotherapy, there are also some conflicting findings on this matter, and the relative importance of this variable in producing change is, as yet, uncertain. It would appear quite probable that some such variable in simple form, or including such related aspects as confidence in the therapist and in the type of therapy, might be a potentially significant one in influencing outcome in psychotherapy. The ubiquitous placebo response may also be related to such components (Frank, 1961: Shapiro, 1971). In a recent review of this phenomenon, Shapiro (1971) evaluates the placebo response in relation to such subject variables as anxiety, suggestibility, expectancies, faith and hope, as well as others. While there is considerable evidence to support the influence of the placebo response on treatment outcome, it has been a too generalized and nonspecific concept, as well as a threatening one, to fully secure advantages from its utilization. However, more precise experimentation to delineate its specific components may be useful.

It would appear, then, that there are some common factors operative in most psychotherapies which conceivably may account for some of the change secured by psychotherapeutic means. However, although some suggestive formulations have been offered by thoughtful observers of the psychotherapy scene, we are a long way off from knowing precisely what these variables are, how they operate, and utilizing them fully in our psychotherapeutic endeavors. It would also appear likely, as Frank (1971) has pointed out, that at least some of the different varieties of psychotherapy may have some specific value for treating particular kinds of problems or disorders. It is possible, although as yet unproved, that long-term insight-oriented therapy may help some rather bright and verbal individuals to attain some kind of orientation or philosophical outlook on life, which is of help to them in meeting their requirements of everyday living. It would also appear likely that behaviorally oriented approaches, such as desensitization or implosion (flooding), are effective procedures for overcoming phobic behavior. However, such views are still suppositions, for we lack definitive evidence concerning the specific variables which supposedly account for the changes secured. Although, for example, there are a number of relatively well controlled studies which would appear to demonstrate the specific values of desensitization and its procedures (Davison, 1968; Paul, 1966), there are other studies which have produced conflicting findings. Several studies, for example, have indicated that omitting relaxation does not impair significantly the results of desensitization (Aponte and Aponte, 1971; Cooke, 1968), and in one investigation neither relaxation nor a graded hierarchy was necessary in reducing phobic behavior as long as subjects imagined the feared object without negative reinforcement (Wolpin and Raines, 1966). Even in behavior therapy the importance of creating expectancy conditions for positive change have been reported (Marcia, Rubin, & Efran, 1969; Leitenberg, Agras, Barlow, & Oliveau, 1969). Two recent reviews by Wilson and Davison (1971) and Davison and Wilson

(1973) also indicate that we are still far from having adequate explanations for why desensitization works. I would like to emphasize, however, that the behavior therapists have been appraising their procedures and formulations critically and, of particular importance, they are trying to ascertain systematically the specific variables that make for change. This I applaud heartily.

Thus far, I have focused almost exclusively on what might be characterized as technique variables or therapist variables. While these are clearly important in our attempts to unravel the variables which are therapeutic in psychotherapy, we must not neglect other potentially significant variables such as the patient or client and his interactions with other therapy variables. Before concluding, however, I do want to allude to the significance of the client in psychotherapy. A fair amount of research has indicated that positive outcome is related to the degree of disturbance and associated aspects of the client. In fact, the status of the client appears to be the variable most predictive of outcome, since the best results appear to be obtained with those clients with minimal disturbance and the strongest personal attributes (Garfield, 1971). As some have said, those clients who secure the best results are those who need treatment the least. Obviously, we must pay attention to client variables and attempt to devise treatment procedures which are best suited for particular individuals with certain kinds of problems. However, we should not be so selective in our therapy endeavors that we work only with a very highly selected population.

In conclusion, I would reiterate that we are faced with the task of ferreting out what are the significant variables which lead to change in psychotherapy. Many of the descriptions of the processes of psychotherapy are rather vague and amorphous and frequently couched in language derived from a particular orientation. We must search for the variables which actually produce positive change, and we can discover these variables only if we define them clearly and then systematically detect what changes they produce.

References

Aponte, J. F., & Aponte, C. E. Group preprogrammed systematic desensitization without the simultaneous presentation of aversive scenes with relaxation training. *Behaviour Research and Therapy*, 1971, 9, 337–346.

Avnet, H. H. How effective is short-term psychotherapy? Appraisals of mental health after short-term ambulatory psychiatric treatment. In L. R. Wolberg (Ed.), *Short-term psychotherapy*. New York: Grune & Stratton, 1965, pp. 7–22.

Bergin, A. E. The effects of psychotherapy. Negative results revisited. *Journal of Counseling Psychology*, 1963, 10, 244–250.

Bergin, A. E. The evaluation of therapeutic outcomes. In A. E. Bergin and S. L. Garfield (Eds.), *Handbook of psychotherapy and behavior change*. New York: Wiley, 1971, pp. 217–270.

Cooke, G. Evaluation of the efficacy of the components of reciprocal inhibition psychotherapy. *Journal of Abnormal Psychology*, 1968, *73*, 464–467.

Davison, G. C. Systematic desensitization as a counter-conditioning process. *Journal of Abnormal Psychology*, 1968, *73*, 91–99.

Davison, G. C., & Wilson, G. T. Processes of fear reduction in systematic desensitization: Cognitive and social reinforcement factors in humans. *Behavior Therapy*, 1973, *4*, 1–21.

Eysenck, H. J. The effects of psychotherapy: An evaluation. *Journal of Consulting Psychology*, 1952, *16*, 319–324.

Eysenck, H. J. *The effects of psychotherapy*. New York: International Science Press, 1966.

Frank, J. D. *Persuasion and healing*. Baltimore: Johns Hopkins Press, 1961.

Frank, J. D. Therapeutic factors in psychotherapy. *American Journal of Psychotherapy*, 1971, *25*, 350–361.

Frank, J. D., Gliedman, L. H., Imber, S. D., Stone, A. E., & Nash, E. H. Patients' expectancies and relearning as a factor in determining improvement in psychotherapy. *American Journal of Psychiatry*, 1959, *115*, 961–968.

Friedman, H. J. Patient expectancy and symptom reduction. *Archives of General Psychiatry*, 1963, *8*, 61–67.

Garfield, S. L. *Introductory clinical psychology*. New York: Macmillan, 1957.

Garfield, S. L. Research on client variables in psychotherapy. In A. E. Bergin and S. L. Garfield (Eds.), *Handbook of psychotherapy and behavior change*. New York: Wiley, 1971, pp. 271–298.

Garfield, S. L., & Bergin, A. E. Therapeutic conditions and outcome. *Journal of Abnormal Psychology*, 1971, *77*, 108–114.

Garfield, S. L., & Wolpin, M. Expectations regarding psychotherapy. *Journal of Nervous and Mental Disorders*, 1963, *137*, 353–362.

Goldstein, A. P. *Therapist–patient expectancies in psychotherapy*. New York: Pergamon Press, 1962.

Heine, R. W. A comparison of patients' reports of psychotherapeutic experience with psychoanalytic, nondirective, and Adlerian therapists. *American Journal of Psychotherapy*, 1953, *7*, 16–23.

Leitenberg, H., Agras, W. S., Barlow, D. H., & Oliveau, D. C. Contribution of selective positive reinforcement and therapeutic instructions to systematic desensitization therapy. *Journal of Abnormal Psychology*, 1969, *74*, 113–118.

Marcia, J. E., Rubin, B. M., & Efran, J. S. Systematic desensitization: Expectancy change or counter-conditioning? *Journal of Abnormal Psychology*, 1969, *74*, 382–387.

Paul, G. L. *Insight versus desensitization in psychotherapy*. Stanford: Stanford University Press, 1966.

Rogers, C. R., Gendlin, E. T., Kiesler, D. J., & Truax, C. B. *The therapeutic relationship and its impact*. Madison: University of Wisconsin Press, 1967.

Shapiro, A. K. Placebo effects in medicine, psychotherapy, and psychoanalysis. In

A. E. Bergin & S. L. Garfield (Eds.), *Handbook of psychotherapy and behavior change*. New York: Wiley, 1971, pp. 439–473.

Stone, A. R., Imber, S. D., & Frank, J. D. The role of non-specific factors in short-term psychotherapy. *Australian Journal of Psychology*, 1966, *18*, 210–217.

Torrey, E. F. What Western psychotherapists can learn from witchdoctors. *American Journal of Orthopsychiatry*, 1972, *42*, 69–72.

Truax, C. B. Effective ingredients in psychotherapy: An approach to unraveling the patient–therapist interaction. Paper presented at the Annual Meeting of the American Psychological Association, St. Louis, 1962.

Truax, C. B., & Carkhuff, R. R. *Toward effective counseling and psychotherapy*. Chicago: Aldine, 1967.

Wilson, G. T., & Davison, G. C. Processes of fear reduction in systematic desensitization: Animal studies. *Psychological Bulletin*, 1971, *76*, 1–14.

Wolpin, M., & Raines, J. Visual imagery, expected roles and extinction as possible factors in reducing fear and avoidance behavior. *Behavior Research and Therapy*, 1966, *4*, 25–37.

Chapter 10

Pathways to Change in Psychoanalytic Therapy[1]

Stephen A. Appelbaum

In the last few years I have lived a double life. In one life I have carried out my usual clinical and teaching responsibilities and have written a just-published book, *The Anatomy of Change*, which reports the test findings of the Psychotherapy Research Project of the Menninger Foundation. In my second life I have explored what are called the new therapies or alternative therapies by way of periodic forays from Topeka to the outer world.

These trips were dizzying experiences. It would have been much easier to explore such things if I had lived in California. I went from one subculture to another, from one set of therapeutic beliefs and practices to another, from one set of testimonials to another. I saw plenty of activities that I thought to be technically and conceptually questionable, but, all in all, I simply could not dismiss them. I could not adduce experimental evidence strong enough to seriously undermine their positions. I could not claim that psychoanalytic practices and points of view are more suitable for all people and all situations of psychological need than any other. I could not claim beyond question that patients with whom I have been acquainted—my own, those of colleagues and friends, those in the research reported in my book—could in every

[1]George Klein Memorial address presented at the meeting of Psychologists Interested in the Study of Psychoanalysis (PISP), San Francisco, California, August, 1977.

Reprinted by permission of the author, Stephen A. Appelbaum, and the publisher from *Bulletin of the Menninger Clinic*, 1978, 42, 239–251.

instance be judged as having greatly benefited from psychoanalytic therapy in the least time and with the least risk possible.

In view of all these observations, I had to consider seriously a variety of means by which change comes about, some of which are clearly outside of psychoanalysis. Whether they can be added to psychoanalysis is worth considering, but that option is outside the purview of this paper. Other factors in change are already inside psychoanalysis; most of them are not new. Yet, in the face of curious and hostile questions and criticisms of psychoanalysis, I have been forced to think, through issues and practices which I otherwise might have taken for granted. I have been made aware of sometimes overlooked or underemphasized factors in psychoanalytic change and forced to see them in sometimes novel ways.

A reexamination of this kind is in the tradition of George Klein. He was a man who loved loyally the pursuit of psychological meaning and, for him, meaning was the essence of psychoanalysis. At the same time he boldly argued on careful, logical grounds for the elimination of the concepts of structure and drive from psychoanalytic thinking and declared metapsychology to be only academic faculty psychology dressed up in a new language (1970). Such precedents as Klein's have sustained me through many anxious moments as I have flip-flopped from the chair behind the couch to the pillow on the floor, from the buzzing of the head to the tingling of the body, from the pointed concentration required for conceptual thinking to meditative reverie. Solid oaks of tradition, such as George Klein, paradoxically make possible the sprouting branches and drifting seeds of new ideas and innovation.

In the next section of this paper I will discuss a number of factors, or pathways, to psychoanalytic change. To therapists who characteristically keep all of these putatively therapeutic factors in mind and select among them designedly, I will have little to say. However, as far as I can tell, by virtue of our training, the nature of psychoanalytic theory, and our personal disposition, many of us tend to be less than evenhanded in our self-surveys and experimentations. We are inclined to favor some approaches and to emphasize some factors over others, not always with a balanced appreciation of the factors based on diagnostic thinking. Many of the factors I will discuss are not exclusive with psychoanalysis. Indeed, they have been called nonspecific. Yet, since psychoanalysis is unlike any other therapy, there is no reason to assume that these factors function in psychoanalysis the same as they do in other therapies. In interaction with psychoanalysis, even nonspecific factors may be unique.

Insight

Unsurprisingly, this overview begins with insight, meaning, self-knowledge. True to Freud's seminal observation that he could help a patient get rid of his symptom through learning of a prior event which gave meaning to the symptom, change in psychoanalysis is chiefly identified with understanding, learning the underlying meanings of thoughts and behaviors, making the unconscious conscious through insight.

By now there should be no doubt that one can empirically gather data which will allow the construction of a pattern of meaning according to the clinical theory of psychoanalysis. Also by now there should be no doubt that, in response to following the rules for ascertaining these data, predictable behaviors will occur; for example, free association will lead to meaningfully connected thoughts, patients will resist the process of self-discovery, etc. When all is well—the right patient with the right analyst in the right supporting environment—patterns of development will inevitably occur, for example, from dependence to independence, from regression to progression, from unrealistic ideas (especially about the analyst) to more realistic ones. This process is clearly and unequivocally moved along by way of felicitous interpretations on the part of the analyst and by meanings cooperatively derived by patient and analyst.

In apparent response to such discoveries, what the patient talks about, the patient's mood, behavior, and experience of life outside the analytic hours tend to change for the better. Because of all this change, the temptation is to assume a one-to-one correspondence between correct insight and therapeutic change. In so doing, however, we overlook the many other possible reasons for change which have participated, designedly or inadvertently, in the process of pursuing insight as well as in the overall process of behavioral change. We also may have elided such issues as whether change comes about through the achieving of insight or insight comes about through the achieving of change, and we may have overlooked other aspects of the relationship between knowledge of the unconscious life and how the conscious life is lived. By assuming too much too soon about the power of insight, we may fail to check systematically, for example, what the patient understands as compared to what the analyst understands. (Most analysts have noticed how often patients remember previous hours differently from the way the analyst remembers them and how hard it is to believe what patients report about any previous analyses they have had.) Finally, how durable is change brought about by way of insight, and is such durability related to other therapeutic factors as well? For many of us, as I think it was to George Klein, psychoanalytic insight is a thing of beauty and a joy forever. We should not, however, allow its power and dramatic appeal to lead to an idealization of it, at the cost of insufficiently studying insight itself and of overlooking and underexploiting other possible means of change.

Corrective Emotional Experience

At one point during my psychoanalytic education, I learned to associate corrective emotional experience with Franz Alexander and just as immediately to dismiss it as nonanalytic. It took a while for me to discriminate between Alexander's special use of corrective emotional experience and the general process. In general terms, corrective emotional experience refers to the nonoccurrence of events which the patient assumes will occur. As a consequence of this nonoccurrence, he learns that his fantasies need not come true. Alexander (1946) recommended that the therapist self-consciously dramatize roles from the patient's repertoire of fantasy figures. But Alexander's procedure is not necessary for corrective emotional experiences to occur. Indeed, if the analyst maintains his neutral, nonjudgmental stance, corrective emotional experiences cannot be prevented.

By the way, the very phrase "correctional emotional experience," is something of a misnomer. It is true that most psychoanalytic learning best takes place when things matter emotionally. But in a corrective emotional experience, ideas and fantasies are corrected fully as much as are emotional reactions. The phrase could just as well be "corrective ideational experience." But whatever phrase is used, some patients tell me that the change in them was brought about because what they had expected to happen did not happen; for example, I did not reject them despite their acknowledging what they thought were dirty wishes, or I did not leave them no matter how obstreperous, boring, or healthy they behaved. As one patient put it, since I took her on as a patient and stayed with her, she must be an all right person; and since she was an all right person, she could then stand up to people when necessary or get in bed with them when she wanted, without fearing the previously fantasied consequences.

Interpersonal Relationship

The term *interpersonal relationship* is another rubbery phrase which has led to much misunderstanding and unneccessary heat. Some psychoanalysts immediately understand the phrase to refer to a relationship in opposition to an intrapsychic one, a transpersonal transaction more akin to social psychology than psychoanalysis. Indeed, it sometimes has such meaning and is used to draw a boundary between psychoanalysis and other schools of therapy or professions. But this polarizing of insight versus interpersonal relationship factors in change can lead to an underemphasis of those interpersonal factors which do take place even in the most thoroughgoing psychoanalysis. To believe that they do not would be to subscribe to the image that many critics of psychoanalysis have of the analyst as an unfeeling calculating machine. Such an image would belie the psychoanalytic values inherent in identification, benevolent modification of the superego, and internalizing a cooperative, understanding partner for purposes of self-analysis and guidance.

The concept of the "real" nontransference relationship is one expression of the understanding of interpersonal relationships in psychoanalytic change. Another is the largely British object relations point of view that psychoanalysis provides a second chance for the patient to grow in a new and improved nurturing environment. The growth-producing qualities of such an environment are said to be more important than the interpretations and understanding which take place in it. A similar emphasis has been set forth in American psychoanalysis by Harry Stack Sullivan, Frieda Fromm-Reichman, and Otto Will, among others. A major finding of the Psychotherapy Research Project of the Menninger Foundation was that those patients who had developed the most insight did best of all. Yet there was another group of patients who, in the absence of much insight and conflict resolution, achieved what was called in the project "structural change," despite the project's conventional assumption that structural change could come about only through conflict resolution (Appelbaum, 1977). One explanation given for such a change was that the patients had benefited primarily from the interpersonal relationship with their therapist (Horwitz, 1974). A new interpersonal context enabled the patient to resume the arrested development which had led to his symptoms.

Overcoming Apartness

An aspect of the interpersonal relationship as a pathway to change, but deserving of notice in its own right, is the difference between feeling alone, so often a distinguishing characteristic of neurosis, as compared to having somebody to turn to. Freud described a neurotic as someone who is unable to establish membership in a group. The neurotic is solipsistic, he relates himself to himself, he interacts with his idiosyncratic population of internal images. In this sense, every neurosis is narcissistic and every neurotic is alone. How much is the distress of neurotic life due to this self-imposed loneliness? How much desperation and pessimism come about because the struggle with ghosts is a solitary one? This state of affairs changes immediately when the patient is accepted for treatment, though patients vary a good deal in the degree to which they accept the interpersonal reality which we call a therapeutic alliance. That "somebody up there loves me," or might love me, probably plays a significant part in bringing about a honeymoon at the beginning of analysis. As reality becomes transference, and transference becomes transference neurosis, the bloom is off the peach. The patient's solitary preoccupation with fantasy figures continues, but now in relation to a real person. Yet with a patient well selected for analysis, there always is, in such a relationship, the recognition of the real person, the real helper. As with many teenagers and their parents, and between many husbands and wives, the participants may act as if there were no satisfying connections between them, no transactions unmarked by idiosyncratic concerns from elsewhere. Yet, at some level of awareness, they know that they are benevolently attached to one another. When all goes well and the patient surmounts his difficulties, he does so in part as a function of the guiding relationship with the analyst, just as some students learn out of love for their teachers. Independent of the content of the analytic hours, this primordial image of a helper, someone to live for and with, someone to work out one's difficulties on, directs outward and makes workable what otherwise might be the circular, festering conundrum of neurosis.

Emotional Release

In the beginnings of psychoanalysis, alongside the abreaction of ideas was catharsis of emotion. The contribution to change of emotional outpouring has survived in psychoanalysis, but for the most part in the context of suffusing the discovery of meaning and the reconstruction of events with emotions. Such emotions give ideas and memories an intrapsychic importance which increases their influence and usefulness. In recent years, Janov (1970) and others have demonstrated dramatically the great intensity of emotion which can be elicited when releasing emotion is taken as the major task of therapy. In so doing, he has implicitly raised the issue for psychoanalysis as to how much emotion is enough emotion. He has widened the range so we now see that in psychoanalysis we ordinarily work with only a small part of that range. Whatever the relative contribution of emotion to change proves to be, in calling our attention to the possibilities of change through intense emotional expression, Janov has refurbished for some of us the recognition that affect ought to be credited explicitly and studied imaginatively.

Suggestion

The word suggestion has several meanings. As most commonly used it means to offer an idea, that is, to make a suggestion. It can also mean to force one's ideas on another as in brainwashing and thought control. Somewhere in between making a suggestion and forcing an idea is the explicit influencing of the patient by backing up a suggestion with authority engendered by the transference.

In all of these uses of the word suggestion, one person does something to another, the difference between them dependent only on the amount of force applied. Many people experience this mode of extending help as unsavory; others object to its being nonanalytic, usually meaning noninterpretive. So, for many psychoanalysts, suggestion is at best a base form of the copper of psychotherapy, at worst, manipulation. But there is another kind of suggestion, one which does not involve this subject/object mode, one in which no one does anything to anyone else. That is the suggestion, alternatively named "placebo," which silently functions in all manner of therapeutic transactions where the need to believe and to benefit is strong. Take the state of mind and feeling of a person pacing around in neurotic circles, knowing he has nowhere to go except where he has unsuccessfully been before, and compare it with the state of mind and feeling of a person engaged in psychoanalysis, in which with the help of another he is offered the hope of breaking out of his neurotic cage. The patient's attention has somewhere new to go, his energy has somewhere else to expend itself. He has made a break with the past simply by undertaking therapy, and he backs up his intention to bring about change with the expenditure of time, effort, and money. He thereby produces in himself an expectation and impetus toward change, an autosuggestion. He is aided in this effort by the implicit suggestion that he is to be helped, as conveyed to him by the cultural sanctions which support the offering to him of psychoanalysis. By way of such sanctions, his peers, his social family, proffer their like-minded expectation that he is to benefit. That suggestion contributes to change in psychoanalysis is, from one point of view, unsettling. Perhaps the patient only reports change because he expects that of himself, or perhaps he behaves differently only because he expects to behave differently; in both instances change would be tied to the treatment and might give way when the treatment is over. But suggestion may also contribute to the analytic process through helping the patient overcome resistances and accept meaning and through tiding the patient over difficult times. By way of suggestion the analyst is given the benefit of the doubt so the work can continue. In this sense, suggestion can be considered as mutative and thus deserving of study and respect. Copper, too, has important uses.

Coherence and Mastery

As can be seen from some altered states of consciousness, and especially in dreams, the unconscious mind is chaotic. The psychoanalytic objectives of making the unconscious conscious, of bringing impulses under the sway of the ego, of shifting from the primary to the secondary process are intended, by definition, to create order. When one takes into consideration that the patient's experience is often one of confusion, dismay, and a loss of moorings, then it follows that whatever brings about a sense of stability contributes to beneficial change. One way such stability can come about is through a compulsive regime—for example, anchoring the week with psychoanalytic appointments and the continual opportunity for self-analysis. As Glover (1931) pointed out, even an inexact interpretation has beneficial effects in that it gives the patient something to focus on, thereby helping him bind anxiety, a sort of internal compulsive regime. Another way of creating order is by learning a coherent story of one's self, an encompassing framework which unites seemingly separate events into meaningful sequences and patterns. Equipped with such coherence, the patient becomes confident that whatever occurs in his life can, in principle, be understood within the framework of his analytic understanding. He knows now that he is less likely to be taken by surprise, to be mystified at what he or others do, think, or feel, that he has a backlog of information on which to base decisions. With all of these contributing to a sense of mastery, he is no longer subject to what Frank (1974) called "demoralization."

Order by way of understanding is not necessarily dependent on the accuracy of explanation. The version of events hammered out by analyst and patient need merely be reassuringly plausible to the patient and powerful enough to explain most things that come his way. One never knows whether any historical reconstruction, as made in psychoanalysis or in any other kind of history, is an accurate representation of how things were. Indeed, histories are regularly rewritten. Yet having the feeling of knowing such a history as if it were correct seems to have clear practical benefits with respect to sought-after change.

The Shift to Activity

Schafer (1976) and others have indicted psychoanalytic theory, and the language in which it is expressed, for contributing to a psychoanalytic technique which encourages passivity. So long as people live in the passive voice or mode, as illustrated by language which posits events as happening to us, we overlook our capacities to influence events. How can the patient change, he wonders, when he learns that he is the victim of powerful drives, complexes, early influences, bad relationships; indeed, why should he even try when he expects psychoanalytic treatment to take three to five years? Bemused by the drama and discovery of the unconscious, we have minimized the study of consciousness. We overlook, sometimes in derision, the power of positive thinking, the capacity to have things go as we want them to through intending that they do so, and acting upon this intention. How often, when the patient says he understands but cannot do anything about it, does a part of us sink into dismay instead of moving with the patient into the arena of intention, decision, execution? Too often perhaps—though not as often as alternative therapists believe. The alternative therapies have developed in substantial part as an antidote to passivity, one of their central tenets being self-responsibility. Gestalt therapists will, for example, adjure a patient to say "I won't" instead of "I can't." Whether or not we exploit it to the fullest, the assumption of self-responsibility, the shift from passivity to activity, is another factor in the psychology of change. The patient does not accept his misery lying down—on the couch or off it.

Let us for the moment consider ourselves as psychoanalytic patients who have developed, by whatever combination of these change factors, a new understanding of ourselves, complete with new beneficial feelings about ourselves and the analytic enterprise in general. We are, nonetheless, faced with continued challenges, from our familiar tendencies toward neurotic behavior and from the ordinary expectable difficulties in living. What does the exanalysand do when he faces trouble? He may first dip back into his store of analytic insight and attempt to understand what is happening in these terms. He may consider what his analyst would think, do, or experience in a similiar situation. These reactions are the technological nuts and bolts of his new striving, coping personality. Another thing to do, as Wheelis (1973) pointed out, is to behave differently, to act upon hard-earned analytic knowledge and so behave one's way to further change.

But "action" does not merely mean large muscle or other easily observable behavior. Action can also include thinking, for example, bringing to bear points of view learned through analysis which make difficulties easier to endure or even to dispel through viewing them differently. Charny (1975) writes:

> . . . it is not simply the unraveling of their hang-ups that makes the difference, but a kind of constant focus on the joy and dignity of being oneself, even as one continues to suffer any number of upsets in discovering the utter insanity and absurdity of one's spouse, children, the entire world (as well as one's dear self). . . . the trick is to see these as the other sides of the beauty and grandeur of all human beings and not be flipped out by the unfairness of life [p. 14].

There is something of Yoga and Zen in this assertion that neurosis is, to some extent, a function of the way one looks at things. As Schafer (1970) has pointed out, a successful psychoanalysis results in a changed view of reality, a new appreciation of layered meanings, a wisdom which transcends mere knowledge. Such a new world view may combine comic, romantic, tragic, and ironic visions. But whatever the specific contents, an enlarged and delineated capacity to experience what otherwise was narrowly, unilaterally, and reductionistically defined in neurotic terms can result in ways of living better for which psychoanalysis can take credit.

Altered Consciousness

Here is a speculative but to me intriguing contribution to this list of factors in psychoanalytic change. We are currently learning from studying altered states of consciousness, as produced by meditation and biofeedback, that in these states of mind people have capacities unavailable to them in other states of mind. Under these atypical conditions, people control what were at one time considered to be involuntary physiological processes. They bring about a variety of somatic and psychological changes through visualizing them, and they learn some kinds of material more efficiently than under other conditions. Such effects are not intended, or even attended to, in the psychoanalytic theory of technique. Yet the practice of psychoanalysis inadvertently may encourage such states of consciousness. The subdued atmosphere of the quiet, darkened office reclining on a couch, the often soft, soothing voice of the analyst, the patient's quasi self-hypnosis from listening to his own voice for long periods of time may all contribute to the altered consciousness which exploits capacities for change.

DISCUSSION

One question which pertains to every pathway mentioned is the degree to which it is cause or effect. Does intrapsychic change bring about changed behavior, or does changed behavior bring about intrapsychic change? Is the shift from passivity to activity, the capacity to benefit from a new interpersonal relationship, the ability to turn mere suggestion into independently held and enduring aspects of self—are all of these how change is brought about or are they the rewards of change?

Or is this question the wrong formulation to begin with? Would it be more correct to think of an interaction of factors contributing to a synergy in which the whole is greater than the sum of its parts? In such a formulation, traditional cause and effect sequences would yield to a complex relationship in which no factors were cause or effect, or were operative only as part of the total configuration. For example, insight may be maximally useful only in interaction with the requisite amount of affect, both becoming maximally useful only in the context of a helping interpersonal relationship, a corrective emotional experience, and so on down through the list of factors.

Once past the partisan preoccupation with one or another factor, we will be in a better position to answer such questions. Nonetheless, one can hardly avoid the issue, stated crudely, of "which factor is most important?" This query reflects the form of argument that one often hears, for example, in alternative therapists' denunciation of verbally derived insight and in psychoanalysts' implicit derogation of working directly on the body as a means of bringing about personality change. One answer to this issue is to try to rank order the factors or pathways according to their effectiveness in general and with respect to specific patient circumstances. A sophisticated way of making such a ranking would be to control for age, sex, birth order, and analyst's personality and skill. With a valid rank ordering, the therapist could better emphasize one or another factor or relationship between factors. He could change emphasis during the analysis as different levels of experience and ego functioning become paramount. For example, as patients work with the more primitive levels of their personality, the relative importance of the interpersonal relationship is increased. It may sound complicated, and would occasion a complicated research design, but I am inclined to think that good analysts make such sophisticated rankings and act upon them, sometimes without even thinking about it, to a greater extent than hortatory discussions might suggest.

Yet all these ways of approaching the assessment and use of the change factors in psychoanalysis may be largely or entirely wrong. The therapist decides in the confines of his conceptual world what is more or less useful to his patient. It may be that this formulation is yet another way we have been led astray by working in the mode of doctor and patient. Could it be instead that there is no such ranking, or that such a ranking is practically irrelevant anyway? Consider this analogy: A person is determined to go somewhere, but he needs time and money. The rich man needs time, and so he sets about getting from the environment time. The poor man who has time sets about getting from the environment money. Could it not be the same with patients? People may have the wisdom not only to know what is lacking, but also to know the means by which they can best overcome these lacks. The patient picks what is useful for him from the congeries of possibilities, just as babies and animals pick the foods that their bodies require. Perhaps all we can do is to facilitate patients' choices by making sure that all possibilities are available. This function may reflect our main clinical expertise.

Our research expertise has hardly been extended in ascertaining means of change. An obvious study would be simple to find out what analyst and patient respectively think brought about change. This and other researches are dependent on follow-up studies of psychoanalytic patients, which we woefully lack at present. Without such studies, we are in the same position as drug companies which sell their products with insufficient testing for efficacy and side effects. To rise above and go beyond that state of affairs, we need to know not only outcome—whether and what change occurs—but how such change comes about.

Such a research comparison would, I am sure, yield much information about the nature of psychoanalytic change. However, one final possibility ought to be considered. It may be that the full story can never be known with our present assumptions, hypotheses, and methods. Perhaps change in psychoanalysis is like creativity. We learn just so much about it; the rest remains ineffable, mysterious. There is always the patient who, despite all odds, changes beneficially. And there is always the patient who, seemingly with much going for him, somehow never quite makes the gains which he should have made. As with literary or musical talent, one can teach, inspire, nurture in manifold ways. Yet what is produced seems to dance to its own tune, follow arcane rules. This possible factor in psychoanalytic change gives us no cause to stop investigating. Indeed, it should stimulate new directions. But it does give us cause for awe and wonder. Awe and wonder, too, may be factors to consider in psychoanalytic change.

References

Alexander, F. The principle of corrective emotional experience. In F. Alexander and T. M. French (Eds.), *Psychoanalytic therapy*. New York: Ronald Press, 1946, pp. 66–70.

Appelbaum, S. A. *The anatomy of change*. New York: Plenum, 1977.

Charny, I. W. The new psychotherapies and encounters of the seventies: Progress or fads? *Reflections*, 1975, *10*, 1–17.

Frank, J. D. Psychotherapy: The restoration of morale. *American Journal of Psychiatry*, 1974, *131*, 271–274.

Glover, E. The therapeutic effect of the inexact interpretation: A contribution to the theory of suggestion. *International Journal of Psychoanalysis*, 1931, *12*, 397–411.

Horwitz, L. *Clinical prediction in psychotherapy*. New York: Jason Aronson, 1974.

Janov, A. *The primal scream*. New York: Putnam, 1970.

Klein, G. The emergence of ego psychology: The ego in psychoanalysis: A concept in search of identity. *Psychoanalytic Review*, 1970, *56*, 511–525.

Schafer, R. The psychoanalytic vision of reality. *International Journal of Psychoanalysis*, 1970, *51*, 279–297.

Schafer, R. *A new language for psychoanalysis*. New Haven: Yale University Press, 1976.

Wheelis, A. *How people change*. New York: Harper & Row, 1973.

Chapter 11

Some Views on Effective Principles of Psychotherapy

*John Paul Brady, Gerald C. Davison,
Paul A. Dewald, Gerard Egan,
James Fadiman, Jerome D. Frank,
Merton M. Gill, Irwin Hoffman,
Walter Kempler, Arnold A. Lazarus,
Victor Raimy, Julian B. Rotter,
and Hans H. Strupp*

Introduction

The argument has been advanced by several writers in the field that with increased experience, therapists tend to become more similar in their actual clinical practice. It has been suggested that there exists a "therapeutic underground," which may rarely appear in the literature, but which nonetheless reflects some common observations among well-seasoned clinicians as to what tends to be effective. If this indeed is the case, then such commonalities are likely to shed light on some very significant principles of

Reprinted by permission of the authors, John Paul Brady, Gerald C. Davison, Paul A. Dewald, Gerard Egan, James Fadiman, Jerome D. Frank, Merton M. Gill, Irwin Hoffman, Walter Kempler, Arnold A. Lazarus, Victor Raimy, Julian B. Rotter, and Hans H. Strupp, and the publisher from *Cognitive Therapy and Research*, 1980, 4, 269–306.

change as they have managed to emerge in spite of the theoretical biases inherent in each of our varying orientations.

In looking for common themes, it is not being suggested that there are no real differences among varying theoretical approaches. The conclusion that "we all do the same thing" would represent a gross oversimplification. Nonetheless, a search for common principles can be of immeasurable help in advancing the effectiveness of our therapeutic procedures.

Toward the goal of searching for common principles, a group of prominent therapists were asked to comment on their observations of what they believed to be the underlying principles or clinical strategies associated with the therapeutic change process, particularly as it was relevant for nonpsychotic patients/clients. We were primarily interested in having them share the results of *their own personal experiences and observations as clinicians*. Clearly, it was assumed that what they believed to be the most effective ingredients in psychotherapy would be heavily determined by their theoretical and philosophical orientations. Nevertheless, theory often allows us ample room to vary in what we do in therapy, so a fair amount of individuality was certainly expected. This is precisely what we were trying to get at, namely, their own personal conclusions, as determined by the interplay of their clinical experience, theoretical orientation, and knowledge of research findings.

Representing varying backgrounds and theoretical orientations, the therapists that participated in this project were as follows: John Paul Brady, Gerald C. Davison, Paul A. Dewald, Gerard Egan, James Fadiman, Jerome D. Frank, Merton M. Gill and Irwin Hoffman, Walter Kempler, Arnold A. Lazarus, Victor Raimy, Julian B. Rotter and Hans H. Strupp. Each of them was asked to respond to the following set of questions:

1. What is the role played by new experiences provided to the patient/client in facilitating change?
2. To what extent does offering patients/clients feedback on their thinking, emotions, and behavior facilitate therapeutic change?
3. In what way do you see the therapist–patient/client relationship as contributing to the change process?
4. How have you used language/cognition/awareness in facilitating change within the therapeutic setting?
5. What clinical strategies or principles of change do you believe to be common across all therapeutic orientations?

In answering these questions, the respondents were asked to make every attempt to avoid use of theoretical concepts. As a useful guideline, it was suggested that they imagine that these questions were being asked of them by an uninformed layperson, who was intelligent but unaware of any theoretical jargon. It was also emphasized that these questions be answered in light of those conclusions drawn from *their own personal experiences and observations* of what tended to work with the majority of nonpsychotic patients/clients. Their responses to each of these questions are outlined below.

Marvin R. Goldfried

1. What is the Role Played by New Experiences Provided to the Patient/Client in Facilitating Change?

JOHN PAUL BRADY: I regard new experiences, that is, experiences of the patient since treatment was initiated, as critical to favorable change. It is only by behaving differently, trying out new responses to old situations, that the patient can hope to alter habitual maladaptive ways of responding. This is true whether the new ways of responding were simply discussed with the patient verbally or whether they were tried out in therapy through role playing or through actually entering situations with the therapist and behaving differently under his guidance and urging. Of course, the therapy itself may be considered "new experiences." However, I suspect these are not as drastically different from other experiences the patient has had as is generally believed. What may make therapy as new experience useful is the accompanying explanation or interpretation of the therapy experience; that is, the patient perceives the experience in a way in which he has not perceived previous interpersonal communications. Of course, there are some highly structured therapeutic techniques, such as systematic desensitization and its variants, that may provide relatively new experiences because of their carefully programmed and structured nature.

GERALD C. DAVISON: I have absolutely no doubt that this factor is absolutely crucial for therapeutic change and that, indeed, it cuts across all therapy orientations. The subtle questions have to do with the *nature* of new experiences as well as with the way such experiences are brought about.

In my own clinical work, I view the therapy situation as one in which the client can try out new ways of thinking, feeling, and behaving both within the therapy relationship (that is, to myself) and outside the consulting room.

My belief is that clients build up over time a set of expectancies about what the world holds for them, what they are capable or incapable of doing. These beliefs about the future may come from a variety of sources, not all of which are important to uncover, in my opinion. But what remains critical is that the client encounter situations (actual, analogue, or symbolic) in which he or she has behaved in a predictable way, but in one way or another is induced to behave differently, to look at the situation differently, or some such thing.

As for *how* such experiences are created, I sometimes cajole clients into trying out something new, and sometimes become more heavy-handed under certain circumstances.

PAUL A. DEWALD: In psychoanalysis and psychoanalytic psychotherapy, new experience plays a crucial role in facilitating change. However, the experience occurs primarily in the two-person field of patient and analyst, and the analyst maintains a relatively circumscribed and constant form of neutral participation. The therapeutic situation and technique are designed to promote a return for the patient of earlier and at times forgotten forms, organization, and levels of behavior previously experienced toward key persons during the patient's earlier life and development. Progressively, these are reactivated and are felt and expressed toward the analyst (transference and transference neurosis).

The patient, however, maintains an adult perspective, while simultaneously experiencing childlike or infantile feelings states, wishes, and fears. These lead him to expect of the analyst responses similar to those that occurred or were fantasied in connection with earlier figures. By maintaining the neutral participant observer stance, the analyst provides the patient with a new experience of acceptance, understanding, and help in coping with conflicts and feeling states. The patient simultaneously experiences at a childlike level the old conflicts and feelings, as well as the new therapeutic experiences *at the same level of childlike regression*. The adult rational and self-observing portion of the patient's personality must then integrate and reconcile the other two levels of experience.

Another new set of experiences for the patient are those of being treated with attention and respect by a parental figure who does not seek to impose upon the patient his own values, behavior patterns, or demands, and who instead encourages independence, autonomy, and freedom of choice in regard to value systems, self-awareness, and the experimenting and practicing of new behavioral responses to old conflicts.

GERARD EGAN: If clients have problems in living and if counseling can be seen, at least in part, as a problem-solving process, then new experiences are called for throughout all the therapeutic steps (see my answer to question 5). Each step calls for some kind of new experience.

I believe that new experiences are critical in facilitating change. New experiences together with new perspectives on self, others, behavior, and environment constitute the challenge dimension of the helping process. Counseling without support is destructive, but counseling with challenge is effete. Through new experiences clients learn that they can live life differently and more fully without being destroyed. "I am not as fragile as I see myself or as some others see me." Some of these new experiences take place inside the counseling relationship; others take place outside but are set up and supported by the counseling sessions themselves. For instance, clients find out that they can talk intimately about themselves, whether to one other person in individual counseling or to a number of others in a group situation, without being destroyed. New experiences introduce clients to dimensions of developmental tasks that they are handling poorly, overlooking, or running away from. For instance, a client can learn that she can let down her guard and experiment with various ways of being intimate with others without surrendering values that are important to her and without being swallowed up by others. Most clients I see are "out of community" in some way and need to establish or reestablish some kind of community. This cannot be done without new experiences. Group counseling can be a start but cannot take the place of community "out there." Developmental tasks such as autonomy, intimacy, and identity and the ways in which they relate to one another can be discussed forever without having any impact on the ways in which clients live their lives. New experiences rather than just new ideas are the essence of the challenge dimension of helping.

JAMES FADIMAN: Without new experiences, there is no change. The central experience is feedback without blame. To be accepted not only for what one has been but for what one is becoming is an ongoing revelation.

Beyond therapy, the critical new experiences occur during moments of testing the insights acquired in therapy. Unless these tests occur, nothing (useful) has been gained but insight

Except for those clients who are in therapy as a hobby, or those who use it as an ironclad defense, the surprises that occur are the core of the experience.

I wish it was my canny wisdom, understanding, and clarity that makes the differences. However, it is only after the client does something that is novel, something outside of therapy, that the insubstantial excitement of understanding is transformed into lasting change.

JEROME D. FRANK: In a sense, all psychotherapy is a new experience in that it provides the patient with a relationship with a helping figure that differs from previous ones and uses procedures that are not part of daily living. A powerful therapeutic force with many clinic patients is being taken seriously and being encouraged by a prestige figure to express their feelings for the first time in their lives. I have seen a patient abandon a socially crippling monosymptomatic delusion of many years' duration simply on the grounds that the doctor seemed genuinely interested in her and encouraged her to talk. Other experiences that may produce change directly through their novelty are arriving at a startling new insight, which causes a shift in the patient's perceptions, or being challenged in a novel way by other members of a therapy group, thereby eliciting a new response.

Much of the therapeutic power of innovative psychotherapeutic procedures, as with new medical and surgical procedures, lies in their novelty, which stimulates patients emotionally, thereby increasing their susceptibility to the therapist, and arouses their hopes.

MERTON M. GILL and **IRWIN HOFFMAN**: There is little doubt that the therapist's personality and his manner of relating can often provide the patient with a new and beneficial interpersonal experience. However, we are convinced that it is of great importance that the patient be encouraged to verbally explicate the details and nuances of his experience of the relationship, including those aspects of it that seem to be new. First of all, sometimes what appears to be new experience turns out, upon critical reflection, to be a new edition of something old or to conceal something about the nature of the therapist's influence that both the patient and the therapist are inclined to deny. Secondly, even when the experience stemming from the effects of the therapist's involvement is entirely positive and genuinely new, there is much to be gained by coupling it with the special new experience that comes with direct communication about the relationship. We believe that changes that are brought about by this particular, unique kind of new experience in the therapy involve a maturation of the patient's reflective self-consciousness as a social being. These changes are likely to be the most far-reaching and enduring. The experience in the therapy increases the patient's self-awareness, which in turn modifies the way in which he experiences and copes with outside situations. These modifications lead, in turn, to new outside experiences, which further consolidate what has been achieved.

WALTER KEMPLER: If by "new" experiences you mean that something happens *within* the person that has not previously occurred—though they may have been through the same scene many times before and said the same things in it before—then yes, new experiences are our essential aspect of changing. When I quit smoking many years ago, I said, as I had said many, many times before, "This time I'm really finished." And as I said it, I experienced my saying it differently and knew I was finished. There was no "new experience" that I could identify outside of me. I was simply ready. Outside circumstances—situations—old and new experiences also lead to qualitative changes.

A therapeutic act is one that supplies the other—whether intentional or fortuitous is not significant—with a presence that enables the other to take the next necessary step. This ingredient, this catalytic agent, has infinite variations. One patient described my attitude toward a given issue (pain) as "not giving a damn," and from that perspective of *his* drew the needed courage to make his next move. Another saw me as "really caring," while yet another described the catalytic agent in my presence as my "willingness to be vulnerable and let it all hang out." Another came unstuck when I was "wrong and told off." The descriptions are endlessly assorted.

ARNOLD A. LAZARUS: By definition, without "new experiences" there can be no change. A successful treatment outcome will reflect a wide range of "new experiences"—new thoughts, feelings, and behaviors, new improved ways of communicating with others.

There are data demonstrating that therapeutic change usually follows methods that are *performance-based*. Purely cognitive or verbal methods are often less effective. I therefore deliberately provide a series of performance-based "new experiences" for my clients to transact or put into effect. At the start of each session I customarily ask, "What new or different things have you done this week?" If the answer is "None!" one can be quite certain that little (if any) progress will have been made. Effective therapists, in my estimation, manage to persuade their clients to take calculated emotional risks. They inspire and encourage them to do different things and to do things differently.

Most people who consult therapists are in an unsatisfactory rut. Their restricted or faulty thinking limits their freedom of choices so that their actions, feelings, sensations, creative outlets, and personal relationships are often conglutinated. Only "new experiences" can provide the flexibility and the reinforcements they require.

VICTOR RAIMY: Almost everything I do in therapy consists of trying to provide the client with new experiences so that he can gain new perspectives on himself and on himself in relation to significant others. Such new experiences or new perspectives are intended to help him to detect and change his misconceptions.

For me, the new experiences form a continuum from the explanations or questions I employ to try to modify the client's thinking directly, through the small experiments I conduct within the interview in which the client can observe his own reactions, to the specific and concrete homework assignments where he can obtain further and often more elaborate feedback about his own reactions and misconceptions in real life.

In my experience, straightforward questioning of the client directed toward helping him to discover and deal with his relevant misconceptions can be an extremely powerful and new experience in bringing about change. In complex emotional problems where the client is inhibited in discussing his often ambivalent thinking, the process can frequently be speeded up by asking him to close his eyes and imagine that the significant other is present but mute; the client then tells the imagined person what his "feelings" are toward him. Homework assignments outside of the interview can also be helpful in providing the client with new perspectives.

All three kinds of new experiences—interview discussion, imaginary interactions within the interview, and self-observed interactions in real life—can provide the client with insight, which I define as recognition of a misconception.

JULIAN B. ROTTER: If one accepts the idea that a new thought is a new experience, then of course, all change follows from new experience. The person may or may not be aware of the new experience or the connection between the new experience and the changed behavior. If the question is being asked in the more restrictive sense of new experiences outside of the therapy room, it makes a great deal of sense from the point of view of social learning theory that such new experiences be heavily emphasized.

According to the social learning theory (Rotter, 1954; Rotter, Chance, & Phares, 1972), a change in the potential occurrence of any behavior is a function of (1) a change in the expectancy for a particular reinforcement to occur as a result of the behavior in that situation and/or (2) a change in the value of any particular reinforcement that is expected to occur in that situation. Consequently, any new experience that changes either expectancy or reinforcement values will change behavior.

While insight into the origins of behavior or insight into the future consequences of behavior can be highly significant for some patients, it seems reasonable that it is important for all patients to try out new behaviors in their present life circumstances and to discover for themselves whether or not they are more adaptive. It seems apparent from the frequent relapses following therapeutic gains (clinically and experimentally established) that the gains produced in the therapy room often do not generalize to outside circumstances. Generalization proceeds along a gradient, and if the therapist is seen as a social agent, he or she is typically much different from others, and the patient's behavior in relationship with the therapist is likely also to be different.

There is no special technique, no special method, no mysterious process that is presumed to accomplish therapeutic change. Verbal discussions, trying out new behaviors, suggestion, and a change in one's life situations all can lead to behavioral change. The major problem is one of suiting the method to the patient so that change is accomplished efficiently and beneficially. It is the therapist's job to get the patient to try out new behaviors or to seek out new environments or, in the case of children, to help produce such new environments; but it is ultimately the patient's choice as to whether to maintain the new behaviors and/or try to control his or her environment himself or herself.

HANS H. STRUPP: Basic to all forms of psychotherapy, whether or not it is acknowledged by the theory to which the therapist subscribes, is the patient's experience with a human being who, for better or worse, becomes a "significant other." Psychotherapy works because (1) all human beings have a strong tendency to "transfer" patterns of interpersonal relatedness[1] from the past to the present, and (2) this transference tendency can be utilized by the therapist to bring about a "corrective experience." Thus the essence of psychotherapy is interpersonal learning, a new significant experience (*Erlebnis*) that, if all goes well, modifies basic aspects of the patient's patterns of relatedness in ways that are called therapeutic.

With reference to (1), Freud's discovery of the universal transference tendency was revolutionary. He demonstrated that human beings learn their most basic patterns of relatedness from care-givers (usually the mother) in infancy and childhood. These internalized experiences form the "deep structure" governing experiences with significant others later in life. The fundamental reason for the pervasiveness of early learning experiences (particularly those pertaining to the receiving and giving of affection that form the substrate of the person's self-image and self-concept) is the small child's biological and psychological dependency on powerful adults. As a result, injurious early experiences (e.g., inadequate mothering, death of a parent, birth of a sibling) that are beyond the child's mastery become the source of conflicts and maladaptive patterns of behavior that tend to repeat earlier traumas.

With respect to (2), the therapist's attitude of understanding, respect, warmth, and acceptance promotes the reenactment of earlier difficulties in interpersonal relatedness. The therapist is helpful by providing a certain amount of genuine nurturance and by refusing to reenact the complementary role unwittingly assigned to him or her by the patient. Furthermore, by making explicit the conflictual and maladaptive patterns energizing in the patient–therapist relationship, the therapist enables the patient to restructure his or her experience in more adaptive and satisfying ways.

To What Extent Does Offering Patients/Clients Feedback on Their Thinking, Emotions, and Behavior Facilitate Therapeutic Change?

JOHN PAUL BRADY: A common practice of psychotherapists (including myself) is to label a bit of the patient's thinking, emotional responses, or behavior with the expectation that the patient will understand himself better and that this will facilitate favorable changes in these three interre-

---

[1]By patterns of interpersonal relatedness I mean characteristic and often stereotyped ways in which a person relates to significant others. Such patterns become apparent particularly in situations that are affectively charged and that activate engrained (overlearned) tendencies of relating to care-givers and authority figures. Patterns of relatedness are often suffused by unconscious fantasies and contradictory strivings. They also tend to repeat traumatic experiences and are frequently troublesome because of hostile components that are experienced by the patient as ego-alien.

lated aspects of psychological functioning. A hazard of this strategy is that the therapist may not correctly identify or interpret the patient's thinking, emotions, or behavior. Another hazard is that the patient will become defensive or offended by the therapist's interpretations. Although I find this strategy useful at times with selected patients, I do not find it a major treatment strategy. In general, I think it is more useful for the patient to identify recurring patterns in his thinking, emotional reactions to certain situations, or characteristic behaviors under particular circumstances and label them himself. Of course, the therapist may indirectly facilitate this process by eliciting the required self-reports from the patient and judiciously asking whether he can identify a recurring pattern and whether a given pattern is adaptive or satisfying.

GERALD C. DAVISON: Over the past several years my clinical practice and beliefs have changed in the direction of acknowledging more and more the importance of what we call feedback to the client. The therapist is in a unique, socially sanctioned situation to tell the client things that other people are unlikely to tell, such as how the client comes across to people. Often I will use myself as a barometer of what other people are likely to feel or think in reaction to the client. (The role of interfering biases by the therapist is obvious.)

All human beings, but perhaps especially those who are deeply troubled, do not have a terribly good idea of how they affect others by the way they think or act. I have often told clients that the therapy situation is a rare and treasured opportunity to learn things about themselves; I do this deliberately to further enhance the legitimacy of things that I will tell them about themselves.

PAUL A. DEWALD: In psychoanalysis and psychoanalytic psychotherapy, feedback is offered primarily in the form of verbal interventions. These are designed to bring to the patient's attention behavior patterns or meaning inferred regarding the patient's verbal communications of which the patient is not consciously aware. To the extent that such verbal feedback to the patient increases the patient's own self-awareness and allows the patient to recognize previously unconscious fantasies, emotions, and conflicts, as well as the ways by which the patient has previously sought to avoid awareness of those mental processes, such feedback is a precursor for facilitation of behavioral change. Interpretation or other forms of feedback alone do not create change. Change occurs as the result of how the patient responds to and uses the feedback offered by the analyst.

GERARD EGAN: If new experiences constitute the "machinery" of behavioral change, then feedback is the oil that keeps it running. Feedback must pervade the entire process. *Ongoing* feedback is critical. Without reliable and valid feedback no one, including the counselor, knows whether the helping process is working. One of the tasks of counseling is to help clients discover sources of ongoing feedback in their lives. There are two very practical issues—the source of feedback and the content.

Initially, the counselor is the principal source of feedback. As soon as possible, however, clients must be taught to give feedback to themselves and to find in their environment natural sources of feedback. Again, group counseling offers a beginning since clients can get feedback immediately from peers in the counseling session itself.

Feedback on what? The answer to this question describes the *content* of feedback. Since I see counseling as a humanistic problem-solving process and the helper as a consultant to this process, the stages of the problem-solving process itself tell me what kinds of feedback are important. Accurate empathy, which is useful throughout the helping process, is a kind of feedback itself. However, clients need direct feedback with respect to (1) how clearly they are understanding their problems and needs, (2) whether they are developing new, problem-related perspectives, (3) the realism of their goals, (4) the comprehensiveness of their program census, and (5) the "fit" of programs, chosen to their style and resources.

Of course, feedback is critical in helping the client evaluate the helping process itself. *Clients* need feedback to answer the three evaluation questions I have listed in my response to question 5.

JAMES FADIMAN: Feedback is offering a peculiar sort of mirror in which clients can observe their reflections. I focus on one or another aspects of peoples' lives to encourage them to take one step beyond their normal reactions to their situation.

A story is told of a cat who complained: "What ingratitude there is in this world! Here I am offering free lessons in catching mice and not a single rabbit has signed up." Outside of therapy and special teaching situations, people are free to be satisfied with the cat's perception of the world.

To be able to examine one's preconceptions—one's filters against experiencing reality—is useful. Keep in mind that the cat's evaluation is accurate *and* incomplete. Feedback leads to completion.

JEROME D. FRANK: Any intervention that brings into conscious focus behaviors that are more or less out of awareness is potentially helpful. Whether or not it actually motivates the patient to change depends a good deal on how it is presented and on the therapist's attitude. For patients who perceive themselves as victims of others' behavior, an especially useful form of feedback is that which clarifies how the patient's behavior or attitudes elicit these reactions. By discovering how they contribute to the difficulty, patients come to realize that they also can do something about it, thereby increasing their sense of competence. Through this kind of feedback the patient discovers that he or she is not a helpless victim of circumstances but has more control than he or she realized. Included in feedback should be the therapist's indication of his or her own reaction to the behavior in question, especially if it arouses the reactions of unfriendliness, boredom, or rejection that the patient experiences from others in daily life.

An aspect of feedback that does not depend so much on the therapeutic relationship is bringing to the center of attention maladaptive habitual behavior or words that are largely out of awareness. As with biofeedback of physiological processes, this helps patients to gain conscious control over them.

MERTON M. GILL and IRWIN HOFFMAN: The kind of feedback we find most effective takes the form, primarily, of tentative interpretations designed to further the process by which the patient becomes aware of and speaks openly about his experience of the relationship. On the whole, we do not favor feedback in which the therapist reveals his own personal reactions to the patient as a means of facilitating change. There may be some exceptions when the therapist is confident that all observers would similarly assess the patient's behavior. Otherwise, there is too much risk that in the process of revealing his own reactions the therapist will take on the mantle of a judge and neglect a joint exploration of how the patient experiences the interaction. Such joint exploration entails a special kind of dialogue. On the one hand, the perspective of the patient, which is subject to self-deception, is complemented by the outside perspective of the therapist. On the other hand, interpretations offered by the therapist are continually checked against what the patient finds through his own introspection.

While change in all psychological therapies depends on the relationship, therapies differ in the degree to which the patient's experience of the relationship is itself explored and explicated. There are barriers to the patient's free communication of his experience of the relationship. To a significant extent the patient's inhibitions are related to what he thinks the therapist is prepared to hear and accept without reacting defensively or in any other adverse ways. One of the most compelling demonstrations of the therapist's receptiveness occurs when he recognizes and interprets the patient's hints about or disguised allusions to his experience of the relationship, including his impressions of the therapist. These interpretations should be offered as hunches to be affirmed, modified, or denied by the patient, never as fact.

WALTER KEMPLER: We do not "offer feedback" as a mirror or an apparatus. We are, and are seen as, living. We "feed back," filtering through our own perceiving, and our voice, manner, attitude, posture, and how we are valued by the receiver are all part of the return arm of the process. "Feedback" is reminiscent of the old nonsense called the "objective" interpretation—both are fiction. We are speaking of our personal responses, or a variation of personal response in which we urge patients to reconsider what they have done or said. It can be done in many ways—by repeating it; with video replay; by asking, "Do you mean . . . . "; by exclaiming, "You must be kidding!!"; by declaring, "That's absurd." How the therapist reacts is important, as is relevance and timing. But let's not pretend the impossible and sterile neutrality that I suspect is intended in the term *feedback*.

ARNOLD A. LAZARUS: Frank, forthright, and honest feedback is a rare commodity. Social protocol often demands a degree of tact and diplomacy that hinges on hypocrisy. Even good friends are often loath to provide one with honest feedback lest the other person take offense. And when loved ones do offer feedback, their perceptions are bound to be biased and may often be questioned. Therapists, on the other hand, are trained observers who can hold up a "psychic mirror" and allow clients to see things about themselves that might otherwise go unnoticed.

Feedback alone, without providing alternate (more adaptive) reactions or responses is limited. Errors in the client's thinking, emotions, and behavior may be clearly articulated in a supportive and empathic manner and still lead nowhere. "Thank you for the feedback. I see exactly what you mean, but I don't know what to do about it." Thus, while corrective feedback is often essential, it is rarely sufficient. The client needs to be able to accept the feedback, validate and integrate it; and finally, he/she needs to be taught to translate it into new actions and transactions.

VICTOR RAIMY: Verbal feedback that graphically encapsulates a client's misconception about himself or his relationships is for me the "therapeutic act" *par excellence*. In the well-known *Gloria* film in which Fritz Perls tells Gloria that she is a "phony," he immediately captures her attention, focuses it upon a misconception that interferes with her interpersonal relations, thus throwing into sharp relief her faulty assumption that she behaves toward others in a rational, genuine fashion.

This instance of uncomplimentary feedback is only an extreme example of how I believe most progress in therapy occurs. Ordinarily the therapist provides feedback when the client has not been able to grasp the significance of his expressed thoughts, emotions, and behavior. Reflections, interpretations, and confrontations are all designed to provide feedback that enables a client to examine his thinking more critically, thus helping him to correct whatever misconceptions are affecting his adjustment. Similar feedback can also be provided for the client by asking him to observe his own behavior, thoughts, and emotions during new experiences arranged by the therapist within or outside of the interview.

Most of the feedback I verbalize is in the form of tentative questions in order to give the client as much latitude as possible so that he can concentrate on the content of the feedback itself without having to deal with the therapist's implied attitudes at the same time. I also try to phrase such feedback as graphically and tersely as possible in order to set it off from the often confused (for the client, particularly) dialogue of the interview.

JULIAN B. ROTTER: This question can be restated in two questions: To what extent is it typical that patients are not aware of their behavior, thoughts, emotions (states of the organism)? The usual criterion for awareness is the ability to verbalize, and it is clear that there is a great deal about the patient's own behavior and ideations that he or she cannot verbalize, although there is also much that he or she can verbalize. Being able to describe one's own behavior, ideas, and emotions, including one's "true feelings," does not necessarily lead to therapeutic change, although it may facilitate it.

One problem is that feedback or insight is often incomplete. For example, the client's responses to a parent are extremely complicated, varying from situation to situation and involving a considerable variety of potential reinforcements, not only love and hostility. Broad, overgeneralized interpretations (reflections) often are not convincing to the patient because he or she is aware that something is missing.

The greater limitation, however, is that such insight or awareness alone is not enough. It can lead to therapeutic change only when satisfying alternatives are available to the client.

The further question is: Is such awareness necessary? I think not. If the patient can learn alternative behaviors and find them satisfying, he or she can adjust quite well without being aware of what he or she is doing, thinking, feeling at all times, just as the rest of us do.

HANS H. STRUPP: In keeping with the foregoing conceptualization, patients benefit particularly from therapist comments ("interpretations") that place their current troublesome patterns of relatedness, particularly those with the therapist, in the context of major themes of their life history and thus highlight the anachronistic, maladaptive, and often self-contradictory character of the patient's goals. The therapist's efforts are consistently aimed at discovering the latent (symbolic) meanings of the patient's verbal and nonverbal communications—in this respect fantasies, reveries, dreams, and other relatively uncensored communications are particularly useful—and bringing them to the patient's attention. Noteworthy here is the universal human tendency to hide painful experiences and their aftermath from oneself, often by fending off (resisting) the person attempting to unravel and understand them. At the same time, the patient's most basic desire (which also provides the "motivation for therapy") is the wish to be accepted and understood.

Therapeutic change is basically structural change; that is, the patient learns to reorganize beliefs about himself or herself, the intentions and behavior of others, and the patient's feelings and behavior in interaction with others. Such reorganizations occur most dramatically and probably most lastingly in the context of *aroused affect*, provided the *nature* and *timing* of the therapist's interventions are "right." In other words, the patient must be in an optimally receptive state in order to benefit from the therapist's communications ("feedback"). For this reason, efforts by the therapist to promote reorganization, insight, and understanding at other times are probably of very limited utility. In short, the therapist's communications must be geared to the patient's current level of understanding, that is, his or her ability to experience them as meaningful. Therapy tends to be slow because these processes often cannot be hastened, although the therapist can endeavor to keep the patient "on track" by maintaining a focus on major conflictual themes and avoiding excursions into side issues.

3. In What Way Do You See the Therapist– Patient/Client Relationship as Contributing to the Change Process?

JOHN PAUL BRADY: There is no question that qualitative aspects of the therapist–patient relationship can greatly influence the course of therapy for good or bad. In general, if the patient's relationship to the therapist is characterized by belief in the therapist's competence (knowledge, sophistication, and training) and if the patient regards the therapist as an honest, trustworthy, and decent human being with good social and ethical values (in his own scheme of things), the patient is more apt to invest himself in the therapy. Equally important is the quality and tone of the relationship he has with the therapist. That is, if he feels trusting and warm toward the therapist, this generally will facilitate following the treatment regimen, will be associated with higher expectations of improvement, and other generally favorable factors. The feelings of the therapist toward the patient are also important. If the therapist feels that his patient is not a desirable person or a decent human being or simply does not like the patient for whatever reasons, he may not succeed in concealing these feelings and attitudes toward the patient, and in general they will have a deleterious effect. There are some exceptions to these generalizations, however. Some patients will feel frightened and vulnerable with a therapist toward whom they feel attracted, particularly if from past experience they perceive such relationships as dangerous (danger of being hurt emotionally). With such a patient, a somewhat more distant and impersonal relationship may in fact be more desirable in that it will facilitate the patient's involvement in the treatment, following the treatment regimen, etc.

GERALD C. DAVISON: This aspect of therapy is of the utmost importance. Even behaviorally oriented clinicians like myself have for some time acknowledged the importance of the relationship. Clients have to trust the therapist to tell the therapist things. Clients have to believe in the therapist to try to do new things, to allow feedback from the therapist to have an impact on them, to feel secure about divulging terrible secrets about themselves or others. A relationship that is not a strong one will not encourage the client to explore alternatives and try out new ways of behaving. A technique will not be any more believable to a client than is the therapist suggesting the use of the technique.

PAUL A. DEWALD: As mentioned in questions 1 and 2, from a psychoanalytic perspective the therapist–patient relationship and interaction are crucial to the entire therapeutic process. As the therapy evolves and unfolds, the patient increasingly experiences in a living situation between himself and the therapist the earlier forms and levels of conflict that had produced or contributed to the patient's psychopathology. In this sense the patient–therapist relationship serves as a paradigm of interpersonal reactions and conflicts from which the patient can recognize and observe similar forms and level of conflict with others in his life and environment. The emergence of these conflicts in the treatment relationship offers a "laboratory" setting in which to explore and practice new forms of conflict expression, containment, or resolution, which can then be generalized by the patient to other relationships outside of the treatment setting. Different from other interpersonal relationships, the therapist avoids imposing new solutions or expectations upon the patient, thus supporting the patient's ultimate autonomy. To some extent this interaction also provides the patient with a model for imitation in connection with the work of the treatment and the willingness to tolerate painful or unpleasant emotional and psychological conflict. But if such imitation and identification by the patient with the therapist begins to limit or constrict the patient's autonomy, this is usually dealt with as a form of interference in the achievements of independent self-development and freedom of choice.

GERARD EGAN: I don't like to either underplay or overplay this relationship. I feel, however, that it is too often overplayed. This relationship does not exist for itself but for the work that is to be done. Very often clients who come are "out of community" in some sense of that phrase. While it is important that they get into community with the helper in order to get about the work of facing developmental issues and the problems in living that face them, it is important that they not get lost in this relationship. When it is obvious that the person coming to me is out of community, one of my objectives from the very start is to help that person find and cultivate human resources in his or her own natural environment. I do not particularly want to become this person's professional friend. One of the reasons I prefer group therapy or counseling is that it demythologizes the role of the helper somewhat and provides a relatively safe forum in which the client can face the issue of relating to others. Even in group counseling, however, I believe that the issue of transferring what is learned in the group to the person's day-to-day environment needs to be tended to from the very beginning.

Certainly the relationship between helper and clients is important in that it gives the latter an opportunity to start from scratch, as it were, and examine precisely how they go about the task of relating to another human being. The helper provides both support and challenge as clients examine their interpersonal style. The skill of immediacy—the ability to reflect mutually on how this relationship is proceeding generally and the ability to take a look at what is happening at any particular moment of relating—is very important for both therapist and client. This, I believe, can be done in a way that contributes to continuing this process in everyday life.

JAMES FADIMAN: The relationship is a mix of blessings and impediments. When the therapist becomes an unrealistic, powerful figure for the client, it can lengthen therapy and obscure the client's concerns. The therapist's support can in itself be what allows fundamental changes to occur, irrespective of the content of the procedures.

I work with individuals and groups often as a consultant, not as a therapist. In that role I listen, interpret, offer feedback, deal with past traumatic events, clarify emotional overreactions, and so on. In these settings the client is encouraged to feel capable. The client is empowered from the beginning and the consultant is always in the place of the one who serves.

In some situations, one-on-one therapy may be an indulgence for the client and an uneconomical use of time for the therapist. Group work often quickly relieves clients of their attachment from the seductive charm of their pathology. As others work, people see a variety of solutions to problems that disconcertingly resemble their own.

I prefer to coach, educate, consult with, and assist people rather than assume the therapist role. My clients are less likely to develop dependency and I am less prone to hubris.

JEROME D. FRANK: This is the cornerstone of all psychotherapy. Without a good therapeutic relationship, any procedure will fail; with it, with most patients, probably any procedure will succeed. (That sometimes computerized self-administered programs may be able to alleviate some circumscribed symptoms is probably only apparently an exception since the therapist–patient relationship was involved in setting up the program and the patient's acceptance of it.) The core of the patient–therapist relationship is the therapist's ability to inspire the patient's confidence in him as being competent and concerned with the patient's welfare. Mere acceptance by the therapist for treatment, then, implies that the therapist values him and believes he can be helpful. This in itself boosts the patient's self-esteem, allays anxieties, and inspires hopes, thereby enabling the patient to become more flexible in his thinking and behaving, to face unacceptable aspects of himself, and to try out alternative ways of behaving and feeling. In addition, hope is probably a healing emotion in itself.

The patient's feeling of dependence on the therapist for help provides the latter with the necessary leverage—that is, it is the reason that the patient accepts the therapist's suggestions, formulations, and procedures. A good therapeutic relationship has been likened to the relationship between an appreciative audience and a performer in that the audience encourages the performer to do his best, and even to excel himself. In this sense, a good relationship also provides a suitable soil for personal growth.

I believe, without being able to document it with scientific evidence, that much of the therapeutic power of the therapist lies in aspects of the therapist's personality, the patient's personality, and their fit, which probably cannot be conceptualized in objective terms.

MERTON M. GILL and **IRWIN HOFFMAN**: We believe that the patient–therapist relationship is the central consideration in the process of change. We prefer to speak in terms of patient's experience of the relationship because we want to dispel any implication that what the relationship actually is can be understood without an examination of how the patient experiences it. We realize that an outside observer can come to fairly good guesses as to how the patient is experiencing the relationship, but we believe the test of any such guesses rests finally on the patient's account of the experience.

It is important to realize that all interventions affect the patient's experience of the relationship in ways that often are not recognized by the participants. When such efforts are left unexplored, there is a considerable possibility that the immediate interaction will be a repetition of an old experience or pattern of interaction. The revival of certain of these old patterns sometimes helps to restore psychological equilibrium and the patient's functioning may well improve. Such change may follow upon the patient's feeling reassured, forgiven, admired, or even punished. If the basis for the change is a repetition that is not recognized, the change may be precarious, because whatever disappointment disturbed the patient's functioning originally could very well recur and have the same deleterious effects again.

WALTER KEMPLER: Exactly the same as any other relationship contributes. All of us—therapists, patients, people—change according to what happens or doesn't happen between ourselves and certain *powerful* or *influential* or *significant* others, whichever term you prefer, and regardless of how those others are empowered—through one's love, one's respect, or the others' force. The how, of course, contributes to the character of the changing. The ingredient essential in the changing process from my perspective is the presence of a worthy other: someone to be reckoned with, someone one can empower to measure oneself by or to lay oneself in the hands of, the worthy witness who knows when and how to give a hand or point a finger. How does one become the catalytic worthy other? It happens when I am relevant, that is, when I see the persons in a way they have not seen themselves and yet are able to recognize the validity of my perspective, *and* when I am able to deliver that relevance that touches them in a larger way than logically, cognitively, graspable by reason alone—often called "a moving experience."

The term *catalytic* agent appeals to me, for the actual *therapeutic act* is not what we do. We can only provide the context, the inspiring atmosphere, the inviting pointing. It is what the patient says and/or does as a consequence of our catalytic presence that is the therapeutic act—or change-producing behavior. I contribute (it's all through the therapist–patient relationship) to my patients' changing by saying and/or being, intentionally or fortuitously, just what the others happened to need at that moment in order to make their move.

ARNOLD A. LAZARUS: A good "working relationship" (rapport) is essential. A client who distrusts his or her therapist and/or questions the therapist's competence and abilities is unlikely to derive much benefit. An effective therapist provides responsible guardianship, inspires hope, and enables the client to achieve self-mastery. Role modeling is often an essential part of this constructive process—by selective self-disclosure and judicious guidance, the client is enabled to "try on the therapist's problem-solving strategies" and then to reshape and mold them to fit his or her own personality and style.

Some therapists maintain that relationship factors embody all the necessary conditions for growth and change. Others play down relationship factors and emphasize methods and techniques. Most, however, would seem to agree that relationship variables are important, often crucial, but are generally insufficient to effect long-lasting positive treatment outcomes.

I notice an interesting variability in the type of relationship different clients tend to form. At one extreme are those who regard me as a loving, indispensable, profoundly significant guru (fortunately, I am able to keep these overzealous enthusiasts to a minimum), and at the other end of the continuum are those who desire a pure "business relationship" with a supposedly competent professional. I would say that the majority of my successful clients have tended to like me (rather than love me) and have considered me competent, trustworthy, concerned, and outspoken. Therefore they were willing to implement my suggestions, which provided the necessary reparative actions, the impetus for risk taking, and the cultivation of new experiences.

VICTOR RAIMY: For many years I believed that therapist characteristics such as warmth and acceptance were of the greatest importance in achieving a therapeutic alliance. More recently I have become impressed with the perhaps greater importance of the therapist's ability to demonstrate concretely his ability to help the client with his specific problems. Acceptance and comfort certainly facilitate communication and maintain treatment, but now I believe that "going for the jugular" is even more important then warmth and acceptance. The jugular is that complex of misconceptions that accounts for the client's problems. If the therapist can convincingly assess the client's misconceptions and then demonstrate their relevance to the client, a good therapeutic alliance can be established and maintained in spite of major lacks in warmth and acceptance. Distortions of the principle probably account for the financial success and sometimes the therapeutic successes of the quack and the charlatan.

The rationale for this principle can be illustrated in the work of surgeons, physicians, and dentists, who often inflict considerable pain and discomfort yet remain adored if not loved by their patients. Most patients and clients prefer restoration of health to warmth and acceptance, although in some therapy clients, such demonstrations by an established, admired professional may undermine a debilitating misconception.

Since the jugular is often embedded in an emotionalized morass of defensive and conflicting misconceptions that may take weeks to disentangle, warmth and acceptance are the everyday workhorses needed to cement the therapeutic alliance.

I also find that making salient the relevant misconceptions in transference behaviors can be helpful to the client by demonstrating their influence in the here and now.

JULIAN B. ROTTER: The patient–therapist relationship is crucial to the patient's developing an expectancy that alternative behaviors will be more satisfying, either in the present or in the future. The effectiveness of the therapist in achieving this attitude depends upon (1) the therapist's strength as a reinforcer, (2) the degree to which he or she is thought of as being objective, i.e., not having some personal stake in the person's change, and (3) the degree to which the therapist is perceived as being knowledgeable, wise, and/or skilled. The willingness of clients to accept new ideas, try out what they consider to be risky new behaviors, and give up the hidden satisfactions of maladaptive behaviors is often dependent upon their trust of the therapist and their desire to obtain his/her approval. In group therapy situations, patients may act as each other's therapists and the same principles would hold. It is not necessary that all patients seek the approval or love of the therapist or that all patients consider the therapist wise or that both conditions hold in order to obtain change; but these are clearly very important characteristics of most therapies. Whether it is more important that the patient feel that the therapist is warm, sympathetic, and concerned or that he or she believe that the therapist has a great knowledge of human behavior depends on the patient. Therapeutic change takes place on the basis of a three-way interaction of therapist, method, and patient.

HANS H. STRUPP: Apart from some dramatic exceptions, the patient–therapist relationship is crucial for therapeutic change. This follows from the basic conception that the patient's difficulties and complaints are typically the product of disturbances in earlier relationships. Therefore, the task of psychotherapy is to bring about corrections in the patient's patterns of relatedness by superimposing a new (better) relationship upon internalized earlier ones. The new relationship with the therapist is curative in two ways: (1) it provides a direct experience in living with a mature and understanding adult, and (2) it uses the new experience as a framework within which the kinds of reorganization I spoke of earlier can occur.

In order for a patient to benefit from such an experience, he or she must have had some previous experience with a satisfying human relationship. By the same token, the more deficient, troubled, and destructive the patient's experience with significant others has been the greater will be the difficulties in achieving a corrective experience in psychotherapy. This is the reason therapy often faces an uphill battle, and it defines the limits of what can be achieved in a given period of time. Patients with severely disturbed earlier relationships frequently have great difficulty in forming a good "therapeutic alliance" with the therapist, a *sine qua non* for therapeutic change.

In addition to the foregoing obstacles, a therapeutic relationship is often deficient because of the therapist's shortcomings. Prominent are lack of empathy, understanding, and sensitivity; deficient interest in and commitment to therapeutic work with the patient; exploitative and destructive tendencies, etc. (Hadley and Strupp, 1976). In short, unless the patient can "click" or "hit it off" with the therapist as another human being, limited progress or failure (negative effects) may be expected (Strupp, Hadley, & Gomes-Schwartz, 1977).

4. How Have You Used Language/Cognition/ Awareness in Facilitating Change Within the Therapeutic Setting?

JOHN PAUL BRADY: Most of the therapy I conduct entails the use of language and includes exploring the way the patient sees himself and his world (cognition). However, the manner in which I do this varies vastly from patient to patient. For example, with some it may entail exploring the manner in which the patient interprets his own behavior and that of other people with whom he comes into contact, including exploring the implied assumptions the patient uses in making such an analysis of himself in the world in which he lives. With another patient, it may entail exploring his fears and by the use of language identifying the environmental cues that seem to elicit it. With still another patient, the emphasis may be upon teaching the patient specific skills for coping better with interpersonal and environmental challenges (overcoming shyness, relaxing in situations that provoke maladaptive physical tension, speaking more fluently by pacing his speech, or reducing anxiety that limits his effectiveness by being more assertive in certain kinds of social situations).

GERALD C. DAVISON: *All* therapy with adults is necessarily cognitive in nature. It is inconceivable to consider a therapy that does not rely on the ability of the client (and of the therapist!) to think, to consider things abstractly, to turn things over in one's mind, and so forth.

Now, whether awareness of the historical origins of one's behavior is necessary is a separate matter, and I do not personally believe that this is always necessary. And yet I must confess that I cannot spell out for you under what conditions it is or is not necessary, nor do I believe anybody else can.

In any event, the obvious truth is that outpatient therapy, at least with nonpsychotic individuals (and probably with psychotic people as well), rests utterly on language and cognition.

But your question asks *how* I use language/cognition, and that is a far more difficult question. The best I can do, without resorting to jargon, is to say that one can replicate virtually the entire range of human experience with language employed in the consulting room. The client is assumed to have the capacity to transform the therapist's language into information that has an impact similar to actual experience. But language can do more than experience itself, it seems to me, by permitting more abstract consideration of things. It is as if the client is enabled to turn over a geometric figure resting on a table so as to examine its underside, and how it appears to a person sitting across the table.

PAUL A. DEWALD: As mentioned under question 2, the therapist's verbal interventions are designed to enhance and increase the patient's own awareness in regard to the meanings and patterns of his psychic life and experience, providing a bridge between present and past behaviors as well as a bridge between behavior in the therapeutic setting and behavior outside the treatment situation. Such cognitive awareness serves as a precursor for change, providing insight and recognition, which the patient may then use from the vantage point of his adult self-observing capacities to recognize when behavior is rational and when irrational, and thus it serves as a tool to be used by the patient in gradually modifying subjective as well as objective behavior patterns. Insight and cognitive awareness do not by themselves produce change but become tools used by the patient to promote change.

GERARD EGAN: People usually do not solve problems unless and until they get new perspectives on what they are currently doing. The assumption is that the way they see things now is not helping them handle developmental crises or problems in living. They get these new perspectives in basically two ways—by new behaviors (this was discussed in my response to question 1) and by new insights or new ways of seeing things, that is, through language/cognition/awareness. For me, one of the principal functions of confrontation is precisely this—to help clients develop the awarenesses they lack. This can take place in simple ways, for instance, through information sharing. Some people act in self-defeating ways because they lack certain information. It can also take place in more complex ways through various kinds of challenge, that is, invitations to consider less subjective perspectives that are being overlooked. A number of different therapies provide very useful methodologies in this process of challenging. For instance, I use rational-emotive techniques quite freely to help clients develop new perspectives. I think that script analysis developed within transactional analysis is also a powerful tool for developing new perspectives. In the problem-solving model I use, these techniques are most useful when the client must make choices, that is, when he or she must choose issues to be explored, set goals, choose programs, evaluate the helping process, and determine whether to continue or terminate the process. Language/cognition/awareness procedures in conjunction with various forms of behavioral challenge are especially useful whenever a client gets "stuck" in some way. For instance, some clients lose heart when they are trying to carry out programs to achieve need- or problem-related goals. Language/cognition/awareness techniques at this stage can help them discover the resources within their environments that they need to carry on. These techniques are very useful with people with flagging motivation.

JAMES FADIMAN: Every way I can think of, read about, observe, and practice. My task is to establish, on a trial basis, alternative realities for the client's consideration. I often pose the idea or a situation in which a client's usual patterns will not be adequate or even plausible. The tension between those patterns and the demands of a novel problem force alternative possibilities into consciousness.

I might ask a person to evaluate the Golden Rule, for example, to consider it as a prescription for damaging relationships and demeaning other people. Grappling with this idea allows people to sift rapidly through their knee-jerk morality, their simplistic religious training, their resistance to authority, their capacity for logical thought and perhaps obtain some insight into those behaviors that display self-hatred. Language is the framework, awareness and flexibility the goal.

Language provides me with clues to the nonfunctional portions of a client's belief system. To the extent that a client is stuck, fixated, attached, or neurotic about some beliefs, he or she will benefit from "shocks" or surprises to that part of the system. Language is an ideal carrier for such shocks.

My intention is to reinforce the capacity for change without punishing the need for continuity, for remaining fixated.

JEROME D. FRANK: I try to help patients become more aware of their patterns of behavior and feelings through identifying their antecedents and consequences, and how they express or attempt to cope with motivational states such as anger or fear. It is often useful to relate present behaviors and feelings to earlier ones, or to point out how feelings appropriate to a past situation are reactivated in a contemporary one. It may be particularly useful to view a symptom as a self-perpetuating and self-defeating attempt at communication through which the patient is trying to control the behavior of others without being aware of or taking responsibility for what he is trying to do. Thus the symptom may be an effort to placate another, to win sympathy, or to get the significant other to gratify a patient in other ways.

All these interventions can be seen as in the service of heightening the patient's sense of self-efficacy or mastery through (1) labeling or attributing meaning to subjective states or behavior that had been inexplicable or mysterious, and (2) encouraging the patient to try out the new behaviors toward significant others that follow from the insights he has gained.

MERTON M. GILL and **IRWIN HOFFMAN:** Interpretations designed to promote self-awareness, whether they are addressed to the patient's experience in the therapy situation or to his experience in outside situations, can be useful and lead to change. However, we find that interpretations addressed to the patient's experience of the immediate interaction with the therapist

are likely to have the most impact for several reasons: First, as a participant, the therapist has more intimate knowledge of the immediate interchange; second, what is being examined is also more immediate in the
patient's experience; third, the therapist's attempt to make explicit what
the patient believed was forbidden to speak of directly, in itself, provides
the patient with a new interpersonal experience (see question 1). When the
patient is encouraged to examine his experience of the relationship, including the therapist's immediate influence or impact, he has the opportunity
for a new understanding stimultaneously. For example, in the very process
of discovering, with the therapist's help, what may be the repetition of an
old pattern of behavior in the interaction, he finds himself engaged in an
interaction that is different from any he has experienced before. Thus the
kind of insight that we want to promote is inseparable from the type of new
interpersonal experience that we think is the most powerful facilitator of
change.

WALTER KEMPLER: *Language*—my words come deliberately, carefully, and
quickly—before I can think about them. I use words, thoughts, phrases for
impact, not for understanding, as a rule—in or out of therapy.

Cognition—sometimes offered as a map to provide courage to take the
trip. Also, sometimes when I'm tired and worthless as a therapist and not
quite aware of it, I offer cognitions.

Awareness—I "use" my awareness to shape my witnessing and pointed
reactions. If I believe the other needs encouragement, harshness, clarification, challenge, my silence, my talking—whatever—I tend to become it.
My awareness and its consequent behavior changes from moment to moment, sentence to sentence, and is usually not in consonance with what the
other believes is needed from me at that moment. Through my awareness
and behavior I incite behavior that leads to change; awareness (theirs) may
or may not follow. If it does, it may not correspond with mine and that's as
it should be. Cure comes through what the other does, says, discovers. I
avoid preempting that with direct disclosures of what I am aware of.

On occasion, and as a last resort, I sometimes provide my awareness
and have seen beneficial results. But then it is presented with my personal
reaction—often desperation, helplessness, or vulnerability—and I suspect
it is my candor rather than the content that carries the impact.

ARNOLD A. LAZARUS: I would like to emphasize again that therapeutic
change usually follows methods that are performance based, whereas
purely cognitive or verbal methods are often less effective. Yet to rely
entirely on performance-based methods is to miss the obvious reality that
our cognitions and images stimulate our actions. Our expectations and
anticipations determine our behaviors. Thus misconceptions, false ideals,
gaps in knowledge, and irrational philosophies may require specific

changes in language/cognition/awareness before new instrumental responses (behavior change) can be promoted.

It needs to be underscored that a shift in language/cognition/awareness
often *follows* a behavior change. But the present question seems to be
addressing those instances where a lack of awareness, semantic errors,
and/or irrational ideas lie at the core of a client's problems. In these instances I have found the caveats about "premature interpretations" somewhat misplaced. It is my custom to forge ahead with a didactic repertoire of
procedures aimed at correcting self-talk, disputing faulty notions, remedy-
ing gaps in self-understanding, and promoting a repertoire of social skills.
The art of effective psychotherapy rests heavily one one's ability to convey
these verbal inputs in a manner that permits the client to assimilate and
integrate them. Otherwise, a change in meaning will not necessarily lead to
a change in functioning. In my own therapy, I rely very heavily on the use
of metaphors and analogies that permit me to "speak the client's language"
and thus facilitate the attainment of constructive ends.

VICTOR RAIMY: All of my efforts in therapy employ language in attempting to
discover and modify those client misconceptions that hinder adjustment. This
principle applies to all phases of treatment from the initial effort to modify
whatever misconceptions the client may have about my approach to therapy,
through trying to discover the relevant misconceptions that maintain his
maladaptive behavior, through modification or elimination of misconceptions
to enable him to attain the goals he seeks. Since misconceptions are the end
product of thinking (cognition), they must exist in the client's awareness. I
make no use of unconscious processes as I have not found the construct
helpful. I may, however, agree with a client that some of his motives may be
unconscious in order to avoid intellectual digressions and arguments.

Some form of thinking, which for me includes manipulation of visual
and kinesthetic imagery as well as words, seems to be basic in bringing
about constructive as well as destructive changes in behavior. My primary
efforts are directed toward helping the client discover those end products
of his thinking that interfere with his adjustment to his reality.

The target misconceptions are often entangled in a variety of defensive
misconceptions as well as complex confusion. The very frequently encountered ambivalence toward significant persons illustrates the presence
of conflicting conceptions as well as confusion. The emotion produced by
ambivalence enhances the confusion. Consciousness, verbal sorting out of
the conflicts and the confusion can be facilitated often by providing new
experiences for the client.

JULIAN B. ROTTER: If it is desirable that any changes in behavior or ideation in response to some specific set of stimuli are to be lasting, generalize to other similar stimuli, or represent the start of a "benign cycle"

leading to other behavior changes, then it is clear that all such changes are enhanced by language. This is probably just as much true of relaxation or behavioral shaping procedures as it is of insight therapies. Language enhances generalization.

In psychotherapy based on social learning theory, problem solving plays a special and important role (Rotter, 1978). Such techniques as looking for alternatives, trying to discover the motives and feelings of others, understanding that one can change his or her environments rather than merely being the victim of them, and consciously exploring the long-term effects of specific behaviors are examples of problem-solving attitudes that can provide the client with the potential to deal with new problems outside of the therapy situation. To develop such attitudes on the basis of non-verbalized experience would take both tremendous control of the client's environment and an enormous length of time. Only by language can such problem-solving skills be developed relatively quickly and be resistant to extinction. This principle holds true for children as well as for adults, although the language and the concepts may have to be simplified, depending upon the age and intelligence of the child. Even where relatively little explanation is made by the therapist, if lasting and relatively generalized changes take place, it is probable that the client himself or herself has verbalized new attitudes. Learning that one does not have to experience anxiety at the sight of snakes or high places may be useful to the client, but it is probably the idea that he or she can control his or her own behavior that is more important and produces the most beneficial effects. It is through language that a patient can become willing to try out new behaviors and persist through painful therapy because the rewards of the effort have been verbalized by the therapist or the client himself or herself.

Behavioral techniques can often be of considerable use as part of a therapeutic regime. But it is likely that their major value is not in establishing new conditioned responses but in establishing new cognitions.

HANS H. STRUPP: I view the good therapist as an exquisitely sensitive and refined clinical instrument whose major contribution to therapeutic change, apart from the not inconsiderable ability to mediate a good interpersonal experience, consists of his or her skill in being keenly attuned to the inner struggles of another human being. The therapist resonates to the patient's experience and places his or her own reactions (associations, fantasies, affects, comparable experience, clinical acumen) in the service of the therapeutic task. The creative use of language is the major vehicle by which the therapist assists in the production of structural change. The therapist's efforts at understanding are often groping and imperfect.

A brief example may serve as an illustration: The patient, a young woman suffering from a fairly severe borderline condition who had been seen in long-term therapy, displayed morose affect during the hour, complained of being used, exploited, and criticized by her boss, and eventually communicated in highly indirect ways that she had similar feelings toward me. In a preceding hour she had expressed the wish for my vacation to start soon (I had announced earlier my plan to take a brief vacation). Seeing herself as the victim of an impending separation (= rejection), she experienced herself as dependent and needy but also as wishing to be needed and exploited. While the parallel to a comparable experience with her father was clear, she rejected my attempt at interpreting her current experience in the context of the earlier one. However, she was unable to deny her anger and resentment at me—these were empirical data we could both see. It was also clear to her that I had not been exploiting her and that she had distorted her present experience with me in terms of constructions she had unwittingly placed on it. By pointing out these facts to her, I believe I was able to accomplish a piece of therapeutic work. This was made possible by (1) our basically good relationship, (2) her enactment of a previous experience in the presence of affect, (3) the presence of incontrovertible data we could both see, and (4) her willingness to listen and be confronted, albeit in a painful way, with facts that demanded a reorganization of her cognitions and emotional reactions.

5. What Clinical Strategies or Principles of Change Do You Believe to Be Common Across All Therapeutic Orientations?

JOHN PAUL BRADY: It is difficult to generalize about this because no clinical principle seems applicable to all treatment situations. Nevertheless, one might generalize about the following strategies and principles:

1. Development of a therapist–patient relationship, characterized by trust, mutual respect, and positive emotional feelings.
2. Procedures and strategies that will increase the patient's expectation of a positive outcome or benefit from the treatment program.
3. Strategies and procedures that will increase the patient's sense of self-worth, mastery of his environment, and general effectiveness.
4. Related to the above, tactics and strategies that will in fact make the patient more effective in handling certain situations and in overcoming maladaptive fears and help him act in a manner or engage in behaviors that, in his own view and that of others, make him a worthwhile, effective person. This may sound circular but it is an important point. For example, a stutterer will generally speak more

fluently if he has more confidence in his ability to communicate effectively. Thus part of the treatment is in fact to improve his fluency rate by whatever means possible. However, it is important that he recognize the increase in fluency as evidence of his greater interpersonal effectiveness. This perception and awareness will further increase his fluency and motivation to change. Thus there is a synergistic effect between actual improved performance in real-life situations and the increase in sense of effectiveness and self-worth.

5. New ways of behaving, thinking, and feeling in therapy, whether through simple discussion, role playing, or the like, need to be practiced in the natural environment to ensure their persistence and generalization, with details of these experiences being brought back to the therapist.

6. The patient should be encouraged to view his behavior, thought, and feelings as ultimately under his own control and must assume responsibility for change in treatment.

GERALD C. DAVISON: A time-honored truth is that much of human behavior is a function of its consequences. While I hardly adhere to the belief that *all* behavior is regulated in this fashion, it seems to be obvious that at least some behavior is sensitive to its payoff in the envronment, or the environment as construed by the client.

I believe also that all therapies—at least sensible ones—help clients introspect about how they *feel* about things, often beyond what is obvious. Therapy, then, requires a fair amount of interference by the therapist and considerable skill in getting the client in touch with affect that is not normally attended to. The Gestalt therapists are at one end of this continuum, behavior therapists using something like systematic desensitization at the other. It is in this way that I myself use "insight."

Another strategy is the "Try it, you'll like it" intervention. The therapist is like a salesperson in a clothing store, encouraging the customer to try things on for size, even if the color and material do not seem right. Clients must be encouraged to attempt something they may never have before considered for themselves, to see how it feels, to consider what benefits and risks it holds for them.

I believe also in the importance of placebo, suggestion. People in pain are usually open to social influence and to having their expectations directed by the therapist.

Finally, it is my abiding belief that therapy overall is a moral enterprise, that we are society's secular priests, that we basically offer clients a philosophy of life, a set of biases not amenable to empircal test. Most of the time we do so unwittingly, which is dangerous and, I believe, in itself unethical.

PAUL A. DEWALD: In a previous paper (Dewald, 1976) I described 10 principles or strategies by which various therapeutic orientations could be compared. Each of the different therapeutic orientations uses these components in its own way, and I see no common strategy that is equally applicable to all forms of therapy.

Even if one looks at this question from such broad vantage points as the therapist's personality or the therapist's faith in his own treatment methods, there are still patients within each of the therapeutic orientations whose responses to treatment are highly variable both within a particular therapeutic orientation and across such orientations.

At the most general level of all might be existence of a relationship between patient and therapist as the setting within which therapeutic change occurs. However, the nature of this relationship and the way in which it is used is highly variable among different therapeutic orientations, and I can see no clinical strategies or principles in this area that unite all therapeutic orientations.

GERARD EGAN: I believe that when any therapist of any orientation is successful, she or he uses, knowingly or unknowingly, a substantial number of principles found in a full problem-soving paradigm. I do not consider something as basic as problem solving as a "therapeutic orientation." But I do see it as a tool for organizing the principles and techniques used in all therapeutic endeavors.

Good therapists, since they are also good problem-solvers or good consultants to those with problems:

- Establish decent, nondependent relationships with clients.

- Help clients explore problems, needs, wants, conflicts, developmental tasks.

- Help clients see which issues are most critical and set priorities.

- Challenge clients to develop new perspectives through discussion and action.

- Help clients set up realistic, behavioral goals related to presenting needs.

- Help clients take a census of possible programs for achieving each goal.

- Help clients choose programs best fitted to their own style and needs.

- Support and challenge clients to invest themselves in chosen programs.

- Help clients find resources "out there" to do all the above.

- Help clients in an ongoing way deal with the three principal evaluation questions:
     Are you investing yourself realistically in goal-related programs?
     Are the programs helping you achieve the goals you set?
     Does achieving the goal or goals take care of the presenting need or problem?

Good therapists provide support and challenge for this entire process. They also realize that the process is not necessarily as linear as presented here. As consultants, they help clients move back and forth in this model in ways that are most in keeping with individual needs.

Finally, good therapists help clients make sense out of and deal with the multiple systems of their lives and the developmental tasks that are worked out in the context of these systems.

JAMES FADIMAN:

1. Change is possible.
2. Change is more likely with support.
3. Support is easily offered, difficult to accept.
4. Therapists derive pleasure, even joy, from seeing people change.
5. We all have unfulfilled needs for omnipotence and unconditional love. These needs carry therapists of all persuasions through the boring, difficult, and repetitive times in therapy.
6. Therapists care. It disturbs each of us that people suffer excessively. Even the most mechanistic or messianic therapist hopes that every individual can be helped; that suffering can be lessened, pain reduced, satisfaction increased, and ignorance dissipated.
7. There is an urge, or a drive, toward health, awareness, wholeness, certainty in each of us. It is this drive that facilitates and underlies the success of all therapeutic interventions.
8. Along with the dogmatism and foolishness that permeate every school of psychotherapy, there is a core of humility that allows learning. Any realistic therapist knows that the tools are imperfect, the theories tentative, and the results ambiguous.
9. It is a difficult, distressing, demanding, and meaningful occupation with considerable opportunity for improvement.

JEROME D. FRANK: The common principles of change include:

1. Inspiring the patient's hopes, which may be healing in itself and also encourages the patient to explore him- or herself and enter situations he or she has previously avoided out of fear, and to try out new ways of dealing with problems.
2. Providing new occasions for both cognitive and experiential learning.
3. Arousing the patient emotionally, which seems to facilitate patients' susceptibility to the therapist's interventions.
4. Heightening the patient's self-esteem and sense of mastery through attributing meaning to previously inexplicable experiences in terms of a coherent conceptual framework and providing experiences of success.

Most therapies may also "extinguish" dysphoric emotions by allowing the patient to experience them repeatedly in a nonreinforcing or actively supportive context.

MERTON M. GILL and **IRWIN HOFFMAN**: A good relationship is probably a common factor in all successful therapy, whatever the orientation. The therapist must inspire trust, at least enough so that the patient can invest and actively participate in whatever therapy is attempted. When therapy promotes new development rather than merely restoring previous states of equilibrium, it undoubtedly is associated with new experience occurring either in the context of the therapy relationship itself or in the context of outside situations. New awareness or insight may also be inevitable, at least to the extent that the patient realizes that his old ways of responding are not absolutely necessary and that new alternatives are possible and within reach.

Therapy can be extraordinarily powerful when the three factors mentioned—a good relationship, new experience, and new awareness or insight—are integrated into a single process. This integration can be approached when the therapist and the patient work collaboratively to explore the patient's experience of the relationship. However, even then, there is an inevitable greater or lesser residue of inadvertent interpersonal effects that escape detection and examination.

WALTER KEMPLER: The desire to be of value to another crosses all therapeutic orientations. But what is inherent in all people is neither a strategy nor really a private principle of therapy.

The principle of engaging, of moving toward or in relation to another, is the essential principle in common—essential because it is only in the context of one another that the possibility for change can live.

The most common strategy in common, unfortunately, is the attempt to be more than one is through the use of tactics, techniques, and strategies.

ARNOLD A. LAZARUS: Given the proliferation of several esoteric and radical departures from traditional psychotherapy, is it nevertheless possible to identify unifying constructs or methods that hold true for *all* therapeutic orientations? Perhaps in a generic sense one can refer to the existence of a viable relationship, even if the relationship is between client and computer. But one element that necessarily transcends all treatment boundaries is the presence of *hope*. Presumably, the analysand who spends years on a psychoanalyst's couch has the hope and expectation that benefits will ensue, just as those who follow the ministrations of Gestalt therapists, behavior modifiers, bioenergetic analysts, rational-emotive therapists, transactional analysts, or whatever, have optimistic beliefs about their therapeutic potential.

VICTOR RAIMY: I suspect that there are four primary principles for producing change that are common across all therapeutic orientations:

1. The therapist's ability to facilitate communication with the client.
2. The development of a therapeutic alliance.
3. The discovery in some fashion of the client's relevant misconceptions.
4. The changing of these misconceptions in some fashion.

Facilitating communication seems to be the *sine qua non* of all therapies ranging from the behavioral through the psychoanalytic.

The therapeutic alliance is necessary to motivate the client to work on his problems, whatever the methods employed, as well as to bind the client to the therapist to ensure his remaining in treatment. The therapeutic alliance is produced by some mix of the therapist's personal characteristics plus his ability to convince the client that he understands his specific problems and can help him.

Misconceptions can be "discovered" in many ways, ranging from behavioral and Gestalt techniques, which concentrate upon the immediate present, to psychoanalytic techniques, which under optimal conditions can trace the same patterns from early life to the present. Inappropriate emotional reactions are excellent clues to significant misconceptions. The same misconception can be made manifest to the client experientially, in the terminology of a particular approach, or in everyday, commonsense language.

Since misconceptions are "ideas" or "conceptions," they can be modified or changed by all the methods that change ideas—by logical explanation, by encouraging the client to examine his own ideas critically, by having the client demonstrate errors in his thinking through contrived or natural experiences, and sometimes by modeling relevant behaviors. Different therapies use different techniques to the same end.

JULIAN B. ROTTER: The variety of techniques that presume to be psychologically therapeutic is indeed great. They range from mediation to constant activity, from anxiety-enhancing to anxiety-reducing, from "deep" insight to massage. It is not clear that anything is common to all of these methods. However, there are a few things that seem to be true of successful therapy regardless of the method employed. One of these is that increasing the patient's belief that he or she will get better, that he or she will be able to achieve a more satisfying adjustment by doing what is required in the therapy, is related to successful outcome. Consequently, it is probably true that in all therapies the therapist either overtly or subtly uses techniques to increase the patient's expectancies for improvement.

It is also true that in most therapies the therapist's caring attitude and acceptance of the patient as a worthwhile person is an important variable. Such behavior is probably necessary in order to build up the therapist's reinforcement value for the patient and to get the patient to try out new behaviors, consider new ideas, take risks, and expend effort, It also is valuable in maintaining persistence of patients over periods when they do not perceive any positive change taking place.

Of course, from a social learning point of view, what all therapies have in common is that they result in changes in expectancies and reinforcement values and, consequently, changes in behavior potentials. However, the variety of techniques used to accomplish this is extremely diverse.

HANS H. STRUPP: I view all forms of psychotherapy as varieties of interpersonal experiences that promote learning (structural change). For such experiences to be successful there must be (1) a therapist (or a group) who is willing and able to provide such an experience and (2) a patient who is willing and able to profit from it. Obstacles to therapeutic change derive from deficiencies in any aspects of the foregoing specification.

The goal of therapy is to help the patient to think, feel, and act differently. The objective can be reached in many different ways, and I question seriously whether there can be a single technique or set of techniques useful to all patients. Instead, what a particular patient can use is highly idiosyncratic; in other words, psychotherapy must always be tailored to the needs of the individual patient and his or her capacity to profit from it. It is difficult if not impossible to write prescriptions for a meaningful interpersonal learning experience, but the following ingredients seem essential:

1. The therapist must be experienced as genuinely interested in the patient as a person and committed to helping him or her.
2. The "lessons" mediated by the therapist must be experienced by the patient as meaningful and helpful. In the process, the patient must have a consistent experience of mastery and success.

3. Psychotherapeutic learning can occur only in the present; thus the patient's *current* transactions with the therapist are of crucial significance.

4. Since maladaptive learning that brings patients to psychotherapy is typically associated with painful earlier experiences that have not been properly mastered and integrated, psychotherapy must be aimed at helping the patient with this task. A corollary of this proposition is that resistances the patient places in the path of therapeutic learning must be systematically confronted and resolved.

Editorial Comment

We are indeed fortunate to have been able to obtain the pooled knowledge and insights from such a group of prominent leaders in the field. Their responses to these several questions clearly provide us with an important step toward obtaining a consensus on clinical principles of change. We hope that further efforts toward this goal will involve ongoing and more direct dialogues among representatives of varying theoretical viewpoints, conducted within a context of cooperative collaboration. And while no attempt will be made here to offer a comprehensive analysis of the material provided by our respondents, a few comments will be offered to highlight some of the more obvious themes that seem to have emerged.

To begin with, one is struck by the very strong emphasis placed on the importance of new experiences in the therapeutic change process, which was referred to as "critical," "crucial," "essential," "basic," and the like. These new experiences have been observed to occur in the relationship between patient/client and therapist, as well as outside of the therapeutic session. Such experiences, according to our respondents, can have the effect of creating changes in the clients' perspective, both toward themselves and toward others. Language was viewed as an important vehicle for facilitating such new perspectives, especially by conjuring up and helping to tie together relevant experiences. It was also noted that a patient's/client's changing perspectives can at times be supplemented by the therapist's feedback. In this regard, several of the respondents reminded us that therapists need to be ever alert to the possibility that their own biases may color such feedback attempts. The therapeutic interaction was also referred to a being "crucial" or "central" to the change process, as it provides patients/clients with a relationship in which they can obtain a new awareness or perspective, a setting in which they can experience a new way of relating to another peson, and a place where they may be encouraged to relate differently to others in their current life situation. Also emphasized was the importance of a caring, trustworthy, and confident attitude by the therapist, who encourages patients/clients to become more autonomous and to experience a greater sense of self-mastery.

In any attempt to outline common themes, we ultimately need to look directly at what clinicians from various orientations actually do, with an eye toward detecting themes that get at a level of abstraction encompassing the diverse techniques one is likely to encounter in the clinical situation. In trying to specify what actually "works" clinically, we need to continually guard against the danger of our theory and research becoming too far removed from the clinical foundations of our generalizations.

Since the relevance of any clinical principle will depend on the particular case at hand, any future dialogues and observations should revolve around the search for common themes that exist in dealing with specific clinical problems (e.g., fears, depression, various addictions, sexual problems). What can emerge from such efforts would be the generation of hypotheses that can serve as the basis for a program of clinically meaningful research. Speaking as a behavior therapist interested in both clinical practice and therapy research, I believe that this is clearly a direction in which we need to go.

M.R.G.

References

Dewald, P. A. Toward a general concept of the therapeutic process. *International Journal of Psychoanalytic Psychotherapy*, 1976, *5*, 283–299.

Hadley, S. W., & Strupp, H. H. Contemporary views of negative effects in psychotherapy: An integrated account. *Archives of General Psychiatry*, 1976, *33*, 1291–1302.

Rotter, J. B. *Social learning and clinical psychology*. Englewood Cliffs, N.J.: Prentice Hall, 1954.

Rotter, J. B. Generalized expectancies for problem solving and psychotherapy. *Cognitive Therapy and Research*, 1978, *2*, 1–10.

Rotter, J. B., Chance, J., & Phares, E. J. (Eds.). *Applications of a social learning theory on personality*. New York: Holt, Rinehart, & Winston, 1972.

Strupp, H. H., Hadley, S. W. & Gomes-Schwartz, B. *Psychotherapy for better or worse: An analysis of the problem of negative effects*. New York: Jason Aronson: 1977.

Part V
Psychodynamic, Behavioral, and Humanistic Therapists Look at Other Approaches

In the process of looking for common features that are shared across all therapeutic orientations, it would be an error to conclude that all therapists "do the same thing." While there is much to be gained in searching for common principles of change, this in no way denies the likelihood that each orientation might offer a unique, if not complementary contribution. Indeed, by providing converging perspectives on the same clinical phenomena, we may be able to build into our therapeutic practices a more comprehensive intervention approach. The complementary nature of different therapeutic orientations is illustrated by the articles in this section. These selections represent the need to look at other approaches as presented from a psychodynamic vantage point (Marmor; Wachtel), from a behavioral point of view (Birk & Brinkley-Birk; Brady), and from a humanistic orientation (Ricks, Wandersman, & Poppen; Landsman). Each of these articles vividly illustrates the manner in which therapists from each of the three major orientations perceive the need to expand their own limited perspectives on clinical problems.

Chapter 12

Dynamic Psychotherapy and Behavior Therapy: Are They Irreconcilable?

Judd Marmor

In the course of psychiatric training and practice our professional identities become so intimately linked to what we have learned and how we practice that we are prone to extol uncritically the virtues of our own techniques and to depreciate defensively those techniques that are different. The dialogue that has gone on between most behavior therapists and dynamic psychotherapists has been marred by this kind of bias, and claims as well as attacks have been made on both sides that are exaggerated and untenable. Science is not served by such emotional polemics but rather by objective efforts to evaluate and extend our knowledge.

Part of the confusion that exists in discussing these two basic approaches to therapy is that they are often dealt with as though each group represents a distinct entity when, in fact, they are anything but monolithic. The various schools of thought among dynamic psychotherapists are too well known to require elaboration. They cover a wide range from classical

An earlier version of this paper was read before the Temple University Conference on Dynamic Psychotherapy and Behavior Therapy, Philadelphia, March 6, 1969.

Freudians, to adherents of other major theorists, to eclectics who borrow from all of them, to still others who try to adapt their concepts to correspond with modern learning theories, information theory, game theory, or general systems theory.

What is less well known is that among behavior therapists also there is a broad range of differences, from adherents of Pavlov and Hull, to Skinnerians, to eclectics, and to those who lean toward information theory and general systems theory. At one end of each spectrum the theories of behavioral and dynamic psychotherapists tend to converge, while at the other end their divergence is very great. It is because adherents of these two approaches tend to define each other stereotypically in terms of their extremes that so much misunderstanding and heat are often generated between them.

It would further serve to clarify the discussion of this problem if we distinguish between investigative methods, therapeutic techniques, and theoretical formulations. A good investigative technique is not necessarily a good therapeutic technique, nor is the reverse true. By the same token, as we have long known, the success of a psychotherapeutic method for any particular condition does not in itself constitute a validation of its theoretical framework; indeed, exactly why and how any particular psychotherapeutic method works and what it actually accomplishes within the complex organization of drives, perception, integration, affect, and behavior that we call personality is itself a major research challenge.

In the remarks that follow, therefore, I shall not concern myself with the knotty issues of the comparison of results between behavior and psychodynamic therapies or of their validation. The problem of how to measure or evaluate psychotherapeutic change is still far from clear and a matter for much-needed research. Moreover, comparisons of results between these two approaches are unsatisfactory because different criteria of efficacy are applied, and different techniques of investigation are employed, even if complete objectivity on the part of the various protagonists could be assumed—which is doubtful!

In addition, I shall not get into the oft-argued issue of whether or not simple symptom removal inevitably leads to symptom substitution. Long before behavior therapists began to question this hoary assumption, hypnotherapists had presented evidence that symptom substitution did not always take place when a symptom was removed by hypnosis (Wolberg, 1955). Indeed, I would agree, on purely theoretical grounds, that symptom substitution is *not* inevitable. Earlier psychoanalytic assumptions concerning symptom substitution were based on what we now know was an erroneous closed-system theory of personality dynamics. If the conflictual elements involved in neurosis formation are assumed to be part of a closed system, it follows logically that removal of the symptomatic consequences of such an inner conflict without altering the underlying dynamics should result in some other symptom manifestation. If, however, personality dynamics are more correctly perceived within the framework of an open system, then such a consequence is not inevitable. Removal of an ego-dystonic symptom may, on the contrary, produce satisfying feedback from the environment that may result in major constructive shifts within the personality system, thus leading to modification of the original conflictual pattern. Removal of a symptom also may lead to positive changes in the perception of the self, with resultant satisfying *internal* feedbacks, heightening of self-esteem, and a consequent restructuring of the internal psychodynamic system.

Psychodynamic theorists have been aware of this possibility for many years, dating back at least to 1946 when Alexander and French published their book entitled *Psychoanalytic Therapy*. In this volume a number of cases of brief psychotherapy are described, some of them involving only one to three interviews, following which the patients were not only dramatically relieved of their presenting symptoms but were then able to go on to achieve more effective adaptive patterns of functioning than they had previously displayed. In the years that followed this important publication, dynamic psychotherapists have become increasingly involved with techniques of brief psychotherapy and of crisis intervention, with a growing body of evidence that in many instances such interventions can have long-lasting positive consequences for personality integration.

Where I part company with most behavior therapists is not in questioning their therapeutic claims—although I would offer the caution that many of them are repeating the error of the early psychoanalysts of promising more than they can deliver—but in what I consider to be their oversimplified explanations of what goes on in the therapeutic transaction between patient and therapist. The explanations to which I refer are those which assume that the essential and central core of their therapeutic process rests on Pavlovian or Skinnerian conditioning and, incidentally, is therefore more "scientific" than the traditional psychotherapies. With these formulations often goes a conception of neurosis that seems to me to be quite simplistic. Thus, according to Eysenck, "Learning theory [note that he uses the singular—actually there are many theories of learning] regards neurotic symptoms as simply learned habits; there is no *neurosis* underlying the symptom but merely the symptom itself. *Get rid of the symptom and you have eliminated the neurosis.*" (Eysenck, 1960). Such an explanation is like evaluating the contents of a package in terms of its wrapping and represents a regrettable retrogression from the more sophisticated thinking that has begun to characterize dynamic psychiatry in recent years—an approach that recognizes that "psychopathology" does not reside solely in the individual but also has significant roots in his system of relationships with his milieu and with other persons within his milieu. Hence the growing emphasis on family therapy, on conjoint marital therapy, on group therapy, and on dealing with the disordered socioeconomic conditions which constitute the matrix of so many personality disorders. To see the locus of psychopathology only in the individual leads to an emphasis on techniques of adjusting the individual to his environment regardless of how distorted, intolerable, or irrational that environment might be. Such an emphasis brings us uncomfortably close to the dangerous area of thought and behavior control.

However, I do not wish to overemphasize this ethical issue. The fact that a technical method may lend itself to being misused does not constitute an argument against its scientific validity. My major point is that the *theoretical* foundation of Eysenck's formulation is scientifically unsound. Even if we deliberately choose to restrict our focus only to what goes on within the individual himself, the Eysenckian point of view has profound limitations. It overlooks all of the complexities of thought, symbolism, and action which must be accounted for in any comprehensive theory of psychology and psychopathology. To assume that what goes on subjectively within the patient is irrelevant and that all that matters is how he behaves is to arbitrarily disregard all of the significant psychodynamic insights of the past 75 years. In saying this, I am not defending all of psychoanalytic theory. I have been as critical as anyone of certain aspects of classical Freudian theory and I am in full accord with those who argue that psychodynamic theory needs to be reformulated in terms that conform more closely to modern theories of learning and of neurophysiology. Current researches strongly suggest that the brain functions as an extremely intricate receiver, retriever, processor, and dispatcher of information. A stimulus–response theory of human behavior does not begin to do justice to this complex process. It is precisely what goes on in the "black box" *between* stimulus and response that is the central challenge of psychiatry, and no theory that ignores the complexities of the central processes within that "black box" can be considered an adequate one. It is to Freud's eternal credit, regardless of the limitations of some of his hypotheses, that he was the first to develop a rational investigative technique for, and a meaningful key to, the understanding of this uncharted realm that exerts so profound an influence on both our perceptions and our responses.

Evidence from learning theories themselves reveals that neurotic disorders are not necessarily the simple product of exposure to traumatic conditioning stimuli or to the operant conditioning of responses. The work of Pavlov, Liddell, Masserman, and others has clearly demonstrated that neurotic symptoms can ensue when an animal is faced with incompatible choices between simultaneous approach and avoidance reactions, or with confusing conditioned stimuli which it is unable to differentiate clearly.

This corresponds to the psychodynamic concept of conflict as being at the root of the vast majority of human neurotic disorders. Once such a neurotic conflict is set up in a human being, secondary elaborations, defensive adaptations, and symbolic distortions may become extensively and indirectly intertwined with almost every aspect of the individual's perceptual, cognitive, and behavioral process.

A behavioral approach alone cannot encompass these complexities. Granting that Skinnerians include verbal speech as an aspect of behavior that may require modification, what shall we say about subjective *fantasies*, concealed *thoughts*, and hidden *feelings?* Are they totally irrelevant? What about problems involving conflicts in value systems, disturbances in self-image, diffusion of identity, feelings of anomie, or even concealed delusions and hallucinations? Are they less important than specific symptom entities of a behavioral nature? No comprehensive theory of psychopathology or of the nature of the psychotherapeutic process can properly ignore these aspects of man's subjective life.

To illustrate my point that much more goes on between therapist and patient than most behavior therapists generally recognize, I should like now to briefly focus on three contrasting behavioral therapeutic approaches: (1) Wolpe's technique of reciprocal inhibition, (2) aversive conditioning treatment of homosexuality, and (3) the Masters and Johnson technique of treating sexual impotence and frigidity. In discussing these three approaches, I wish to emphasize that it is not my intention to denigrate their usefulness as therapeutic modalities or to question their results, but solely to present some of the diverse variables that I believe are involved in their therapeutic effectiveness.

Wolpe has elaborated his technique in many publications as well as in at least one film that I have seen. Although he considers the crux of his technique to be the development of a hierarchical list of graded anxieties which are then progressively dealt with by his technique of "reciprocal inhibition," the fact is that a great deal more than this takes place in the patient–therapist transaction in the Wolpe technique. Most significantly, in the orientation period of the first session or two the patient is not only informed of the treatment method per se, but also of the fact that it has yielded successful results with comparable patients, and it is indicated implicitly, if not explicitly, that the patient can expect similar success for himself if he is cooperative. Wolpe, moreover, is warm, friendly, and supportive. At the same time he is positive and authoritative in such a way as to reinforce the patient's expectations of therapeutic success. During this introductory period a detailed history is taken and even though the major emphasis is on the symptom with all of its manifestations and conditions for appearance, a detailed genetic history of personality development is usually taken also.

Following this a hierarchical list of the patient's anxieties is established. The patient is then taught a relaxation technique which is remarkably similar to what is traditionally employed in inducing hypnosis. After complete relaxation is achieved, the patient is instructed to create in fantasy these situations of graded anxiety beginning at the lowest level of anxiety, and is not permitted to go to the next level until he signals that he is completely relaxed. This procedure is repeated over and over again in anywhere from 12 to 60 or more sessions until the patient is able to fantasize the maximally phobic situation and still achieve muscular relaxation. Throughout this procedure the patient receives the strong implication, either explicitly or implicitly, that this procedure will cause his symptoms to disappear.

Wolpe attributes the success of his technique to "systematic desensitization" and explains it on the basis of Pavlovian counterconditioning. He asserts that any "activities that might give any grounds for imputations of transference, insight, suggestion, or de-depression," are either "omitted or manipulated in such a way as to render the operation of these mechanisms exceedingly implausible." (Wolpe, 1958). This kind of claim that Wolpe repeatedly makes in his writings clearly reflects his failure to appreciate the complexity of the variables involved in the patient–therapist transaction. I cannot believe that anyone who watches Wolpe's own film demonstration of his technique would agree that there are no elements of transference, insight, or suggestion in it. Indeed, one could make as plausible a case for the overriding influence of suggestion in his technique as for the influence of desensitization. In saying this I am not being pejorative about Wolpe's technique. Suggestion, in my opinion, is an integral part of every psychotherapeutic technique, behavioral or psychodynamic. It need not be overt; indeed, it probably works most potently when it is covert. Suggestion is a complex process in which elements of transference, expectancy, faith, and hope all enter. To the degree that a patient is receptive and perceives the therapist as a powerful help-giving figure, he is more likely to accept the suggestions he is being given and to try to conform to them. This process is most obvious in hypnosis but it is equally present in all psychotherapeutic techniques, where the suggestion is usually more covert. Wolpe's technique abounds in covert as well as overt suggestion. It is questionable, moreover, whether the fantasies that Wolpe has his patients create are actual substitutes for the phobic reality situations, as he would have us believe. It may well be that what is really taking place is not so much desensitization to specific stimuli, as repeated reassurance and strong systematic suggestion, within a setting of heightened expectancy and faith.

However, even the combination of *desensitization* (assuming that it is taking place) and *suggestion* do not begin to cover all the elements that are present in the Wolpe method. There is also the *direct transmission of values* as when Wolpe says to a young patient, "You must learn to stand up for yourself." According to Ullmann and Krasner (1965), Wolpe hypothesizes that if a person can assert himself, anxiety will automatically be inhibited. (Parenthetically, one might question whether this is inevitably so. One frequently sees patients who assert themselves regularly, but always with enormous concomitant anxiety.) In any event, Ullmann and Krasner say: "The therapist provides the motivation by pointing out the irrationality of the fears and encouraging the individual to insist on his legitimate human rights" (Ullmann & Krasner, 1965). Obviously this is not very different from what goes on in dynamic psychotherapy and it is not rendered different by virtue of the fact, according to Ullmann and Krasner, that it is "given a physiological basis by Wolpe who refers to it as excitatory" (Ullmann & Krasner, 1965). Still another variable which cannot be ignored is Wolpe's manner, which, whether he realizes it or not, undoubtedly facilitates a "positive transference" in his patients. In his film he is not only kindly and empathic to his female patient, but occasionally reassuringly touches her. Does Wolpe really believe that a programmed computer repeating his instructions to a patient who had had no prior contact with the doctor himself would achieve the identical therapeutic results?

The second behavioral technique that I would like to consider briefly is that of the aversion treatment of homosexuals. I had occasion to explore this technique some time ago with Dr. Lee Birk, of the Massachusetts Mental Health Center, who was kind enough to demonstrate his technique and go over his results with me.

Dr. Birk's method is based on the anticipatory avoidance conditioning technique introduced by Feldman and MacCulloch (1965). The patient is seated in a chair in front of a screen with an electrode cuff attached to his leg. The method involves the use of patient-selected nude and semi-nude male and female pictures which are flashed onto the screen. The male pictures (and presumably the fantasies associated with them) become aversive stimuli by linkage with electric shocks which are administered to the leg whenever these pictures appear on the screen. On the other hand, the female pictures become discriminative stimuli signaling safety, relief, and protection from the schocks.

In Dr. Birk's hands, as in others, the use of this method has apparently produced a striking reversal of sexual feelings and behavior in more than one half of the male homosexuals so treated. On the face of it, this would seem to be the result of a relatively simple negative conditioning process to aversive "male" stimuli, with concomitant positive conditioning to "female" stimuli.

Closer inspection will reveal, however, that the process is considerably more complex. I wonder whether most psychiatrists realize what is actually involved in such aversive conditioning. I know that I, for one, did not, until I asked Dr. Birk to permit me to experience the kind of shock that he administered to his patients—the least intense, incidentally, of the graded series that he employed. I can only say that if that was a "mild" shock, I never want to be subjected to a "severe" one! I do not have a particularly low threshold for pain, but it was a severe and painful jolt—much more than I had anticipated—and it made me acutely aware of *how strongly motivated toward change a male homosexual would have to be to subject himself to a series of such shocks visit after visit.*

The significance of this variable cannot be ignored. Once it is recognized, the results of aversive therapy, although still notable, become less remarkable. The fact is that if other forms of psychotherapy were limited only to such a select group of exceptionally motivated homosexuals, the results also would be better than average. Although one might assume that in dynamic psychotherapies the cost of therapy in itself should insure equally good motivation, this is not always the fact. Costs of therapy may not be sacrificial, or they may be borne or shared by others, but no one else can share the pain involved in the aversive conditioning process.

Again, then, it becomes clear that we are dealing with something that is much more complicated than a simple conditioning process. The patient's intense wish to change, and his faith and expectation that this very special technique will work for him—as the doctor himself implicitly or explicitly suggests—are important factors in the total therapeutic gestalt of this aversive technique, as they are in successful dynamic psychotherapies also.

But more than this, the transference-countertransference transaction between therapist and subject is also of paramount importance. Dr. Birk communicated two interesting experiences he had which underline this point. Two of his subjects who had had very favorable responses to the "conditioning" procedure suffered serious relapses immediately after becoming angry at him. The first patient became upset because of what he considered a breach in the privacy of his treatment. Before this, he had not only been free from homosexual contacts for the first time in many years, but also of conscious homosexual urges. When he became angry, he immediately went and sought out a homosexual partner because he wanted to see "how really good" the treatment was. Dr. Birk was aware that his patient obviously wanted to show him up and prove that the treatment was no good. Although the patient remained improved as compared to his previous homosexual behavior, *he was never again,* despite many more conditioning treatments, completely free from conscious homosexual urges and continued to act them out although less frequently than in the past. The second patient became angry with Dr. Birk because he concluded that the therapist seemed to be more interested in the results he was obtaining than he was in the patient as a person. Immediately after expressing this irritation the patient regressed to a series of homosexual encounters.

These striking examples illustrate that a simple conditioning explanation does not fit the complex process that goes on in such techniques of therapy. Aversive conditioning that has been solidly established would not be expected to disappear on the basis of such experiences unless there is something that goes on centrally in the patient that is a very important factor in the therapeutic modifications achieved. A basic aspect of this central process is in the patient–physician interpersonal relationship and it cannot and must not be ignored even in behavior therapies. I have recently encountered a number of instances where patients who were referred to behavior therapists failed to return to them after the initial sessions because the behavior therapists involved ignored this essential factor and related to the patients as though they were dealing with experimental animals.

Let us now turn to a consideration of the Masters and Johnson (1965) technique of treating disorders of sexual potency. In many ways this technique falls midway between a behavioral and a psychodynamic approach and illustrates one of the ways in which a fusion of both can be successfully employed. The Masters and Johnson technique is behavioral in the sense that it is essentially symptom-focused, and that one of its most important technical tools is desensitization of the performance anxieties of the patients.

Conceptually, however, the Masters and Johnson approach to their patients goes considerably beyond simple conditioning or desensitization processes. For one thing, Masters and Johnson recognize that the problem of impotency or frigidity does not exist merely in the symptomatic individual but in his relationship with his partner. Therefore, they insist on treating the couple as a unit, and the symptom as a problem of the unit. This constitutes a systems approach in contrast to a strictly intrapsychic or behavioral one.

Secondly, Masters and Johnson are acutely aware of the influence of psychodynamic factors on the sexual behavior of their couples. In their preliminary interviews they carefully assess and evaluate the importance of these factors, and if they consider the neurotic components or interpersonal difficulties to be too great, they may refuse to proceed with their method and will refer the couple back to their physicians for appropriate psychotherapy.

This kind of selective procedure has an effect, of course, on their percentage of successful results, as does the high degree of motivation that their patients must have to come to St. Louis (who, after all, goes to St. Louis for a two-week vacation?) and to commit themselves to the considerable expense and inconvenience that is involved.

The fact, also, that Masters and Johnson insist that the therapeutic team consist of a man and a woman reveals their sensitivity to the transference implications of their relationship to their couples. They function as a sexually permissive and empathic mother-surrogate and father-surrogate who offer not only valuable technical advice and suggestions concerning sexual behavior, but also a compassion and understanding that constitute a corrective emotional experience for their patients.

Finally, the tremendous charisma and authority of this highly publicized therapeutic team must inevitably have an enormous impact on the expectancy, faith, and hope with which their patients come to them. This cannot help but greatly accentuate the suggestive impact of the given instructions in facilitating their patients' therapeutic improvement. This improvement is then reinforced by subsequent follow-up telephone calls which, among other things, confirm to the patient the empathic interest, concern, and dedication of these parent-surrogates.

I am all too aware that these brief and summary remarks cannot begin to do justice to the three above-mentioned behavioral techniques. I hope, however, that I have succeeded in making the point that in each of these instances, complex variables are involved that go beyond any simple stimulus–response conditioning model.

The research on the nature of the psychotherapeutic process in which I participated with Franz Alexander beginning in 1958 has convinced me that all psychotherapy, regardless of the techniques used, is a learning process (Marmor, 1962, 1964, 1966). Dynamic psychotherapies and behavior therapies simply represent different teaching techniques, and their differences are based in part on differences in their goals and in part on their assumptions about the nature of psychopathology. Certain fundamental elements, however, are present in both approaches.

In any psychotherapeutic relationship, we start with an individual who presents a problem. This problem may be in the form of behavior that is regarded as deviant, or it may be in the form of subjective discomfort, or in certain distortions of perception, cognition, or affect, or in any combination of these. Usually, but not always, these problems motivate the individual or someone in his milieu to consider psychiatric treatment. This decision in itself establishes an *expectancy* in the individual which is quite different than if, say, "punishment" rather than "treatment" were prescribed for his problems. This expectancy is an essential part of *every* psychotherapeutic transaction at its outset, regardless of whether the patient presents himself for behavioral or dynamic psychotherapy. The patient, in other words, is *not* a neutral object in whom certain neurotic symptoms or habits have been mechanically established and from whom they can now be mechanically removed.

Expectancy is a complex process. It encompasses factors that Frank (1961) has demonstrated as being of major significance in psychotherapy— the degree of faith, trust, and hope that the patient consciously or unconsciously brings into the transaction. It is based in large part on previously established perceptions of authority or help-giving figures, perceptions that play a significant role in the degree of receptivity or nonreceptivity that the patient may show to the message he receives from the psychotherapist. Psychoanalysts have traditionally referred to these presenting expectations as aspects of "transference," but regardless of what they are called, they are always present. Transference is not, as some behavior therapists seem to think, something that is "created" by the therapist—although it is true that transference distortions may be either increased or diminished by the technique the therapist employs. The way in which the therapist relates to the patient may reinforce certain maladaptive perceptions or expectations, or it may teach the patient that his previously learned expectations in relation to help-giving or authority figures are incorrect. The latter teaching is part of what Alexander and French (1946) called the "corrective emotional experience."

Even in "simple" conditioning studies, experimenters like Liddell, Masserman, and Pavlov have called attention to the significance of the relationship between the experimental animal and the experimenter. In humans the problem is more complex, however. Thus, a therapist who behaves in a kindly but authoritarian manner may confirm the patient's expectancies that authority figures are omnipotent and omniscient. This increases the patient's faith and may actually facilitate his willingness to give up his symptoms to please the powerful and good parent-therapist, but it does *not* alter his childlike self-image in relation to authority figures. Depending on the therapist's objectives, this may or may not be or importance.

What I am indicating, in other words, is that a positive transference facilitates symptom removal, but if the patient's *emotional maturation, rather than just symptom removal, is the goal of therapy*, what is necessary eventually is a "dissolution" of this positive transference—which means teaching the patient to feel and function in a less childlike manner, not only in relation to the therapist but also to other authority figures.

Closely related and interacting with the patient's motivations and expectancies is the therapist's social and professional role, by virtue of which the help-seeking patient endows him with presumptive knowledge, prestige, authority, and help-giving potential. These factors play an enormous role in strengthening the capacity of the therapist to influence the patient and constitute another element in the complex fabric that makes up the phenomenon of positive transference.

Also, the *real persons* of both patient and therapist, their actual physical, intellectual, and emotional assets and liabilities, and their respective *value systems* enter into the therapeutic transaction. Neither the patient nor the therapist can be regarded as stereotypes upon whom any particular technique will automatically work. Their idiosyncratic variables are always an important part of their transaction.

Given the above factors, a number of things begin to happen more or less simultaneously, in varying degrees, in behavior therapies as well as in dynamic psychotherapies. I have discussed these factors in detail elsewhere and will merely summarize them here. They are:

(1) *Release of tension* through catharsis and by virtue of the patient's hope, faith, and expectancy. (2) *Cognitive learning*, both of the trial-and-error variety and of the gestalt variety. (3) Reconditioning by virtue of *operant conditioning*, by virtue of subtle reward-punishment cues from the therapist, and by corrective emotional experiences. (4) Identification with the therapist. (5) Repeated *reality testing*, which is the equivalent of the *practice* in the learning process. These five elements encompass the most significant factors on the basis of which change takes place in a psychotherapeutic relationship (Marmor, 1966). As I have mentioned above, suggestion takes place in all of these, covertly or overtly. Furthermore, as can be seen, a conditioning process takes place in dynamic psychotherapies as well as in behavior therapies, except that in the latter this process is intentional and more structured, while in the former it has not been generally recognized. In focusing on this conditioning process, behavior therapists have made a valuable contribution to the understanding of the therapeutic process. It is the thrust of this paper, however, that in so doing they have tended to minimize or ignore other important and essential elements in the therapeutic process, particularly the subtle but critical aspects of the patient–therapist interpersonal relationship.

In the final analysis, the technique of therapy that we choose to employ must depend on what aspect of man's complex psychic functioning we address ourselves to. If we choose to focus on the patient's overt symptoms or behavior patterns, some kind of behavior therapy may well be the treatment of choice. On the other hand, if the core of his problems rests in symbolic distortions of perception, cognition, affect, or subtle disturbances in interpersonal relationships, the source and nature of which he may be totally unaware, then the more elaborate reeducational process of dynamic psychotherapy may be necessary.

Moreover, indications for one approach do not necessarily rule out the other. Marks and Gelder (1965, 1966) and Brady (1968), among others, have demonstrated that the use of both behavior therapy and dynamic therapy in the same patient either concurrently or in sequence often brings about better therapeutic results than the use of either approach alone. Indeed, many dynamic psychotherapists have for years been unwittingly using such a combination of approaches when they prescribe drugs for the direct control of certain symptoms while concurrently pursuing a psychotherapeutic approach.

To conclude, then, in my opinion behavior therapies and dynamic psychotherapies, far from being irreconcilable, are complementary psychotherapeutic approaches. The line of demarcation between them is by no means a sharp one. As Breger and McGaugh (1965) and others have shown, behavior therapists do many things in the course of their conditioning procedures that duplicate the activities of dynamic psychotherapists including ". . . discussions, explanation of techniques and of the unadaptiveness of anxiety and symptoms, hypnosis, relaxation, 'nondirective cathartic discussions,' and 'obtaining an understanding of the patient's personality and background' " (Breger & McGaugh, 1965). The process in both approaches is best explicable in terms of current theories of learning which go beyond simple conditioning explanations and encompass central cognitive processes also. The fact that in some disorders one or the other approach may be more effective should not surprise us and presents no contradiction. Just as there is no single best way of teaching all pupils all subjects, there is no single psychotherapeutic technique that is optimum for all patients and all psychiatric disorders.

Since completing this paper, I have come across the excellent article by Klein, Dittman, Parloff, and Gill (1969) in which many of the conclusions I have set forth are confirmed by them as a result of five days of direct observation of the work of Wolpe and his group at the Eastern Pennsylvania Psychiatric Institute. The authors also point out that as a consequence of their increasing popularity, behavior therapists are now beginning to treat a broader spectrum of more "difficult" patients (complex psychoneurotic problems, character neuroses, or borderline psychotic problems) with the result that their treatment procedures are "becoming longer and more complicated with concomitant lowering of success rates."

Summary

Behavior therapists deserve much credit for having opened wide the armamentarium of therapeutic strategies. By so doing they have forced dynamic psychotherapists into a reassessment of their effectiveness—a reassessment that in the long run can only be in the best interests of all psychiatrists and their patients. The psychotherapeutic challenge of the future is to so improve our theoretical and diagnostic approaches to psychopathology as to be able to apply knowledgeably and flexibly to each patient the particular treatment technique and the particular kind of therapist that together will most effectively achieve the desired therapeutic goal.

References

Alexander, F., & French, T. M. *Psychoanalytic therapy*. New York: Ronald Press, 1946.

Brady, J. P. Psychotherapy by a combined behavioral and dynamic approach. *Comprehensive Psychiatry*, 1968, 9, 536–543. [Reprinted in this volume.]

Breger, L., & McGaugh, J. L. Critique and reformulation of learning theory approaches to psychotherapy and neurosis. *Psychological Bulletin,* 1965, *63,* 338–358.

Eysenck, H. J. *Behavior therapy and the neuroses.* New York: Pergamon Press, 1960.

Feldman, M. P., & MacCulloch, M. I. The application of anticipatory avoidance learning to the treatment of homosexuality. *Behaviour Research and Therapy,* 1965, *2,* 165–183.

Frank, J. D. *Persuasion and healing.* Baltimore: Johns Hopkins Press, 1961.

Klein, M. H., Dittman, A. T., Parloff, M. B. & Gill, M. M. Behavior therapy: Observations and reflections. *Journal of Consulting and Clinical Psychology,* 1969, *33,* 259–266.

Marks, I. M., & Gelder, M. G. A controlled retrospective study of behavior therapy in phobic patients. *British Journal of Psychiatry,* 1965, *111,* 561–573.

Marks, I. M., & Gelder, M. G. Common ground between behavior therapy and psychodynamic methods. *British Journal of Medical Psychology,* 1966, *39,* 11–23.

Marmor, J. Psychoanalytic therapy as an educational process. In J. Masserman & L. Salzman (Eds.), *Modern concepts of psychoanalysis.* New York: Philosophical Library, Inc., 1962.

Marmor, J. Psychoanalytic therapy and theories of learning. In J. Masserman (Ed.), *Science and psychoanalysis (Vol. 7).* New York: Grune & Stratton, 1964.

Marmor, J. The nature of the psychotherapeutic process. In G. Usdin (Ed.), *Psychoneurosis and schizophrenia.* New York: J. B. Lippincott Co.; 1966.

Masters, W. H., & Johnson, V. E. *Human sexual response.* Boston: Little, Brown & Co., 1965.

Ullmann, L. P., & Krasner, L. (Eds.). *Case studies in behavior modification.* New York: Holt, Rinehart & Winston, 1965.

Wolberg, L. R. Hypnotherapy. In J. L. McCrady (Ed.), *Six approaches to psychotherapy.* New York: Dryden Press, 1955.

Wolpe, J. *Psychotherapy by reciprocal inhibition.* Stanford: Stanford University Press, 1958.

Chapter 13
Behavior Therapy and the Facilitation of Psychoanalytic Exploration

Paul L. Wachtel

Limits of time, money, patient's frustration tolerance, etc., frequently lead psychoanalytically oriented therapists to rely considerably on kinds of interventions other than interpretations, which are the preferred therapeutic interventions from the psychoanalytic point of view. It is generally acknowledged in the psychoanalytic literature that such extra-interpretive interventions often provide considerable help to patients and that for many patients only by altering standard psychoanalytic procedures in this way can useful therapeutic aid be provided. But such divergences from purely interpretive therapy are frequently discussed as a kind of necessary compromise, which though often of substantial value, nonetheless limit the depth of treatment and cannot produce as extensive and permanent personality change (e.g., Luborsky & Schimek, 1964).

The therapeutic interventions developed by behavior therapists tend to be particularly eschewed by dynamically oriented practitioners. These methods have arisen out of a tradition which not only does not stress exploration of unconscious motives and conflicts, but is in many respects self-consciously *opposed* to the psychodynamic point of view. Not surprisingly, use of behavioral techniques is regarded by many analysts as strongly antithetical to the psychoanalytic method and as seriously in-

Reprinted by permission of the author, Paul L. Wachtel, and the publisher from *Psychotherapy: Theory, Research and Practice*, 1975, *12*, 68–72.

terfering with the kind of exploration analysts view as essential to major personality reorganization.

A number of trends in psychodynamic thought, however, seem to suggest that efforts to directly alter certain problematic behavior need not be antithetical to the fuller development of insight and self-confrontation. Alexander, among others, has suggested that insight might well follow behavioral change, and much of the writings in the interpersonal psychodynamic tradition, following the lead of thinkers such as Horney and Sullivan, also points to the ways in which our actual day-to-day behaviors, and the responses they evoke from others, help to maintain and perpetuate the neurotic conflicts which are evident in character neuroses. Much of the writing in psychoanalytic ego psychology also considers the reciprocal interaction between behavior and its consequences on the one hand and intrapsychic structures on the other.

It will nonetheless be clear to the reader familiar with current writings in the interpersonal and ego psychological literature that even here explicit or implicit opposition to the use of behavioral methods is the rule. To fully consider all the objections which have been raised would require a rather extensive examination of the history of psychodynamic thought, its necessary and non-necessary assumptions, alternative interpretations of psychoanalytic data, etc. Such an examination is currently being undertaken. The present contribution, however, will limit itself to an illustration of how behavioral intervention might facilitate psychodynamic exploration in a particular case.

Illustrative Case Material

The patient to be discussed was not someone in treatment with the author, but a rather young man whose case I heard presented at a case conference and about whom I conferred with his therapist several times for purposes of this paper. He was student who lived at school all week and returned home to his mother on weekends. The time he spent at school was fraught with anxiety. He was extremely isolated, avoiding contact as much as possible because of the considerable anxiety he felt whenever he was with another person, whether the janitor, his classmates, his teachers, or anyone else he might encounter. He went right from class to his room, ate alone, and would walk considerably out of his way to avoid seeing anyone he might have to say hello to.

Being home with mother on the weekends, while not particularly joyful either, was nonetheless rather a reprieve for him. He was relatively free from anxiety at home, and relaxed most of the day, often in front of the TV set. His relationship with his mother was described as involving seductive behavior on her part, but rejection when he got too close.

Much of the therapist's effort was directed toward elucidating the patient's strong erotic and symbiotic ties to his mother. It was expected that resolution of his core conflicts regarding parental figures would be a central means of creating the change necessary for improvement in other relationships in his life and a reduction of his intense anxiety at school. The patient's strong and conflictful tie to his mother was viewed primarily as an independent variable, changes in which would lead to changes in the other troubling aspects of his life.

While I would agree that this patient's particular ties and conflicts with his mother were probably *historically* primary (i.e., earlier), the relationship he had with his mother at the time he began therapy may be seen as a *product* of how he was living his life away from her as much as a *cause*. The cumulative effect of his developmental history found him at a point where, for all the conflict he experienced regarding her, his mother was by then the only person he could relate to with even a modicum of gratification and freedom from anxiety. Because of this, attempts to clarify the irrational and inappropriate aspects of the patient's relationship to his mother might be expected to be made difficult by her current *real* importance. Like a child, he was turning to mother for safety from a world both bewildering and frightening. His anxiety when he was away at school (whatever the original reasons for it) prevented him from forming any alternative ties which could serve as a base for leaving mother in any sense. For this reason it seemed to me that unless early direct efforts were made to reduce his daily burden of anxiety and facilitate interaction with others at school, exploration of the patient's feelings toward his mother was likely to be limited.

The Therapy Relationship and the Problem of Intense Demands

To some extent one might expect that his dilemma could be mitigated, without the introduction of behavioral methods, by the development of a strong relationship with the therapist. By providing the patient with an *alternative* to the mother as an important object, the therapist can help make the relationship with the mother less urgent, and thereby make it more possible for the patient to experience "forbidden" feelings toward her which he didn't dare experience when she was all he had.

Additionally, in this new relationship with the therapist, feelings similar to those experienced toward the mother might be expected to arise, but this time in an atmosphere in which their exploration and fuller understanding could occur. By responding differently to the patient's expression of feelings than the parents originally did, and by aiding the patient to recognize the differences between his helpless position as a child and his present situation of *self*-created dependency, the therapist can create conditions in which the patient can establish new and more growth-facilitating patterns.

These latter considerations tend to buttress the traditional strategy of focusing on the development of the patient–therapist relationship and regarding improvement in his day-to-day behavior as a more distal consequence of the therapeutic interaction. But if the alleviation of the misery and emptiness in the daily life of a man such as this is viewed as an ultimate outcome rather than a more immediate and direct goal, the therapeutic relationship itself may not develop in an optimally useful way; for to the degree that the patient's needs go unmet in his daily living, his demands on the therapist are likely to be more intense, and extremely intense demandingness by the patient poses a number of problems for the therapist.

Now, of course, intense demands by patients are not unfamiliar to analytic therapists. At the height of the transference neurosis in a classical analysis the demands made by the patient are often remarkably intense and primitive. In the face of such demands, the therapist must be very skillful to avoid either confirming infantile and neurotic patterns or being rejecting in response to them. Wolf (1966) has described vividly how therapists may at times intensify the patient's difficulties by responding in ways evoked by the patient's neurotic behavior. It is in large measure to prevent such an occurrence that the guidelines have developed which limit contact with patients outside of therapy hours and also place limits on full mutuality within the sessions. The technical guidelines help the therapist to be able to *interpret* instead of *acting* on the patient's demands. But it has been increasingly recognized that the stance of emotional neutrality which the analyst takes can be experienced by the patient as cold and rejecting, and if not tempered by sufficient indications of warmth and interest may limit the patient's ability to usefully participate in a process of therapeutic change (Greenson, 1967; Stone, 1961).

When the patient's neurotic demands are especially intense and persistent, it is difficult to maintain a useful balance of neutrality and empathic engagement. To avoid falling into countertransference traps the therapist may have to distance himself more than usual from the patient, with the danger of aloofness and lessened responsiveness to the patient's emotional communications. Such distancing is also problematic by virtue of being even more *different* from ordinary social intercourse, and hence exacerbating the always troubling issue of whether whatever change does occur in the therapy sessions will generalize to the patient's life situation.

Problems deriving from intense demands did arise in the case under discussion. For the first few months of therapy the therapist was pleased with the progress being made. In the early spring, the patient took a leave from school and felt somewhat better, seeing some old friends occasionally and experiencing less of the overwhelming anxiety he had felt when at school. But he still was never really relaxed with others and couldn't maintain a conversation. The main improvement evident was in his relationship with the therapist, where greater trust was clearly evident. The therapy continued to focus largely on the transference relationship.

After the therapist's vacation, the treatment began to unravel. Rather early in the treatment the patient had become very attached to his therapist and had revealed wishes to live with him, follow him around, and learn from him, etc. These had been within manageable bounds, however, and seemed to the therapist to provide fruitful areas for exploration. After the vacation these desires and fantasies became so intense that they were disruptive. The patient would plead with the therapist to "take me home and teach me how to live." He would tell the therapist that he was the only nice person in the world, literally the only one worth being with, and would combine this with strong complaints that the therapist wasn't helping enough, wasn't giving enough. The therapist began to feel flooded by the patient's demands and frustrated by the patient's *complete unwillingness to reflect upon what he was expressing*.

The patient's behavior became increasingly bizarre. He exhibited strange obsessions and depersonalized experiences, frequently checking and feeling himself to see if he was still there. His fantasies of incorporating the therapist became more overt and literal and more destructive. He made biting grimaces in the sessions and said he wanted to eat the therapist's head, swallow him up, etc. All the while he would continue to demand that he be taken into the therapist's home and be with him all day and to bitterly complain that the therapist was holding out on him by not doing so. Eventually, the patient left the therapist and checked himself into a psychiatric day hospital.

Such an unsuccessful course of therapy can be understood in many ways. Questions about the therapist's countertransference reaction to the patient's demands are appropriate, as are considerations of the most skillful and effective way to handle the situation within a traditional mode of therapeutic interaction. But the considerations advanced earlier suggest it may also be fruitful to ask whether an exploratory mode of therapy was impeded by the degree of anxiety and inhibition which were manifest in the patient's everyday life, and whether efforts to directly intervene in his day-to-day problems might have increased his freedom to explore and reflect upon those inclinations which he had been finding to frightening to face. One might anticipate a number of positive synergistic cycles following upon assistance in interacting more comfortably with the people he sees during the day: (1) The more success with people, the less anxiety, the more further success, etc. (2) the better his relationship to others, the less desperate and irrational the ties to mother and to therapist, the better his relationships to others, etc. (3) the less pressured the ties to mother and to therapist, the greater the possibility of *exploring* feelings regarding them, the greater the freeing from those ties, etc.

One approach to intervention might be to attempt to reduce his extremely intense anxiety about being with people via systematic desensitization. In considering how one might go about constructing a hierarchy for desensitization with such a man, it is interesting to note that the layering of inclinations, fears, and avoidances which is familiar to the analytic therapist may be perceived in this context as well. Early in the therapy, while he was still in school, the patient first indicated his anxiety whenever he saw others in the hall. It intensified as the other person approached, especially if it were someone the patient knew, who might attempt to engage him in a conversation. The patient would try to avoid such an encounter, because he was even more afraid that a conversation might start and that he wouldn't be able to think of anything to say. He imagined himself standing there feeling awkward and immobilized, yet unable to either leave or talk, and he felt very anxious at the thought that he would then seem very odd to the other person. Further probing by the therapist revealed that the patient would be silent in such situations because he was afraid he would have to tell the other person he was "full of shit," that they were just making small talk, and he didn't believe the other person was really interested in him.

Several alternatives for desensitization seem possible here. On the one hand, one might proceed via scenes of increasing approach of the other person, or greater familiarity with the person approaching, increasing the likelihood he would stop and talk and the anticipated embarrassment at appearing foolish. Images of standing there with nothing to say would be very high on the hierarchy. On the other hand, one might proceed in the manner of Feather and Rhoads (1972), emphasizing conflict over aggressively accusing the other person, and encouraging the person to combine muscular relaxation with imagery of acting out his most frightening fantasies.

An additional aid in helping the patient to reduce the social anxieties which plague him might be provided by role playing or behavior rehearsal. Providing the patient with opportunities for modeling and practice in conducting small talk would enable him to develop skills which his life history has inhibited his acquiring. It would also enable his early trial and error efforts to occur with the *therapist*, where there would be far less damaging consequences, and an opportunity to "take it from the top" when something seems to go wrong. In everyday social intercourse, such awkwardness is not as likely to meet with a sympathetic response, and he could readily have his anxieties confirmed and intensified instead of diminished. It is likely that a good deal of undermining and failure in psychotherapy is due to the retraumatizing effect of trying out new behavior patterns with others before they have been developed to the point where they are likely to lead to a rewarding interaction. This is a particularly important issue, which will be examined in greater detail in a book now in preparation.

Antithesis or Complement?

Such efforts to directly assist in the change of specific troubling life patterns are typically viewed as an *alternative* to the exploratory and interpretive methods of psychodynamic therapists. It is held by many analytic therapists that such methods are manipulative and that they necessarily limit the possibilities of exploration and of resolution of underlying core conflicts. On the other hand, much of the behavior therapy literature argues for the *exclusive* use of such direct change methods and sees the events of the psychoanalytic interview as merely prescientific mumbo-jumbo, or at best inadvertent and inefficient behavior therapy.

It is recognized by most clinicians, regardless of theoretical orientation, that anxiety is strongly implicated in a wide range of maladaptive behavior patterns, and that avoidances, including alterations of attentional focus, can readily obscure the source of anxiety and prevent opportunities for its extinction. The interpretation of defenses in analytically oriented therapies is designed to reveal those avoidances and help the patient attend to the real source of his anxieties. To the extent that anxiety gradients persist and remain undetected, they can continue to motivate avoidances and restrict the range of possible adaptive behaviors. In such circumstances, recurrences or new instances of neurotic behavior are likely. Reports by behavior therapists that their direct interventions into specific maladaptive behavior patterns do not frequently lead to symptom substitution or recurrence of the troubling behavior suggest that a larger range of maladaptive behavior may be independent of underlying unconscious conflict than was originally assumed by psychodynamic theorists. Apparently, the opportunity to experience new contingencies in one's day-to-day life is often sufficient to maintain new patterns, regardless of the origins of the patient's problems. The question of whether such gain is at the expense of subtle and undetected negative characterological change, or of intensification of childlike fantasies of protection by powerful authorities, is an important one which cannot be considered in this brief presentation. The observations of behavior therapists thus far have suggested that there are *positive* changes in other aspects of the patient's daily living. Whether more subtle probing will reveal opposite tendencies remains to be seen.

But even strong proponents of exclusively behavioral approaches to therapy have acknowledged that the success of such efforts is considerably greater with a limited range of isolated phobias or the fears of volunteer college students than with the more pervasive and intense difficulties of most psychiatric patients (e.g., Eysenck and Beech, 1971). And Lazarus' (1971) recent reports regarding relapse in behavior therapy patients suggest that behavior therapists have tended in the past to underestimate the importance of underlying characterological features in the generation and perpetuation of neurotic patterns.

Much further investigation is needed to determine how readily psychodynamic inquiry into hidden aspects of patients' adaptational dilemmas can be combined with direct efforts to relieve specific troubling behaviors and how much each approach can enhance the effectiveness of the other. The case discussed here is one that analysts would be unlikely to regard as a "good analytic case," and thus the question is also raised as to whether, even if helpful with cases such as these, behavioral methods would also facilitate work with the kind of patients now in classical analysis. Psychoanalytic writers have stressed the ways in which direct intervention can limit the scope and depth of exploration. But as illustrated above, there are barriers to exploration stemming from *not* intervening as well. The development by behavior therapists in the past decade of useful specific interventions requires a rethinking of the rationale for the traditional psychodynamic stress on nonintervention in light of the countervailing considerations which have been discussed.

References

Eysenck, H. J., & Beech, J. R. Counterconditioning and related methods. In A. Bergin & S. Garfield, (Eds.), *Handbook of psychotherapy and behavior change*. New York: Wiley, 1971.

Feather, B., & Rhoads, S. Psychodynamic behavior therapy: II. Clinical Aspects. *Archives of General Psychiatry*, 1972, 26, 503–511.

Greenson, R. *The technique and practice of psychoanalysis*. New York: International Universities Press, 1967.

Lazarus, A. A. *Behavior therapy and beyond*. New York: McGraw-Hill, 1971.

Luborsky, L., & Schimek, J. G. Psychoanalytic theories of therapeutic and developmental change. In P. Worchel & D. Byrne, (Eds.), *Personality change*. New York: Wiley, 1964.

Stone, L. *The psychoanalytic situation*. New York: International Universities Press, 1961.

Wolf, E. Learning theory and psychoanalysis. *British Journal of Medical Psychology*, 1966, 39, 1–10.

Chapter 14
Psychoanalysis and Behavior Therapy

Lee Birk
and Ann W. Brinkley-Birk

Most readers of this journal are already sufficiently familiar with the historical developments of psychoanalysis and behavior therapy to recognize the extent to which the theoretical and methodological divergence of the two traditions is due to the different scientific/epistemological biases of their founders. That psychoanalysis and behavior therapy developed from and were formally determined by separate, seemingly incompatible methodological and metaphysical underpinnings is by now a well-established commonplace in the history of science. But that the two traditions should continue to generate essentially separate and uncooperative clinical schools can no longer be supported by differences in their philosophical/scientific determinants; there *is* a conceptual interface between psychoanalysis and behavior therapy. In this paper, we will be focusing on the prospects for broadening this nascent interface into an effective theoretical synthesis of these two traditions—a synthesis that eventuates clinically in the mutual potentiation of psychoanalytic and behavioral techniques.

Real and widespread synergistic cooperation between advocates of the two schools has been slow in developing (Birk, 1972; Birk, Stolz, Brady, Brady, Lazarus, Lynch, Rosenthal, Skelton, Stevens, & Thomas, 1973, pp. vii–ix; Glover, 1955; Cushing, 1952; Tabachnick, 1973; Marmor, 1973;

This paper was written at the invitation of the Editor of the *American Journal of Psychiatry*.

Reprinted by permission of the first author, L. Birk, and the publisher from *American Journal of Psychiatry*, 1974, *131*, 499–510. Copyright 1974 by the American Psychiatric Association.

Allen, Hart, Buell, Harris, & Wolf, 1964; Ayllon & Azrin, 1965; Baer & Wolf, 1968; Shapiro & Birk, 1967); at present, the integration of behavioral and psychoanalytic techniques[1] in the treatment repertoire of the single clinician is the result of ad hoc adaptations and is still without a solid conceptual foundation. For about half a decade, however, there have been at least a few modest steps toward de facto convergence on a practical, clinical level. The joint session of the American Academy of Psychoanalysis and of the American Psychiatric Association at APA's 1973 annual meeting is typical of this trend. Moreover, it is no longer unusual for psychoanalysts and behavior therapists to refer patients (even including themselves!) to each other or to collaborate in the treatment of difficult cases. Despite this and a series of papers over the past 10 years that have emphasized their common features (Alexander, 1963; Wolf, 1969; Porter, 1968; Aronson, 1972), coexistence (Marmor, 1971; Sloane, Staples, Cristol, Yorkston, & Whipple, 1975), and even convergence (Sloane, 1969), real conceptual integration has barely begun and it remains true that "on the whole, both behavior therapists and dynamic psychiatrists seem to have been unwilling to inform themselves sufficiently to be able to consider the observations presented by the other approach" (Birk, Stolz, Brady, Brady, Lazarus, Lynch, Rosenthal, Skelton, Stevens, Thomas, 1973, p. 6).

There have been a few instances, however, in which writers have gone beyond a merely hortatory approach to this integration. One of the earliest papers illustrating this trend toward true integration and synthesis was a 1966 paper by Crisp that presciently discussed both "transference" and effects as in "social repercussion effects" due to successful behavior therapy. A few years ago one of us (L.B.) presented a brief but much-rebutted paper, "Behavior Therapy: Integration with Dynamic Psychiatry" (Birk, 1970), and in early 1972, Feather and Rhoads published an important paper entitled "Psychodynamic Behavior Therapy." This nascent trend toward true integration reached its fullest development to date with two papers presented in May 1973 at the joint session mentioned above: one by Rhoads and Feather (1974) and one by one of us (Birk, 1974). These two papers are noteworthy for the amount of conceptual and practical integration they embody; each described the work of single clinicians alternately (Rhoads & Feather, 1974) or even simultaneously (Birk, 1974) using both behavioral and psychoanalytic concepts and methods in the treatment of the same patients, the first using relatively short-term individual therapy and the second using intensive five-day-per-week group therapy.

[1]Following Glover (1955), Cushing (1952), Tabachnick (1973), and Marmor (1973), we see no clear-cut criteria (especially conceptually) for differentiating between psychoanalysis and psychoanalytic psychotherapy. In this article we use the term "psychoanalysis" to refer not just to classical psychoanalysis (dyadic, four to five times a week, on the couch) but also to the many variants of psychoanalytic therapy—including group, family, and couple therapy—that are largely derived from psychoanalysis.

What is really required at this stage, however, is dialogue between clinicians of both schools whose aim is genuine rapprochement, mutual understanding, and the tentative forging of a new clinical learning theory for psychotherapy—a conceptual framework that can embrace and contain the raw data (clinical phenomena) of both psychoanalysis and behavior therapy.

Assumed Differences

The Philosophical Paradigms

Psychoanalytically derived psychotherapies and the behavior therapies are assumed to differ essentially in two ways: in the mechanisms of therapeutic change deemed effective by each school and in the primary areas in which change is assumed to become manifest. These differences are derived from the contrasting sets of assumptions that underlie the theoretical structure of each school. That is, each school was bound to a large extent to the philosophical/scientific parameters that were operating at each stage in its development, since these determined not only what was accepted as workable and true but what were the very standards of truth itself. Insight-oriented psychotherapy, for example, derived its theoretical impetus from the "knowledge-is-power" model underlying post-Newtonian science. That insight should be presumed to be the mark of—and catalyst for—therapeutic change is only a corollary of that model's basic premise. Moreover, the emphasis on insight-mediated change is also perfectly consistent with the primary focus of other scientific models of the time: until the early 1900s, rational reconstruction of the phenomenal world ("making sense of the data") was regarded as the principal concern of the scientific community—more so, that is to say, than mastery or manipulation of the phenomenal world.

The triple-layered (conscious, unconscious, and preconscious) mental structure postulated and accepted by the adherents of Freudian and neo-Freudian psychotherapeutic theory and practice served as a referential base[2] for the collection of technical explanations and operations that they advocated, at the same time that it was assumed to be a second-order source of validation for the choice of therapeutic mechanisms underlying the retrospective-associative methods of psychoanalytically oriented psychotherapists.[3] For

---

[2]This is equally true of the earlier (pre-1920s) "topographical" model of psychoanalysis and of the later "structural" model.

[3]On reflection, it will be clear that this is circular; in very simple terms, the existence of the unconscious as a receptacle for repressed conflicts and wishes is predicated on the assumption that the content of slips of the tongue, dreams, and so on make indirect reference to unconscious material, but that these mechanisms in turn are believed to be the vehicles of transit between the two mental levels is itself a hypothesis that requires confirmation directly by the above-mentioned existence postulate.

this reason, the primary mechanisms of therapeutic change were believed to serve a dual purpose: on the one hand, to act as signs or indications to the patient and therapist of the current (albeit ameboid) interface between conscious and nonconscious (preconscious or unconscious) and, on the other hand, to be the vehicles for that transit between unconscious and conscious that was assumed to be the major, indeed the necessary, condition for therapeutic change in psychoanalytic psychotherapy.

Slips of the tongue, dreams, and unexpected associations (to name only a few of these mechanisms) are presumed to be interpretable and self-consistent, not primarily within the context of conscious experience but within the expanding framework supplied by the content of conscious and previously unconscious thought together. Indeed, by virtue of this same theoretical ontology, neurotic symptoms are the presumed explicanda of repressed conflicts, wishes, memories, and motivations. The ultimate mark of a successful retrospective probe is not just the recovery of repressed material, therefore, but is also the discovery of subjectively acceptable explanations for the otherwise inexplicable phenomena of ordinary conscious thought and affect, unconscious verbal or motor slips (accidents), and dreams—explanations, that is, that do not so much merely expose the repressed conflicts as make sense of phenomena that appear at first glance to be inconsistent (Freud, 1949, 1953; Fenichel, 1945; Nemiah, 1975).

The emergence of unconscious processes into consciousness—via dreams, slips, associations, affective links, etc., to the hidden conflict or motivation—is mediated by the phenomenon of transference. To recreate the past in the present or react to the present as if it were just like the past is already to have made accessible to interpretation the early learning experiences from which were constructed the matrix of rules operating within the perceptual-interpretive apparatus. It is by means of these "rules" that individuals establish an idiosyncratic pattern in the screening, coding, and storing of experiences.

In working through the transference one might be said to be redetermining the boundary conditions for past and present in the service both of exposing and eliminating the systematic perceptual distortion that the individual brings to his current environment and of shifting or modifying the basic rules by which he typically codes and integrates new experiences. Secondarily and concomitantly, of course, one should expect to change the reality-perception-feeling sequence to the point that cognitive and emotional reactions to external stimuli work with and not against each other. This implies the resolution of conflict, some aspects of which had not previously been fully conscious; in short, it can be said that merely exposing the internal consistency of the items in an individual's psychological inventory is not adequate to the task of bringing into harmony with external reality that individual's emotional and cognitive responses without a corrective emotional experience (Alexander, 1956) concurrent with the resolution of the transference neurosis.

In spite of well-specified theoretical and practical differences, behavior therapy and psychoanalytically derived psychotherapy show a marked and similar congruence in the amount of circular reinforcement between operative metaphysical assumptions (or any lack thereof) and the derivation of therapeutic mechansims. While psychoanalytic psychotherapy can be said to operate within a context in which metaphysical assumptions (i.e., the "mental model" with its triple-layered view of consciousness) both determine and are derived from a carefully chosen set of phenomena that have been granted *a priori* significance, it must be said of behavior therapy that its principles are presumed valid within a context in which, by prescientific decision, *no metaphysical assumptions* are allowed to operate. These are the contexts that validate the choice of treatment mechanisms and that determine the priorities assigned to different outcome criteria.

The Clinical Models

These differences in the two philosophical paradigms are reflected in the dissimilarity in clinical models. Whereas psychoanalysis focuses on learning about previously unconscious motivation and conflicts, emphasizes free association, dream interpretation, and the handling of the interpersonal relationship between the analyst and the patient, and focuses on making the correct cognitive interpretation to the patient (Marmor, 1973, p. 1197), behavior therapy generally has not attempted to deal with unconscious mental processes, nor has it ever really acknowledged their relevance— even, in some quarters, their existence. Moreover, behavior therapy focuses on the patient–therapist relationship only to the extent that this is seen to be important in securing the patient's cooperation with the therapist's treatment plan (Birk et al., 1973, pp. 27–28) and in enhancing the therapist's effectiveness as a "social reinforcer" (Krasner, 1962). With only sparse and limited exceptions, originating mainly from those who have an analytic background (Beck, 1970) or who have otherwise been tainted by analytic apostasies (Stampfl & Lewis, 1967), behavior therapists have not attached therapeutic value to cognitive interpretations, correct or incorrect, nor have they in general even acknowledged the possibility of dealing with cognitive material (what the patient says he thinks or feels) with sufficient scientific objectivity to make this a worthwhile endeavor. This theoretical stance strikes a strangely discordant note[4] in view of the practi-

---

[4]In fact, one of us (Birk, 1972) has pointedly criticized the paradoxical tendency among some behavior therapists to base entire therapeutic strategies wholly on assumed cognitive processes—"covert" imaginal stimuli, "covert" reinforcement, and "covert" punishment—quite without any adequate objective data, even self-report data, to confirm that the therapist's commands to imagine stimulus scenes and to imagine

cal fact that most behavior therapists, especially those more in the tradition of Wolpe than Skinner, *use* self-report data about cognitive matters in carrying out, for example, systematic desensitization and in the construction of hierarchies (Locke, 1971).

The emphasis by behavioral theorists on observable, objectively manifest data is a consequence of the phenomenological bias inherent in the scientific model that was prominent at the time of the development of behavioral principles. Manipulation of the external environment to effect behavior change is the modus operandi of behavior therapists and is consistent with the parsimony of metaphysical accretions that is characteristic of phenomenologists and others of a behavioral bent who regard observability, objectivity, and repeatability as the hallmark of criteria for existence and truth. In this, clinical behaviorists have taught us much about the importance of extinction in the therapeutic process and about competitive response (Birk, 1968) and behavioral-shaping strategies (Wolpe, 1958; Skinner, 1938, 1953; Krasner, 1971; Ferster, 1972; Ayllon & Azrin, 1968). With their emphasis on the processes of operant conditioning that pervade everyday life, normal, neurotic, and even psychotic, they have opened up self-control and treatment mechanisms that depend on bringing selected behaviors under "stimulus control" (Lindsley & Skinner, 1954; Ferster & DeMyer, 1961; Harris, Johnston, Kelley, & Wolf, 1964; Allen, Hart, Buell, Harris, & Wolf, 1964; Ayllon & Azrin, 1965; Baer & Wolf, 1968) through the planned use of discriminative stimuli, punishment, and reinforcement. In so doing, they have also added depth, subtlety, and power to the clinician's ability to understand and therapeutically limit what analysts call "secondary gain" (Birk, 1968; Shapiro & Birk, 1967; Liberman & Raskin, 1971).

Both schools have recognized the great importance of what analysts call identification (Knight, 1940; Koff, 1961) and what behaviorists call modeling (Bandura & Walters, 1963), although the analysts have been much more alert to the fact that therapeutic (and other) identifications can exert profound, pervasive, and life-long effects, while the behaviorists have been much more productive in studying modeling experimentally and in manipulating it as a process for the achievement of focused therapeutic goals, such as overcoming specific phobias.

Marmor has recently summed up the "fundamental aspects of Freud's contribution . . . generally accepted by all psychoanalysts"—

---

reinforcing and/or punishing events in fact lead to those events within the patient's brain. Psychoanalysis, in contrast, (1) does not attempt to directly manipulate cognitive content, but rather attempts to deal naturalistically with existing cognitive content, and (2) amasses as much self-report data as possible, including data that come from observed verbal slips and associative connections, to support any theories the analyst may have about cognitive content, conscious and unconscious.

On the theoretical side . . . that human behavior is motivated, that our personalities are shaped by the interplay of biological potentials and life experiences, that functional psychiatric disturbances are the result of developmental vicissitudes and contradictory and conflictual inputs and feedbacks, and that early childhood experiences are of special significance in shaping subsequent perceptions and reactions in later life (Marmor, 1973, p. 1197).

And one might say of behavior therapy that it, too, emphatically acknowledges the undeniable role of past learning experiences, recent and remote, in the formation of an individual's adaptive and maladaptive (symptomatic) behavioral repertoire. Thus, in fact, psychoanalytic and behavioral theories are both learning theories; it follows that in effect *psychoanalysis and behavior therapy are both learning therapies*.

In other words, past experience (learning) shapes current behavior and personality, including "neurosis" or "functional psychiatric disturbance," and the role of therapy is to reverse this faulty learning. With this in mind it might really be more accurate to refer to both psychoanalysis and behavior therapy as un-learning and re-learning therapies.

Strengths and Limitations of the Two Therapeutic Methodologies

We have discussed above the theoretical causes for divergence between the psychoanalytic and behavioral traditions. We will turn our attention now to the types of successful therapeutic change and the mechanisms by which those changes are achieved, based on the pure theoretical models of psychoanalytic and behavior therapy, respectively. To this end, we have prepared a series of diagrams to represent the pure models of psychoanalysis and behavior therapy and their combination in schematized form.

Psychoanalysis

In successful psychoanalysis or psychoanalytically oriented psychotherapy, one can predict a necessary and significant change in the patient's level of self-understanding or self-awareness. One mark of successful therapy of this type is the recovery of forgotten or repressed material through the gradual exposure, clarification, interpretation, and extension of associative-affective links between present and past. By means of these emotion-mediated insights, the patient is gradually made aware of his particular psychodynamic inventory—in philosophical terms, of the cognitive assumptions underlying his personal world view. This is the *sine qua non* of a successful analysis. In addition, the patient would predictably begin to feel better about himself, to experience less guilt and more pleasure, to be freer to work efficiently, and to achieve a greater degree of social integration without concurrent or later self-punishment. In Figure 14.1, we have indicated this causal nexus by the broad arrow from "insight" to "subjective sense of improvement." This is meant to suggest that if insight occurs—as it must if psychoanalysis is to effect its proper end—subjective confirmation of improvement follows. It goes without saying, however, that objectively manifest behavioral change is not at all a necessary product of insight and insight-based changes in the patient's self-evaluation: "we have learned the difficult lesson that rational understanding alone is not enough, that people can understand only why they behave in certain ways and yet be unable to alter their unsatisfactory patterns" (Marmor, 1968).

Case 1. A 25-year-old male graduate student with a 12-year history of a disabling fear of gagging (or actual uncontrolled gagging) in public-speaking situations uncovered the origin of his phobic symptom during group therapy. In a particularly emotional moment, he gained the insight that this problem had to do with his fear of disclosing the guilty secret of his long-practiced habit of playing with his own feces, originally as an imagined substitute for the siblings that he (an only child) lacked. Memory confirmed this insight: the patient's first trouble with gagging (to the point of vomiting) had occurred at age 13 when, during a Sunday-school Bible reading in front of the entire congregation, he was called upon to read the words "and all his bowels spilled out" (at this age he thought "bowels" meant feces). In

Figure 14.1.   The Narrow Psychoanalytic Model

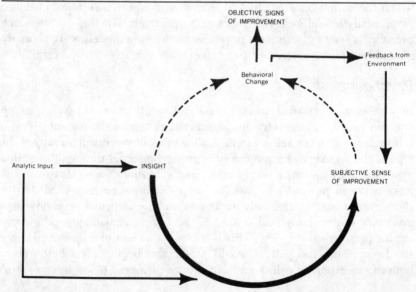

spite of extensive therapeutic efforts to "work through" this insight, he experienced no relief whatever from the symptom. This patient has now been referred for systematic desensitization; he is also continuing in group psychotherapy.

Behavior Therapy

It is now well recognized that discrete behavioral symptoms—for example, specific fears and inhibitions; compulsive habits; obsessive, ritualized, or self-destructive, self-punitive, or self-defeating behaviors; specific behavioral deficits; and certain psychophysiological symptoms (Birk, 1973a)—are amenable to modification by a variety of behavioral techniques that do not rely in any way on insight but instead make use of external feedback mechanisms. As Figure 14.2 indicates, insight and heightened self-awareness are not part of a pure behavior therapy strategem; instead, the behavior therapist undertakes careful "behavioral analysis" of the leading behaviors in the symptomatic matrix in order to determine what the current sources of reinforcement are that perpetuate these target behaviors. This leads naturally to the design of a specific behavioral program to modify the behaviors that constitute the patient's chief complaints.

Figure 14.2. The Narrow Behavior Therapy Model

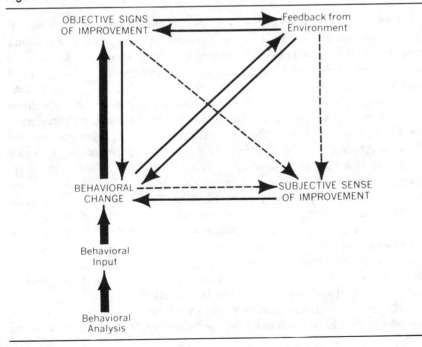

Thus, if the behavioral analysis is correctly done, behavioral change and objective signs of improvement will necessarily occur (if they do not, one can legitimately assume an error, omission, or oversimplification in the original behavioral analysis). Both behavioral change per se and its observable or measurable manifestation in objective signs of improvement should elicit greater social rewards, which in turn lead to further shaping of the desired behavioral change, as Figure 14.2 indicates. According to behavioral theory, maladaptive behavior is defined as just that behavior which routinely elicits punishing responses from the environment and adaptive behavior as that which effects appropriately rewarding social consequences. Although behavioral change and its objective manifestation may be sufficient to cause a subjective sense of improvement, the latter is not a necessary effect.

This happens when the patient's internal reinforcement/punishment system is sufficiently skewed, because of an unanalyzed neurotic distortion in the value system or the perceptual-interpretive apparatus, to permit behavioral change to occur in the absence of the patient's really experiencing subjective improvement. The natural system of rewards and punishments alone may not be effective in modifying maladaptive behavior when there is systematic (neurotic) distortion in the patient's perception or valuation of reward/punishment. In such cases, a systematic amplification of the normal reward/punishment consequences may not be helpful and may even be countertherapeutic.

Case 2. A 45-year-old teacher and mother of four with a 20-year history of multiple severe compulsive habits, manipulative depressive affect, and periodic quasi-suicidal behavior was seen in treatment with her husband by an experienced behavior therapist. She had already had many years of unsuccessful psychotherapy. The therapist noted that the patient's complaints were shifting and migratory following successful work in a given area. Ultimately his efforts with her foundered in the face of his straightforward (noninsight-seeking) efforts to help bring some genuine nonneurotic pleasure into her life. She was then referred to one of the authors (L.B.) for combined behavioral-psychoanalytic work. Previous insight-oriented psychotherapy had failed as well, although the patient had come to recognize the intensity of her guilt over the death of her father. He was an inveterate gambler—in her eyes, an assertive, charming man—with whom she had been incestuously involved as a young woman. His death by suicide followed an argument with her about money. Despite her earlier psychotherapy the patient continued to feel guilty and to heap punishment on herself and those around her by manipulating and provoking her all-too-compliant and passive husband into low-key but hurtful attacks.

Her previous psychotherapy did not work because, despite considerable insight, it did not interrupt her self-punitive life style. Her behavior

therapy, on the other hand, did not work because it attempted simplisti-
cally to eliminate her multiple self-punitive behaviors without altering her
basic world view, which provided a cognitive justification for her pervasive
need to punish herself. She was in a sense doomed to continue paying off
her guilt for her father's suicide until she could achieve sufficient insight
into the relationships among her old sexual feelings about her father, her
anger at him, and her unconscious wishes for his death. It was the punish-
ment-seeking drive produced by this patient's guilt that distorted her response to what would ordinarily have been reinforcing/punishing events in
her environment.

As Figure 14.2 also indicates, another drawback of pure behavior therapy is that desirable behavioral change can occur either in the absence of a
subjective sense of improvement or even in the face of increasingly negative self-report data.

Case 3. A 25-year-old passive-dependent office worker sought behaviorally oriented couple therapy in order to resolve his inhibitions against
further involvement with a woman he was otherwise on the verge of marry-
ing. The assignment of graded behavioral tasks accomplished the ostensible
goals for which therapy was undertaken, but it resulted in a simultaneous
worsening of the patient's chronic success-anxiety to the point that he was
experiencing frequent attacks of nausea and vomiting. Insight-oriented
probing exposed the patient's previously unconscious fear of his father's
retaliatory jealousy. Once exposed, these fears were treated with imaginal
desensitization in combination with a flooding and extinction technique of
"symptom scheduling." With this combined behavioral-psychoanalytic approach, the patient not only continued to *do* better but also began to *feel*
better.

Figure 14.3 shows the therapeutic power that is gained when, in the
treatment of the same patient, there is both an analytic input and a behavioral input. Fundamentally, this is the combined (but not integrated) paradigm that operates when analyst–behavior therapist teams collaborate successfully in the treatment of individual patients.

A Proposed Paradigm for the Clinical and Conceptual Integration of Psychoanalysis and Behavior Therapy

One of the fundamental reasons that psychoanalysis and behavior therapy
have such apparently well-entrenched differences in their modi operandi,
it seems to us, is that their goals are different. That is to say, successful

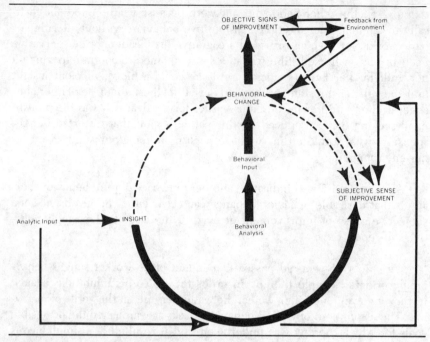

Figure 14.3.   The Combined Model

psychoanalysis is marked by the maximization of self-awareness, "making sense of" increasingly profound levels of psychological data as they become accessible to conscious interpretation. Behavior therapy, on the other hand, is primarily concerned with *modifying* behavior according to external, socially determined standards, by means of the manipulation of environmental contingencies. Both are consistency-oriented therapies in the sense that each attempts to fit together its choice of significant phenomena under an integrating theoretical superstructure but, since these phenomena make up categories that need not be coextensive, the goals and therapeutic results remain essentially disparate. Psychoanalysis works to bring the internal data of consciousness into some sort of harmony mediated by the logic and self-consistency of mental events; behavior therapy, on the other hand, works to bring the individual (characterized by the externally manifest phenomena of his behavior) into greater harmony with the physically and socially determined consequences of his own deliberate and idiosyncratic (habitual) actions.

Our proposed model seeks to combine the internal and external aspects of human activity—to regard self-awareness as a potentiator of behavioral change and to view an increasingly realistic assessment of natural social rewards and punishments as a motive for continuing insight-based self-realization. That is, if insight and external feedback systems can be used together to expose, clarify, and change an individual's perceptual and reactive patterns when those have proved ineffective, one has indeed found a way to maximize the fit between an individual, his self-evaluation, his perceptions of external reality, his response to that reality, and his actual existential position.

To be more specific, it is our belief, on the basis of our clinical experience, that psychoanalysis and behavior therapy need no longer represent two warring belief systems or two separate clinical traditions but that, as techniques, each can be used to reinforce the weakest links in the therapeutic input–outcome chain of the other.

For example, even in the specific case of dealing with loss and grieving, usually regarded as an area in which behavioral ideas can contribute little, therapists can learn something of value from both the behavioral and the psychoanalytic traditions. The behavioral literature contains some excellent conceptual contributions to the understanding of the phenomena of acute depression (Liberman & Raskin, 1971; Ferster, 1973), learned helplessness and chronic depression (Seligman, 1974, Miller, 1973), chronic social (maternal and peer) deprivation (Suomi, Harlow & McKinney, 1972), and even a few promising studies of the treatment of depression (Liberman, & Raskin, 1971; Lewinsohn, Weinstein, & Shaw, 1969; Lewinsohn, 1975). Notwithstanding all this, it can still be said that, for obvious ethical reasons, loss and grieving have not been subjects that lend themselves naturally to truly experimental study and, therefore, that those who have pursued the more naturalistic scientific methods, ranging from Freud (1957) to van Lawick-Goodall (1971), have made a relatively greater contribution.

Faced with helping a patient to deal with the loss of a child or of a life partner, the therapist may find it useful, to some extent, to conceptualize this in terms of an existentially unhappy state, e.g., an "abrupt loss of available reinforcers," but in our opinion there is no humane and ethical alternative to the therapist's "sharing it, bearing it, and helping the patient to place it in perspective." In this endeavor, we have found this clinical admonition of Semrad's, along with Freud's classic paper "Mourning and Melancholia" (1957) and Lindemann's paper on the management of acute grief (1944), to be among the most helpful in the literature and lore of psychotherapy.

Integrated Model

In the integrated model, an insight is regarded not so much as one piece in the puzzle uniquely representative of every individual's psychological identity, but rather as a clue to the developmental origins of a particular emotional/behavioral/cognitive response that is, in the patient's current life,

symptomatically overgeneralized from past learning experiences. If it becomes clear to the patient—through insight—what the details of the original situation were and why the response may have been an adaptive one *in
that situation*, it becomes increasingly easy for him to learn to discriminate
between new experiences that no longer call for the same response/feeling/
idea and those that resemble past learning experiences so closely as to be
appropriate stimuli for the previously habitual response. Insight, in short,
functions as a vehicle for the retraining of an individual's discriminative
abilities (Dollard & Miller, 1950). One might even say insight *is* discriminative learning, evaluated subjectively.

To reexperience childhood traumata or conflicts as completely as possible is to become convinced of the *particularity* of early learning experiences. Thus, the patient relives past traumatic experiences in order to
establish (learn) the particulars of these experiences and in order to minimize the likelihood of continued faulty generalization in later similar situations. Insight based on the exploration and interpretation of transference
phenomena is not the only mechanism for promoting recognition of the
natural human (and biologic) tendency to recreate past situations in the
present[5] and to respond to them as if universalization of experience were a
valid cognitive/emotional induction. In fact, a change in behavior can supply a compelling counterinstance to the prevailing faulty cognitive or emotional set.

All therapists have one objective in common, and that is to help patients respond internally and externally in more adaptive ways, to bring
feeling states and behavioral responses into closer alliance. In pursuing this
end, psychoanalytic therapists concentrate on improving the patient's perceptual clarity and acuity through the analysis of distortional transference
phenomena; behavior therapists direct their efforts toward teaching the
patient to stop doing what is maladaptive and begin doing what is situation-
ally adaptive.

Development of Appropriate Responses

With pure analytic therapies a patient may come to see the need for
changing his behavior without being able to do so; with pure behavior
therapy, a patient may change his behavior without learning to see the
need for modifying the new learned responses when the subtleties of new
situations warrant and demand this modification. A response that is fully
adaptive to the nuances of particular new situations depends, therefore, as

---

[5]Biologically, stimulus generalization is an important learned involuntary component in this process but, in
our opinion, there is another demonstrable wish-component in the human situation: a stubborn nostalgic
longing for things to be as they were in the "good old days" of comfortable childhood dependence, as well
as for the original parental objects of a person's love/hate (Birk, 1973b).

much on accurate perception of the situation as it does on attention to the natural social feedback consequent to the response. Thus, psychoanalytic psychotherapy and behavior therapy are naturally complementary and resonant (Birk, 1973b); within the psychoanalytic therapies a patient learns to use insight as an incentive for a potentiation of behavior change and within the behavior therapies a patient learns how to change his behavior.

Behavior therapy is not only a technique to modify behavior; because of its emphasis on contingencies of reinforcement/punishment, it is also a profoundly effective technique for teaching people to consider the consequences of their behavior and to reconcile their internal reward/punishment systems with those of the natural social environment (this is especially true of behaviorally oriented group, family, and couple therapies). Even more important is the fact that behavior therapy is an approach capable of teaching patients to be able to provide themselves with effective counterinstances to their own faulty (anachronistic or primitive) views of world and self.

For example, a man in analysis may "know" that his wife is not his mother but if, because of a deficit in his own capacity for effective assertive behavior, she dominates him as his mother did, he will still feel like a little boy with her until this deficit in assertiveness can be remedied. In analytic psychotherapy, in such matters, the patient essentially is left to "work out his own salvation with fear and trembling."[6] The analyst may repetitively point out that his wife and his mother are quite different, may proddingly question why he did or didn't say X or Y, and may support (and reinforce) him emotionally for nascent efforts at assertiveness, but he *does not teach him how to be assertive*. A behavioral-psychoanalytic therapist would do all of these things and, *if needed*, would also use the behavioral technique of assertive training to teach him how to be assertive with his wife. This would typically include sessions with the wife; such sessions combine the therapeutic advantage of *in vivo* behavioral shaping, enhanced identification/modeling effects, and the systematic undermining of his old "little boy" feelings with his wife.

Not only does the patient learn to change his behavior, but he is also compelled to give up the faulty assumptions, often unconscious or preconscious, about himself and about his wife, that were part of the cognitive/emotional matrix out of which his maladaptive behavior with her arose, grew, and was neurotically nourished by him in the first place. If uninterrupted, this maladaptive behavior continues to reinforce the erroneous, albeit unconscious, coalescence of wife and mother. When the old behavior is interrupted and replaced by new assertive behavior, however, the new

---

[6]We do not mean here to derogate the didactic advantages, *in classical psychoanalysis*, of the analyst's limiting himself in a disciplined way to the pure task of analysis.

pattern stands in direct contradiction, as a counterinstance, to the chronic unconscious equation of wife and mother. In other words, the patient is behaving as if he no longer believed in this equation. The consequent shift in cognitive set and attendant increase in self-esteem serve as internal reinforcers for the continuance and increasing adaptiveness of the new behavior patterns.

Some of the powerful advantages of such an integrated model are illustrated in Figure 14.4. This is the paradigm that applies when a single clinician, as in the papers cited earlier by Rhoads and Feather (1974) and by one of us (Birk, 1974), integrates within his own clinical approach be-havioral *and* psychoanalytic principles and techniques.

This clinical integration is indicated by the circle labeled "therapist" that contains within it "psychoanalytic understanding and interpretation" and "behavioral analysis." Insofar as the therapist is able to direct the cogni-tive content of what he says toward insight while simultaneously managing to keep the behavioral valence (reinforcing/punishing) and timing (contingen-cies) of his therapeutic interactions consonant with the plan set up during the behavioral analysis, he can effect a significant behavioral change; to that

Figure 14.4.   The Integrated Model

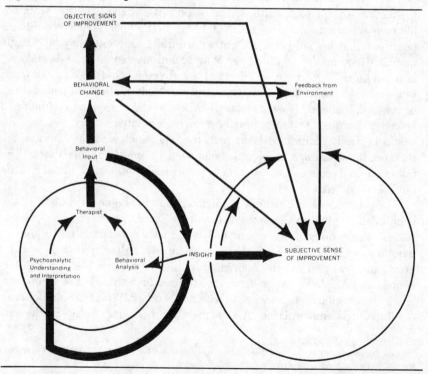

extent he is able to function simultaneously as a behavioral and a psychoanalytic therapist. Thus, there is an arrow leading from "therapist" to "behavioral input" as well as an arrow from "behavioral input" to "behavioral change" and one from "behavioral input" to "insight." That is, the therapist may also elect to try to impart cognitive understanding (insight) by means of psychoanalytic comments, questions, and interpretations; although these do not sabotage the behavioral regimen, they are not meant to subserve a particular function in that regimen. This accounts for the arrow leading directly from "psychoanalytic understanding" to "insight."

Another advantage of the integrated single-therapist model is that insight provides the therapist with data about the patient's internal processes, which may serve as internal reinforcers and punishers for behavior that may otherwise consistently defy skillful management of modifications by only external contingencies (for example, a masochistic patient may have a covert guilt-linked need to suffer, so that presumed punishing stimuli are in fact reinforcing). This is indicated by the arrow from "insight" to "behavioral analysis." Finally, as the other three smaller arrows from "insight" indicate, insight can be used to promote movement toward "subjective sense of improvement" from "behavioral change," "objective signs of improvement," and "feedback from the environment." In earlier figures, these were connected only by broken lines: in the absence of the patient's correctly recognizing the value of each of these (because of unanalyzed transference distortions or unresolved self-punitive needs, for example), the three do not *necessarily* lead to a subjective sense of improvement.

Transference and Countertransference

Naturally, considerable skill and experience are required for the therapist to be able to act explicitly as a reinforcer/punisher of certain patient behaviors while also managing to silhouette and interpret transference distortions. Basically, in order to do this the therapist must shift his stance away from the traditionally sought analytic neutrality, against the backdrop of which the transference is first developed and later experienced by the patient as a distortion. Instead, the therapist deliberately and openly attempts to promote the explicit behavioral goals toward which the patient and he together have agreed to work. Within such a therapeutic alliance, intruding transference feelings can be experienced and recognized (with concomitant therapeutic benefit) as a distortion by the patient.

It should be emphasized, however, that the *elicitation of transference phenomena is not a goal* during behavioral-psychoanalytic therapy, although it is certainly a proper and indispensable goal in classical psychoanalysis. The transference phenomena that do occur in the course of behavioral-psychoanalytic therapeutic programs tend to be very strong eruptions of

feeling in direct relation to the therapist's interventions. Resolution of transference conflict depends on the patient's being able to see the distinction
between the therapist and the early object of his strong and by now overgeneralized feelings. Recognition of the distinction is made considerably easier
by the patient's having a real sense of the therapist's individuality—a sense
that will, with proper interpretation and help from the therapist, defy further overgeneralized reactions from the patient. The therapist must therefore be a real person to the patient, not only in the sense of being a more
effective "social reinforcing machine" (Krasner, 1962) but also in order to
help correct the faulty cognitive/emotional responses that patients bring
from their past learning experiences and incorrectly apply to new individuals
and new situations.

Since there need be no concern about impeding the full development
of a traditional transference neurosis, transference behavior can be interpreted and managed in a straightforward and open way.

Case 4. A 46-year-old university professor, after almost a year of treatment in intensive behavioral-psychoanalytic group therapy, became quite
angry with the therapist (L.B.) when the therapist announced his plan to
take a two-week summer vacation. The patient wanted to take a four-week
vacation. This discrepancy, he said, would ruin his whole summer. His
anger deepened despite the therapist's offer not to charge for the extra two
weeks he wanted to be away. Open interpretive group discussion of this
led him to an early intellectual acknowledgment of the irrationality of these
deep strong feelings—which he continued to struggle with—and of their
rootedness in his anger at his wealthy but withholding father over money,
at his warmly affectionate but domineering mother over her controlling-
ness, and at both his parents and himself for his still-unresolved dependency needs ("I just wouldn't want to be away on vacation if the group
were meeting!").

Countertransference issues are also of course complicated by the decision to use reinforcement or punishment[7] as part of the therapeutic strategy. The therapist is compelled to examine his choice of behavioral contingencies in the light of his own (perhaps unconscious)[8] predisposition to
reward certain behaviors out of his own needs, rather than because of their
social adaptiveness for the patient, or to punish other behaviors as an acting
out of his own anger.

---

[7]The use of punishment may (rarely) include frank aversive procedures; more commonly, however, punishment takes the form of negative interpretations (Birk, 1974).
[8]For this reason, we believe that therapists who use behavioral techniques have even more reason than
traditional therapists to explore thoroughly their own unconscious processes, ideally within the setting of a
classical psychoanalysis.

For example, a female therapist with unanalyzed castration impulses may unconsciously wish to undermine the assertive traits in her male patients. Thus she may discourage (subtly punish) his assertive responses, while simultaneously overtly reinforcing counteraggressive behaviors in the service of promoting "gentleness" or "sensitivity." Similarly, a therapist with unresolved (perhaps unrecognized) sadistic or angry feelings may choose punishment strategies for personal gratification rather than therapeutic utility.

To sum up, it should be said that the behavioral-psychoanalytic therapist is accepting a great ethical responsibility and should be vigilantly on guard against using learning theory and learning therapies as a way of rationalizing and justifying the acting out of impulses that serve his own needs rather than the patient's.

"Saving the Phenomena"[9]

In the preceding parts of this paper we have tried to highlight the potential therapeutic power that results from broadening the criteria used to determine the set of clinically relevant psychological data and to propose a comprehensive framework into which clinical data of all sorts can be fitted. One of the major features of our proposal is the built-in exhortation neither to overlook phenomena nor to deliberately exclude practical operations merely because they do not conform to preconceived metaphysical or methodological standards of a particular theoretical stance—not to exclude, for example, subjective reports on the grounds that they are not amenable to objective quantification, nor behavior modification by contingency scheduling on the grounds that it does not contribute directly to heightened self-awareness.

We do recognize, however, that the sets of data circumscribed by the strict behavioral and psychoanalytic models constitute categories of differing ontological status. It is a well-acknowledged fact that subjective reports are *about* mental events, feelings, and fantasies but are not the events, feelings, or fantasies themselves. Mental events, sensations, or feelings are private, to the extent that only the individual whose consciousness they shape has privileged access to them. Behaviors, on the other hand, are in a sense their own report and are therefore amenable to scientific description and confirmation by observation, measurement, and quantification. And we recognize that these two categories of phenomena require two essentially different approaches, designed to effect two different ends.

---

[9]"Saving the phenomena" (*tithenai ta phainomena*) is a short-hand name for the philosophical argument that originated with the Greek philosophers between those who sought to ignore anomalous "facts" in favor of theoretical purity and those who sought to preserve the facts against an imposed theoretical distortion.

Experimental psychologists can employ as a scientific strategy a necessarily restricted view of the "significant phenomena," i.e., of what there is that underlies rigorous scientific theory. But it is not the same for the phenomenological and operational underpinnings of clinical psychiatry; there *are* behaviors and there *are* feelings, dreams, fantasies, fears, ideas, and a collection of techniques for dealing with them that have not yet been conceptually integrated. To exclude any of these in order to preserve intact a favored ideal of methodological rigor is a luxury of scientific strategy that clinical psychiatry cannot properly afford.

***

The insight-seeking methodology of psychoanalytic psychotherapy and the change-producing techniques of behavior therapy form a complementary system; the former serves to uncover the early developmental learning experiences that shaped the later maladaptive and overgeneralized emotional/cognitive/behavioral habits, thereby providing therapeutically powerful counterinstances to the patient's prevailing faulty world-view and self-evaluation.

Summary

Psychoanalysis and behavior therapy developed within separate, contrasting, and seemingly incompatible scientific/epistemological traditions. Psychoanalysis was founded by clinicians who were trying to "make sense of" introspective self-report data, while behavior therapy was founded by experimentalists who were employing the data of direct observation, explicitly excluding consideration of private (subjective) events. Over the past decade, a growing acknowledgment of the clinical utility and scope of behavioral methods has reduced chauvinistic sparring and has led to greater mutual respect, as well as to some pioneering collaborative work. Although the theoretical determinants of psychoanalysis and behavior therapy are both historically and philosophically context-dependent and represent no absolute deterrent to genuine theoretical synthesis, until now there has been no real consensus about the need for or form of a conceptual integration. The authors here propose that this is not only possible but necessary in order to preserve all the data of the clinical therapeutic process.

References

Alexander, F. *Psychoanalysis and psychotherapy*. New York: W.W. Norton & Co., 1956.

Alexander, F. The dynamics of psychotherapy in the light of learning theory. *American Journal of Psychiatry*, 1963, *120*, 440–448. [Reprinted in this volume.]

Allen, K. E., Hart, B. M., & Buell, J. S., Harris, F. R., & Wolf, M. M. Effects of social reinforcement on isolate behavior of a nursery shool child. *Child Development*, 1964, 35, 511–518.

Aronson, G. Learning theory and psychoanalytic theory. *Journal of the American Psychoanalytic Association*, 1972, 20, 622–637.

Ayllon, T., & Azrin, N. The measurement and reinforcement of behavior of psychotics. *Journal of the Experimental Analysis of Behavior*, 1965, 8, 357–383.

Ayllon, T., & Azrin, N. H. *The token economy*. New York: Appleton-Century-Crofts, 1968.

Baer, D. M., & Wolf, M. M. The reinforcement contingency in pre-school and remedial education. In R. D. Hess & R. M. Baer (Eds.), *Early Education*. Chicago: Aldine, 1968, pp. 119–129.

Bandura, A., & Walters, R. H. *Social learning and personality development*. New York: Holt, Rinehart & Winston, 1963.

Beck, A. Cognitive therapy: Nature and relation to behavior therapy. *Behavior Therapy*, 1970, 1, 184–200.

Birk, L. Social reinforcement in psychotherapy. *Conditioned Reflex*, 1968, 3, 116–123.

Birk, L. Behavior therapy: Integration with dynamic psychiatry. *Behavior Therapy*, 1970, 1, 522–526.

Birk, L. Psychoanalytic omniscience and behavioral omnipotence: Current trends in psychotherapy. *Seminars in Psychiatry*, 1972, 4, 113–120.

Birk, L. *Biofeedback: Behavioral medicine*. New York: Grune & Stratton, 1973. (a)

Birk, L. Psychoanalysis and behavioral analysis: Natural resonance and complementarity. *International Journal of Psychiatry*, 1973, 11, 160–166. (b)

Birk, L. Intensive group therapy: An effective behavioral-psychoanalytic method. *American Journal of Psychiatry*, 1974, 131, 11–16.

Birk, L., Stolz, S., & Brady, J. P., Brady, J. V., Lazarus, A. A., Lynch, J. J., Rosenthal, A. J., Skelton, W. D., Stevens, J. B., & Thomas, E. J. Behavior therapy in psychiatry, Task Force Report no. 5. American Psychiatric Association, Washington, D.C., 1973.

Crisp, A. J. Transference, symptom emergence, and social repercussion in behavior therapy. *British Journal of Medical Psychology*, 1966, 39, 179–196.

Cushing, J. G. N. Report of the committee on the evaluation of psychoanalytic therapy. *Bulletin of the American Psychoanalytic Association*, 1952, 8, 44–50.

Dollard, J., & Miller, N. E. *Personality and psychotherapy*. New York: McGraw-Hill, 1950.

Feather, B. W., & Rhoads, J. M. Psychodynamic behavior therapy. *Archives of General Psychiatry*, 1972, 26, 503–511.

Fenichel, O. *The psychoanalytic theory of neurosis*. New York: W. W. Norton, 1945.

Ferster, C. B. Clinical reinforcement. *Seminars in Psychiatry*, 1972, 9, 101–111.

Ferster, C. B. A functional analysis of depression. *American Psychologist*, 1973, 28, 857–870.

Ferster, C. B., & DeMyer, M. K. The development of performances in autistic children in an automatically controlled environment. *Journal of Chronic Disorders*, 1961, 13, 312–345.

Freud, S. *An outline of psychoanalysis*. New York: W. W. Norton, 1949 (Translated by J. Strachey).

Freud, S. The interpretation of dreams (1900). In *Complete psychological works* (Vols. 4–5), standard edition. London: Hogarth Press, 1953. (Translated and edited by J. Strachey).

Freud, S. Mourning and melancholia (1917). In *Complete psychological works* (Vol. 14), standard edition. London: Hogarth Press, 1957, pp. 243–259. (Translated and edited by J. Strachey).

Glover, E. *The techniques of psychoanalysis*. New York: International Universities Press, 1955, pp. 261–350.

Harris, F. R., Johnston, M. K., Kelley, C. S., & Wolf, M. M. Effects of positive social reinforcement on regressed crawling of a nursery school child. *Journal of Educational Psychology*, 1964, 55, 35–41.

Knight, R. P. Introjection, projection, and identification. *Psychoanalytic Quarterly*, 1940, 9, 334–341.

Koff, R. H. A definition of identification: A review of the literature. *International Journal of Psychoanalysis*, 1961, 42, 362–370.

Krasner, L. The therapist as a social reinforcement machine. In H. H. Strupp & L. Luborsky (Eds.), *Research in psychotherapy* (Vol. 2). Washington, D.C.: American Psychological Association, 1962, pp. 61–94.

Krasner, L. Behavior therapy. *Annual Review of Psychology*, 1971, 22, 483–532.

Lewinsohn, P. M. The behavioral study and treatment of depression. In M. Hersen, R. M. Eisler, & P. M. Miller (Eds.), *Progress in behavior modification* (Vol. 1). New York: Academic Press, 1975, pp. 19–64.

Lewinsohn, P. M., Weinstein, M. S., & Shaw, D. A. Depression: A clinical approach. In R. Rubin & C. Franks (Eds.), *Advances in behavior therapy*. New York: Academic Press, 1969, pp. 231–240.

Liberman, R. P., & Raskin, D. E. Depression: A behavioral formulation. *Archives of General Psychiatry*, 1971, 24, 515–523.

Lindemann, E. Symptomatology and management of acute grief. *American Journal of Psychiatry*, 1944, 101, 141–153.

Lindsley, O. R., & Skinner, B. F. A method for the experimental analysis of behavior of psychotic patients. *American Psychologist*, 1954, 9, 419–420.

Locke, E. A. Is "behavior therapy" behavioristic? (An analysis of Wolpe's psychotherapeutic models). *Psychological Bulletin*, 1971, 76, 318–327.

Marmor, J. *Modern psychoanalysis: New directions and perspectives*. New York: Basic Books, 1968.

Marmor, J. Dynamic psychotherapy and behavior therapy. *Archives of General Psychiatry*, 1971, 24, 22–28. [Reprinted in this volume.]

Marmor, J. The future of psychoanalytic therapy. *American Journal of Psychiatry*, 1973, 130, 1197–1202.

Miller, N. E. Interactions between learned and physical factors in mental illness. In D. Shapiro, T. X. Barber, L. V. DiCara, J. Kamiya, N. E. Miller, & J. Stoyva (Eds.), *Biofeedback and self-control*. Chicago: Aldine, 1973, pp. 460–476.

Nemiah, J. Psychodynamic psychotherapy. In G. L. Usdin (Ed.), *Overview of psychotherapies*. New York: Brunner/Mazel, 1975, pp. 36–50.

Porter, R. *The role of learning in psychotherapy*. A Ciba Foundation Symposium. Boston: Little, Brown, 1968.

Rhoads, J. M., & Feather, B. W. Application of psychodynamics to behavior therapy. *American Journal of Psychiatry*, 1974, *131*, 17–20.

Seligman, M. E. P. Depression and learned helplessness. In R. J. Friedman & M. M. Katz (Eds.), *The psychology of depression*. Washington, D.C.: Winston-Wiley, 1974, pp. 83–113.

Shapiro, D., & Birk, L. Group therapy in experimental perspective. *International Journal of Group Psychotherapy*, 1967, *17*, 211–224.

Skinner, B. F. *The behavior of organisms*. New York: Appleton-Century, 1938.

Skinner, B. F. *Science and human behavior*. New York: Macmillan Company, 1953.

Sloane, R. B. The converging paths of behavior therapy and psychotherapy. *International Journal of Psychiatry*, 1969, *7*, 493–503.

Sloane, R. B., Staples, F. R., & Cristol, A. H., Yorkston, N. J., & Whipple, K. *Psychotherapy versus behavior therapy*. Cambridge: Harvard University Press, 1975.

Stampfl, T. G., & Lewis, D. J. Essentials of implosive therapy: A learning—theory-based psychodynamic behavioral therapy. *Journal of Abnormal Psychology*, 1967, *72*, 496–503.

Suomi, S. J., Harlow, H. F., & McKinney, W. T., Jr. Monkey psychiatrists. *American Journal of Psychiatry*, 1972, *128*, 927–932.

Tabachnick, N. Research committee report on psychoanalytic practice. *The Academy*, 1973, *17*, 3–5.

Van Lawick-Goodall, J. *In the shadow of man*. Boston: Houghton Mifflin, 1971.

Wolf, E. Learning theory and psychoanalysis. *International Journal of Psychiatry*, 1969, *7*, 525–535.

Wolpe, J. *Psychotherapy by reciprocal inhibition*. Stanford: Stanford University Press, 1958.

Chapter 15

Psychotherapy by a Combined Behavioral and Dynamic Approach

John Paul Brady

Behavior therapy refers to an approach to psychological disorders which stresses a behavioral analysis of the patient's adjustment difficulties and employs a number of psychotherapeutic techniques which focus fairly directly on the removal or amelioration of maladaptive behaviors or psychological states. Many of these techniques, such as the systematic desensitization treatment of neurosis (Wolpe, 1958) and the anticipatory avoidance treatment of homosexuality (Feldman & MacCulloch, 1965), involve the direct application of principles derived from experiments in learning (learning theory). Others, such as the treatment of tics and stuttering by "negative practice" seem more empirical in nature although they too are often rationalized in learning theory terms.

In contrast, the psychotherapeutic approach currently in most common use in the United States focuses less on the patient's presenting symptoms than on the intrapsychic conflicts and interpersonal relationships which are presumed to give rise to his specific neurotic difficulties. This group of techniques also has some empirical basis but is derived to a large extent from psychoanalytic theory and practice. Treatment in which these techniques are emphasized is usually termed dynamic or psychoanalytically oriented psychotherapy.

This research was supported in part by Research Scientist Award K3-MH-22.682 from the National Institute of Mental Health, U. S. Public Health Service. This chapter originally appeared in *Comprehensive Psychiatry*, 1968, 9, 536–543. Reprinted by permission of Grune and Stratton, Inc., and the author.

Differences in Theory

Some therapists of exclusively psychodynamic or behavioral orientation hold that the assumptions which underlie the two treatment approaches are antithetical and mutually exclusive. These therapists often suggest that the considerable overlap in the way patients are actually treated by exponents of behavioral and dynamic methods is the basis for the fact that each form of treatment produces favorable results in some patients. Thus it has been argued that favorable results in behavior therapy are due to suggestion, transference, or other processes rather than specific conditioning procedures (Glover, 1959). Others attribute the improvement associated with dynamic psychotherapy to the unplanned reciprocal inhibition of neurotic responses (Wolpe, 1958). However, many authors hold that the psychological theories which underlie the two approaches are not mutually exclusive but rather different levels of conceptualization and analysis of the same phenomena. Apropos of this view are efforts to reexamine concepts and principles of psychoanalytic theory and practice from the viewpoint of learning theory. Concepts such as displacement, repression, and insight which are central to dynamic theory have been meaningfully analyzed in conditioning terms (Brady, 1967; Dollard & Miller, 1950; Miller, 1948). The purpose of such reformulations has not been to replace one terminology or frame of reference with another. Rather, the object has been to gain new perspectives on psychotherapeutic phenomena which may help clarify important theoretical issues and suggest innovations in treatment which are amenable to clinical investigation.

Many psychoanalytic writers also have argued for reformulations of analytic theory by means of learning models. However, these writers generally prefer more cognitive theories of learning than the conditioning or "stimulus–response" models which form the basis of most behavior therapists' concepts of neurosis and treatment procedures (Alexander, 1963; Marmor, 1964; Miller, Galanter, & Pribram, 1960; Piers & Piers, 1965). However, these knotty problems of theory will not be discussed further; rather, attention will be turned to differences in practice between the two approaches.

Differences in Practice

Dynamic psychotherapists have often recommended techniques and procedures which, in somewhat different form, constitute one or another procedure of behavior therapy. In fact, Freud stated that the patient with severe agoraphobia hardly ever overcomes his problem "if one waits till the patient lets the analysis influence him to give it up" (Freud, 1953). Rather, concurrent with analytic treatment, the patient must go out alone and struggle with his anxiety. This suggestion of Freud touches upon a group of behavior therapy techniques in which the anxiety elicited by certain situations is gradually reduced by having the patient expose himself to the situation, in real life or in imagination, in a gradual manner and under conditions in which the anxiety may be inhibited by other responses (Freeman, 1965). In recent years many therapists have described techniques conducted within the framework of traditional dynamic psychotherapy which are closely akin to behavior therapy procedures. For example, Stevenson described such techniques as assigning a patient the task between sessions of asserting himself more in a relationship in which he is usually overly passive (Stevenson, 1959). This kind of direct instigation of behavioral change is closely related to a behavioral technique usually termed assertive training (Wolpe, 1958). Such innovations in traditional dynamic therapy are becoming more frequent (Freeman, 1965). Of course the difference between these innovations and behavior therapy proper is that in the latter learning principles are applied in an explicit and systematic manner to fashion more effective methods of behavior modification.

It has been pointed out by a number of writers that the influence of the behavior therapist on the course of his patient's illness is not restricted to the specific conditioning procedures involved (Crisp, 1966; Marks & Gelder, 1966). In obtaining a detailed account of the patient's difficulties and adjustment before specific treatment is instigated, the patient may obtain a clearer picture of his illness and factors that are important in its maintenance. In addition, much emotional support and suggestion may be conveyed. Such factors continue to operate during the course of treatment as there is usually considerable therapist–patient interaction in addition to the administration of conditioning procedures. Much of this interaction is potentially therapeutic and may include interpretative as well as supportive elements. Thus techniques which are used in a more focused and systematic manner in dynamic therapy are present here as well and doubtlessly contribute to the efficacy of behavior therapists' treatment.

From the foregoing it appears that the degree to which the treatment of a particular patient involves indirect techniques which relate to the patient's feelings, thoughts and relationships versus efforts toward the direct modification of symptom-behavior varies on a continuum. Idealized psychoanalytic therapy would be at one end of this continuum and therapy conducted solely by an inanimate conditioning machine at the other. It would seem reasonable that different patients have different needs and might best be treated by approaches corresponding to different points on this continuum.

Some therapists believe that behavior therapy is best suited for certain patients but that dynamic therapy is the method of choice for others. In the course of careful clinical investigations Marks, Gelder, and their colleagues have attempted to delineate some of the relative indications for each approach in the treatment of phobic patients (Gelder & Marks, 1966; Gelder, Marks, & Wolff, 1967; Marks & Gelder, 1965; Marks & Gelder, 1966). A number of writers have described the use of both behavior therapy and dynamic therapy for the same patient, either concurrently or in sequence (Crisp, 1966; Gelder, Marks, & Wolff, 1967; Lazarus, 1963a; Marks & Gelder, 1966). The flexibility inherent in these approaches to the treatment of neurotic patients is appealing. However, the problem of establishing criteria for choice of treatment approach is a difficult one, involving complex theoretical issues which probably can be solved only by careful clinical investigations. This is also difficult because behavior therapists and dynamic therapists are often unfamilar with the terminology and procedures each other use. Further, they often differ in their methods of evaluating patients, assessing improvement, and in fact, what they consider the illness to be. In this paper, no comprehensive discussion of these problems will be attempted but one issue of special importance will be briefly discussed. This concerns the notion of neurosis.

The Concept of Neurosis

The controversy in the literature over the relative efficacy of behavior therapy and dynamic therapy has been confused by different uses of the term *neurosis* (Bookbinder, 1962). Behavior therapists usually mean by neurosis the collection of specific behavioral and psychological symptoms the patient displays. For example, a housewife with a typical agoraphobia may report and display anxiety in a variety of situations, such a leaving her house alone and riding on public conveyances, which restricts her movements and activities a great deal. Of course not everyone is equally disposed to develop a neurosis of this kind, even under the same degree of "environmental stress." This predisposition to neurosis, whether it be primarily genetic or experiential in origin, some behavior therapists term *neuroticism*. Thus, the patient with agoraphobia may be a generally anxious and dependent person. Indeed, the agoraphobia may be maintained in part by its effects on her husband, tending to keep him at her side and thus fulfilling some of her excessive dependency needs. The behavior therapist would focus his treatment on the agoraphobic symptoms, perhaps in a treatment program to decondition the anxiety associated with going out alone, being on a public conveyance, etc. Some behavior therapists would in addition deal directly with patient's dependency on her husband. In any case the therapist would anticipate that relieving the specific agoraphobic symptoms would facilitate general improvement in the patient's adjustment. Self-confidence and self-esteem would be increased by mastery of the problem and more adaptive means of dealing with current stresses would be expected to emerge.

In contrast, the dynamic therapist would not consider the agoraphobic symptoms the neurosis but merely a manifestation of the neurosis. Rather, the neurosis would be regarded as certain underlying conflicts. Depending on the clinical details of the case (and to some extent on the therapist's theoretical orientation), these conflicts might be viewed as chiefly sexual in nature or primarily as conflicts arising from unresolved dependency needs and aggressive strivings. An understanding of these conflicts would in turn involve an understanding of the patient's character structure. Thus it seems what the behavior therapist terms neuroticism is close to what the dynamic therapist terms the neurosis—in both instances the propensity to develop certain maladaptive feelings and behaviors which compromise the patient's adjustment. The dynamic therapist would focus his treatment on these propensities and work toward their diminution. Again depending on his orientation, style of dynamic therapy, and the intensity of therapy planned, he might think more in terms of altering the patient's character structure or resolving current intrapsychic and interpersonal conflicts. His expectation would be that the specific agoraphobic symptoms will improve when progress is made with the underlying conflicts and/or character structure.

It is essential to keep these differences in mind in assessing the relative efficacy of behavioral and dynamic treatments. Otherwise, lack of agreement on what constitutes the illness and adequate assessment of change precludes any meaningful comparison of results. This indicates the necessity of evaluating multiple aspects of patients' adjustment in comparative studies since it may be that behavior therapy techniques bring about improvement in some areas whereas the impact of dynamic psychotherapy is greater on other areas of the patient's life. Indeed, some comparisons of the results of behavior therapy and dynamic therapy in the treatment of phobic patients suggest that this is the case (Marks & Gelder, 1965). This suggests further that some patients might be best treated by a combined approach. Perhaps in certain instances this would mean behavioral techniques for specific neurotic symptoms which are currently restricting the patient's activity and are an immediate source of discomfort and concern. Dynamic psychotherapy might be directed at less focused maladaptive tendencies the patient demonstrates in his relationships with others.

A Combined Behavioral and Dynamic Approach

The present writer has developed an innovation in the systematic desensitization treatment of severe sexual frigidity which involves the use of subanesthetic doses of I.V. Brevital (methohexital sodium) to facilitate the deconditioning process (Brady, 1966a, 1967). It has been the only treatment in those cases in which primary sexual inhibition seemed central to the patient's adjustment difficulties. Marital and other adjustment problems are usually present in these women as a consequence of their frigidity. Successful treatment of the frigidity is usually followed by general improvement in these other areas of the patient's life.

In other patients with a complaint of frigidity it is apparent that current sexual difficulties are not primary or central, but rather the result of other neurotic problems, especially ones involving the marital relationship. In these instances, progress in resolution of marital or other difficulties by psychotherapy is often accompanied by improvement in sexual adjustment.

However, there remains women in whom both primary sexual inhibition and unresolved nonsexual conflicts play a major role in the frigidity. A case will be briefly described to illustrate this situation and its treatment by a combined behavioral and dynamic approach.

The patient was a 25-year-old nurse who was frigid during the two years of her marriage. Petting before marriage produced some embarrassment and distress, but she did not anticipate the severe negative reactions which occurred during intercourse after marriage. At times these reactions were mild, permitting her to complete coitus but rarely bringing pleasure and never ending in orgasm. At other times intense anxiety would develop, making it necessary to terminate relations. Sometimes during these latter encounters, fantasies of a sadomasochistic nature would intrude themselves in which she would see herself being "abused" by her husband with other men looking on. Although accompanied by sexual arousal, the fantasies would lead to more anxiety and termination of coitus. After a year with little change in symptoms, the patient entered psychotherapy which focused on early experiences and her relationship with her husband. It seems that her father had been an impatient and physically abusive man who ran the family in an autocratic manner and demonstrated affection toward no one. The patient's mother reacted to these abuses with the attitude of a martyr and was close and affectionate with all her children. The patient recognized that her sexual problems were probably related to the poor model her father presented of a husband and lover and, at the same time, unresolved aspects of her relationship with him. She recognized also her tendency to overreact to her husband's somewhat critical manner. An accountant with many obsessive-compulsive personality traits, the husband was inclined to be a little demanding and controlling with his wife but was a generally warm and affectionate person.

The frigidity did not yield to psychotherapy, however, and other aspects of their adjustment worsened. The patient felt progressively more discouraged and inadequate, and her husband became less tolerant of the problem as he, too, experienced a growing feeling of frustration and inadequacy. Therapy was terminated after nine months because the couple moved to Philadelphia.

The problem remained the same during the four months before the couple was seen by the present writer. After assessing the present status of the problem, it was decided to make a direct approach to the frigidity since progress in other areas seemed unlikely so long as this very disruptive symptom persisted. To this end the frigidity was treated by systematic desensitization as described by Wolpe (1958) and Lazarus (1963b) but modified by the use of I.V. Brevital. This procedure has been reported elsewhere and will not be described in detail here (Brady, 1966a, 1966b, 1967). In brief, the patient was gotten into a deeply relaxed and tranquil state with the aid of Brevital. Then she was instructed to vividly imagine a series of sexual scenes with her husband beginning with the initial sexual approach and ending with coitus. However, she was permitted to progress from one scene of the series or hierarchy to the next only if no appreciable anxiety was experienced. With this patient it required 17 sessions of 30 minutes each over a period of three months for her to be able to vividly imagine continuing coitus with her husband without negative affects of any kind. During the course of the desensitization therapy, there was steady improvement in her sexual adjustment. By the time the desensitization treatment was completed, the couple regarded their sexual adjustment as satisfactory for the first time. Negative emotional reactions were no longer occurring but the patient was yet to experience an orgasm. This improvement in the sexual relationship was accompanied by a general improvement in both wife and husband and in the marriage. However, some residual problems were still in evidence, centering around the husband's overly controlling tendencies. The author then saw the patient in weekly sessions over a period of four months in which her relationship with her father was reexplored with an effort to work through those feelings which seemed to be contributing to her sensitivity to the husband's behavior. The husband was also seen several times to help him understand his wife's needs for independence and autonomy. Following this period of short-term psychotherapy, the total situation improved further, including the sexual adjustment. The patient experienced an orgasm for the first time during the last month of therapy and has continued to do so with coitus about 90 percent of the time. At present, two years after both courses of treatment were completed, the sexual and general marital adjustment has remained good, as has the individual adjustment for both man and wife.

Needless to say, this one case does not prove the efficacy of combined treatment of this sort. It is cited merely to demonstrate its feasibility. It is possible that all aspects of the problem presented by this patient and her husband could have been treated by behavior therapy procedures. It is possible also that a good result would have been attained by a longer trial of dynamic psychotherapy alone. However, the data of the case strongly suggest that the combined approach was an efficient way to deal effectively with the problem presented by this patient.

Summary

Much of the psychological theory underlying behavior therapy and dynamic therapy are not contradictory or mutually exclusive but are different levels of conceptualization of the same phenomena. There seems to be much overlap in the way patients are actually treated within the frameworks of these two approaches. It is argued that for some patients an effective therapeutic regimen may be one that includes both a behavioral and a dynamic course of treatment. The feasibility of such a combined approach is illustrated by a case report of a woman whose severe frigidity was first treated by Brevital-aided systematic desensitization. This brought about an increase in her sexual responsiveness and improvement in her general adjustment. Following this, problems in relationships with her husband and others were the focus of short-term dynamic psychotherapy. This was followed by further improvement in her sexual functioning as well as improvement in other aspects of her adjustment.

References

Alexander, F. The dynamics of psychotherapy in the light of learning theory. *American Journal of Psychiatry*, 1963, *120*, 440–448. [Reprinted in this volume.]

Bookbinder, J. J. Simple conditioning versus the dynamic approach to symptoms and symptom substitution: A reply to Yates. *Psychological Reports*, 1962, *10*, 71—77.

Brady, J. P. Brevital-relaxation treatment of frigidity. *Behaviour Research & Therapy*, 1966, *4*, 71–77. (a)

Brady, J. P. Brevital-relaxation treatment of neurosis. Proceedings of the Symposium on Higher Nervous Activity. Madrid, Spain, September 9, 1966. (b)

Brady, J. P. Comments on methohexitone-aided systematic desensitization. *Behaviour Research & Therapy*, 1967, *5*, 259–260. (a)

Brady, J. P. Psychotherapy, learning theory, and insight. *Archives of General Psychiatry*, 1967, *16*, 304–311. (b)

Crisp, A. H. Transference, symptom emergence, and social repercussions in behavior therapy. *British Journal of Medical Psychology*, 1966, *39*, 179–196.

Dollard, J., & Miller, N. E. *Personality and psychotherapy*. New York: McGraw-Hill, 1950.

Feldman, M. P., & MacCulloch, M. J. The application of anticipatory avoidance learning to the treatment of homosexuality. *Behaviour Research & Therapy*, 1965, *2*, 165–184.

Freeman, H. The current status of behavior therapy. *Comprehensive Psychiatry*, 1965, *6*, 355–368.

Freud, S. Turnings in the ways of psycho-analytic therapy. *Collected papers* (Vol. II). London: Hogarth Press, 1953, pp. 399–400.

Gelder, M. G., & Marks, I. M. Severe agoraphobia: A controlled prospective trial of behaviour therapy. *British Journal of Psychiatry*, 1966, *112*, 309–319.

Gelder, M. G., Marks, I. M., & Wolff, H. H. Desensitization and psychotherapy in the treatment of phobic states: A controlled inquiry. *British Journal of Psychiatry*, 1967, *113*, 53–73.

Glover, E. Critical notice. *British Journal of Medical Psychology*, 1959, *32*, 68–74.

Lazarus, A. A. the results of behaviour therapy in 126 cases of severe neurosis. *Behaviour Research & Therapy*, 1963, *1*, 69–79. (a)

Lazarus, A. A. The treatment of chronic frigidity by systematic desensitization. *Journal of Nervous and Mental Disorders*, 1963, *136*, 272–278. (b)

Marks, I. M., & Gelder, M. G. A controlled retrospective study of behaviour therapy in phobic patients. *British Journal of Psychiatry*, 1965, *111*, 561–573.

Marks, I. M., & Gelder, M. G. Common ground between behaviour therapy and psychodynamic methods. *British Journal of Medical Psychology*, 1966, *39*, 11–23.

Marmor, J. Psychoanalytic therapy and theories of learning. In J. H. Masserman, (Ed.), *Science and psychoanalysis (Vol. VII)*. New York: Grune & Stratton, 1964.

Miller, G. A., Galanter, E., & Pribram, K. H. *Plans and the structure of behavior*. New York: Henry Holt, 1960.

Miller, N. E. Theory and experiment relating psychoanalytic displacement to stimulus–response generalization. *Journal of Abnormal and Social Psychology*, 1948, *43*, 155–178.

Piers, G., & Piers, M. W. Models of learning and the analytic process. Sixth International Congress of Psychotherapy, London, 1964. Basel: S. Karger, 1965.

Stevenson, I. Direct instigation of behavioural changes in psychotherapy. *Archives of General Psychiatry*, 1959, *1*, 99–107.

Wolpe, J. *Psychotherapy by reciprocal inhibition*. Stanford: Stanford University Press, 1958.

Chapter 16

Humanism and Behaviorism: Toward New Syntheses

David F. Ricks, Abraham Wandersman, and Paul J. Poppen

Our goal in *Humanism and Behaviorism* (Wandersman, Poppen, & Ricks, 1976) has been to stimulate a discussion between humanism and behaviorism and to examine its implications. Beginning with systematic presentations of the ideas and therapeutic approaches of two exemplary therapists, one a humanist and the other a behaviorist, we have carried through a dialogue between the two men, two ways of thought, two ways of collecting and interpreting information. Do we now know both approaches better, and can we see signs of mutual respect and possible mutual help? The reader will answer this for himself, and different readers will reach different conclusions. We will present our own conclusions here, but we will expect and welcome different judgments of the papers in *Humanism and Behaviorism*.

Our principal interest will be the degree to which the humanist and behaviorist positions, each of which has its own integrity and theoretical coherence, may be converging into a new synthesis. We do not expect humanism and behaviorism to come completely together, nor do we think it would be productive if they did. But as we worked on this project we

Reprinted by permission of the first author, David F. Ricks, and the publisher from A. Wandersman, P. J. Poppen, and D. F. Ricks (Eds.), *Humanism and behaviorism: Dialogue and growth*. New York: Pergamon Press, 1976, pp. 383–402.

were surprised to find much more agreement than either common stereotypes or our own original judgments could have predicted. Both groups are
clearly beyond the name calling, suspicion, and rhetoric that polarized
humanists and behaviorists from the middle 1950s to the early 1970s. We
seem to be on the verge of a creative synthesis that can unite the two
approaches, or at least large parts of them, into a *broader social developmental view of the human being as an active organizer of his own particular environment over time*. The intellectual power of such a new synthesis,
already suggested in recent work by Krasner and Ullmann (1973) and by
Bandura (1976) is impressive in its own right. It promises to revitalize our
understanding of human nature, choice, freedom, and the meanings we can
give to life. It has also given a new vitality to thinking about psychotherapy
and behavior change.

Attempts have been made to diminish or disregard the dichotomies
that have separated humanism and behaviorism. Some of the efforts have
merely tacked on the term humanism to a behavioristic program when they
apparently meant humanitarian, while others have attempted to integrate
ideas from humanism and behaviorism. Thoresen and Mahoney (1974)
point in the direction of a "behavioral humanism" which is "a scientific
approach to human behavior that neither ignores nor de-emphasizes cognitive phenomena" (p. 6). Work in this area has been progressing under the
social learning label. Thoresen (1973) has attempted to translate humanistic
ideas into admittedly simple statements of human action. For example, the
humanistic idea of having new and unusual thoughts, physical sensations,
and images is translated into increasing the frequency and variety of low
probability responses. Despite its oversimplistic appearance, Thoresen suggests that this approach may be empirically useful. In Wandersman et al.
(1976) we have encouraged a dialogue which included a synthesis of parts of
humanism and behaviorism as a goal, e.g., behavioristic methods for humanistic goals (Goldstein, 1976) and programs including humanistic methods
and goals and behavioristic methods and goals (Gold, 1976). In Wandersman et al. (1976), which viewed humanism and behaviorism in broader
perspective, the potential of integrating humanism and behaviorism with
other perspectives is suggested with the aim of producing a more comprehensive understanding of the relationship between man and society and
more efficient and functional interventions toward the improvement of the
quality of life.

Most of the papers assembled in Wandersman et al. (1976) have emphasized interpretation and understanding, getting ideas into perspective
and thinking them through, rather than gathering new data. This emphasis
might mislead a reader into thinking that we see only a small role for new
research data and information. Not so. Unlike those theorists who believe
that the paradigm clash between humanism and behaviorism can only be

resolved on nonempirical grounds, we hold for the solution of controversy by careful search for evidence. In part, the evidence can come from new experiments such as Alker (1976) developed for self-observation and Rychlak (1976) invented for studying reinforcement value. In part it can come from clinical research on the pragmatic values of helping children label and control their own emotional arousals (Gold, 1976) or helping an institution become a more person-centered place (Curtiss, 1976). "I would maintain that science in the broadest sense can and does discover what human values are, what the human being needs in order to live a good and happy life, what he needs in order to avoid illness, what is good for him and bad for him" (Maslow, 1966, p. 125).

Devereux (1976) argued to the same type of conclusion, that the fulfillment of values, and to some extent the values themselves, could be studied empirically. Psychotherapy and behavior change provide a real life observation post for the study of human nature. Readers interested in the research background of the ideas debated here can find increasingly sophisticated research reports of what goes on in psychotherapy, and what its outcomes are, in Bergin and Garfield (1971), Bergin and Suinn (1974), Franks and Wilson (1974), and Orlinsky and Howard (1975).

We will now put our conclusions into four simple declarative sentences and show some of the evidence for each.

1. *Neither behaviorism nor humanism is reducible to the other, and neither can be completely incorporated into the perspectives or language of the other.* A popular strategy among behaviorists has been to translate other approaches into the presumably more precise language of behavioral theories (Sears, 1943; Dollard & Miller, 1950; Thoresen, 1973). This approach has some values. It may be useful, for instance, to study empathy as a particular kind of positive reinforcement. The problem is that the narrow scope of behaviorism has trouble encompassing much that is important to humanists, such as self-realization, self-evaluation, and emotional involvement.

There is clearly a movement toward incorporation of cognition, fantasy, affect, and self-awareness into behavior theory, and in the articles in Wandersman et al. (1976) these tend to be called by their common English names, not the neologisms of earlier behavior theory. This growth in the scope of behavior theory is probably due to its current involvement in real life problems. As behavior therapy grapples with the problems of anxious children, depressed adults, and complicated human relationships, it can be expected to show increased comprehesion of traditionally humanistic concerns. But similarity is not incorporation, and many humanistic ideas, such as self-actualization, can still be best expressed in humanistic language.

One striking illustration of this lack of specificity when behaviorists try to deal with humanistic concerns is the continued use of the global term "nonspecific factors" to describe the therapist's personal contribution to psychotherapy. Since humanistic therapists have been able to be quite specific and operational about what they mean by warmth, empathy, genuineness, transparency, etc., behavior therapists should now follow their lead, discard this tired old umbrella term, and try to be as precise about the person of the therapist as they are about his methods.

Humanists have argued that their ideas are necessary in order to understand how human beings can live proactively as well as reactively, can transcend immediate environments through memory and imagination, and can create their own environments through choices over time. Like G. H. Mead contemplating Watson, they can say that they find the behavior of the psychologist studying the rat more interesting than they find the rat itself. It does not seem likely that behavioral perspectives and language can soon encompass all of this range of inner life.

Behaviorism cannot be reduced to humanism because the humanistic position has no way of incorporating the many techniques of behavior therapy, at least without being considerably changed in the process. The humanist claim to incorporation of behaviorism within a more comprehensive understanding of human nature differentiates behavior in different environments. Behavioristic notions are interpreted as valuable only in showing how organisms respond to clearly structured, coercive environments, such as a Skinner box or Mischel's (1976) example of a red traffic light. In Maslow's hierarchy of needs, the bodily needs studied by behaviorists are not denied, but the organism is seen as responsive to higher needs as soon as these simple needs are satisfied. The trouble with this position is that the behaviorism it incorporates is too often a simple stereotype, rather than the more comprehensive and flexible scheme of a Bandura or a Mischel. These theories not only provide a technology for behavior change; they are complex paradigms in their own right, and while humanists can learn from them, no humanistic theorist has succeeded in comprehending social learning theory within his own broader system.

The essays in Wandersman et al. (1976) suggest a halt to further efforts at territorial aggrandizement. The field of therapy would be diminished without humanists such as Jourard, and it would be equally diminished without behaviorists such as Wolpe. People who come to treatment want "to be left alone or talked to as a human being," as Jourard (1976) says, but they also want to be relieved of their symptoms, inhibitions, and anxieties. What is needed is not submission of one system to the other, or translation of the language of one approach into the language of the other, but a creative synthesis of the two. Alexander, Dreher, and Willems (1976) suggest that this is already under way, with each system complementing and filling in weaknesses in the other.

2. *Humanism and behaviorism are reconcilable.* We offer this conclusion in opposition to those who argue that the two represent diametrically

opposite views, as well as those who argue that coexistence or detente is the closest approach the two can tolerate. Consider the Rychlak–Mischel debate (Wandersman et al., 1976). Both the humanist and the behaviorist point the way to understanding each human being as an active, aware problem solver, accommodating to his environment, but also assimilating it in his own way, influenced, but also influencing.

Whether this active organism must require a final cause, and this cause must be a self, remains open to debate. We have tried to hear both sides, the dialectical approach that Rychlak (1976) advocates in difficult situations. But we do not need to keep on seeing the two sides as opposites if we can find areas of agreement. The mainstream of modern thought is breaking down old dichotomies such as male vs. female, black vs. white, us vs. them. Are the humanist and behaviorist still so far apart? Isn't it likely that both are concentrating on complementary parts of some larger ecological or social or life span whole?

Of the several possible syntheses, the most popular continues to be one with a long history, the use of behavioristic techniques to reach humanistic goals. This strategy is most explicit in the program Curtiss (1976) used to redevelop a traditional mental hospital. Token economies have often been seen as the purest form of Skinnerian behaviorism. But in the hands of a humanist, these techniques were used to modify and enliven a tradition-dominated ward. Supporting Skinner's contention that behaviorism is a humanism that works, staff with behavioristic orientations were more optimistic about patient outcomes and preferred to spend more time with patients. "Those staff who were most humanistic in theory were least humanistic in practice" (p. 240). The goals set in this program, "internalizing controls" and "developing spontaneity," were thoroughly humanistic. And while the technology used was primarily behavioristic, the method of individual contracts based on mutual decisions of patient and therapist shows the respect for individual choice that is the hallmark of humanism.

Goldstein (1976) also demonstrates a reconciliation of humanistic goals, in this case emotional awareness and expressiveness, with a behavioral technology. Mischel (1976) and Bandura (1976) bring cognition into the 'empty organism" of classical behaviorism. Goldstein goes further, introducing not only emotion (which may or may not be expressed), but also a self (which is asserted in self-assertion). From the patient's point of view, there may not be much difference between Goldstein's behavioral instruction to try to begin statements with "I feel" and Rogers' empathic humanistic "You feel." A long-run comparative study might make the prediction that both techniques would result in people focusing on feelings and becoming increasingly aware of their own emotional states.

Gold's (1976) use of behavior therapy methods, interpreted within a cognitive developmental framework and directed toward the humanistic goal of helping the child reach accurate understanding of his emotional arousals, is an even more strongly bonded synthesis. Humanistic theorists have focused on emotion as their particular concern, but they can hardly ignore the effectiveness of Gold's behavioral methods in making emotions open to awareness, discussion, and control (though they might argue for transparency and expression rather than control, once the child is aware of the feeling). Since Gold's whole concept of human nature is so consistent with humanistic positions, we might even think of her approach as a synthesis of a humanistic *therapist* with a cognitive behavioral technology.

Coexistence will of course continue to flourish, with thoughtful therapists exploring combinations of methods that will emphasize behavior therapy for behavior problems and humanistic therapy for problems of experience and meaning. This mutual toleration will probably continue to take the form of "You treat your patients and I'll treat mine, and may we both be helpful." Or it can take the form of comparative studies of the efficiency of the two methods in reaching common goals, such as self-regulation, without too many unwanted side effects. This is the dominant stance of true believers in both fields today, but we believe that several of the authors in this volume have been able to go beyond collaboration toward integration and synthesis. Gold's comparative data, small scale as they are, suggest that even the most dedicated Rogerian, confronted with an actively aggressive child, might well adopt her behavioral methods.

Lambert and Bergin (1976) show another way in which reconciliation is coming about. Early debates on method had a childish "My therapist can lick your therapist" flavor. As therapy research moved from dramatic case reports to careful data collection and controlled studies, claims became less strident and extreme. The field of psychotherapy research now seems finally ready to begin providing reliable answers to what we might call its fundamental question. "What specific therapeutic interventions produce change, in what particular clients, under what specific conditions?" Psychotherapy research has had at this point a disturbingly small impact on practice. At one time this might have been due to the small amount of relevant research and its poor quality. At this point, however, any remaining inability to use research results in refining the therapeutic effort must be seen as at least in part to ingrained habit, stupidity, or dogmatism on the part of practicing therapists. The facts are beginning to be obvious, and those unwilling to use them have to ask themselves why. The importance of the issue is especially clear in the case of deterioration effects. If therapy doesn't help, we can at least feel that we have tried—but if a therapist harms his patient because of his own unwillingness to learn and grow, he really has no place in the therapeutic endeavor.

If we can begin to understand the varieties of therapists, not according to ideological labels, but according to what they are and do, we can go on to study their particular effects. Ricks and Fleming (1976) offer evidence that case studies of therapists can help us to understand their varieties, and perhaps even select appropriate therapists for particular patients. If they are correct, the best type of therapist for one population may be quite different from the optimal therapist for another. In one of his finest papers, Jourard (1971) described the lethal factors in the male role in American society. There may be comparable lethal factors in striving to be a therapist who can help everybody. The intense effort at self-improvement evident in Jourard's paper is matched in some of the papers by Rogers (1967) and in papers by humanistic therapists like Raskin (1975). It would probably be more practical for each therapist to take a long hard look at his work and its effects, and say something like: "All right, I am not really much help to this set of people (narcissistic depressives, delinquent boys, bored middle-aged housewives, or whatever) but I really seem to understand and help these others. So be it. This is where my future efforts will go."

   3. *Existing areas of agreement provide the growing points around which new syntheses of humanism and behaviorism are already developing. Both are concerned with humane goals.* While it is easy to exploit the clang association that equates "humanism" with "humane," the evidence in Wandersman et al. (1976) indicates that behaviorists are just as interested in alleviating suffering and promoting development as their humanistic peers. In fact, reading Wolpe (1976), one can gain new respect for the much maligned medical model, which really seeks control over pain, not over people, and removal of symptoms, not removal of the patient's autonomy or pride.

   Both humanists and social learning therapists are concerned with the person as an active organism. As Curtiss (1976) shows, a concern with behavior does not necessarily exclude efforts to promote spontaneity and self-control of one's own environment. Recent developments in social learning theory, which emphasize self-awareness and social effects of behavior, put an even stronger emphasis on the person in the person–environment interaction.

   The methods of humanists and behaviorists may lead to quite similar results. We mentioned earlier the common outcomes we might expect from Goldstein's (1976) and Rogers' (1967) particular ways of focusing on emotions in therapy. The analysis can be carried much further. Suppose, for example, we agree that it is well for people to feel less inhibited and anxious, and that one common sign of this is a feeling of increased freedom and openness, of having more alternatives open in one's life and more ready access to those alternatives. This freedom might be reached through several different therapy approaches. Gold (1976) might produce it by helping people to recognize their emotional states and gain control over them; Goldstein (1976) might help them to become more appropriately expressive; Rychlak (1976) might help them to recognize the reinforcements they were working for. An increased sense of freedom might also come from a Maslovian examination of one's need hierarchy, or from work with an empathic Rogerian therapist concerned with feelings.

A fourth area of agreement is the willingness to subject clinical impression and experience to the sobering test of research results. Rogers and his students pioneered the empirical study of therapy and its outcomes, but behavior therapists have been even more willing than the Rogerians to submit their ideas to the discipline of natural consequences and to be governed by these consequences, not by dogma.

4. *Broader perspectives may incorporate both humanism and behaviorism into more comprehensive positions.* Both traditional humanism and laboratory-based behaviorism were in trouble as soon as they tried to conceptualize the interactions of the person with his natural environment. The current sophisticated work of social learning theorists and those behaviorists interested in the design of environments is making up for this deficiency in the behavioral approaches. Other than Laing's residences and groups like Esalen, humanists seem to have no corresponding development. This lack of concern for the environment may account for the solipsistic quality of many humanistic interior journeys. Humanists might do better here if they remained aware of the human environment and of man as a social animal whose autonomy grows as he increases his options in society, not as he withdraws from it.

Goldstein (1976) offers a good example of the value to the behaviorist of seeing people in context. Some of the early assertiveness training and rational-emotive therapy brought about an unmitigated aggressiveness that later associates of the patient found extremely grating. A therapist has not helped his patient a great deal if he has only changed him from a person who gets ulcers to a person who gives them.

The main argument in each of the larger perspectives is "the postulate of empirical interconnectedness" (Devereux, 1976), which may also be expressed as the ecologist's "you can never do just one thing." All of the papers in the last section of Wandersman et al. (1976) were concerned with what both behaviorism and humanism fail to account for or leave out of their systems. They argue that Wolpe (1976) leaves out the context of the symptom he is removing—not the immediate behavioral context, but the human context (what function this symptom plays in the overall life of the patient) and the social context (its role in the family life and work life he is involved in or retreating from). Suppose, to use one of Wolpe's examples, a therapist removes a young man's fear of approaching women, but fails to help him to become socialized in the complicated rituals of sexual conduct. He might have cured an inhibition, but at the cost of freeing a potential rapist. Humanistic ignorance of the environment has often led to a naive radicalism, in which the environment is simply treated as an obstacle to self-realization, rather than the arena in which the self will either be realized or lost.

All of the broader perspectives are oriented around some conception of the person's development over time, "the complex and developing interdependence of the personality structure," in a society that is itself changing. Desire to remove the human being from his everyday context, the better to control and change him, has a long history. Asylums were originally supposed to provide a retreat from life's demands, and became in time the human warehouses we now call mental hospitals. Jails were originally "time out" for troublesome people, and became our current institutions for training in crime. We have learned from these experiments and others like them that there is no alternative to trying to cope with the person's problems where he is, in his own context. In practice this proves to be less convenient for the therapist but more effective for the patient. A systems view looks to change the system anywhere it shows inadequate functioning and some elasticity. Sometimes this may be in the parents, the school, or the job situation, not in the designated patient.

The broader perspectives remind us that a really shocking lack in current theories of psychotherapeutic change is their insulation from the growing corpus of knowledge about biological, cognitive, and social development. The life history perspective particularly emphasizes locating problems early and working with high-risk populations to lower the odds on later trouble rather than waiting for fully developed problems to be presented to the passively waiting therapist.

The most developed framework is the ecological perspective outlined by Alexander, Dreher, and Willems (1976). An ecological systems approach appears to comprehend all of the narrower systems, and it not only puts them in relation to each other, but gives each part a new specificity and relevance by including it into a larger, more articulated whole. A proper respect for the ways in which people fit into their biological and social systems prevents the ecologist from falling into the "anti-society" stance of the more radical humanists. The ecologist will strive to improve a society, but he will never assume that his patient can live without one.

One of the converging areas for learning theory, life history research, and ecology is study of the changing nature and availability of reinforcements through the life span. These seem to begin with attachment, safety, and appetitive needs, proceed through development of social and cognitive competence, culminate in mating and parenthood, then trail off into the milder reinforcements of later maturity and old age. A learning approach has to recognize that any organism learns what it is biologically biased and maturationally primed to learn. Study of different species suggests that primates, including humans, have the same propensity for learning relationships with fellow primates that rats have for learning mazes and dogs have for learning to salivate on cue. A therapy based on human learning then, will have to make learning about human relationships a primary focus. Older learning theories based on rats or dogs or pigeons are not likely to be so relevant. And as learning theories focus on how relationships are learned they converge toward areas traditionally considered humanistic.

Implications for Psychotherapy and Behavior Change

Who is to do psychotherapy? If we hold to traditional ways of thought, we have no general answer. Those trained in psychoanalysis hold that only the analytic route makes one fully analyzed, learning theorists argue that only their training makes one fully effective, and humanists may say that only their approach can make the therapist and his patient fully human. (If this sounds like parody, the authors are prepared to point to statements by true believers in each school that are even more extreme.) We believe that the evidence in Wandersman et al. (1976) justifies a belief that no one approach is likely to have the breadth of applicability, the flexibility, or the therapeutic effectiveness achieved by a judicious combination of methods. The best therapists are likely to be people who have a thorough grounding in psychoanalysis, humanism, and behaviorism. Unlike traditional behaviorists, they are likely to be quite precise as to how they themselves enter into the therapeutic experience of their clients—and, unlike traditional psychoanalysts and humanists, they are likely to be able to do a good many kinds of active intervention.

In training, humanists have tended to emphasize encounters, experiences, growth within the therapist. Behaviorists have emphasized a range of methods. Training programs for psychotherapists have a challenging task ahead as they try to combine training in technical skills with experiences that promote personal growth.

How is therapy to be done? The message of Wandersman et al. (1976) is clear: get beyond paper credentials and schools and take what helps people from each approach, without undue regard for intellectual paternity. The most creative therapists will find excitement in developing individual approaches that fit the age and problems of each patient and the setting of the therapeutic program. The section on broader perspectives suggests, however, that therapists ought to check carefully for the generalizability of their findings before applying them on a large scale in new settings and with new age groups. Maturation and environment are powerful influences that easily defeat insensitive transfer of methods from one age group or local setting to another.

Much of the most important new work in therapy will be design of environmental programs, in which the whole institution or agency is planned on therapeutic principles. In such settings the therapist can become an activist, an advocate for those he wants to help.

The growing literature on psychotherapy research indicates that the responsible therapist must find out whom he helps, whom he leaves untouched, whom he hurts. And he must ask further whether some aspect of his personality is responsible for his effect, or whether some aspect of his methods or of the therapeutic setting is more important.

How are we to judge what help and hurt are, and how they can be measured? Are any criteria general enough to apply the outcomes of all schools of therapy, in ways that will not bias comparisons? Some criteria for change, e.g., insight and recovery of early memories, are identified with psychoanalysis, while others, such as spontaneity and immediateness, are identified with some humanistic approaches. Our search has been for a more general framework.

The ordinary medical criteria for cure provide a starting point for the criteria we will discuss. Medical treatment is expected to preserve life, to decrease pain and other symptoms, to restore normal function, and to strengthen the organism so that the disorder will not recur. If we add to these treatment criteria the public health goals of early intervention to reduce risk for later disorder and of preventing the conditions that cause the disorder in the first place, we have a comprehensive ecological model for looking at intervention efforts. We will try to adapt this model to the problems of psychological intervention. We will propose a hierarchy of goals, ranging from simple, minimal criteria with extremely broad applicability to other criteria that are still broader than those in general use.

Criterion I. Survival. Expected survival rates can be calculated for any defined group of people. For some groups, such as elderly patients, suicidal and depressed people, and those who are addicted to drugs or alcohol, death rates are strikingly high. Robins (1972) and Groeschel (1974) have demonstrated that they are also high in groups not often thought to be at risk for early death, such as young delinquent boys.

It seems likely that any therapy that reduces the weight of depression can lower the rates for suicide (and for addiction to pain muffling drugs). Cognitively oriented therapies and assertion training, for instance, can apparently change the ways one evaluates one's self and the kinds of cues one evokes from other people. If desensitization or insight reduces anxiety, and so reduces the risk of high blood pressure in stress situations, it should reduce the frequency of sudden breakdown of heart functions. Therapies that make emotion conscious and bring impulses under control probably reduce the likelihood that a person will get himself knifed or shot during an uncontrolled aggressive outburst. Sexual therapies that keep the elderly active by night as well as by day are likely to result in happier and longer lives.

Eysenck (1952) included people who had died in his category of therapeutic failures. We do not have to agree with Eysenck's other ideas to note that here he seems to have made a thoughtful decision.

Criterion II. Effective reproduction, parenting, and survival of the culture or subculture the patient group represents. Survival of the culture may seem a value beyond the modest goals of psychotherapy, but people as diverse as Freud, Skinner, and Devereux (1976) agree on its value as a criterion for the broad effects of psychotherapy. Effective reproduction and parenting is a general criterion for biological viability. One criterion for therapy, then, would be its capacity to remove the inhibitions and anxieties that prevent effective reproduction and competent mothering or fathering. The criterion does not lend itself to simple counting—the issue is not how many children are produced, but whether patients can have the children they want and raise them well. Weissman and her colleagues (1972), among others, have indicated some of the criteria for adequate mothering, and some of the ways in which psychological handicaps can interfere with mothering.

Criterion III. Decreased vulnerability to inner and outer sources of stress. Vulnerability is measurable in terms of physiological indicators like pulse rate, breathing rate, skin conductance, and chemical changes in the blood. It is also commonly reported to therapists, e.g., "After yesterday, I just don't think I can go out and face another customer." A huge body of research, ably summarized by Garmezy (1974), has described the characteristics of children vulnerable to schizophrenia. Risk rates can be calculated for various groups, such as those born to schizophrenic parents, children with low intellectual ability, those rejected by peers, and those involved in intense family conflict. If psychotherapy can reduce the risk for breakdown in such children it makes a major social contribution. Evidence from the Judge Baker studies (Ricks, 1974), the Wisconsin studies of Rogers and his colleagues (1967), and Myers and Bean's (1968) follow-up of discharged patients suggests that good therapists can strikingly reduce the risk for schizophrenia. It seems likely that desensitization to help one cope with anxiety, behavior rehearsal for situations of upcoming stress, insight into old roots of present problems, and growth of self-awareness and secure identity can all have the effect of reducing vulnerability.

Vulnerability to antisocial behavior has also been extensively studied (Robins, 1972; Roff, 1972). These children are vulnerable in a different sense than those vulnerable to schizophrenia. While many have a tough veneer, they generally feel unable to conform to the demands of families, schools, and employers well enough to make a go of life and get what they want legally. For these children, a practical criterion of decreased vulnerability is getting back into the ordinary spectrum of developmental tracks well enough to stay out of trouble with the law and out of jail.

Criterion IV. Increased competence and "good fit" to one's behavioral niche in the environment. There are many arenas in which competence or lack of competence can show itself: school, work, social relationships, family living. Society provides a useful measure of competence in the employment history—whether an ex-patient has been able to get jobs, hold them, be promoted, and take responsibility are important criteria for outcome. Social competence can be measured by sociometric methods in childhood (Roff, Sells, & Golden, 1972) and by social activities in adult life. Myers and Bean (1968) show that ability to hold a job is a better predictor of ex-patients staying out of mental hospitals than any other single criterion. The therapies that most emphasize competence have been the various educational methods. Massimo's vocational guidance techniques, and those behavioral therapies that have emphasized self-awareness, self-regulation, and teaching alternatives to long-term patterns of learned helplessness.

Criterion V. Feeling better. Strupp, Wallach, & Wogan (1962) asked people why they had entered therapy and what changes they had experienced. Generally, people had come to therapy because they felt bad; depressed, anxious, guilty, sick, and so on. What they got from therapy was decreased depression and anxiety, increased enjoyment, and greater feelings of satisfaction, well-being, and self-esteem, together with a general increase in awareness of all emotions. Balkin (1974) used a set of feeling scales, filled out every night for a month, to measure more precisely how people felt before and two years after psychotherapy. His results suggest that therapy can result in marked improvement in daily feelings. In rare moments, at their best, the pre-therapy group reached the level of happiness, energy, sociability, and so on that the post-therapy group felt most of the time.

Criterion VI. Improved social system preformance. The behavioral ecology approach suggests that the consequences of therapy for the social systems in which the individual participates must be evaluated. Devereux (1976) provides criteria of efficiency, effectiveness, and functional adequacy by which system functioning can be evaluated. For example, an acting out child who is taught self-control may not only feel better himself but may enable the systems in which he participates e.g., family, classroom, and neighborhood, to function better.

Criterion VII. A reorganized personal world. The devout humanist or psychoanalyst might at this point say something like this: "So, what have you showed? You can count the numbers of ex-patients who end up in hospital or jails, and you can perhaps estimate vulnerability or competence or feeling better. But what therapy is really about is reorganization of the patient's personal world. Can you measure whether a person now perceives his mother in a totally new way, whether he has successfully resolved his Oedipus complex, whether his personality is now integrated into a new structure?" Our answer is that all of these changes are to some extent measurable now, and all are potentially measurable.

Take transference. Suppose we get from you, the reader, a set of names of all the people who have been important in your life. We might do this by getting you to give us your autobiography, and then pulling from it every name you had to mention in order to describe your own life. When we have tried this (Ricks, 1972) we have gotten from 50 to 100 people, and currently this set often contains one or more therapists. We can then ask you to Q-sort these names according to all sorts of criteria—whom you feel most comfortable with, who means the most to you, whom you respect the most, can communicate the best with, and so on. We now correlate the sorts, factor them, and there before us we have the factorial crossroads of your unique interpersonal world, with everybody assigned his location by his positions in your various Q-sorts and the loadings of those sorts on the factors. If we do this procedure several times as you proceed through psychotherapy we can chart the emotional neighborhoods of your parents, therapist, and other significant figures. If your therapist is seen as much like Mommy or Daddy in the first year of therapy, and after therapy is seen as rather similar to a particularly valued dentist or history teacher, we have charted the emergence and dissolution of transference reactions. Our results so far suggest that there is nothing particularly mysterious or unmeasurable in this idea of restructuring of the personal world. (The method is general in scope, so that not all of the changes it can show will necessarily involve a therapist.)

Take "integrated into a new structure." Here Cartwright (1972) has developed methods for studying consistency across a set of relationships. The client is given precise ways for answering the question, "Am I the same person with my mother as with my father, my boyfriend, my boss, etc.?" Psychotherapy resulted in increased consistency in 9 out of 10 clients in one study, and these findings were confirmed and extended on replication. Cartwright's results demonstrate that the concept of structure can be empirically related to consistency, order, and stability.

According to these criteria, a long-term follow-up of therapy, by therapists of any persuasion, should show that a treated group has greater survival rates than matched controls. They should also show more effective reproduction and parenting, should show less vulnerability to breakdown or extremes of acting out, be more competent in learning work, and social life, and be more able to deal with stress. Finally, they should feel better, and they should have reorganized their personal lives in ways that show more integrative structure. All of these have been measured in one or more studies, and the bulk of the evidence on all of the criteria is at least mildly confirmatory of the value of psychotherapy. However, these results are group trends, and in almost all studies research can also detect some patients who fail to move toward the criteria and some who deteriorate. No study of therapeutic trends is adequate without attention to these therapeutic failures. Our successes confirm us in our work, but it is from our failures that we learn the lessons we most need to learn.

Applied together, these criteria can provide a comprehensive assessment of any program in psychotherapy, either individual therapy or intervention in a system. The criteria are doctrine free—they can apply equally to all forms of psychotherapy and behavior change, even though each owes its origins mainly to one or another school. The idea of feeling better as a result of psychotherapy, and the various measures of self-ideal correspondence, self-satisfaction, etc., are associated with humanistic therapies, but it may be that behavioristic methods can help patients reach these goals faster and more efficiently than humanistic therapies can. Humanistic therapies may decrease extreme sensitivities (e.g., to ridicule) more than behavior therapies can. These are empirical issues calling out for research solutions.

Presentation of this set of criteria does not imply that we think that all of the criteria will apply equally in all therapeutic situations. Any particular program of therapy might emphasize certain criteria, drop others, and modify those that they keep to fit their particular patient population. We would also suggest that therapy can be seen in terms of interest groups, and that the interests of patients, which we concentrated on here, may not always coincide with the interests of therapists or of funding agencies.

The criteria are proposed primarily for evaluating psychotherapy and behavior change. However, we do not believe that they are limited only to this area. They may provide standards for evaluation of many kinds of human change programs, e.g., innovations in education and in community design.

Where Are We Headed?

The optimism and the strength to struggle and change systems that Curtiss (1976) noted in the behavioral unit in her study seems to permeate much of the discussion of behavior therapy in Wandersman et al. (1976) and in the current world of psychotherapy. Behavioral methods are in a heady period of innovation, growth, and proliferation into new areas. As they broaden their scope, they seem to cope as well with the complex systems of institutions and social expectations as they did earlier with the simpler surroundings of the laboratory. Much of what behaviorists are doing can only be viewed with admiration for their vitality and their innovations.

The situation in humanism does not justify so much optimism. the great men and women of humanism often came to their full development late in life, and currently Bühler, Maslow, Rogers, and Perls are either dead or retired. In the work of younger humanists such as Jourard (whose untimely death occurred while *Humanism and Behaviorism* was in progress) there is an admirable movement toward a greater operationalism and specificity, some fine scholarship, and some interesting research—but few really new ideas or programs. We do not see among current humanists the enthusiastic therapeutic explorations of the behaviorists. Many of their new explorations are in directions that broaden therapeutic methods in ways that are hard to describe or study. Other than their explorations of new ways for selecting and training therapists (Carkhuff, 1971) and the occasional studies of therapist personality and talent, there is little new work going on. Changes in humanistic theory seem to be neither systematic nor cumulative. It is hard not to agree with Koch, himself a humanist, that current humanism is showing signs of simultaneously hardening into intellectual dogmatism and deteriorating into methodological anarchy (Koch, 1969). Encounter groups and sensitivity training may offer a way out of this cul de sac. Like the written work of Rogers, May, Maslow, and Perls, they bring many recruits to humanism. But humanism seems more in need of new ideas than of new recruits. Rychlak (1976), Jourard (1976), and Alker (1976) offer some new directions, and perhaps these models can be a basis for an evolving humanism over the next few years. Another basis for an enlarged humanism is developmental psychology and the psychology of the life span of human development—a fact that Bühler grasped a long time ago, but one that has not yet had its full impact in humanistic thought.

Learning From Each Other

The main function of dialogue is mutual learning, and the test is whether we now see familiar facts in new ways. What behaviorists can learn from humanists, and vice versa, might be suggested by what we have learned from each other and from our authors in the course of doing *Humanism and Behaviorism*.

The broadening scope of behaviorism is evidence that behaviorists are learning from psychoanalysts, humanists—and perhaps most of all, from their patients. But we believe that they have not yet fully digested the research news that the whole personality and life style of the therapist is relevant to therapeutic process and outcomes. Behaviorism badly needs to study the therapist and his own reinforcers.

Like other people intoxicated by the partial victories of technology, behaviorists need to develop a greater respect for the system properties of human nature and the social order. Skinner's "humanism that works" requires two further questions: Works for what? Works for whom? Here behaviorists can learn from humanists, who have always been concerned with human nature and human values. Ecological research shows that it is impossible to isolate real life change. Changes in symptoms lead to changes in family life, in jobs, in all sorts of human relations. As behaviorists become more aware of this they are less likely to go on developing programs that arouse the fury of civil libertarians.

Humanists need to learn from behaviorists a respect for doing as well as being. What the therapist is cannot fail to be important, but what he does is crucial to the well-being of his patient. Suppose a particular therapist is genuine, transparent, and incompetent. Will he help his patients, or only meddle in human lives in an enthusiastic but uninformed way?

Related to this is a second lesson, flexibility in methods. Current behavior therapists have many methods available, and if one does not work they can switch to another. Gold (1976), for example, could show that when Axline methods failed to work with aggressive children she could switch to active affective teaching, which did work.

After an impressive early start in research on psychotherapy, with Rogers and his students, humanistic research in psychotherapy has in recent years fallen behind behavioristic research. This seems to us to be a regressive movement. Humanists can learn from behaviorists, or learn once again, that there is no substitute for patient investigation. Although behaviorists are not strangers to personal antagonisms and irrelevant controversy, their record here is a good example to humanists interested in maintaining viable systems of human service.

So long as we stay out of the day-to-day work of psychotherapy, in the quiet of the study or library, it is easy to think of psychotherapists as exponents of competing schools. When we actually participate in psychotherapy, or observe its complexities, it loses this specious simplicity. Our work in this area, and our own experience, convinces us that the old dichotomy of humanism vs. behaviorism is dead. *Humanism and Behaviorism* has explored several of the syntheses that result when behaviorists and humanists talk and work together.

We have also tried to look at both approaches to therapy from the broader perspective of life history research, sociological systems, and ecology. Observing human beings growing up to adulthood, in the intricate biological and social systems in which all of us develop, we get a sense of what an enormous task it is to try to influence, change, and help another human being. We share Jourard's belief that humanists and behaviorists are both admirable, even heroic. We hope the viewpoints presented in Wandersman et al. (1976) will help them in their work together. Beyond that, we hope it will help the people into whose lives they reach.

References

Alexander, J. L., Dreher, G. F., & Willems, E. P. Behavioral ecology and humanistic and behavioristic approaches to change. In A. Wandersman, P. J. Poppen & D. F. Ricks, (Eds.), *Humanism and behaviorism: Dialogue and growth.* New York: Pergamon Press, 1976.

Alker, H. A. The incommensurability of humanistic and behavioristic approaches to behavior change: An empirical response. In A. Wandersman, P. J. Poppen & D. F. Ricks, (Eds.), *Humanism and behaviorism: Dialogue and growth.* New York: Pergamon Press, 1976.

Balkin, J. Once more with feeling: Moods before and after psychotherapy. In D. F. Ricks, M. Roff, & A. Thomas (Eds.), *Life history research in psychopathology* (Vol. III). Minneapolis: University of Minnesota Press, 1974.

Bandura, A. Behavior theory and the models of man. In A. Wandersman, P. J. Poppen, & D. F. Ricks (Eds.), *Humanism and behaviorism: Dialogue and growth.* New York: Pergamon Press, 1976.

Bergin, A. E., & Garfield, S. (Eds.), *Handbook of psychotherapy and behavior change: An empirical analysis.* New York: Wiley, 1971.

Bergin, A. E., & Suinn, R. M. Individual psychotherapy and behavior therapy. *Annual Review of Psychology,* 1975, *26,* 509–556.

Carkhuff, R. R. *The development of human resources.* New York: Holt, Rinehart & Winston, 1971.

Cartwright, R. D. The Q method and the intrapersonal world. In S. R. Brown & D. J. Brenner (Eds.), *Science, psychology, and communication.* New York: Foresight Books, Teachers College Press, 1972.

Curtiss, S. The compatability of humanistic and behavioristic approaches in a state mental hospital. In A. Wandersman, P. J. Poppen, & D. F. Ricks (Eds.), *Humanism and behaviorism: Dialogue and growth.* New York: Pergamon Press, 1976.

Devereux, E. C. Models for man, value systems, and intervention strategies: A sociological critique of Wolpe and Jourard. In A. Wandersman, P. J. Poppen, & D. F. Ricks (Eds.), *Humanism and behaviorism: Dialogue and growth.* New York: Pergamon Press, 1976.

Dollard, J., & Miller, N. E. *Personality and psychotherapy: An analysis in terms in learning, thinking, and culture.* New York: McGraw-Hill, 1950.

Eysenck, H. The effects of psychotherapy: An evaluation. *Journal of Consulting Psychology,* 1952, *16,* 319–324.

Franks, C. M., & Wilson, G. T. *Annual review of behavior therapy: Theory and practice.* New York: Brunner/Mazel, 1974.

Garmezy, N. Children at risk: the search for the antecedents of schizophrenia. Part I: Conceptual models and research methods. *Schizophrenia Bulletin,* 1974, 8.

Gold, G. H. Affective behaviorism: A synthesis of humanism and behaviorism with children. In A. Wandersman, P. J. Poppen, & D. F. Ricks (Eds.), *Humanism and behaviorism: Dialogue and growth.* New York: Pergamon Press, 1976.

Goldstein, A. Appropriate expression training: Humanistic behavior therapy. In A. Wandersman, P. J. Poppen, & D. F. Ricks (Eds.), *Humanism and behaviorism: Dialogue and growth.* New York: Pergamon Press, 1976.

Groeschel, B. Social adjustment after residential treatment. In D. F. Ricks, M. Roff, & A. Thomas (Eds.), *Life history research in psychopathology* (Vol. III). Minneapolis: University of Minnesota Press, 1974.

Jourard, S. M. *The Transparent Self*. New York: Van Nostrand, 1971.

Jourard, S. M. Changing personal worlds: A humanistic perspective. In A. Wandersman, P. J. Poppen, & D. F. Ricks (Eds.), *Humanism and behaviorism: Dialogue and growth*. New York: Pergamon Press, 1976.

Koch, S. Psychology cannot be a coherent science. *Psychology Today*, Sept. 1969.

Krasner, L., & Ullmann, L. P. *Behavior influence and personality*. New York: Holt, Rinehart & Winston, 1973.

Lambert, M. J., & Bergin, A. E. Psychotherapeutic outcome and issues related to behavioral and humanistic approaches. In A. Wandersman, P. J. Poppen, & D. F. Ricks (Eds.), *Humanism and behaviorism: Dialogue and growth*. New York: Pergamon Press, 1976.

Maslow, A. H. *The psychology of science*. New York: Harper & Row, 1966.

Mischel, W. The self as the person: A cognitive social learning view. In A. Wandersman, P. J. Poppen, & D. F. Ricks (Eds.), *Humanism and behaviorism: Dialogue and growth*. New York: Pergamon Press, 1976.

Myers, J. K., & Bean, L. L. *A decade later: A follow-up of social class and mental illness*. New York: Wiley, 1968.

Orlinsky, D. E., & Howard, K. I. *Varieties of psychotherapy experience*. New York: Foresight Books, Teachers College Press, 1975.

Raskin, M. J. Becoming a therapist, a person, a partner, a. . . . Unpublished manuscript, 1975.

Ricks, D. F. Dimensions in life space: Factor analytic case studies. In S. R. Brown & D. J. Brenner (Eds.), *Science, psychology, and communication: Essays honoring William Stephenson*. New York: Foresight Books, Teacher College Press, 1972.

Ricks, D. F. Supershrink: Methods of a therapist judged successful on the basis of adult outcomes of adolescent patients. In D. F. Ricks, M. Roff, & A. Thomas (Eds.), *Life history research in psychopathology* (Vol. III). Minneapolis: University of Minnesota Press, 1974.

Ricks, D. F., & Flemming, P. Humanistic and behavioral approaches from a life history perspective. In A. Wandersman, P. J. Poppen, & D. F. Ricks (Eds.), *Humanism and behaviorism: Dialogue and growth*. New York: Pergamon Press, 1976.

Robins, L. N. An actuarial evaluation of the causes and consequences of deviant behavior in young Black men. In M. Roff, L. N. Robins, & M. Pollack (Eds.), *Life history research in psychopathology* (Vol II). Minneapolis: University of Minnesota Press, 1972.

Roff, M. Childhood antecedents of adult neurosis, severe bad conduct, and psychological health. In D. F. Ricks, A. Thomas, & M. Roff (Eds.), *Life history research in psychopathology* (Vol. I). Minneapolis: University of Minnesota Press, 1972.

Roff, M., Sells, S. B., & Golden, M. *Social adjustment and personality development in children*. Minneapolis: University of Minnesota Press, 1972.

Rogers, C. R. Carl Rogers. In E. G. Boring & G. Lindzey (Eds.), *A history of psychology in autobiography*. New York: Appleton-Century-Crofts, 1967.

Rogers, C. R., Gendlin, G. T., Kiesler, D. J., & Truax, C. B. (Eds.), *The therapeutic relationship and its impact: A study of psychotherapy with schizophrenics.* Madison: University of Wisconsin Press, 1967.

Rychlak, J. F. Is a concept of "self" necessary in psychological theory, and if so why? A humanistic perspective. In A. Wandersman, P. J. Poppen, & D. F. Ricks (Eds.), *Humanism and behaviorism: Dialogue and growth.* New York: Pergamon Press, 1976.

Sears, R. R. *Survey of objective studies of psychoanalytic concepts.* New York: Social Science Research Council, 1943.

Strupp, H. H., Wallach, M. S., & Wogan, M. Psychotherapeutic experience in retrospect: Questionnaire survey of former patients and their therapists. *Psychological Monographs,* 1962, 76.

Thoresen, C. E. Behavioral humanism. In C. E. Thoresen (Ed.), *Behavior modification in education,* 72nd yearbook of the National Society for the Study of Education. Chicago: University of Chicago Press, 1973.

Thoresen, C. E., & Mahoney, M. J. *Behavioral self-control.* New York: Holt, Rinehart & Winston, 1974.

Wandersman, A., Poppen, P. J., & Ricks, D. F. *Humanism and behaviorism: Dialogue and growth.* New York: Pergamon Press, 1976.

Weissman, M. W. The depressed woman as a mother. *Social Psychiatry,* 1972.

Wolpe, J. Behavior therapy: A humanitarian enterprise. In A. Wandersman, P. J. Poppen, & D. F. Ricks (Eds.), *Humanism and behaviorism: Dialogue and growth.* New York: Pergamon Press, 1976.

Chapter 17

Not an Adversity but a Welcome Diversity[1]

Ted Landsman

Out of the pains of the past, the realities of the present, and the threats of the future, there is good reason to be fearful, suspicious, and even angry about behaviorism.

This past year, particularly, has been an ominous one.

1. START is the acronym for Special Treatment and Rehabilitative Training, a behavior modification program for prisons. The Federal Bureau of Prisons also planned for a behavioral research center at Butner, North Carolina. Six governors in the New England area were also to participate in the planning for a new regional prison at Portsmouth, New Hampshire, which would include a major behavior modification program. On February 7 and 11, 1974, William Claiborne of the *Washington Post* and Lesley Oelsner of the *New York Times* reported that the Federal Bureau of Prisons had decided to dismantle the Springfield, Missouri, behavior-modification project.

Oelsner reported: "In the project, prison guards and doctors tried to alter the conduct of troublesome inmates by first locking them in cells for hours and depriving them of all privileges, then rewarded them if they behaved properly by restoring their privileges."

According to Claiborne of the *Washington Post*, "Prisoners began a fixed term of solitary confinement in a small, tile walled cell behind a steel

[1]Presented at the 82nd Annual Convention of the American Psychological Association, New Orleans, August 30, 1974, as part of symposium entitled "Behaviorism and Humanism: Can There Be a Rapprochement?"

Reprinted by permission of the author, Ted Landsman.

door with a small window. Gradually, the convict earned time out of his
cell, depending on his attitude and his willingness to adapt to rules."

Returning now to Oelsner's report in the *New York Times:* "The project had become an object of fear and hatred to inmates in federal prisons
across the country. Some inmates, hearing of START in the prison grape-
vine, staged hunger strikes against the program.

"Inmates and former inmates wrote letters and articles describing
START. . . . as Pavlovian and *Clockwork Orange.*"

One publication put out by former inmates reported that a prisoner
had committed suicide rather than be put in START. Some inmates in the
project filed lawsuits in federal court, contending that it violated a host of
civil liberties and was "cruel and unusual punishment." (*Gainesville Sun,*
1974, p. 1).

The behavior therapists consistently imply that reinforcement techniques are more economic in time and effort in contrast to talking therapies. You will sense a touch of irony in the additional report by Mr.
Theodore Swift, assistant to the director of the Bureau of Prisons, who
insisted that the program was *ended* for "economic" reasons. The number
of prisoners had dwindled to four and the staff–inmate ratio made the
program too costly to justify.

2. On May 26, 1974, the Associated Press released a report raising the
possibility that Patty Hearst had been behaviorally modified. An inadvertent revelation was proferred by Dr. Zev Wanderer, head of the Center for
Behavior Therapy in Los Angeles, who was quoted as saying, "If the SLA
(Symbionese Liberation Army) were such fine behavioral modifiers, I'd like
to offer them a job here." I believe he escaped the further irony in his own
statement.

3. The LEAA (Law Enforcement Assistance Administration) announced
in March 1974 that it would no longer support any programs involving
behavior modification, psychosurgery, chemotherapy, or medical research
(*APA Monitor,* Vol. 5, No. 4, p. 1, April 1974, Sharland Trotter and Jim
Warren). But the humanists are cheated of victory. Donald E. Stantarelli,
LEAA administrator, gives as his reason not that these approaches have
failed but rather "because there are no technical and professional skills on
the LEAA staff to screen, evaluate or monitor such projects."

4. As a result of these and other distant thunders, in July (*APA Monitor,* Vol. 5, No. 7, p. 3) APA's president, Albert Bandura, announced the
appointment of a "blue ribbon" Commission on Behavior Modification to
develop guidelines which may be used in formulating an official APA policy
on the use of these psychological procedures in a variety of settings.

But these are only newspaper reports and as a humanistic psychologist
I would perhaps rather believe my own experience. I have three brief
experiences: (1) Some three years ago at Sunland Training center, our

institution for the mentally retarded in Florida, a doctoral graduate of our University, functioning as a school psychologist, was dismissed for forcing a program of behavior modification upon residents which included requiring them to inhale the aromas from their own soiled underwear. (2) The second experience involved a young lady whom I had known as a student and who was put into a psychiatric ward for some rather bizarre behavior. Some of my colleagues and I had attempted to visit her, only to be informed by a young psychiatrist, who was trying behavioral techniques on her, that she was to receive absolutely no visitors (that is, reinforcement) except her confused parents. I was incensed and considered plans to carry my protest to the courts. One strange day, I received a desperate, sobbing phone call from the girl. She had slipped into an office in the ward, found a phone, and called me. She told me she had been thrown earlier into a room with no furniture, only a mattress on the floor. I asked her if it was okay for us to take the question of visiting her into the courts. She was terrified and begged me not to do it. She felt sure she would be punished for it. In the middle of the phone call, I heard a door open, heard a stern male voice say, "Jane, what are you doing here. Now put that phone down. . . ." There was a click and the line was dead. This was real life drama of the late TV movie quality!

My final personal example (3) comes from two colleagues whom I have observed, both of whom are dedicated behavioral modifiers and both of whom have been making valiant efforts to stop smoking with charts and wrist counters. Both of them (and Leonid Brezhnev, who has the same problem and the same solution) after months of charting are still pouring clouds of smoke into all of their professional meetings.

Who Gets Behavior Therapy?

Some years ago an excellent study pointed out that the rich get psychoanalysis and the poor get shock therapy. And who gets behavior therapy? The Law Enforcement Assistance Administration and the U. S. Bureau of Prisons discovered in a computer printout that some 400 of their projects seemed to involve behavior modification in one form or another. The greatest single category in the published literature, however, seems to deal with retarded children in institutions. Perhaps the most publicized reports of success have to do with autistic children. The rich get psychoanalysis, the poor get shock therapy, and the prisoners and institutionalized retardates get behavior modification. This is not the result of a careful count of recipients, and it is true that the captive college sophomores are often beneficiaries of this great gift from our science, but it appears that behavior modification is fast approaching application in the form originally feared by the humanists—for increasing control, management, and shaping of human beings. These are the clear and present dangers. And what of such grave threats in the past?

And the Threat out of the Past

Here and Now Humanists, while they can afford to neglect the past of their clients, forget the past of their own profession at the pain of reliving its mistakes. In 1918, 1919, and 1920 when Watsonian Behaviorism first brought a clean breath of reason and order into the chaos of introspectionism, a burn-the-house-down kind of cleaning passion overwhelmed American psychology to the point that introspectionism, phenomenology, humanism, and all forms of subjectivism including experience were eventually banished, exiled, and disgraced and disappeared from all APA journals, graduate programs, and other respectable laboratories and salons for perhaps 30 to 40 years. McDougall engaged in the famous "Battle of Behaviorism" with Watson in 1929 and was voted the winner by the sweet and tender undergraduates at Radcliffe, only to be overwhelmed by obscurity.

Behaviorism became the official psychology of the professional establishment. Only the tremulous, persistent, and unbowed efforts of a growing post–World War II clinical psychology brought about the restoration and created an ambience in the establishment which enabled the rebirth of a new subjectivism in psychology called humanistic psychology. In this rebirth of Skinnerian and Wolpian behaviorism are we again to be cast out into obscurity?

Does then the past portend and the present fail to preclude a future of disappearance and disaster out of the Battle of Behaviorism II?

But Are There Dangers in Humanism?

Can there be a real rapprochement with such a villain? Does one compromise with such evil, with electro-shockers, with tortures of helpless, institutionalized children, with cruel and inhuman punishers of those defenseless and imprisoned? Must we compromise with, be reconciled with those who mindfully but heartlessly destroy, ignore, and sneer at the soul of our science: freedom and dignity?

While we are in such a state of high dudgeon, while our ideals and indignation at righteousness are at their most shining and noble, let us take a careful look at ourselves, at the position with which the behaviorists are being asked to merge and mingle.

Humanistic psychology has resulted in the creation of a number of

institutions almost equal to the number of behaviorism projects in LEAA—
the growth of the Growth Centers. These, our finest jewels, offer a bewildering array of exotic mixtures, of sexuality unfettered, spirituality, meditation,
and transcendence into infinity, solutions for the blahs, for American materi-
alism, nude, erotic and nonerotic massage, the most colorful exotic, light-
headed excitements of all cultures and all times—and selling for about $75 to
$150 per intimate, irresponsible weekend. A colleague and I founded one
such center, The Center of Man, and we have grown astounded at how it
won't die as well as how our own interest in it has perished. Hardly ever was
a black to be seen at any of our programs, students came only when we
reduced the cost to below our cost, poor whites were never to be seen. The
Growth Center is an upper-middle-class white weekend phenomena—the
new country club with a much-expanded program. It is often reckless and
irresponsible, offering promises of joy and bliss and ecstasy. Esalen catalogues are the souvenir Sears catalogues of the future.

At our San Francisco meetings, panelists for a symposium who had
been asked to prepare half hour talks were stunned when the chairman
instead invited members of the audience forward to give spontaneous presentations. I listened, fascinated and dismayed while a young man in the
official uniform of the counterculture, told with quiet pride of an experimental college where schizophrenics were invited to do the teaching.

At the Miami meetings a large group exercise in body freedom was
somewhat damaged in mood when a young couple, who were readying to
carry the exercise to its logical conclusion, was swatted on the rear end (the
one on top) by an obscene and prudish boor of over 30. An uproarious
party for the total association at the San Francisco meetings opened, continued, and closed, with gleeful idiocisms seemingly dedicated to the
funniest thing the group needed to cathect: intercourse with the mother.

At the southern institute where I presented a serious program on
Hassidism, a young man walked in, sat admiringly at my feet, smoking pot,
mindlessly hearing nothing, knowing nothing, but feeling everything, with
great, loving admiration, I guess for the sound of my voice. At our living
quarters later that night, only another pot smoking session quieted the
insistent request of two girls for an orgy. One of our best-reported annual
programs involved the proposal of intercourse with the client for therapeutic purposes. Rollo May, one of our founding fathers, sensing the portent of
these vagaries, has made known his pain at the excesses of the association
in an anguished letter to the bulletin.

A behaviorist might well ask, is this sex-maddened, drugged group of
antiscientists, worthy of rapprochement? Do these whimsical weekend
lovers of humanity have anything other than freedom in them, and no
dignity, no truth, no knowledge, no understanding, certainly no control,
and are they innocent of interest in prediction?

Now who would like to be the first to say, that "yes we have these kooks but this is the price we pay for freeing the mind. We do have scientists among us; we do have clear precise brilliant thinkers, Maslow, May, Rogers." And to paraphrase an ancient proverb of Senator Goldwater, extremism in the service of freedom is no vice.

Both of these positions, the humanist's complaint and the behaviorist's contempt, are examples of reason by extremes. More important, they both represent the dreadful dangers of monolithic theoreticians, fashioned by reasonably good thinkers but possessed of the self-confidence of giants, bolstered and edged on by followers looking for a single, incontrovertible truth who are happy to have found someone with sufficient self-assurance to point it out for them.

For the longest of times it seemed to me that we humanists were far more susceptible to this professional monotheism than were the behaviorists. A few months ago I discovered one of my most respected behavioristic colleagues, about to announce a school psychology training program which was to be exclusively behavioristic. I chided him on his abandonment of the impartiality of science, and now we have a program with two parallel tracks, one behavioristic and one humanistic.

It is a beautiful and blissful feeling to be surrounded by faculty, colleagues, and even secretaries and students who are all of a like mind with oneself. It results in a great camaraderie, great flights of fantasy as well as illusions of truth. It is but a few short years to great rivalries for superorthodoxy and the ridiculous excesses of loyalty and devotion to a single party line best described by Solzhenitsyn in *The Gulag Archipelago* (1974), when a village conference stood to applaud a mediocre party official who spoke in glorious praise of Stalin and found no one dared stop the applause. And the one man who finally tired of that nonsense and did sit down was soon in prison.

Humanism is not a complete, total, and proven personality theory in and of itself, and neither is behaviorism. One is hard put to find more zealots of less than total, mindless, and senseless devotion in one or the other. But they have both become sorely afflicted with the passion for monotheoristic systems, for the one and only truth.

I am sure all of us share a similar indignation at the crude interference with the dignity of the prisoner in the START program. The *APA Monitor* report (April 1974, p. 1 by Sharland Trotter and Jim Warren, Vol. 5, No. 4) also sets us up for a logical tour de force. Professor James V. McConnell, professor of psychology at the University of Michigan is quoted in *Psychology Today* as saying:

> I believe the day has come when we can combine sensory deprivation with drugs, hypnosis and astute manipulation of reward and punishment to

gain almost absolute control over an individual's behavior. . . . We'd assume that a felony was clear evidence that the criminal had somehow acquired full-blown social neurosis. . . . We'd send him to a rehabilitation center where he'd undergo positive brainwashing. . . . We'd probably have to restructure his entire personality.

At this point all of us would argue privacy, dignity of the individual, individual freedom, constitutional freedom, big brother, 1984, legal rights, civil rights, ethics. McConnell is unimpressed and offers us this point of view, so different from our own as to have an aura of fascination about it, the fascination of the victim watching the serpent rear back its head to strike.

"I don't believe," continues McConnell,

the constitution of the United States gives you the right to commit a crime if you want to: therefore, the constitution does not guarantee you the right to maintain inviolable the personality it forced on you in the first place—if and when the personality manifests strongly antisocial behavior.

In other words, your personality was never yours anyway—society gave it to you in its entirety. Now this I find to be an example of behavioristic reasoning, unchecked, uninfluenced by competitive ideas, at its most dangerous nadir. Since your personality was fashioned entirely by society, it has the right to take it back and give you one which it feels fits you and society better.

These statements are perhaps exemplary in that they represent not too much what is feared most but what can most likely occur from a theory, any theory, or any theoretician who is carried away by the promises of his most ambitious dreams. It illustrates what errors we need to avoid. These statements are logical derivatives of a monolithic theory, of surrounding oneself with like-mindedness and with studies ignoring alternative explanations (also known as "ignorance"). I am reasonably assured that Professor McConnell has never given anybody, even a rat, and including the flatworms, who were his first clientele, a whole, newly fashioned personality. Nor can he muster acceptable evidence that the personalities of prisoners nor of preachers were forced upon them by the constitution nor even by our society, which I believe is what he really meant to say.

These remarks of McConnell are unmerited from the vantage point both of science and of art. They are good science fiction. I urge you to take them not as examples of what we have to fear from behaviorism but as examples of what both behaviorism and humanism have to fear from any official theory, from any monotheory, from any theory unchallenged by alternatives.

Including even religious and political systems, thinking, creating, testing and applying theories best proceeds under a pluralism, with diversity, with intellectual competition for soundness and meaningfulness of concepts, ideas, laws, and principles. Ideas are sharpened *against* contrasting concepts. Pencils sharpen against knives, pictures are focused by lights against darks, sounds are most clearly heard against silences, and are particularly pleasant as rhythm, an alternation or rapprochement of sounds against silences.

Do we want an "official" psychology such as the official Lysenko biology of Stalin? Do we insist that such a psychology succeed in our party journals even if it fails in the wheat fields? Of course we don't want behaviorism to be such an official psychology—but neither do we want such bliss for ourselves. For it would make us fat, complacent, and, worse, completely kookie—like some of us already are, in our orgies of humanistic freedom, spiritual shallowness, and methodological madness.

There is no need for a melding into a single humanistic behaviorism or behavioristic humanism. We need a pluralistic, vigorous, uncompromising intellectual dialogue, a sharpening of each other's ideas against one other.

What Kind of a Treaty?
What Kind of a Peace?

Can we achieve rapprochement? The symposium asks (how did we manage to avoid the word *detente*?). What are the possible forms of relationship between these noisy, quarrelsome, children?

1. We could continue the tradition of sarcasm and mutual excommunication which has marked the quarrels between objectivists and subjectivists in both philosophy and psychology since the dialogues of Plato, up through the British empiricists to the Rogers and Skinner debates.

2. We could bend our efforts toward the banishment of one or the other from science and even from the country. Past history would suggest that even in our democracy, governments somehow or other favor the manipulators.

Aside from the glaring example of the Lysenko years in Russia, a similar phenomenon now is found in China, where acupuncture has become the anesthetic of choice in many, not all, Chinese hospitals. Acupuncture had all but faded from Chinese medicine until the so-called cultural revolution and only a return to a modicum of governmental sanity prevented acupuncture from being an "official" anesthetic in Chinese medicine.

As another example, we have the good fortune to have as our director of the division of health and rehabilitation in Florida a gentleman who has been professionally trained in the Glasser approach to counseling. While he was head of our programs for delinquent youth, under his benign leadership, Guided Group Interaction became the "therapy of choice" in all state institutions under his supervision. True or not, the word was that grant programs in that department were not likely to be approved unless they included heavy doses of GGI. To continue up the ladder of subtle exclusivity, I recall with some embarrassment many courses in which I learned and taught a highly orthodox client-centered counseling but which were entitled "counseling and psychotherapy." And I don't recall any student or faculty member ever raising a question about it.

3. Rapprochement as a third alternative implies, in this instance, an understanding and appreciation for the merits of the adversary's position. It is often expressed in pious words and even in written agreements but is palpable only in the form of changes in the practices of the therapists.

When we look, with friendly eye, upon present-day practice of behavior therapy by experienced professionals, there is a surprising manifestation of some of the best out of the hosts of humanistic therapies.

    a. Behavior modification rejects the historical, developmental approach of psychoanalysis and emphasizes the present, the "here and now," in common with almost all contemporary existential approaches, including client-centered therapy and Gestalt therapy.

    b. It permits the client to set the goals for himself rather than having them chosen by his parents, the school, or the society. This is a familiar procedure to rational-emotive, client-centered, gestalt, etc.

    c. It rejects labels, diagnoses and simply sees maladaptive behavior as a function of its consequences. That is, the individual has learned behavior which is unsatisfactory to him. It thus by implication rejects the concept of "blame."

    d. A major technique involves the reinforcement of adaptive approach behavior and extinction of maladaptive avoidance behavior. These are closely parallel to Lewinian concepts of positive and negative valences.

    e. In selecting reinforcement, phenomenology plays a significant role. M & M's may be perceived as reinforcing by a child, while the orgasm is enormously reinforcing for a homosexual adult who has chosen as his goal heterosexuality. While the reinforcement is admittedly defined in circular logic as any consequence or event which increases the probability that the behavior will recur, in actuality the behaviorist must fall back on the phenomenological procedure of determining what is pleasurable—perceived as pleasurable by the client. Incidentally, the term *client* is preferred rather than *subject* or *patient*, as is the case in most existential therapies.

 f. The processes of shaping, a term I agree we all find distasteful, and of successive approximation involves reinforcements for tiny, minute efforts which bring the client closer and closer to his own chosen goals. This is not at all unlike the "working through" process of talking therapies, Freudian, client-centered, and others, where in actuality the reinforcements come either from the approval of the therapist in what I consider low-level skilled client-centered therapy or from the client himself, who discovers himself coming closer to full understanding and self-adequacy.

 g. The contract which is prepared and signed by both therapist and client is in a fashion a development out of the concept of structuring or limits, which are a necessary part of all talking therapies. The contract, usually written, states the therapist's commitments (such as to be on time for sessions, to be available for phone calls, etc.) and the client's commitments, such as to perform the assignments between sessions.

 h. And finally a fundamental concept in such professional, experienced behavior therapy is that the client is responsible for his behavior and for modifying his behavior. This should be familiar to us.

There is then much rapprochement already among the responsible, experienced behavior therapists. Now let us ask what we have learned from behaviorism?

In some of our therapies we employ harsh confrontations where once we waited patiently for the client to explore them. In others we employ exercises in front of a group, ignoring the embarrassment of the chosen subject of the exercise, such as in the "hot seat" technique, and the embarrassments of the group members who sense the pain. The experienced behavior therapists may try a role rehearsal in private but with great care will chose a situation in the successive approximation mode which the client can readily handle. In some of our approaches we subject the client to lengthy, logical harangues, insisting that logic and not satisfaction govern the choice of behavior. Group approval and group disapproval are applied with little relationship to the client's ability to take it at that particular time. I cannot defend the origination of these techniques in behaviorism, but they seem to me to be moves of frustration with slowness on the part of the client, which are borrowed from what we think behaviorists do.

Many of the responsible, experienced behavior therapists took their early training in the humanistic therapies, or at least they have read them, sensitive as they are to the unpleasant charge of their being manipulators. I find very few of us humanists who have enough patience with behavior therapists to study their thinking and their methodology in detail. In other words, I suspect they have taken the best of what we have to offer and we have taken the least of what they proffer.

What are the best things which they have to offer? First, calibrated, careful application of reinforcements which can involve previous knowledge or simply what we call clinical sensitivity; second, attention to detail, minuteness, awareness that big feelings and behaviors are made out of more nuclear feelings; third, recording and charting, counting of which we so often make fun. This is a great comfort to the client, gives him evidence of his own progress or lack of it, and facilitates his observation of self—he is encouraged by it to note when certain aspects of his behavior occur and therefore finds himself introspective with an arithmetic base, if you will. Finally, useful to us is the emphasis on accountability, research, and evaluation, which, if it is any comfort to us, is as often violated and ignored by self-congratulatory behavior therapists as it is among the rest of us softies.

The response of humanistic psychology to the second coming of behaviorism need be neither rapprochement nor warfare with words. If humanists are truly confident that they have much to offer, then they ought to welcome what is being offered by the responsible behaviorists—attention to specifics, to details, careful quantification, modesty in claims, demonstrable results. And even beyond this we welcome its challenge, its role as stimulator to make the dreams of humanistic psychology more of the substance of reality, the spur to demonstrate our promises. The runner needs a pace setter for motivation to break records; the boxer needs his sparring partner. Humanism needs behaviorism as neither enemy nor ally but as a respected adversary to which we listen, carefully. The current popularity of behaviorism is not an adversity. In the chaos of the human condition we are both exploring pluralism; diversity is our best proof against complacency, against sloppiness, against the excesses of self-righteousness, and against kookiness, if you will. I welcome its advocacy whether it be of the devil or of the divine. Its effect will be of neither, but will rather serve the cause of earthly knowledge—which is what we are all about.

Part VI
A Brief Look at Psychotherapy Outcome Research

The ultimate answer to the question of what therapeutic procedures are most effective in any given instance is clearly empirical in nature. Although the practice of psychotherapy has been in existence for some 100 years now, it is only within the past three decades that we have seen very much in the way of actual research into its effectiveness. And while research efforts in this area have been plagued with numerous shortcomings, there is a growing sentiment in the field that important conceptual and methodological gains have been made in recent years. Frank, who has long been an advocate of common factors that cut across all therapeutic orientations, has more recently acknowledged that specific intervention procedures have been demonstrated to be effective with certain kinds of clinical problems. In outlining the conclusions of the Presidential Commission on Mental Health, Parloff brings to bear his extensive experience with and knowledge of the current status of psychotherapy research. Certain directions need to be taken, argues Parloff, especially since governmental policymakers and other interested "third parties" are making increasing demands for information on the efficacy of our procedures.

Chapter 18

The Present Status of Outcome Research[1]

Jerome D. Frank

After decades of research, the amount of well-established, clinically relevant knowledge about psychotherapeutic outcome still remains disappointingly meagre. Although some relationships between determinants and outcome have attained statistical significance, few are powerful enough to be clinically relevant, and most of those that have achieved this status are intuitively obvious. An example is the finding that patients who begin therapy at a high level of functioning terminate at higher levels than those who begin at low levels. In other words, the healthier one is to start with, the healthier one is at the end (Garfield, 1978).

The reasons for this state of affairs are so familiar as to require only brief mention. Criteria for selection of patient samples are inadequate; therapies are so loosely defined that they permit large but undefinable variations in application by different therapists using ostensibly the same techniques; and measures of outcome are not standardized sufficiently so that results of different studies can accumulate. Furthermore, the choice of variables to be studied has been guided too much by the need to produce a publishable result and not enough by the search for significance. Thus, massive amounts of work have been done on variables determining acceptance of therapy and attendance, which at best are prerequisites to improve-

[1]This article is a slightly modified version of a paper delivered at the Ninth Annual Meeting of the Society for Psychotherapy Research, Toronto, Canada, June 22, 1978.

Reprinted by permission of the author, Jerome D. Frank, and the publisher from *Journal of Consulting and Clinical Psychology*, 1979, 47, 310–316.

ment. At worst, the tacit assumption that dropping out indicates failure of therapy is often misleading, in that many brief attenders may drop out because they have improved sufficiently so as not to feel the need of further treatment. The independent variables are too often actuarial ones, like age, sex, and social class, which at best are indirectly related to responsivity.

This presentation reviews four generalizations that outcome studies seem to have reasonably well established and then considers the main areas about which more information is needed and could be obtained, with occasional hunches as to the most promising lines to pursue.

The Current State of Knowledge

By now it seems reasonably well established that all forms of psychotherapy—that is, planned, systematic efforts of a socially sanctioned, trained healer to relieve psychologically caused distress and disability through words and other symbolic interactions—are somewhat more effective than informal, unplanned help. Unfortunately, as appears from the studies of Sloane, Staples, Cristol, Yorkston, and Whipple (1975) and Smith and Glass (1977), these efforts are not impressively more effective. The latter found that the average difference between treated and untreated patients was about two-thirds of a standard deviation. Since it is unclear how many of the studies included in reaching this figure were poorly controlled, the actual difference may be less.

The second generalization is that—except for the short-term superiority of behavior therapy for phobias, compulsions, obesity, and sexual problems, and possibly of cognitive therapy for the relief of depression—no one therapy has been shown to be overall significantly superior to any other, especially over the long term.

Third, follow-up studies seem to show consistently that whatever the form of therapy, most patients who show initial improvement maintain it (Lieberman, Yalom, & Miles, 1973). Moreover, when two therapies yield differences in outcome at the close of treatment, with rare exceptions these disappear over time, and the closing of the gap seems to depend more on patients who received the less successful therapy catching up to the others than on both groups regressing equally toward the mean. This suggests that the main beneficial effect of psychotherapy may be to accelerate improvement that would have occurred eventually in any case.

Even if therapy did no more than speed up natural recovery processes, however, appreciable shortening of the duration of a patient's distress and disability would nevertheless be sufficient to justify therapeutic efforts. To take an example of another form of treatment, electroconvulsive treatment for depression does not prevent relapses, but few would therefore deny its value.

The differences between immediate and long-term outcomes of psychotherapy suggest the probable importance of attempting to distinguish more sharply factors that produce improvement from those that maintain it (Liberman, 1978a).

Finally, the results of outcome research strongly suggest that more of the determinants of therapeutic success lie in the personal qualities of the patient and the therapist and in their interactions than in the therapeutic method.

The conclusions that all therapies do somewhat better than no therapy and that for the vast majority of patients one method has not been proven to be more effective than another rest on measures of central tendency or nose-counting. In view of the relative lack of clarity of most studies with respect to important variables, failures to obtain significant differences between populations should not be interpreted as indicating that such differences do not exist. As Garfield (1978) has put it:

A host of idiosyncratic studies of poorly defined populations with vaguely described therapies and exceedingly variable outcome criteria will not produce findings of any substance [p. 225].

A particular source of weakness in outcome measures is their failure to do justice to the striking benefits achieved by a few patients under many forms of psychotherapy. Most therapists have witnessed improvement justifying the overused phrase "basic personality change" in an occasional patient—in fact, on the principle of intermittent reinforcement, these patients are probably what keep most of us going. Most improvement scales express mental health in terms of diminished disability—that is, they do not do adequate justice to these gratifying patients. The challenge is how to devise scales for appraising outcome and statistical procedures that take adequate account of rare but huge successes. To illustrate with a close analogy, although many attenders find participation in revival meetings psychologically rewarding, it is estimated that only 2 to 5 percent make a "decision for Christ" at a meeting, and only about 15 percent of them (less than half of 1 percent of the total) remain permanently converted (Argyle, 1958). Applying conventional outcome measures, we would probably class those who enjoy the experience as slightly improved, the maximally 5 percent who are temporarily converted as moderately improved, and the miniscule number of permanent converts as markedly improved, or perhaps even recovered. Thus, by statistical criteria, as producers of both immediate and long-term changes, the record of revival meetings is abysmal. Yet the tiny fraction who are permanently converted would justifiably claim that for them revival meetings are extremely effective.

This line of thinking suggests that instead of continuing to pursue the relatively unrewarding enterprise of statistically comparing the effectiveness of different therapies, we should focus on particular forms of therapy that seem to work exceptionally well with a few patients and seek to define the characteristics of both the therapy and the patients that lead to this happy result. David Malan's (1976) persistent and profitable pursuit of the determinants of the differential responses of patients to short-term psychoanalytically oriented therapy is an example.

Considerable progress is being made with two other aspects of outcome research. The first is the development of measures of outcome that permit comparison of therapies with each other. Considerable progress has been made with this, particularly by the publication of *Psychotherapy Change Measures* (Waskow & Parloff, 1975). As a result, we can confidently expect increasing comparability of the outcome measures used by different researchers. Secondly, more detailed specification of different forms of therapy is making it possible to feel relatively confident that therapists who claim to be using the same method actually are doing so. Manuals have been devised for some behavioral and cognitive therapies and for crisis management, and this effort should certainly be encouraged. Both standardized measures of outcome and manuals may be largely irrelevant, however, to long-term open-ended therapies, especially those with an existential orientation. To the extent that the spontaneity of the therapist's actions is considered crucial and the patient's improvement is defined solely by changes in his or her subjective state, it is hard to see how either the therapy or the measures of benefit could ever be standardized. However, there is still so much to be learned from brief, highly structured psychotherapies that this caveat need not worry us for a long time to come.

Problems of Patient Selection

Since research results to date suggest that the major determinants of therapeutic success appear to lie in aspects of patients' personality and style of life, the development of better criteria for their assignment to different therapies is a crucial need. A first step would be to try to purify the sample, as it were, by screening out candidates who would be expected to respond favorably to any form of help. These include patients with fluctuating conditions who enter therapy in the trough of a cycle, those in the midst of a crisis who can be expected to regain their equilibrium when it passes, and patients possessing good ego strength who are motivated by subjective distress to seek help. Incidentally, it may be that inclusion of patients who respond to any form of help accounts for the persistence of all schools of therapy. Patients naturally attribute their improvement to whatever they happen to be doing at the time, so they give credit to the therapy they are in, even though any other might have been equally successful. Since practitioners of all therapeutic schools have many such successes, their belief in the superiority of their method is similarly reinforced.

Another way of approaching the question of patient selection derives from the hypothesis that what brings patients to psychotherapy is a combination of specific symptoms plus demoralization, and that much of the improvement in all forms of psychotherapy results from the improvement in patients' morale brought about by features shared by all forms of therapy. Based on an epidemiological study of a stratified sample of city dwellers, Dohrenwend (1978) developed a demoralization index consisting of nine subscales: poor self-esteem, sadness, dread, anxiety, perceived physical health, unspecific psychophysiological complaints, possible psychogenic complaints, helplessness–hopelessness, and confused thinking. It would be a simple matter to apply this scale to all patients seeking psychotherapy and to eliminate from research studies all those suffering from demoralization of brief duration, because they would probably respond to any form of help. One would have to also consider eliminating those whose demoralization is so prolonged and severe that they would be poor candidates for any therapy. Having excluded both these groups, we might not have enough patients left to study, to be sure, but this approach deserves to be tested.

Having eliminated patients who would or would not do well regardless of therapy, we need ways of classifying the remainder in terms of categories more relevant to different forms of therapy than the present diagnostic scheme, which has been based primarily on clinical descriptions. Three leads toward more psychotherapeutically relevant diagnostic categories have some experimental support, to which may be added a couple of purely speculative suggestions. It seems probable, first, that verbal, psychologically minded patients who have motivation for insight (Malan, 1976) do well in insight therapies, whereas those who are oriented to solving their problems by actions may do better in behavioral ones. Second, patients' expectations seem to have something to do with responsiveness to different forms of therapy. This is suggested by the well-established observation that once therapy is under way, all therapists, subtly or openly, indoctrinate patients into their therapeutic rationales and procedures. Furthermore, therapeutic success has been found to be related to congruence between patients' and therapists' expectations as to the therapeutic process, although this congruence with respect to outcome seems to be irrelevant (Wilkins, 1973).

The third promising lead is classification of patients in terms of locus of control. In our own research we stumbled on an interaction between locus of control and whether patients were led to believe that their improvement in therapy was the result of their own efforts or of a placebo pill. The internally controlled patients did significantly better than the externally controlled ones in the first condition, whereas the results were reversed in the second (Liberman, 1978b).

Other studies with related findings are emerging. One, for example, found that cognitive relaxation procedures resulted in a greater decrement in heart rate and subjective distress in internally controlled than in externally controlled subjects, who responded better to muscular relaxation (Ollendick & Murphy, 1977). A study of reactions of test-anxious students to counseling and behavior therapies found that the internally controlled students preferred an optional amount of control in counseling, whereas the externally controlled felt that they were in too much control of therapy (Friedman & Dies, 1975). Mere straws in the wind, to be sure, but they may be harbingers of a gale!

Two other questions come to mind about possible personality attributes of patients related to choice of therapy, on which, to my knowledge, no research has been done. One is, Do persons who have strong investments in their bodies, such as athletes, physical education instructors, and actors, do particularly well in therapies that stress altering mental states through bodily manipulations and exercises such as bioenergetics?

The second question is, What characterizes persons who respond exceptionally well to abreactive techniques? These procedures have been used in the West at least since Mesmer, and they have never died out, but neither have they proved sufficiently effective overall to prevail. Rather, they seem to enjoy spurts of popularity interspersed with long periods of relative neglect. Presumably, this is because for most patients the improvement is not lasting, or perhaps because those who do experience marked and lasting benefits are too small a proportion of the patients treated by these methods to establish a statistical claim for the methods' validity. Could the success of emotional flooding therapies perhaps be related to the degree to which persons undergoing them are emotionally arousable? If so, would they be most useful with the most emotionally labile, the most phlegmatic, or is the optimal level of arousability somewhere between these extremes?

Problems of Therapist Effectiveness

Two hypotheses concerning the qualities of therapists related to their therapeutic power, which are battered but refuse to die, are the "active personal participation" concept of Whitehorn and Betz (Dent, 1978; Razin, 1977; Whitehorn & Betz, 1975), operationalized by the A–B scale, and the warmth, genuineness, and empathy framework of Rogers and his colleagues (Truax & Carkhuff, 1967). Incidentally, since the ability of the therapist to offer high levels of either active personal participation or the Rogerian conditions seems largely to depend on the patient's responses, these elements are probably more appropriately viewed as properties of the therapist–patient interaction. The most encouraging findings using Rogerian dimensions have been reported by educators, who have found them to be positively related to student achievement (Aspy, 1969). Education is close enough to therapy to justify continuing exploration of the Rogerian dimensions' relation to therapeutic outcome.

Another lead is supplied by the study of Lieberman et al. (1973), which found that the most successful leaders of encounter groups, as measured by beneficial changes in members, displayed a combination of moderate stimulation, high caring, high meaning attribution, and moderate executive function.

Aspects of therapists that are difficult to pin down but may possibly be very relevant to their success are persuasiveness and what may be called healing ability. Pursuit of the latter leads quickly into the quicksands of the paranormal, such as clairvoyance, telepathy, and ability to speed plant growth or activate enzymes or produce spectacular auras on Kirlian photographs. Attempts to study such phenomena involve grave threats to the researcher's reputation as a sober scientist, so their pursuit can be recommended only to the most intrepid; but the rewards could be great.

It should be added that any research into the personal qualities of therapists related to their therapeutic efficiency is, of course, extremely threatening. The discovery that one lacks therapeutic personality characteristics could be disastrous, not only to one's pocketbook but also to one's self-esteem.

Finally, there is the promising area of goodness of match between patient and therapist along relevant dimensions. The word *relevant* needs to be stressed. Most of the matching that has been attempted has been on personality attributes determined by psychological tests or on demographic variables, which at best are only indirectly related to therapeutic success. The most promising lead that I have come upon in this area is level of conceptualization, developed by educators. A scale has been devised to measure the complexity with which persons conceptualize their subjective worlds (Carr, 1970). Although no conclusive studies have emerged, there is some evidence, which deserves to be pursued, that persons with lower conceptual levels respond best with structured therapy and a structured environment. Studies of smokers (Best, 1975), psychiatric outpatients treated by medical students, and alcoholics, as well as college students and delinquents, found that patients whose conceptual level was similar to that of their therapists did better than those in which there was a mismatch (Posthuma & Carr, 1975).

Limits to Outcome Research

Given enough ingenuity, time, and effort, researchers could make considerably more progress with respect to the therapeutically relevant attributes of patients, therapists, and their interaction, and I personally believe this would be potentially the most rewarding line to pursue. There seem to be several built-in limits to the success of research on the outcome of psychotherapy, however, which I should like to mention in closing. The first is that since therapy does not occur in a social vacuum, many of the determinants of outcome lie outside the patient–therapist dyad, and therefore, no matter how sophisticated the focus on it, important sources of variance will be missed. Of these, intercurrent events in long-term therapy are especially significant, particularly with respect to maintenance of change (Voth & Orth, 1973). Whether these can ever be systematized remains to be seen. Even more difficult to evaluate—so much so that I can do no more than mention it as a possibility—is the role of the world view of the society in which the therapy occurs. At the very least, differences in world views of different cultures would be expected severely to limit the cross-cultural generalizability of findings. For example, Peruvian psychiatrists who work with the Indians have pointed out that attainment of mastery, cited by almost all North American psychotherapists as a major goal of treatment, would make no sense to their clientele. For them, the goal would be rather to learn to accept their fate or to restore their harmony with the spirit world. In addition, and perhaps more important, as this example suggests, the world view shared by patient and therapist may have more to do with the choice of procedures, selection of patients, and criteria of outcome than any of the variables I have already mentioned.

With respect to patients, the types of distress and disability for which many seek help are expressions of habitual maladaptive efforts to resolve internally or externally generated stresses. These efforts and the types of distress and disability they generate are protean, often idiosyncratic, and shift from time to time in the same patient. To the extent that this is so, it sets limits to any scheme of classification as related to therapy.

With respect to psychotherapeutic methods, until recently methodological problems have slowed research into group and family approaches, which may well be more powerful, by and large, than dyadic ones. As group creatures, humans are highly susceptible to group forces, especially if these are brought to bear by a strong leader operating within a belief system shared by the group members. Insofar as psychotherapy seeks to produce beneficial attitudinal and behavioral changes, group methods would appear to be more powerful than dyadic ones, a supposition supported by the fact that in most of the world, analogues of psychotherapy are conducted in groups.

Group therapy research involves a forbidding number and complexity of variables that must be taken into account. With the rapid advances of computer science, this problem is becoming more tractable. Lieberman et al. (1973) have blazed the way in their studies of encounter groups, and this should encourage similarly sophisticated research into therapy groups.

Other therapies that pose particular difficulties for the researcher are those termed *humanistic* or *existential*. As already mentioned, they are conceptualized in ways that resist application of the scientific method, which consists of the systematic collection and analysis of shared data. To the extent that their effectiveness lies in a unique encounter between each patient and the therapist—an encounter, moreover, characterized by therapeutic improvisations—their scientific evaluation may permanently elude our efforts.

My overall conclusion is that the years of research on outcome, while they have yielded little in the way of definite and significant findings, have led to considerable advances with respect to the most fruitful questions to ask and the most appropriate methods for going about trying to answer them. Although we have not yet found many answers, we are becoming able to ask more cogent questions and to answer them in a more systematic and sophisticated fashion. This development supplies ground for hope that therapy research will make considerably more progress in the future than it has in the past.

Summary

Outcome research, despite progress in standardization of change measures and specification of therapeutic procedures, continues to fail to demonstrate significant differences in the effectiveness of these procedures for most conditions, suggesting that a more hopeful direction of research would be to explore therapeutically relevant qualities of the patient, the therapist, and their interaction. Based on clinical impressions and scattered research findings, suggestions are offered as to potentially promising research approaches to these areas.

References

Argyle, M. *Religious behaviour*. London: Routledge & Kegan Paul, 1958.

Aspy, D. N. The effect of teacher-offered conditions of empathy, positive regard, and congruence upon student achievement. *Florida Journal of Educational Research*, 1969, *11*, 39–48.

Best, J. A. Tailoring smoking withdrawal procedures to personality and motivational differences. *Journal of Consulting and Clinical Psychology*, 1975, *43*, 1–8.

Carr, J. E. Differentiation similarity of patient and therapist and the outcome of psychotherapy. *Journal of Abnormal Psychology*, 1970, *76*, 361–369.

Dent, J. K. *Exploring the psychosocial therapies through the personalities of effective therapists* (Publ. No. ADM 77-527). Washington, D.C.: U.S. Government Printing Office, 1978.

Dohrenwend, B. Personal communication, January 1978.

Friedman, M. L., & Dies, R. R. Reactions of internal and external test-anxious students to counseling and behavior therapies. *Journal of Consulting and Clinical Psychology*, 1975, *42*, 921.

Garfield, S. L. Research on client variables in psychotherapy. In S. L. Garfield & A. E. Bergin (Eds.), *Handbook of psychotherapy and behavior change* (2nd. ed.). New York: Wiley, 1978.

Liberman, B. L. The maintenance and persistence of change: Long-term follow-up investigations of psychotherapy. In J. D. Frank, R. Hoehn-Saric, S. D. Imber, B. L. Liberman, & A. R. Stone, *Effective ingredients of successful psychotherapy*. New York: Brunner/Mazel, 1978. (a)

Liberman, B. L. The role of mastery in psychotherapy: Maintenance of improvement and prescriptive change. In J. D. Frank, R. Hoehn-Saric, S. D. Imber, B. L. Liberman, & A. R. Stone, *Effective ingredients of successful psychotherapy*. New York: Brunner/Mazel, 1978. (b)

Lieberman, M. A., Yalom, I. D., & Miles, M. B. *Encounter groups: First facts*. New York: Basic Books, 1973.

Malan, D. H. *Toward the validation of dynamic psychotherapy: A replication*. New York: Plenum, 1976.

Ollendick, T. H., & Murphy, M. J. Differential effectiveness of muscular and cognitive relaxation as a function of lucus of control. *Journal of Behavioral Therapy and Experimental Psychiatry*, 1977, *8*, 223–228.

Posthuma, A. B., & Carr, J. E. Differentiation matching in psychotherapy. *Canadian Psychological Review*, 1975, *16*, 35–43.

Razin, A. A–B variable in psychotherapy: Still promising after 20 years? In A. S. Gurman & A. M. Razin (Eds.), *Therapists' handbook for effective psychotherapy*. New York: Pergamon Press, 1977.

Sloane, R. B., Staples, F. R., Cristol, A. H., Yorkston, N. J., & Whipple, K. *Psychotherapy versus behavior therapy*. Cambridge: Harvard University Press, 1975.

Smith, M. L., & Glass, G. V., Meta-analysis of psychotherapy outcome studies. *American Psychologist*, 1977, *32*, 752–760.

Truax, C. B., & Carkhuff, R. R. *Toward effective counseling and psychotherapy: Training and practice*. Chicago: Aldine, 1967.

Voth, H. M., & Orth, M. H. *Psychotherapy and the role of the environment*. New York: Behavioral Publications, 1973.

Waskow, I. E., & Parloff, M. B. (Eds.). *Psychotherapy change measures* (DHEW Publication No. ADM 74-120). Washington, D.C.: U.S. Government Printing Office, 1975.

Whitehorn, J.C., & Betz, B. J. *Effective psychotherapy with the schizophrenic patient*. New York: Aronson, 1975.

Wilkins, W. Expectancy of therapeutic gain: An empirical and conceptual critique. *Journal of Consulting and Clinical Psychology*, 1973, *40*, 69–77.

Chapter 19

Can Psychotherapy Research Guide the Policy Maker? A Little Knowledge May Be a Dangerous Thing[1]

Morris B. Parloff

From time to time, psychotherapy researchers have complained that their findings have not impacted sufficiently on the practitioner or on the policy-maker. We have carped that our voices have not been heard in high councils and that our wisdom has gone unrecognized and unrequited by government decision makers. I regret to inform you that those idyllic days are now gone. We can no longer be confident that our papers will be read only by fellow researchers. Policymakers are reading our reports, and the clinicians are listening.

Some may be cheered, as I am, to learn that our research efforts are being attended to in the real world rather than merely in the cloistered halls and minds of academia. It is my purpose, however, not to dwell on the celebration but to invite the consideration of some of the sobering implications of having even our most tentative and preliminary findings

[1]This article was originally presented as the Presidential Address at the meeting of the Society for Psychotherapy Research, Toronto, September, 1978.

Opinions expressed herein are those of the author and do not necessarily reflect the official position of the National Institute of Mental Health.

Reprinted by permission of the Author, Morris B. Parloff, from *American Psychologist*, 1979, *34*, 296–306.

interpreted directly, not by sophisticated, research-wise investigators, but by novices. Of particular concern is the potential soundness or unsoundness of the inferences that the policymaker may draw from research evidence in making decisions that may materially affect the field of psychotherapy. I say *materially* because I mean to include a range of consequences but especially the crassly material ones—health costs, grant funding opportunities, third-party reimbursements, and so forth. The policymaker's decisions may affect clients, patients, practitioners, and researchers today and in fiscal years to come.

Policy decisions will be made in part on the basis of our research and in part on value judgments regarding need and technical and political feasibility. I anticipate that the researcher need now be less preoccupied with the fear that the clinician will not take his or her evidence seriously than with the likelihood that the policymaker will!

I propose here to review the issues that have stimulated this un-precedented interest in our work and to identify the urgent questions that clinicians and policymakers are addressing to the researcher. I shall then review and anguish a bit about the answers that have recently been made available to the questioners by the *Report* of the President's Commission on Mental Health (PCMH), and finally I shall offer some recommendations for identifying research priorities and for developing mechanisms for providing the decision makers with carefully evaluated research evidence.

Members of our new audience are raising very pragmatic, prosaic, yet profound questions regarding the efficacy of the wide range of psychosocial interventions currently offered to the public. Clinicians and government officials are experiencing mounting pressures from such not easily disregarded sources as the courts, insurance companies, and national health insurance planners. Third-party payers—ultimately the public—are demanding crisp and informative answers to questions regarding the quality, quantity, durability, safety, and efficiency of psychosocial treatments provided to an ever-widening range of consumers and potential consumers.

As long as individuals were prepared to pay for their own "therapy" it was a matter of considerable indifference—benign and otherwise—to society for what purposes the client sought treatment in the practitioner's office, clinic, classroom, and more recently, hotel ballroom. It is an individual's inalienable right to seek therapy, self-enhancement, education, enlightenment, and titillation as long as he or she is willing to pay for it.

Now, however, when society is being asked to pay for psychotherapy, it proposes to exercise its right and responsibility to determine how the terms *health* and *need for services* will be defined, who is qualified to provide such services, and how effective such services are. Society reserves the right to differentiate between problems that are of public concern—and therefore eligible for public support—and those that are viewed as frivolous, cosmetic, or capriciously elective.

Particularly in a period when the costs of health care continue to soar, private and public health insurance planners will seek to impose clear and restrictive rules of eligibility on both patient and psychotherapist.

Currently, psychotherapists appear wittingly to treat, manage, and enlighten an increasing range of clients or patients: the disturbed, the disturbing, the demoralized, the disadvantaged, the abused, and the disabused. The aim of normalizing has been augmented by the task of treating the miseries of normalcy, namely, boredom, stagnation, blocked spontaneity, meaninglessness, and the imperfect sense of personal identity. In addition, the psychotherapist treats the emotional concomitants and sequelae of physical distress and injury. Psychotherapists have more recently responded to calls to use their skills in assisting individuals to control their self-abusive, life-threatening habits of sedentary living, reckless driving, overeating, smoking, drinking, and excessive use of drugs. Psychotherapists are also asked to "treat" the social problems of crime, delinquency, rape, and racism. Indeed, psychotherapy is viewed as the treatment for all reasons and unreason.

It is currently estimated that 15 percent of this nation's population may have diagnosable mental disorders per year although only 3 percent of the population receives specialized mental health services in any given year (Regier, Goldberg, & Taube, 1978). With the expansion of private and public support of health care it may be anticipated that we will see a sharp increase in the number of patients seeking specialized mental health treatment within the next decade.

The administrator has long been preoccupied with the problems of health services delivery. The aims are to bring community mental health services to the people and the people to the services. This frenetic and costly effort has been predicated on the assumption that the treatments to be delivered have previously been established as useful and effective. The question now being belatedly asked is, How effective are these therapies, even under the ideal conditions in which the therapist and patient actually share common language, cultural background, and biases?

Such questions from policymakers and administrators are inevitably translated into pressure on the practitioners, who in turn find themselves faced with a related set of questions. Of perhaps the greatest concern to the psychotherapist is the evidence of a growing skepticism regarding the utility of psychotherapy as a treatment approach. Psychotherapists, regardless of their own skepticism about research, are increasingly turning to the researcher in the hope of receiving encouraging and supportive answers to four basic questions persistently raised by the critics of the field: (1) Does the change effected by psychosocial treatments exceed that which may be attributable to the mere passage of time or to the individual's own recuperative powers, that is, what is the role of *spontaneous remission?* (2) Are the effects of psychotherapy attributable to the use of specific techniques clearly differentiable from the influences of so-called nonspecific techniques of suggestion, persuasion, or commonsense advice, that is, what is the role of *placebo effects?* (3) Does the therapist's effectiveness vary with mastery of specialized techniques and a related body of knowledge, that is, what is the role of *training?* (4) What is the nature, speed, durability, pervasiveness, safety, and efficiency of the therapeutic amelioration and change that may be effected in the treatment of mental disorders of public health interest, that is, how *effective* is psychotherapy?

The questions posed to the researcher by the policymaker and clinician overlap, particularly in the area of treatment effectiveness; however, the policymaker has special concerns, among them patient eligibility.

It is recognized that the ultimate decision regarding eligibility for insurance coverage of treatment does not depend on a research-based resolution of the mental health–illness/problems-in-living dichotomy. Eligibility for *reimbursement* is a social policy decision. Eligibility for *treatment* is a clinical judgment.

The health insurance eligibility questions is primarily one of value judgment, usually reinforced by political and professional presures. Although I have preferences and convictions, they are not pertinent to my present purpose and will not be further discussed here.

I propose to summarize some answers that research has provided to the aforementioned four questions of the clinician and the policymaker. Comments on the first three issues, spontaneous remission, placebo effects, and training, will be based on our own assessment of the research literature (Parloff, Wolfe, Hadley, & Waskow, 1978) and on the *Report* of the President's Commission on Mental Health (1978). The fourth issue, effectiveness with particular categories of disorders, will be addressed by information derived solely from the Commission's report.

Spontaneous Remission

The persistent question of whether psychotherapy effects are greater than those attributable to spontaneous remission continues to be resurrected. This sort of global question presupposes that the improvement rates of all psychotherapy forms, independent of the techniques employed or the particular patient classes treated, are comparable and that all patient classes have comparable rates of so-called spontaneous remission. No such assumptions are warranted. Just as there is no single entity of mental disorders, there is no single spontaneous remission rate (see Beiser, 1976;

Bergin, 1971, pp. 240–242; Lambert, 1976; Subotnik, 1972). The rate of improvement without formal treatment varies from patient category to category and with the criteria used (Malan, 1973), source of rating (Strupp & Hadley, 1977), and measures (Kiesler, 1973; Mintz, 1972).

A considerable body of research evidence has now been amassed based on studies in which relatively homogeneous groups of patients were randomly assigned to treatment or to no-treatment or waiting-list control groups. Such studies attempt to control for the spontaneous remission effect as well as the possible "regression toward the mean" effect. Regression toward the mean is a plausible concern, since it is recognized that patients tend to enter therapy when they are at a low point with regard to their own chronic, spontaneously fluctuating disorder.

A review of controlled studies permits the conclusion that psychodynamic therapies, client-centered psychotherapy, cognitive therapies, and behavioral therapies have achieved results that are superior to no-treatment procedures. The findings, based on diverse studies using diverse criteria, offer an affirmative global answer to the question of whether psychotherapies are more effective than spontaneous remission rates (Beutler, 1976; Luborsky, Singer, & Luborsky, 1975; Meltzoff & Kornreich, 1970; Sloan, Staples, Cristol, Yorkston, & Whipple, 1975; Smith & Glass, 1977).

A recent review summarized nearly 700 published and unpublished studies, each of which included an untreated group. This design permitted the estimate of relevant rates of spontaneous recovery in each study. It was found that in over 90 percent of the experiments, the psychotherapy group improved more than the control group. The median person receiving psychotherapy was better off than 80 percent of the untreated controls (Glass & Smith, 1978). The authors concluded that their survey of research findings overwhelmingly validated the benefit of psychotherapy (Smith, Glass & Miller, 1980).

Placebo Effects

The observation that research has demonstrated that a range of psychotherapies are more effective than is the mere passage of time leaves open the question of whether the effects are due primarily to a placebo, for example, suggestion, expectation, hope, cajolery.

This is an area that has not yet been well studied. However, such literature as is available does suggest that treatment effects are usually more powerful than those found in the placebo-control group (Bergin & Lambert, 1978; Luborsky et al., 1975; Meltzoff & Kornreich, 1970; Smith & Glass, 1977). The review of psychotherapy research summarized by Glass and Smith (1978) concluded that the placebo effect was less than half as large as the effects of the other elements in the psychotherapy relationship.

Efforts to control for the placebo effect are nonetheless difficult, since they presuppose knowledge of the precise mechanisms whereby the so-called specific treatment intervention achieves its potency (Miller, 1978; Shapiro, 1971). Such knowledge is not in fact usually available. The placebo in psychotherapy research should ideally be inert with regard to such hypothesized specific mechanisms. The usual placebo control study attempts to control for the effects of attention, but this may not be an adequate control either for the other nonspecific elements (Frank, 1973; Marmor, 1975; Rosenzweig, 1954) that appear to characterize all forms of therapy or for the hypothesized specific elements of the particular therapy under examination.

One of the important dimensions that appear to increase the potency of placebo controls is the placebo's degree of plausibility as a treatment form to the subjects of the study. The more credible the placebo control intervention, the more closely the placebo effects resemble those of the treatment form with which the placebo is compared (Kazdin & Wilcoxon, 1976). Of increasing interest is the identification of the mechanisms whereby placebos achieve their effects.

It is generally assumed that placebo effects are artifacts and that their positive influences must be subtracted from the observed effects of treatment to arrive at the effects attributable to treatment per se. This presupposes that placebos operate only in one direction, namely, improvement. Yet it has been observed that some patients in placebo groups tend to become worse (see, e.g., Frank, 1973; Goldstein, Heller, & Sechrest, 1966; Shapiro, 1971). Could not some of the reported negative effects of psychotherapy also, then, be due to placebo effects? Since placebo effects are presumed to be due to suggestion, might not the cognitively oriented therapist now reason that some patients who fail to respond to treatment may simply be giving themselves suggestions that counter the potential effectiveness of psychotherapy? (Shades of psychoanalytic invective regarding the resistant patient!)

My point is simply that the control of placebo effects is quite a complex problem. The definitive answer to the question of the relative role of the placebo in various forms of psychotherapy has yet to be achieved.

Perhaps my favorite comment on the difficulty of differentiating the role of the placebo, that is, separating the nonspecific from the so-called specific elements of psychotherapy, is that of Martin Orne (1975), who pointed out that in order for the nonspecific elements to be effective in psychotherapy, the patient must first believe in the potency of its specific elements.

Training and Experience

Psychotherapy is not a profession but a varied and sometimes ill-defined set of practices engaged in by members of a number of different professions. Each profession requires that its members be trained first and primarily to do something else: medicine, psychology, social work, nursing, or religious ministering. In short, psychotherapy represents ancillary activities engaged in by various professionals whose preparation in the area of psychotherapy may be quite variable.

It is therefore not surprising that in the absence of a standardized training program for all psychotherapists across the various professions, the public and the policymaker should seek assistance from the researcher in distinguishing the possible differences in effectiveness among schools and professions due to differences in training.

Research, unfortunately, provides but little sound evidence on this matter. Comparisons across professions and schools have revealed no characteristic differences (e.g., Bergin & Suinn, 1975; Henry, Sims, & Spray, 1971; Meltzoff & Kornreich, 1970). Those trained in the application of specific techniques in the treatment of specific problems appear to be more effective in the use of such techniques than those not so trained, but there is little evidence that experts of different schools are differentiable in their relative treatment effectiveness (Bergin & Lambert, 1978; Sloane et al., 1975). Even more troublesome are the findings that some professionally trained therapists, when contrasted with some untrained or minimally trained therapists, appear to achieve comparable results with comparable patients (Strupp & Hadley, 1979).

Quite apart from the nature of the therapist's training, it is widely believed that length of experience enhances the therapist's expertness. Careful reviews of the literature suggest only that the therapist's experience level is related to the quality of the therapeutic relationship, and evidence regarding its association with outcome is far less clear (Auerbach & Johnson, 1977; Parloff, Waskow, & Wolfe, 1978).

Effectiveness With Specific Categories of Patients

The following is based on psychotherapy research evidence summarized in the *Report* of the President's Commission on Mental Health (1978). In abstracting the salient research findings from the commission's report, I purposely abstain from offering any critique in order better to approximate the information as it may appear to the lay reader in its pristine unqualified form.

Schizophrenia

"Treatment [of schizophrenia] by various types of psychotherapy is as yet of unestablished efficacy, although in combination with drug treatment psychotherapy may facilitate recovery and social adaptation" (p. 1694). Examination of

> many psychosocial forms of intervention, including milieu therapy, formal individual psychotherapy, formal group therapy, activity groups and "total push" programs [reveals that] these programs have generally failed to yield results that are equivalent or superior to chemotherapy. In combination with drugs, certain additive or interactive effects appear possible. However, improved personal and social adjustment in the hospital tend to have little or no relationship to subsequent adjustment or length of time in the community. An encouraging exception is a combination of chemotherapy and social learning that has recently been shown to yield improved post-hospital as well as in-hospital functioning with chronic inpatients. For the most part, however, the durability of inpatient treatment effects has been disappointing [p. 1763].

The foremost contribution of psychosocial treatments has been shown to be improvement in social adjustment, which occurs only when these treatments are combined with maintenance chemotherapy. The benefits of the additional psychosocial treatment, however, seem to take many months to emerge. "There is some evidence that suggests that certain chronic schizophrenics respond adversely to psychological treatments" (p. 1766).

Affective Disorders

> The application and modification of social learning theories to depression have yielded not only etiologic theories, but specific treatment approaches. Although the evidence is in preliminary form, careful experiments have yielded very promising results with depressed patients using such techniques as cognitive/behavioral therapy and social skill therapy. . . .
>
> Serious interpersonal conflicts persist long after resolution of symptoms of depression in women, and perhaps in men also. Treatments are currently being designed and tested which address these interpersonal and social problems that are associated with depression [pp. 1702–1703].

Alcoholism

"Follow-up studies generally indicate that failure or success appears independent of the type of treatment received, whether inpatient or outpatient" (p. 1731). It is a general impression that self-help groups such as Alcoholics Anonymous (AA) offer the most successful treatment, but scientific evidence is lacking. What is clear, however, is that many alcoholics are unsuited for AA (p. 1731). There is no ready cure for this severe and pervasive problem.

Drug Abuse

The effectiveness of psychological treatments independent of drug treatment is not established. "The efficacy of innovative treatments such as biofeedback, behavior modification, and behavior therapy has yet to be definitively assessed" (p. 1740).

Neuroses and Personality Disorders

Fears and Phobias. Moderate to severe disabling fears may now be treated by some forms of behavior modification. Systematic desensitization and *in vivo* desensitization or exposure appear to be especially effective. Treatment appears to be more effective when provided in group rather than individual treatment settings. Agoraphobia appears difficult to treat but may be responsive to treatment consisting of two or three days of prolonged exposure to feared situations. Treatment may be facilitated by the administration of minor tranquilizers, which are then gradually withdrawn (p. 1715).

Obsessive-compulsive neuroses. "Although treatment successes are occasionally reported in the literature, there is very little evidence suggesting that drugs or psychotherapy are successful with severe obsessions or compulsions. . . . The evidence from initial controlled experiment [*sic*] indicates that preventing the rituals from occurring in a benign atmosphere is an effective treatment for compulsive behavior." There is less evidence for the effectivenss of this technique in treating obsessions (p. 1717).

Childhood Disorders

Infantile autism. "Behavioral techniques have been used with dramatic effect for teaching spoken language. However, the procedures are extremely time consuming and costly and, worse yet, may be limited to teaching the child to imitate sounds rather than to develop the complex communicative skills he lacks. Clearly, no great or even modest treatment promise can be held by mental health professionals for children with Infantile Autism" (p. 1708).

Antisocial disorders. It is estimated that 35 to 40 percent of antisocial youngsters will become antisocial adults. The use of the usual psychotherapeutic interventions to prevent this course seems to be of little use. Effective treatment may require a complete environmental restructuring. "So far, short of removal from an antisocial family, no early psychiatric intervention has been shown to alter the course of this serious disorder" (p. 1709).

Hyperactive children. Behavioral treatment programs have been of some use, but medication has repeatedly been shown to be more effective in dramatically reducing the most disabling symptoms of hyperactive children. "There is no cure nor prevention for the disorder" (p. 1709).

Anxiety disorders of childhood. "Though tradition holds that insight psychotherapy is especially well-suited to the treatment of anxiety disorders in children, research data bearing on this important clinical issue are lacking" (p. 1709).

Behavioral techniques have been useful in the treatment of childhood phobic disorders and separation anxiety. In cases of severe separation anxiety, brief periods of antidepressant medication have been found effective (p. 1709).

Depression in childhood. "There is no established therapy for so-called depressed children" (p. 1709).

Learning disabilities. "In the few studies which have examined the long-term benefits of treatment, gains obtained immediately after the intervention fail to be maintained over time, even for as brief a period as 6–9 months" (p. 1709).

In short, according to the research summaries prepared by the President's Commission on Mental Health, evidence regarding the effectiveness of psychotherapy suggests that with patients who present some of the most severe social and public health problems, psychotherapy appears to play but a supportive, habilitative, and rehabilitative role rather than a primary treatment role; psychotherapy does not alone appear to be an effective treatment for the symptoms of schizophrenia, manic–depressive psychosis, autism, alcoholism, or drug abuse. Further, psychotherapy has not yet been shown to be particularly effective in the treatment of severe obsessive-compulsive behaviors in adults or in the treatment of children with hyperactivity, anxiety, depressive problems, or learning disabilities. The disorders with which psychotherapy may be particularly useful are anxiety states—fears and phobias, for example—and some nonpsychotic forms of depression. Note, however, that here the reviewers refer primarily to the effectiveness of behavior therapy rather than the usual psychotherapies.

Let us quickly review the answers that researchers have given to these four major questions of the practitioner and the policymaker: (1) Spontaneous remission effects do not account for the changes observed in treated patients. (2) Studies that have controlled for placebo effects have suggested that changes associated with treatment are greater than those attributable to the placebo. The concept of a placebo control remains ambiguous and, therefore, so does its testing. (3) The role in outcome played by specialized training and length of therapist experience has not been empirically confirmed. (4) Although psychotherapy is applied to a wide range of emotional and social disorders, it appears to be most effective as a treatment approach with some forms of anxieties and nonpsychotic depressions. Psychosocial interventions may also be useful in teaching social skills and in habilitating and rehabilitating patients requiring such assistance. Used in combination with drugs, it may also be of help in the treatment of more severly ill patients.

Discussion

How may these findings impress members of the researchers' new audience? Practitioners will not and should not easily accept the modest assessment of their effectiveness. I anticipate that many practitioners will protest that the listing of problems by discrete diagnostic categories tends to obscure the fact that the preponderance of patients present problems of depression and/or anxiety—problems that the PCMH acknowledged appear to be treated quite effectively. A further problem that inheres in the use of classical diagnostic rubrics is that such classification fails to accommodate the vast numbers of patients/clients treated by most psychotherapists in their day-to-day practice, namely, those who seek and receive assistance for "disabling problems in living," including marital difficulties and vocational uncertainties.

These anticipated objections have merit, but we can hardly blink the fact that many classes of patients (albeit comprising a relatively small number) are not satisfactorily treated.

Administrators may not find the available research answers reassuring. The evidence may, indeed, merely create a further dilemma. Research findings may not appear to endorse the efficacy of some service programs, but there is mounting social pressure to increase the availability of such services.

In addition, the research evidence regarding the indeterminant role of training will do little to clarify the relative roles of the professional and the paraprofessional. It is not surprising, but is nonetheless dismaying, that a member of the President's Commission on Mental Health has already announced his decision to "extract mental health and mental health caregiving from the clutches of professionalism" (Willie, quoted in Herbert, 1978, p. 6).

The policymaker and the clinician share the unhappy responsibility of having to make important decisions on the basis of inadequate data. Indeed, they cannot suspend their obligations pending the hoped-for but elusive day when the researchers will provide them with ultimate and definitive answers. In the absence of clear and credible scientific evidence in support of the unique and effective contributions of each of the disciplines offering psychotherapy—psychiatry, psychology, social work, psychiatric nursing, and the clergy—it is inevitable that these disciplines will

seek other means of persuading the policymaker. Each discipline will seek
to ensure its professional integrity and economic survival by offering its
most persuasive arguments, including political pressure. To be sure, pressure will be couched in terms of concern with the welfare of the patient/cli-
ent. Such ethical motivations have usually led to efforts to guard the public
from the presumed deficiencies and inadequacies of members of the helping professions other than one's own. Each discipline—including, of
course, our own—may be anticipated to strive to mobilize the forces of
sheer numbers, prestige, and political influence. I regret that the various
disciplines, particularly psychology and psychiatry, appear to be headed for
a cyclic renewal of their periodic internecine scuffles. We seem destined to
pursue, for yet a while longer, our all too familiar "dogma eat dogma"
existence.

The tacit assumption that underlies much of the anxiety provoked by
the promise and threat of national health insurance is that the protagonists
will be the members of the currently recognized mental health professions.
This view overlooks the potential major role of the nonpsychiatrically
trained physician. It has been reported that in the United States nonpsychiatrically trained physicians see approximately 60 percent of all patients who have been identified as suffering from diagnosed mental health
problems (Regier et al., 1978). Most of the care provided is pharmacologi-
cal or supportive (e.g., "therapeutic listening"), and few referrals to mental
health practitioners are ever made. The implications of this for the quality
of patient care and the costs to society of national health insurance bear
pondering.

How can the researcher more usefully respond to the PCMH autopsy
of what most of us believed was still a healthy body of research? Since the
field of psychology has contributed disproportionately to the production of
the available research corpus, we may understandably take a rather propri-
etary interest in its proper care and treatment.

What guidance can we offer the policymaker and the practitioner to
assist them in interpreting the responses that research has given to their
questions? Our advice depends, of course, on how seriously we take our
own pronouncements and generalizations. The problem of the credibility of
generalizations in the field of psychotherapy is shared by all disciplines
within the behavioral and social sciences, which must function primarily in
the inductive mode. By careful examination of individual instances we
attempt to arrive at generalizations that appear to fit the data. Since we
cannot hope to study all instances and cannot be certain that our sampling
of the population is adequate, our conclusions must remain tentative.

In my view the problem is particularly acute in the field of psychotherapy because of the inherent difficulty in deriving supportable conclusions
from a literature that is essentially noncumulative. It cannot now be known

with any degree of certainty whether the patients, interventions, goals, and measures are comparable from study to study. In view of this fact I am prepared to place but modest reliance on the present conclusions of the PCMH *Report* regarding psychotherapy. I think that we can assure the nonresearchers that psychotherapy has shown some evidence of potency; however, our research has not yet been designed or conducted in a manner that can provide truly responsive answers to their questions. The best I can say after years of sniffing about in the morass of outcome research literature is that in my optimistic moods I am confident that there's a pony in there somewhere.

The basic question, then, is, What must we as researchers do in order to respond more usefully to the pragmatic questions that now face the field? First, I think it is necessary for us to accept the responsibility to provide more responsive research data to the practitioner and the administrator. We cannot, as a field, remain in the aloof stance caricatured in the familiar picture of the basic scientist who prefers to seek after truth untrammeled by the yammerings of the secular world. The fact is that in the practical world in which we must find support for our research, we can only hope to settle for half-aloof.

I now offer some recommendations which I believe may provide the field with a greater likelihood of achieving more useful and interpretable research data regarding psychotherapy outcome.

Emphasis on Clinical Trials Research

I propose that the National Institute of Mental Health (NIMH) be authorized to support and implement new initiatives in the conduct of such clinical trials research as may now be feasible and to support research that will increase the feasibility of subsequently conducting clinical trials studies. Such research should reflect the maximum involvement of the research community in the advisory process. The support of such research should in no way deflect from the continued support of independently initiated, high-quality research on the mechanisms of psychological interventions, nor should it reduce the support for the development and preliminary testing of new and established treatment forms. Such continued independent research is prerequisite to the more definitive clinical trials research program. It is cautioned that the NIMH does not have, nor should it seek, any regulatory functions. It is further urged that policymakers recognize that clear and compelling research evidence, which constitutes only one of the bases for policy decisions, will not quickly become available. Careful long-term research is required to produce answers to complex research questions. A crash program cannot be expected to yield definitive answers.

I base this lengthy recommendation in part on my conviction that small-scale, independently initiated and conducted, uncoordinated research is inherently unable to provide reliable answers to the urgent "applied" questions of the field. Independently initiated research projects have contributed substantially to a body of basic knowledge regarding the processes and mechanisms of therapy, provided clinical insights, developed hypotheses, contributed to the refinement of research methodologies, and provided preliminary tests of promising treatment techniques and approaches.

Such studies have not, however, provided answers to the questions now being asked with increasing insistence: What kinds of changes are affected by what kinds of techniques applied to what kinds of patients by what kinds of therapists under what kinds of conditions? The problem inheres not in any limitations of the independent investigator's competence, nor even in the complexity and difficulty of the research area. The problem lies instead in the lack of the coordinated planning that can permit the gradual acquisition of cumulative knowledge. No single study, no matter how carefully designed and executed, can hope to control for or investigate systematically the plethora of variables whose influences on outcome may be confounded with and obscure the effects of treatment.

It is necessary that cooperating investigators each adopt an agreed-upon minimal set of standardized measures for describing and assessing such variables as the nature of the problem being treated, the characteristics of the treatment interventions, and the techniques for assessing the nature, quality, speed, and durability of patient change. The conduct of such large-scale studies requires centralized coordination following the achievement of technical consensus based on extensive consultation with the most knowledgeable investigators in the field.

A research program illustrative of this approach may be found in a currently planned, NIMH multi-institutional collaborative study aimed at assessing the effectiveness, efficiency, and safety of two or more pretested psychological approaches to the treatment of carefully defined classes of disabling depressions. The effects of the selected interventions, offered singly or in combination with a designated pharmacologic agent, are to be studied and contrasted with suitable control groups.

Increased Research Attention to the Standard Forms of Psychotherapy

It is specifically recommended that the researcher attempt to study psychotherapy as it is practiced within community facilities and in private practice. Particular emphasis should be placed on assessing the effects with specified patient groups of well-described brief and long-term treatment interventions.

This recommendation grows partly out of the observation that there appears to be a remarkable disparity between the amount of research conducted on behavior therapy and on psychotherapy. This may be due to the fact that behavior therapies are more amenable to rigorous study than are the psychotherapies. In any event, there appears to be an inverse relationship between the frequency with which a treatment form is actually used by practitioners and the frequency with which that treatment is studied. A related point is that research tends to be conducted primarily in academic institutions, laboratories, or chronic patient wards in large public hospitals, yet most of the psychological treatments are offered in multiservice clinics, military clinics, community mental health centers, general medical care settings, general hospitals, and private practice. The effect of this disparity is that different kinds of patients and perhaps even different qualities of treatment may be characteristic of the research settings. To make our research findings more useful to the practitioners and the policymakers, this discrepancy should be corrected.

Facilitation of Research on Innovative Therapies

The NIMH should undertake to fund the independent study of those new treatment techniques deemed promising. The mechanisms of grants and contracts should be used in establishing community psychosocial treatment research organizations competent to provide such services. Such research organizations should have the technical ability to investigate the mechanisms and processes associated with the new treatment procedure, as well as its effectiveness. No standard-setting or regulatory functions would be implied or authorized.

This recommendation is aimed at dealing with the fact that clinicians who develop new procedures and techniques frequently do not have ready access to researchers who can collaborate with them in scientifically testing the benefits of their innovations.

Unlike the fields of drug and somatic interventions, the psychotherapies (as distinct from behavior therapies) are almost always developed by clinicians rather than researchers. The developers, for the most part, do not usually have the skills, resources, or opportunities to subject their therapy form to objective, independent study. At present, the initiative is left to the clinician, who must voluntarily seek a collaborative relationship with researchers at universities. Cooperation of investigators is often difficult to obtain.

The need for independent assessment of newly developed treatment techniques is frequently overlooked in the field of psychosocial interventions. It is a well-recognized principle that the inventor or developer of a technique cannot be expected to be free of bias, yet in psychological treatment research it is generally the innovator of a technique who is expected to undertake to demonstrate the utility of his or her procedures.

It is appropriate that the clinician who *volunteers* to cooperate in such a study should have the opportunity to do so, provided, of course, that preliminary study suggests that the technique is of potential value.

Acquisition, Evaluation, and Dissemination of Research Information

The Alcohol, Drug Abuse, and Mental Health Administration and the NIMH should be supported in their initiative to create advisory groups to assess and evaluate on a periodic basis the published research in the field of psychosocial treatment and to prepare appropriate evaluative reports. Such activity should represent the involvement of the research community to a maximum degree in order that such assessments and recommendations represent the best technical consensus rather than the views of a particular federal agency, individual scientist, or professional interest group.

Scientific communication is currently best among researchers and academicians, or those with a direct incentive to keep up with the latest information in their areas. Scientific communication with practitioners, policymakers, and the public is attenuated. Though the researcher may be able to interpret published research findings and to recognize the limits of generalizability and interpretability, the clinician and the lay person may be less equipped or less inclined to do so. It is therefore necessary to establish a mechanism for providing authoritative information to the practitioner, the policymaker, and the public, regarding the validity and significance of new findings from research and their readiness for wide clinical application.

Specifically, it is necessary to assess the clinical significance of new findings and the adequacy of the research that underpins it. It is necessary to establish a system whereby the informed opinions of the most knowledgeable authorities in the field can be brought to bear on the assessment of current and past research output. On the basis of such a consensus, evaluated information should be disseminated regularly to practitioners and the public regarding such questions as the generalizability of findings to other samples of patients, therapists, and settings; implications regarding costs; and ethical and social considerations.

Apart from the content, readers may have noted two facts about this list of recommendations that may strike them as odd: First, the recommendations appear to be primarily addressed to federal administrators, and second, I appear to have successfully resisted the opportunity to exhort my colleagues to go forth and do better. The fact is that our individual research efforts are good and are getting better. I do, however, reserve the right to offer a primarily strategic suggestion. Before doing so, I wish to return to the first point—the fact that my recommendations appear to be directed primarily toward officials of the federal government and only secondarily to fellow researchers.

I have done so wittingly, mindful of the fact that the federal government is in a very real sense the source of research support not only for those of us on the payroll but for all investigators whose work is supported by grants and contracts. The federal government supports approximately 89 percent of all research in the field of mental health, state governments contribute but 8 percent, and private sources account for only 3 percent. As researchers, therefore, we are all immediately and sometimes painfully affected by governmental laws and policy decisions.

And now a word primarily to the researcher rather than our collective sponsors: Though I am reluctant to dwell on technical issues with this audience, which is all too intimately acquainted with the technical problems that beset our field, there is one issue that bears underlining. It appears that some of our studies may inadvertently be designed in a manner that may effectively preclude the investigator's having the opportunity to reject the null hypothesis. I refer to the fact that group comparison studies often include fatuously heterogeneous groups and measures of low reliability and uncertain validity. Measurement error, coupled with the variance due to differences among patients within the groups being studied, tends to produce estimated population variances of such size as to reduce the likelihood that statistically significant differences between group means can be found. An apparent finding of "no differences" may take on unfortunate significance to the policymaker who lusts after cost-effectiveness evidence. Thus, comparisons of the relative effectiveness of short-term and long-term therapies, or of drugs and psychotherapies, or of professional and nonprofessional therapists may by virtue of inadequate research designs lead to profound overinterpretation of a "no difference" finding.

I have laid heavy emphasis in one of my earlier recommendations on the conduct of clinical trials research, but I do not wish to give the impression that I am unaware of its complexities and dangers. More particularly, I wish to urge that such studies not be designed simply as "horse races" to see which therapy wins. It is past time for us to abandon research aimed solely at identifying "the most effective form of therapy." We must seek instead to determine what kinds of interventions produce what kinds of changes in particular patients. (Readers are by now familiar with the rest of that litany.) Clinical trials research will be useful to the degree that it permits the study of interactions among patients, therapists, and therapies, and the identification of relevant process variables. Research evidence that promises the greatest generalizability is that which furthers our understanding of the mechanisms whereby particular kinds of changes are effected. Generalizations to discrete mechanisms may be even more useful than efforts to generalize findings to schools of therapy, professions, or diagnostic categories of patients.

In the past, in confronting some of the problems I have posed here, researchers have proposed that it was premature to study outcome until the processes and mechanisms were better understood. Others have suggested the opposite—that it may be premature to focus on process studies until we have clearer evidence of the nature and quality of outcome. I believe they are both right. In view of this, I believe we have no choice but to pursue process studies actively as part of well-coordinated outcome studies. In this manner a coherent body of knowledge in this field may finally begin to emerge.

Summary

Policy decisions affecting third-party reimbursements and the continued support of psychotherpay research will be based in part on research evidence developed by researchers in the field. This article considers some of the sobering implications of having available research reports interpreted not by sophisticated research-wise investigators but by lay policymakers. I have discussed currently available answers to the policymaker's questions concerning the role of spontaneous remission, the placebo, and the nature of therapist training. I have summarized the reported effectiveness of psychosocial interventions in the treatment of mental disorders, as assessed by the President's Commission on Mental Health. Finally, I have offered recommendations for developing mechanisms for providing the decision makers with a scientifically sound data base.

References

Auerbach, A. H., & Johnson, M. Research on the therapist's level of experience. In A. S. Gurman & A. M. Razin (Eds.), *Effective psychotherapy: A handbook of research*. New York: Pergamon Press, 1977.

Beiser, M. Personal and social factors associated with the remission of psychiatric symptoms. *Archives of General Psychiatry*, 1976, *33*, 941–945.

Bergin, A. E. The evaluation of therapeutic outcome. In A. E. Bergin & S. L. Garfield (Eds.), *Handbook of psychotherapy and behavior change*. New York: Wiley, 1971.

Bergin, A. E., & Lambert, M. J. The evaluation of therapeutic outcomes. In S. L. Garfied & A. E. Bergin (Eds.), *Handbook of psychotherapy and behavior change* (2nd ed.). New York: Wiley, 1978.

Bergin, A. E., & Suinn, R. M. Individual psychotherapy and behavior therapy. In M. R. Rosenzweig & L. W. Porter (Eds.), *Annual review of psychology* (Vol. 26). Palo Alto, Calif.: Annual Reviews, 1975.

Beutler, L. E. *Psychotherapy: When what works with whom.* Unpublished manuscript, Baylor College of Medicine, Houston, 1976.

Frank, J. D. *Persuasion and healing: A comparative study of psychotherapy* (Rev. ed.). Baltimore, Md.: Johns Hopkins University Press, 1973.

Glass, G. V. & Smith, M. L. Statement to the U.S. Senate Finance Committee regarding the benefits of psychotherapy, August 15, 1978.

Goldstein, A. P., Heller, K., & Sechrest, L. B. *Psychotherapy and the psychology of behavior change.* New York: Wiley, 1966.

Henry, W. E., Sims, J. H., & Spray, S. L. *The fifth profession.* San Francisco: Jossey-Bass, 1971.

Herbert, W. President's panel: Three inside views. *APA Monitor,* May 1978, pp. 6–7.

Kazdin, A. E., & Wilcoxon, L. A. Systematic desensitization and nonspecific treatment effects: A methodological evaluation. *Psychological Bulletin,* 1976, *83,* 729–758.

Kiesler, D. J. *The process of psychotherapy.* Chicago: Aldine, 1973.

Lambert, M. J. Spontaneous remission in adult neurotic disorder: A revision and summary. *Psychological Bulletin,* 1976, *83,* 107–119.

Luborsky, L., Singer, B., & Luborsky, L. Comparative studies of psychotherapies. *Archives of General Psychiatry,* 1975, *32,* 995–1008.

Malan, D. H. The outcome problem in psychotherapy research: A historical review. *Archives of General Psychiatry,* 1973, *29,* 719–729.

Marmor, J. The nature of the psychotherapeutic process revisited. *Canadian Psychiatric Association Journal,* 1975, *20,* 557–565.

Meltzoff, J., & Kornreich, M. *Research in psychotherapy.* New York: Atherton Press, 1970.

Miller, N. E. Biofeedback and visceral learning. In M. R. Rosenzweig & L. W. Porter (Eds.), *Annual review of psychology* (Vol. 29). Palo Alto, Calif.: Annual Reviews, 1978.

Mintz, J. What is "success" in psychotherapy? *Journal of Abnormal Psychology,* 1972, *80,* 11–19.

Orne, M. Psychotherapy in contemporary America: Its development and context. In D. X. Freedman & J. E. Dyrud (Eds.), *American handbook of psychiatry* (2nd ed., Vol. 5). New York: Basic Books, 1975.

Parloff, M. B., Waskow, I. E., & Wolfe, B. E. Research on therapist variables in relation to process and outcome. In S. L. Garfield & A. E. Bergin (Eds.), *Handbook of psychotherapy and behavior change* (2nd ed.). New York: Wiley, 1978.

Parloff, M. B., Wolfe, B. E., Hadley, S. W., & Waskow, I. E. *Assessment of psychosocial treatment of mental health disorders: Current status and prospects.* Report to the National Academy of Sciences, Institute of Medicine, Washington, D.C., 1978.

President's Commission on Mental Health. *Report to the President, 1978* (Vol. 4). Washington, D.C.: U.S. Government Printing Office, 1978.

Regier, D. A., Goldberg, I. D., & Taube, C. A. The de facto U.S. mental health services system: A public health perspective. *Archives of General Psychiatry*, 1978, 35, 685–693.

Rosenzweig, S. A transvaluation of psychotherapy: A reply to Hans Eysenck. *Journal of Abnormal and Social Psychology*, 1954, 49, 298–304.

Shapiro, A. K. Placebo effects in medicine, psychotherapy, and psychoanalysis. In A. E. Bergin & S. L. Garfield (Eds.), *Handbook of psychotherapy and behavior change*. New York: Wiley, 1971.

Sloane, R. B., Staples, F. R., Cristol, A. H., Yorkston, N. J., & Whipple, K. *Short-term analytically oriented psychotherapy vs. behavior therapy*. Cambridge: Harvard University Press, 1975.

Smith, M. L., & Glass, G. V. Meta-analysis of psychotherapy outcome studies. *American Psychologist*, 1977, 32, 752–760.

Smith, M. L., Glass, G. V. & Miller, T. I. *The benefits of psychotherapy*. Baltimore, Md.: Johns Hopkins University Press, 1980.

Strupp, H. H., & Hadley, S. W. A tripartite model of mental health and therapeutic outcomes: With special reference to negative effects in psychotherapy. *American Psychologist*, 1977, 32, 187–196.

Strupp, H. H., & Hadley, S. W. Specific versus nonspecific factors in psychotherapy: A controlled study of outcome. *Archives of General Psychiatry*, 1979, 36, 1125–1136.

Subotnik, L. Spontaneous remission: Fact or artifact? *Psychological Bulletin*, 1972, 77, 32–48.

Part VII
The Interplay
of Practice
and Research

Just as previous sections have emphasized that no one theoretical orientation can provide us with all the answers, so does the theme of this section suggest that neither the clinician nor the researcher, working alone, can be successful in advancing the field. While the ultimate determination of therapeutic effectiveness rests on research findings, the phenomena that are studied empirically—if they are to have any ecological significance—must be based on what actually goes on clinically. In writing about psychological research in general, Maslow argues that firsthand experience with and observations of certain events are needed before we put in the time and energy involved in carrying out research on such events. Maslow cautions that we need to guard against the danger of our theoretical conceptualizations becoming too far removed from the phenomena we encounter directly. Focusing more specifically on the rift between the clinician and the researcher, Goldstein similarly emphasizes that without some coordination between the two, clinical practice will continue to have weak empirical foundations, and research will continue to proliferate on relatively trivial issues. In the end, everyone suffers, including the patients/clients we work with clinically. Strupp has observed the rift between clinicians and researchers since the beginning of his career, noting that each group tends to stereotype the other. Writing from the point of view of someone who has been actively involved in *both* therapy research and clinical practice, Strupp maintains that a combination of firsthand clinical experience and objective evaluation is the path that will ultimately improve our therapeutic effectiveness.

Chapter 20
Abstracting and Theorizing

Abraham H. Maslow

Now that I have expounded on the virtues, the necessities, and the priority of experiential knowledge to abstract knowledge, I turn to the virtues and beauties and necessities of abstract knowledge as well. By now my general point must be clear. It is the dichotomized, solely abstract knowledge that is so dangerous, the abstractions and the systems that are opposed to or dichotomized from experience instead of being built upon it and integrated with it. If I may say it so, abstract knowledge dichotomized from experiential knowledge is false and dangerous; but abstract knowledge built upon and hierarchically integrated with experiential knowledge is a necessity for human life.

Abstractness begins with all orderings of experience, all interpretations of it, and all the hierarchical and Gestaltlike arrangements of experiential knowledge that make it possible for the limited human being to encompass it, grasp it, not be overwhelmed by it. In the same way that our immediate memory span for separate objects is about seven or eight or so, it is also known that six or seven or eight groups of separate objects may also be perceived and encompassed in an immediate perception. This is the simplest example of the holistic hierarchizing of many objects that I can think of. Make these groupings more and more inclusive, and finally it is possible for a human being, limited though he is, to encompass the whole world in a single unified perception. The contrast is with total anarchy, total chaos, a total lack of ordering, or clustering, or of relationships among all these separate things. This is the world, perhaps, of the newborn baby in some

Reprinted by permission of the publisher from Abstracting and theorizing, in A. H. Maslow (Ed.), *The psychology of science: A reconnaissance*. New York: Harper & Row, 1966, pp. 66–71.

respects, or like the world of the panicky schizophrenic in another respect. In any case, it is hardly possible to live with for any length of time or to endure (although it can be enjoyed for a short time). This is even more true if we take into account the necessity for pragmatic living within the world, surviving in it, dealing with it, and having commerce with it. All the means–end relationships, and all the differential perception of ends and means also come under the head of abstractness. Purely concrete experience does not differentiate one experience from another experience in any way, certainly not in terms of relative importance or of relative hierarchy of means and ends. All classifications of our experiences of reality are abstractions, and so is all awareness of similarities and differences.

In other words, abstractness is absolutely necessary for life itself. It is also necessary for the fullest and highest development of human nature. Self-actualization necessarily implies abstractness. It is not even possible to conceive of human self-actualization without whole systems of symbols, abstractions, and words, i.e., language, philosophy, world view.

The attack upon abstractness dichotomized from concreteness must never be confused with an attack upon abstractness hierarchically integrated with concreteness and experience. We might remind ourselves here of the contemporary situation in philosophy. Kierkegaard and Nietzsche, to take two major examples, attacked not philosophy in general but the great abstract systems of philosophy that had long since cut themselves off from their foundations in actual living experience. Existentialism and phenomenology are in large part also a repudiation of these huge, verbal, *a priori*, abstract, total systems of philosophy. This is an attempt to get back to life itself, that is to say, to concrete experience upon which all abstractions must be based if they are to remain alive.

It will help here to make the distinction between an empirical generalization or theory and an *a priori* generalization or theory. The former is simply an effort to organize and to unify experiential knowledge so that we can grasp it with our limited human brain. An *a priori* theory makes no such effort. It can be spun entirely inside one's own head and can proceed without reference either to experiential knowledge or to areas of ignorance. Generally it is presented as a certainty. In effect it commits the great sin of denying human ignorance. The true empiricist or the empirical-minded layman is always aware of what he knows and what he doesn't know and of the relative reliabilities and different levels of validity of what he does know. An empirical theory is in a real sense humble. The classical, abstract, *a priori* theory need not be humble; it can be and often is arrogant. One might also say that the abstract theory or abstract system becomes functionally autonomous in the sense of divorcing itself from its empirical foundations, from the experiences upon which it rests and which it is supposed to explain or give meaning to or organize. It proceeds thereafter to live its own life as a theory per se, sufficient unto itself, having its own life. In contrast the empirical theory or empirical system remains connected with the experiential facts that it organizes into a manageable, graspable unity and in close parallel with these facts. As a consequence it can shift and change and easily modify itself as new information becomes available. That is, if it purports to interpret and organize our knowledge of reality, then it must of necessity be a changing thing, since our knowledge of reality keeps on changing, and it must be adaptable and flexible in the sense of adapting itself to this foundation of changing and increasing knowledge. There is a kind of mutual feedback involved here between theory and facts, a feedback which can be totally lacking in the functionally autonomous abstract theory or system which has become self-borne.

To add a final touch to this differentiation, I refer to a previously made distinction between reduction to the concrete as Goldstein (1939) described it and reduction to the abstract as I described it (Maslow, 1963). I will then contrast both of these with the finding in self-actualizing people that characteristically they were able to be both concrete and abstract.

I can push the whole matter even further. In a certain sense I see the acceptance of the prepotency and the logical priority of experience as another version of the spirit of empiricism itself. One of the beginnings of science, one of the roots from which it grew, was the determination not to take things on faith, trust, logic, or authority but to check and to see for oneself. Experience had shown how often the logic or the *a priori* certainty or Aristotle's authority failed to work in fact. The lesson was easy to draw. First, before everything else comes the seeing of nature with your own eyes, that is, experiencing it yourself.

Perhaps an even better example is the development of the empirical or scientific attitude in the child. Here the major injunction is "let's take a look for ourselves," or "go and see with your own eyes." For the child this contrasts with taking things on faith, whether from daddy or mommy or from the teacher or from the book. It can be phrased in the harshest terms of "don't trust anyone, but look with your own eyes." Or else it can be phrased more mildly: "it's always a good idea to check just to make sure. There are individual differences in perceiving; somebody else might see it in one way, and you perhaps will see it in another." This is to teach the child that one's own perceptions usually constitute the court of last resort. If the empirical attitude means anything at all, it means at least this. First comes "knowing" in the experiential sense; then come the checks on the fallibilities of the senses and of experiential knowledge; then come the abstractions, the theories, i.e., orthodox science. As a matter of fact, the concept of objectivity itself (in the sense of the need to make knowledge public and to share it and not to trust it completely until it has been shared by at least several people) may be seen as a more complex derivative of a primary empirical rule, i.e., to check by one's own experience. This is so because public knowledge constitutes an experiential check by several people on your report of your private experience. If you go into the desert and discover some unexpected mine or some improbable animal, your experiential knowledge may be certain and valid, but you can hardly expect others to believe you entirely and on faith. They also have a right to see for themselves, that is, to acquire the ultimate validity of their own experiential knowledge. And that is just what objective public checking is, i.e., an extension of "see for yourself."

This insistence upon the priority of the empirical theory over the *a priori* theory or system and the consequent insistence upon a close parallelism of the empirical theory with the facts that it ties together in a unity, differentiates between the person with the empirical attitude on the one hand and the doctrinaire on the other. For instance, Max Eastman in his autobiography thinks of himself, by contrast with the Soviet intellectuals, as a "vulgar empiricist who saw Socialism as a hypothesis, an experiment that ought to be tried." He was restless with the Soviet theorists, among whom he felt "an atmosphere of theology rather than of science." I have criticized the religious establishments on a similar basis (Maslow, 1964). Since most of them have claimed to be revealed religions, that is, to be based upon an original prophets' vision of the perfect, final, and absolute truth, there is obviously nothing more to learn. There is no need for openness, for checking, for experimentation, not even for improvement (since it is already perfect).

This is as sharp a contrast with the empirical attitude as I can find. But in a milder form it is widespread and perhaps we could say almost universal in the mass of humankind. And I am not even inclined to exempt all professional scientists from this indictment. The empirical attitude is in its essence a humble attitude, and many or most scientists are not humble except in their own chosen areas of professional work. They are, many of them, as likely to charge out of their laboratory doors with *a priori* faiths and prejudgments of all kinds as are some theologians, if only about the nature of science itself. This humility that I consider to be a defining characteristic of the empirical or scientific attitude includes the ability to admit that you are ignorant and that mankind in general is ignorant about many things. Such an admission has the necessary consequence of making you in principle willing and eager to learn. It means that you are open rather than closed to new data. It means that you can be naïve rather than all-knowing. And all of this means, of course, that your universe keeps on growing steadily in contrast to the static universe of the person who already knows everything.

This is a long way off from the point at which I started, that is, of simply insisting on a place in knowledge and in science for experiential data. But I believe that making a respectable place for experiential data finally strengthens the empirical attitude and therefore strengthens science rather than weakens it. It expands the jurisdiction of science because of its faith that the human mind need not be shut out of any area of life.

References

Goldstein, K. *The organism*. New York: American Book Company, 1939.

Maslow, A. H. Notes on innocent cognition. In L. Schenk-Danzinger & H. Thomae (Eds.), *Gegenwartsprobleme der entwicklungspsychologie: Festschrift fur Charlotte Buhler*. Gottingen: Verlag fur Psychologie, 1963.

Maslow, A. H. *Religions, values and peak-experiences*. Columbus, Ohio: Ohio State University Press, 1964.

Chapter 21

Psychotherapy Research and Psychotherapy Practice: Independence or Equivalence?

Arnold P. Goldstein

All is not well in the world of contemporary psychotherapy, and, perhaps somewhat paradoxically, much of the difficulty is of an interpersonal nature. We speak here of the manner in which the advancement of psychotherapy is inhibited by discrepancies between practitioners and researchers interested in its investigation. There is, perhaps, little novelty in this observation that practitioner–researcher relations are often lacking in harmony—to the detriment of both our understanding and the efficiency of psychotherapy. The recent report of the Joint Commission on Mental Illness and Health (1961) notes, "Practitioners find that they cannot understand the research reports nor see their relevance to their daily problems. Research workers, on the other hand . . . cannot understand the resistance of the practitioner to such elementary and necessary principles of good research as experimental controls and adequate sampling procedures."

In a similar manner, Strupp (1960) has commented:

> Psychotherapy is a focal point of the ongoing debate between the operationally-empirically minded investigator and the seeker of intuitive understanding. The former often dismisses the insights of the latter as insufficiently validated or

Reprinted by permission of the author, Arnold P. Goldstein, and the publisher from S. Lesse (Ed.), *An evaluation of the results of the psychotherapies*. Springfield, Ill.: Charles C. Thomas, 1968, pp. 5–17.

even as incapable of unambiguous validation. The latter, if he is a clinician, may fail to see how results statistically validated "at the .05 level of confidence" can help him deal with unique and complex troubled persons . . . whom he is trying to help.

As noted, observations such as these are not uncommon (Chassen, 1953; Reznikoff & Tooney, 1959; Soskin, 1968). Further, the extremely slight impact, to date, of therapy research upon therapy practice stands as direct, behavioral evidence of just how unconsummated is the marriage of therapy research and practice. Dispassionate attempts to identify and correct the bases for this state of affairs have pointed toward several likely responsible agents, involving researchers and practitioners alike. The therapy research community, for example, has shown a marked lack of concern over applied implications and applications of investigative findings. In 1958, as an example, the country's leading psychotherapy researchers, representing both psychology and psychiatry, met in a conference to share research plans and recent findings which were current at that time. A statement by Parloff and Rubinstein (1959), in a paper summarizing the conference transactions, represents the position of the majority of the conference participants. It speaks for itself:

> A recurrent theme was that to be concerned with outcome of therapy was to identify oneself with the simple pragmatic concerns of the practitioner rather than the more fundamental and more respected interests of the scientist. This differentiation carried a certain amount of admitted intellectual snobbery and a tendency to look down upon applied investigations.

The continued lack of interest in outcome research evident in a second and similar conference (Strupp & Luborsky, 1962), as well as Astin's (1961) recent discussion of the functional autonomy of psychotherapy research, underscores just how widespread is the negative view of such "applied" psychotherapy outcome research.

Researchers are oftimes unreponsive to the needs of practitioners in other ways. Mitchell and Mudd (1957) observe, "He [the researcher] often does little to resolve the problem of terminology or semantic differences between clinician and researcher. He is frequently hesitant to take time to acquaint the clinician with fundamental principles of his tests, questionnaires and statistical techniques." Hamburg (1961) and Landfield (1954) have commented upon similar breakdowns in communication, and in particular have underscored the degree to which such faulty communication can decrease the likelihood of subsequent involvement in research by the clinician.

Yet another factor contributed by the therapy researcher may be suggested. Much of the psychotherapy research which has been conducted has been high in precision but low in psychological significance. Frank (1961) observes in this regard:

> The researcher is faced with the problem of delimiting an aspect of psychotherapy that is amenable to experimental study and at the same time includes the major determinants of the problem under consideration. . . . Under these circumstances there is an inevitable tendency to guide the choice of research problems more by the ease with which they can be investigated than by their importance. . . . This has led to a considerable amount of precise but trivial research.

The overabundance of research on duration of psychotherapy, almost all of which very carefully leads nowhere, is one outstanding example of such research.

The practitioner's contribution to this progress-inhibiting state of affairs is similarly many sided. Shoben (1953) comments, for example,

> Working on the basis of necessity and with little help from their experimentally inclined colleagues, they [clinicians] have built up a body of "intuitive" techniques which have been reinforced by a sense of inner certitude and quasi success. . . . Where certainty exists, no matter how tenuously based, there is little motive for investigation.

A related consequence of a singular commitment to an exclusively clinical approach has been pointed to by Luszki (1957):

> Regardless of whether the research worker is interfering with the ongoing work of the practitioner, there is the possibility of threat in the very fact that the research may bring new knowledge that will lead to changes in practice. The researcher is implicitly questioning present practices, and this in itself leads to some opposition.

Thus, Shoben has underscored the clinician's relative need for certainty, his intolerance of ambiguity; Luszki emphasizes possible feelings of threat which may be engendered by research challenges to current therapeutic techniques or assumptions.

Brody (1957) has suggested a number of other "psychodynamic" bases for negative responses on the part of many clinicians to invitations for research participation:

1. Hostility against being forced into a new and unwanted role.
2. Guilt associated with using the patient for research as equivalent to serving the therapist's needs and not the patient's needs.
3. Hostility due to new status problems among members of the research-clinical group (i.e., the introduction of a professional re-

searcher may increase the awareness of clinical personnel of their relative inadequacy in this area of functioning).

4. Threatened loss of self-esteem following the removal or lowering of accustomed defenses which operate when the therapist works in privacy.

The observations noted to this point describe well, we feel, our current dilemma. When viewed as a group, the obstacles to a more productive working relationship between clinicians and researchers are both quite real and quite substantial, and it is clear that these are obstacles to both more successful practice and more meaningful research. Practice suffers from a grossly insufficient number of substantive research findings by which its efficiency might be enhanced. Practice continues to rest primarily upon. what many feel is the rather weak foundation of clinical lore and intuition. Research suffers from want of sufficient opportunity to examine aspects of psychotherapy of potential use to the practitioner, and particularly from insufficient opportunity to do so with experienced therapists. As a result, development of a sounder understanding of the psychotherapeutic process and the growth of associated theoretical formulations are retarded. As for the patient, he suffers too—and this time in a literal sense, on both counts. Where then do the answers lie? What means may be utilized in an attempt to bring practitioner and researcher closer together on a more common conceptual and operational base?

A possible solution may lie in an increased awareness on the part of both groups that therapy practice and therapy research are, in many real and essential respects, one and the same. On several important dimensions, research *is* therapy; therapy *is* research.

Research as Therapy

Awareness of the therapeutic implications of psychotherapy research, like many subtle research implications, has grown gradually while evidence from diverse research settings has accumulated. Rosenfeld and Orlinsky (1961), in the process of studying the problem of premature patient termination of psychotherapy, found that termination rate decreased to such a marked degree during the course of the study that it could no longer be used as a meaningful criterion variable. Ekman (1961), in a study of what he termed the "Fort Dix Phenomena," attempted to evaluate a new approach to the prevention of military delinquency. During the course of his investigation, a dramatic reduction in the number of courts-martial took place. Two independent investigations (Psychopharmacology Service Center, 1962), studying the effect on release rates of tranquilizer medication administered to hospitalized schizophrenic patients, found an increase in such rates in *both* treated and untreated patients during the drug administration trial. As the research report states, "It may well be that drugs, by effectively controlling symptoms of seriously ill schizophrenic patients, contribute to a general improvement of hospital milieu leading to a better response in schizophrenic patients not so seriously ill as to warrant drug treatment."

With more direct relevance to our present concerns, a series of studies has similarly indicated research-induced positive personality changes in "untreated" patients participating in psychotherapy research. Frank (1961) and Levin (1959), for example, have independently reported significant behavioral improvement in patients following the introduction of a research project and in the absence of formal psychotherapy or medication. Goldstein (1962), and Barron and Leary (1955) report similar symptom reduction and personality change in patients on wait-list research groups not participating in formal psychotherapy. Rashkis (1961) has presented similar findings. Slack (1960), and Schwitzgebel and Kolb (1964), in the same vein, have studied what they term "experimenter-subject" psychotherapy. They report major behavioral change in highly resistant adolescent delinquents who participated for pay in an extended series of experimental sessions—sessions in which introspection was the major demand made upon subjects. Thus, there is growing evidence that patients' participation in certain classes of research is in itself a powerful tool in bringing about personality change; its therapeutic effects appear to be both real and relatively substantial.

Several complementary explanations have been offered as bases for the therapeutic nature of research participation. On a general level, the "Hawthorne effect" forms an appropriate starting point. In the now famous Hawthorne study (Roethlisberger, 1941), a great deal of attention was focused upon a group of telephone assembly workers. Their production rose consistently, in spite of the fact that many of the work environment changes which were instituted more typically have resulted in production decrements in other setings. For example, both an improvement in workroom illumination and a subsequent restoration to the original illumination level resulted in increased production. These findings have been classically interpreted as Zubin (1953) has noted: "Apparently the mere fact that the company was doing something for the workers was in itself sufficient to raise the level of production."

As time passed and this phenomenon was observed in a wide variety of settings, it became elaborated into the concept of *milieu effect*. With regard to research participation, this position would hold that concomitant with the imposition and conduct of a research project are such relative intangibles as interest, attention, enthusiasm, and related behaviors directed at patients by staff members, and that these nonspecific, research-motivated behaviors, *which are also present in formal psychotherapy*, can themselves bring about personality change.

A small number of investigations have attempted to specify in more detail the bases for such therapeutic research effects. Goldstein (1962) has presented evidence pointing toward favorable expectation of improvement as one such variable. In a group of 15 wait-list research patients, a significant relationship emerged between the degree of favorableness of such patient-prognostic expectancies and the amount of personality change taking place during the waiting period. Attention accorded these research patients, in the forms of an intake interview and psychological testing, was held constant across patients. Thus, one basis for the therapeutic effects of research participation may involve the patient's expectation that such nonspecific procedures will eventuate in therapeutic change.

In a second study involving the same research patients, Heller and Goldstein (1961) found suggestive evidence that the degree of patient attraction toward psychotherapy and psychotherapists in general may be of similar importance as a therapeutic research variable. In the absence of formal psychotherapy, and while undergoing only research procedures, there was a significant relationship between the degree of such attraction in these wait-list patients and their growth in independence over the course of the waiting period.

A research project conducted by Rashkis (1960) has pointed toward additional explanatory directions. His sample consisted of a group of inpatient, psychotic women. This study rests on the theoretical assumption that the essence of psychotic disturbance is inadequate cognitive structure or disorganization of the patient's phenomenological field. This position holds that organized and systematically conducted research procedures provide a new cognitive field permitting phenomenological reorganization. Rashkis states,

> I contend it is not mere chance that our patients improve in the course of a research project. . . . The imposition of a research design has produced more structure in the system, better functional organization in at least that part of the hospital involved in the research. To the extent that this increased structure exists in the immediate milieu of the patient, i.e., among the clinical staff on his ward, that which is to be perceived by the patient requires less perceptual organization on his part in order for it to appear organized to him.

And further,

> Thus we see the essential unity of the research and therapeutic process. In both cases the nature of the transaction is imposed by the experimenter-therapist. Participation of the subject patient is achieved through selective reinforcement of a class of responses to the exclusion of others. A central

cognitive state, the phenomenological field, is restructured through the conditioning of attitudes which generalize to other attitudes. Thus structuring serves to reduce anxiety, and hence tends to interrupt the . . . circus action which diminishes the patient's ability . . . to organize his phenomenological field, while concurrently increasing the amount of organization in the input from the external world. This characteristic increases external organization; research designed to create disorganization, and research which inadvertently produces environmental chaos, is antitherapeutic.

A start at the conceptualization of research as therapy thus appears to be well documented. Further, beginning leads are becoming available which appear to permit one to view such research-participation effects in the context of more general knowledge about methods of inducing behavioral change.

Therapy as Research

In contrast to the therapeutic aspects of psychotherapy research and other research, the research aspects of psychotherapeutic practice have been implicitly recognized for many years. It has long been acknowledged that formal research hypotheses are often more meaningfully generated by clinical insights based upon patient behavior in actual therapeutic practice. Schaffer and Lazarus (1952), for example, comment,

> We obtain most of our hypotheses from direct contact with people . . . who are having difficulty making adjustments. In psychotherapy . . . as we see important samples of human behavior, we are led to hypotheses about personality mechanisms. This is the stuff that clinical research begins with . . . it is important to recognize that the two sources of ultimate knowledge—the clinic and the experimental laboratory—are indispensable to each other.

Thus, one major research aspect of psychotherapeutic practice lies in the leads, hunches, and informal predictions to which it daily gives birth.

Of further relevance to our attempt to offer potential solutions to clinician-research divergencies is a second manner in which therapy may be viewed as research (i.e., the degree to which the therapeutic interaction itself may be conceptualized as adhering to the course of inference and the procedural sequence which are the heart of formal research design). Phillips (1956) has also pointed to the manner in which therapy research and therapy practice are inferentially and procedurally equivalent. He states,

> Our position is that the idiographic-nomothetic controversy is spurious. We submit that the two are aspects of the same method of scientific inference, that

they represent different emphases at different points in the scientific enterprise, and that it is fundamentally irrelevant whether one is dealing with one case or many cases as to the *course of inference* from data to theory (or conceptualization) . . . both nomothetist and clinician infer from the data they discern (observe, record) certain conceptualizations (descriptions, additional hypotheses, predictions, theories) regarding the client (subject, patient) to the end that summary statements, theories, hypotheses, may be made, confirmed, rejected and so on.

Table 21.1 makes this comparison more explicit and takes it several steps beyond. This table seeks to highlight that the course of inference in the two orientations, as well as the general nature and sequence of specific procedures, demonstrates a very marked degree of correspondence.

Thus, Table 21.1 illustrates the parallel inferential paths followed by clinicians and researchers. The intergroup differences which do exist are, in large measure, differences in the content of procedural steps. Clinicians, for example, of necessity do not limit their choice of data as explicitly and rigidly as formal research requires. Their task also demands that the degree of standardization of data-gathering procedures be considerably more flexible in the clinical setting, and so forth. If it is true, however, that one of the major research contributions which practitioners can make to advancing psychotherapy lies in their hypothesis-generating potential, then there is little need to aim at altering the procedural differences outlined above, for most such differences serve to permit and encourage the very kinds of therapist–patient interactions which are fertile soil for growth of such hypotheses.

There are, on the other hand, certain clinician-researcher differences which may be abstracted from our comparison which function to inhibit the birth and growth of research hypotheses. One such difference, and a most important one, as Ausbell (1956) and Ellis (1950) note, is the tendency in some clinical quarters to stop the investigative process prematurely and to accept faulty or incomplete data as "final" evidence. Ellis comments, "What is frequently done in this type of analytic 'research' is the utilization of the few facts (or the analyst's impression of these facts) which led to the original hypothesis as the observed evidence to sustain this same hypothesis." Or, as Wolpe and Rachman (1960) comment, in relation to Freud's analysis of Little Hans,

In general, Freud infers relationships in a scientifically inadmissible manner: if the enlightenment or interpretation given to Hans are followed by behavioral improvements, then they are automatically accepted as valid. If they are not followed by improvement we are told the patient has not accepted them, and not that they are invalid.

Table 21.1. Procedures and Course of Inference in Practice and Research[1,2]

Procedure	Clinicians	Researchers
1. Search for regularities	Within a patient	Across patients
2. Tentative prediction based on observed regularities	Within a patient	Across patients
3. Trial intervention	Tentative interpretation or other planned therapist intervention	Pilot study
4. Initial test of prediction	Therapist's judgment of patient reaction to trial intervention	Analysis of pilot data
5. Decision regarding further potential of prediction	Based upon initial test of prediction	Based upon initial test of prediction
6. Revision and restatement of prediction	Based upon initial test of prediction	Based upon initial test of prediction
7. Standardization of data-gathering procedures	Free association, reflection of feeling, etc.	Selection of psychometric or other measurement devices
8. Manipulation of independent variable	Interpretation or other planned therapist intervention (Overlaps with step 7)	Manipulation of independent variable across patient sample
9. Measurement on dependent variable	Therapist's judgment of patient reaction to intervention	Scores on psychometric or other measurement devices
10. Decision regarding prediction	Based upon step 9	Based upon statistical analysis of step 9 and statistical confidence limits
11. Replication	"Working through" with same patient	With other patient samples
12. Generalization	To other aspects of the same patient's behavior and, at times, to other patients in his practice	To other patients in the universe sampled

[1]We are not proposing that all therapies involve all steps indicated, nor in the exact sequence presented. Neither are we proposing that all research programs are either similarly inclusive or ordered. The steps and sequence represent more of a model or abstraction, most of whose steps find characteristic expression—in the general sequence presented—in both practice and research.

[2]Manipulation is used here in its broadest sense and subsumes any planned, deliberate therapist activity which is purposefully employed for its intended effects on patient behavior. Thus, not only are interpretations, therapist role playing, and other overt therapist behaviors manipulation, but so are silence, restatement of content, simple acknowledgments, and other more passive therapist behaviors—when used in such a planned manner.

In summary, I have made what is essentially an intellectual or cognitive appeal in an attempt to resolve what is primarily an emotional-interpersonal problem. That is, I have suggested that heightened awareness that the investigation and practice of psychotherapy are largely equivalent processes may serve to reduce the frictions which exist between researcher and practitioner. Whether such awareness will, in fact, have this harmonizing effect remains an open question. That the advance of psychotherapy fairly demands such an improved working relationship there can be no doubt.

References

Astin, A. W. The functional autonomy of psychotherapy. *American Psychologist*, 1961, *16*, 75–78.

Ausbell, D. P. Relationships between psychology and psychiatry: The hidden issues. *American Psychologist*, 1956, *11*, 99–113.

Barron, F., & Leary, T. Changes in psychoneurotic patients with and without psychotherapy. *Journal of Consulting Psychology*, 1955, *19*, 239–245.

Brody, E. B. Discussion of Mitchell, H. E., and Mudd, E. H. Anxieties associated with the conduct of research in a clinical setting. *American Journal of Orthopsychiatry*, 1957, *27*, 327–330.

Chassen, J. B. The role of statistics in psychoanalysis. *Psychiatry*, 1953, *16*, 153–165.

Ellis, A. An introduction to the principles of scientific psychoanalysis. *Genetic Psychological Monograph*, 1950, *41*, 147–212.

Ekman, P. Research as therapy. *Journal of Nervous and Mental Disorders*, 1961, *133*, 229–232.

Frank, J. D. *Persuasion and healing*. Baltimore, Md.: Johns Hopkins Press, 1961.

Goldstein, A. P. *Therapist–patient expectancies in psychotherapy*. New York: Pergamon Press, 1962.

Hamburg, D. A. Recent trends in psychiatric research training. *Archives of General Psychiatry*, 1961, *4*, 215–224.

Heller, K., & Goldstein, A. P. Client dependency and therapist expectancy as relationship maintaining variables in psychotherapy. *Journal of Consulting Psychology*, 1961, *25*, 371–375.

Joint Commission on Mental Illness and Health: *Action for mental health*. New York: Wiley, 1961.

Landfield, A. W. Research avoidance in clinical students. *American Psychologist*, 1954, *9*, 240–242.

Levin, M. L. A comparison of the effects of phenobarbital promethazine, chlorpromazine, and placebo upon mental health patients. *Journal of Consulting Psychology*, 1959, *23*, 167–170.

Luzski, M. B. *Interdisciplinary team research: Methods and problems*. New York: New York University Press, 1957.

Mitchell, H. E., & Mudd, E. H. Anxieties associated with the conduct and research in a clinical setting. *American Journal of Orthopsychiatry,* 1957, *27,* 310–323.

Parloff, M. B., & Rubinstein, E. A. Research problems in psychotherapy. In E. A. Rubinstein & M. B. Parloff (Eds.), *Research in psychotherapy.* Washington, D.C.: American Psychological Association, 1959.

Phillips, E. L. *Psychotherapy, a modern theory and practice.* Englewood Cliffs, N.J.: Prentice-Hall, 1956.

Psychopharmacology Service Center Program—1961: *Psychopharmacology Service Center Bulletin,* 1962, *2,* 1–15.

Rashkis, H. A. Cognitive restructuring: Why research is therapy. *Archives of General Psychiatry,* 1960, *2,* 612–621.

Rashkis, H. A. Does clinical research interfere with treatment? *Archives of General Psychiatry,* 1961, *4,* 105–108.

Reznikoff, M., & Tooney, L. C. *Evaluation of changes associated with psychiatric treatment.* Springfield, Ill.: Charles C. Thomas, 1959.

Roethlisberger, F. *Management and morale.* Cambridge: Harvard University Press, 1941.

Rosenfeld, J. M., & Orlinsky, N. The effect of research on practice. *Archives of General Psychiatry,* 1961, *5,* 176–182.

Schaffer, G. W., & Lazarus, R. S. *Fundamental concepts in clinical psychology.* New York: McGraw-Hill, 1952.

Schwitzgebel, R., & Kolb, D. A. Inducing behaviour change in adolescent delinquents. *Behavior Research and Therapy,* 1964, *1,* 297–304.

Slack, C. W. Experimenter-subject psychotherapy. *Mental Hygiene,* 1960, *44,* 238–256.

Shoben, E. J. Some observations on psychotherapy and the learning process. In O. H. Mowrer (Ed.), *Psychotherapy, theory and research.* New York: Ronald Press, 1953.

Soskin, W. F. *Research resources in mental health.* New York: Basic Books, 1968.

Strupp, H. H. Some comments on the future of research in psychotherapy. *Behavioral Science,* 1960, *5,* 60–71.

Strupp, H. H., & Luborsky, L. *Research in psychotherapy.* Washington, D.C.: American Psychological Association, 1962.

Wolpe, J., & Rachman, S. Psychoanalytic "evidence": A critique based on Freud's case of Little Hans. *Journal of Nervous and Mental Disorders,* 1960, *131,* 135–148.

Zubin, J. A. Evaluation of therapeutic outcome in mental disorders. *Journal of Nervous and Mental Disorders,* 1953, *116,* 95–111.

Chapter 22

Psychotherapists and (or versus?) Researchers

Hans H. Strupp

I am grateful for John Warkentin's invitation to discuss some of my thinking on research in psychotherapy. He went on to say: "As you know, most active therapists are, by nature, unwilling to take an interest in serious research, and make do with their clinical experience. If you could say something that would make the word 'research' more enticing and less threatening to therapists, that would be a major contribution to the field of psychotherapy." I think John correctly perceived a certain rift—perhaps even animosity—between psychotherapists and researchers, something of which I have been keenly aware ever since I entered the field some 15 years ago. This feeling existed then, it still exists, and I regret its existence. It reflects a deep-seated prejudice on both sides, and like all prejudices it is doing a great deal of harm. Above all, it presents a serious obstacle to the pursuit of the primary goal in which all of us are—or should be—interested: The advancement of knowledge and the development of better techniques for helping people cope with their emotional problems.

My work over the years has brought me in close contact with psychotherapists and researchers, and from personal experience I know something about the patient and therapist roles. Most of us are engaged in the work we are doing for deeply personal reasons, and our therapeutic techniques like our theoretical preferences are dictated more by our life style than by intellectual or scientific considerations. I am firmly convinced that we are

Reprinted by permission of the author, Hans H. Strupp, and the publisher from *Voices: The Art and Science of Psychotherapy*, 1968, *4*, 28–32.

analysts, client-centered therapists, existential therapists, or behavior therapists for reasons largely unrelated to the scientific or pragmatic merits of
these approaches, and our attitudes toward research or clinical practice are
colored by similar factors. The line should be drawn not between researchers and therapists, any more than it should be drawn between
"basic" and "applied" scientists. There are therapists who are very fine
scientists even though they never used an analysis of variance design or
computed a chi square. Freud, to my mind, remains the most outstanding
example of this kind of man. At the other extreme, the field today is full of
individuals who correctly use all the available tools of science; their controls are impeccable, and their results are significant at the one percent
level; nevertheless, they are completely impervious to the concerns of the
psychotherapist, the essence of the subject matter, and their publications
are a sterile exercise. The therapist frequently subscribes to this stereotype
of the researcher, whereas the researcher tends to view the therapist as a
woolly thinker, a mercenary practitioner, or worse. While objective research in psychotherapy has undergone unprecedented growth since the
forties, there are as yet very few contributions which the psychotherapist
would find helpful in his daily work with patients. On the other hand, it
cannot be asserted that therapists have achieved significant breakthroughs
in understanding or technique during the past quarter of a century.

Is psychotherapy a science? Can it become a science? The analyst
Kenneth Mark Colby (1962), for one, does not think so. He compares it to
an art like wine-making, which, however, can be passed on from master to
apprentice. The trouble with research, according to him, is this:

> A practitioner needs a "causal relation" or variable he can manipulate *with this
> particular patient*. Research thus far has not given him a reliable guide in this
> direction because it has mainly been in the tradition of an extensive design.
> Extensive designs yield only weak group averages, not specific causal mechan-
> isms (cf. Chassan, 1967).

And further:

> [The clinician] wants help with failures, with troubles, with lapses from the
> expected . . . Guided by the artisan, a scientist must select a certain crucial
> problem in the art and judge whether the problem is ready and accessible to a
> systematic inquiry using currently available procedures. A scientist hopes to
> reduce the degree of (blind) empiricism in the art by finding that some acute
> problem in it can be solved through understanding an underlying explanatory
> principle [p. 95].

What acute problems can future psychotherapy research profitably elucidate? Says Colby:

We are not trying to solve the problem of justified inductive generalization. Physics, chemistry, and medicine (e.g., heart transplants in single patients) progressed without representativeness of samples. They relied on repeatability of observations by independent observers and the development of a series of cases one by one. The population of observations we should be interested in at this time is a series of single-case populations. It is hopeless to generalize about "all" patients. No "all" exists about anything (personal communication).

One of the things this suggests to me is that there needs to be closer collaboration between psychotherapists and researchers. The researcher, at least in principle, can help the practitioner in resolving "acute problems in the art." By the same token, no therapist should rest content with the current level of practice. Who would be foolhardy enough to assert that his techniques are beyond improvement, even if the conditions are rigorously specified? Many practitioners have turned their back on systematic inquiry—and this charge, I regret to say, must be leveled particularly at psychoanalysts—while quoting liberally from the work of Freud as if it were the Bible. Freud would have been the first one to reject such codification. Exemplifying the spirit of open inquiry, Anna Freud (1954) wrote:

> If all the skill, knowledge and pioneering effort which was spent on widening the scope of application of psychoanalysis had been employed instead on intensifying and improving our technique in the original field [hysteric, phobic, and compulsive disorders], I cannot help but feel that, by now, we would find the treatment of the common neuroses child's play, instead of struggling with their technical problems as we have continued to do [p. 610].

No one, of course, is opposed in principle to the advancement of knowledge, and we can readily agree that we have much to learn. There is one issue, however, which has done more than any other to alienate psychotherapists and researchers from each other. I am referring to the time-honored question of the effectiveness of psychotherapy. Essentially, it seems to me, one can approach this problem with three different preconceptions: On a deep emotional level, reinforced by personal experience and therapeutic work with patients, many therapists consider the question a pseudo issue; that is, they are firmly convinced that in an appreciable number of instances, sufficiently large to sustain their faith and self-respect, psychotherapeutic work benefits their patients. Such therapists need no "demonstrations" from scientists or anyone else. Secondly, there are cynics, not infrequently disillusioned by personal experience, who are dedicated to the proposition that psychotherapeutic changes are either illusory or due to placebo effects but in any case unimpressive. A variation on this theme is represented by those whose zeal causes them to reject violently one theoretical system while espousing the alleged virtues of another. Finally, there are those who make a

serious effort to approach the problem as dispassionately as possible. To be
sure, it is difficult to lay one's preconceptions aside, but one can try. If one
takes this approach, it becomes possible to raise such questions as: Under
what conditions does this particular technique work well? What kind of
changes can one expect from a given form of therapy in the hands of a
particular therapist with a particular patient? Are alternative approaches
perhaps more promising under a given set of circumstances? This listing is
purely illustrative but it suggests a spirit of open inquiry, which is all the
scientist should be committed to. Theoretical boundaries as such are of no
intrinsic interest to him, but he is vitally concerned with elucidating the
conditions under which therapeutic learning occurs, what kind of learning
occurs and when, and he takes it for granted that the last word has not been
spoken on any issue. It is heartening to note that today there is a growing
trend in this direction. Therapists and researchers are becoming more open-
minded, despite many signs to the contrary; they are becoming more sophisticated about each other's endeavors and more tolerant of ambiguity; and
they approach controversy in a somewhat less doctrinaire spirit. I am not
suggesting that the millenium has arrived. Far from it. But the above developments do bode well for the future.

I have consistently maintained that we are not yet in a position to deal
meaningfully with the question of therapeutic outcomes, at least not in the
manner in which this problem has usually been approached. The psychotherapeutic interaction is far too complex to lend itself readily to comparisons which can be translated into percentage figures of success. The popu-
larization of such "statistics" published under the aegis of "Science" in
magazines has done a tremendous disservice and has misled the public.
First the reader is told that one cannot compare apples and oranges, but as
soon as this has been said, outcomes of different forms of therapy are being
compared anyway, with the added assertion that some 70 percent of all
patients "recover" from neurotic disorders "spontaneously." The therapist
is thus challenged to prove the effectiveness of his procedures against
almost impossible odds whose validity he rightly questions.

It has been asserted by somewhat more friendly critics that, if psychotherapy were indeed a very potent method, it should not be difficult to
demonstrate its effectiveness. That is, granted the methodological and
practical difficulties in carrying out controlled research, if dramatic changes
were a regular occurrence, they should be self-evident. To be sure, both
patients and therapists in several studies have reported "improvements" in
the 75 to 90 percent range, but such assessments cannot be taken at face
value, nor can the potency argument be blithely dismissed.

The fact is that, like it or not, we must live with the outcome problem,
and the critics, despite some of their ill-founded allegations, have prevented the field from sinking into a state of complacency and stagnation. As

researchers or therapists, it is our responsibility to face the issue, not to evade it.

A therapist of whatever theoretical persuasion is certainly at liberty to define his goals and the outcome criteria he is willing to accept. As one of my colleagues aptly put it, criteria are purely a matter of taste. One therapist may rest content, if a snake phobic patient can hold a snake for 10 seconds following certain therapeutic interventions; another therapist may want to help his patient develop better interpersonal strategies; a third therapist may work toward the mastery of existential despair. Assuredly, one cannot compare these outcomes with each other, nor can one argue that one is trivial and another profound. Therapies must be tested on their own home ground, but testable they must be. In other words, the criteria must permit specification and communication in the sense that impartial observers can reach agreement on the presence or absence of change. The field is abandoning the view that a little bit of (undefined) psychotherapy may be good for everyone; instead, the more pertinent questions are raised: What kind? For whom? Under what conditions? No form of psychotherapy is a panacea, nor need it be. But we should become increasingly explicit about its potential as well as its limitations.

The researcher's job does not end there because he is equally interested in the kinds of therapeutic interventions which lead to specific changes. He is concerned with the psychology as well as the technology of change. This is a task of gargantuan proportions, for which he needs all the help he can get—and then some.

Personally, I don't think it is possible to do meaningful research on any aspect of psychotherapy without extensive firsthand experience as a therapist or patient; on the other hand, one can practice the art of psychotherapy without being aware of the principles one is employing. Ideally, the researcher should approach the phenomena of psychotherapy with a clinical attitude, and the therapist should have a critical and inquiring mind. In this way, there may also develop greater rapprochement between researcher and clinician.

At its best, psychotherapy is not faith healing, religious conversion, or brainwashing, nor does it traffic in the sale of friendship, as has been alleged. Admittedly, it may share some elements with all of these activities, but that is not its defining characteristic. What sets psychotherapy apart from other forms of "psychological healing"—and of course medicine—is the planful and systematic application of psychological principles, concerning whose character and effects we are committed to become explicit. As psychotherapists and researchers, we want to learn more about what we are doing; we want to be able to do it better; we strive to be objective; and we are willing to work hard toward this end. To me, these are the beginnings of science, if not its essence.

References

Colby, K. M. Discussion of papers on therapist's contribution. In H. Strupp & L. Luborsky (Eds.), *Research in psychotherapy* (Vol. 2). Washington, D.C.: American Psychological Association, 1962.

Freud, A. The widening scope of indications for psychoanalysis. *Journal of American Psychoanalytic Association*, 1954, 2, 607–620.

Part VIII
A Common Language for Dialogue

Any attempt at dialogue or collaboration among the psychotherapies must confront the not insignificant problem that each literally speaks a different language. The use of varying language systems not only interferes with the ability to comprehend what other therapists are saying but also serves to create emotionally laden barriers when certain "taboo" concepts are used in the course of conversation. Although an interim step in the attempt to create a meaningful dialogue might make use of everyday, nontechnical language, there ultimately will come a point when a common set of professional terms and concepts is needed. Anyone who has ever struggled with the task of learning a second language knows how difficult this can be, a factor that no doubt will impede any efforts at finding a common language for the psychotherapies. If we address ourselves to what currently available language system has the potential for serving this common ground, however, it appears as if concepts from the field of experimental cognitive psychology should be considered most seriously. Indeed, this conclusion has been independently drawn by several writers in the field, such as Ryle, Sarason, and Goldfried. Inasmuch as cognitive psychology has turned its attention to the study of implicit meaning structures and their tendency to color an individual's perception of the world, there is much that theory and research in this area can say to practicing therapists and therapy researchers of varying orientations. In addition to addressing themselves to this point, the articles in this section indicate how concepts from cognitive psychology may be useful in better understanding the interplay between cognition and experience as contributors to therapeutic change.

Chapter 23

A Common Language for the Psychotherapies?[1]

Anthony Ryle

The aim of this paper is to examine how far the procedures and theories of therapists working in the psychoanalytic and behavioral traditions may be referred to a common core of psychological understanding and expressed in a shared language based upon cognitive psychology. Imperfect research into therapy in the two traditions indicates that workers in both are capable of helping people; in a few studies, such as that by Sloane, Staples, Cristol, Yorkston, & Whipple (1975), it establishes relatively equal claims for the two methods, at least as far as time-limited treatment is concerned. There is even the beginning of agreement about the appropriate domains of the two approaches.

Since factors unrelated to the therapist's theory play a very large role in therapeutic success, it could be argued that theory does not matter very much and that practitioners might be left to draw upon their different traditions and to work in terms of their own preferences, personalities, and pragmatically acquired skills. Such a dismissal of theory would, however, be a pity. There is a need for a better theory to guide us in choosing and evaluating the effects of our interventions, and there is a need for a theory that does not, subtly or obviously, deny aspects of the humanity of those we set out to help.

[1]Based on a paper given to the Psychotherapy Section of the Royal College of Psychiatrists on October 12, 1977.
Reprinted by permission of the author, Anthony Ryle, and the publisher from *British Journal of Psychiatry*, 1978, *132*, 585–594.

In this paper it is proposed to offer an outline of the framework offered by cognitive psychology for the enterprise of psychotherapy, and to consider psychoanalytic theory in the light of this, noting in particular some of the developments and criticisms which have emerged from within psychoanalysis and seem to support the thesis, and offering some translations or restatements of aspects of that theory in cognitive terms. Following this, behavior therapy will be similarly, but more briefly, considered, with particular attention to the increasing interest shown by some writers in the space between the stimulus (S) and the response (R).

Cognitive Theories of Man

The word *cognitive* as used here does not carry the implication of "opposed to affective." Cognitive processes are those whereby meaning is accorded to experience, and hence they are inseparably linked to affects. Our cognitions of events are derived from sense perceptions and their relation to our memories, feelings, needs, and intentions.

The origins of cognitive theories of man are diverse and include experimental studies of perception, memory, and thinking, observational and experimental studies of cognitive development, and, latterly, the developing interest in artifical intelligence and the computer simulation of cognitive processes. From this tradition, attempts have been made to propound more general theories. One early example of this is Hebb's (1949) attempt to propose a model on a neurophysiological basis; a later one, not attempting a direct link with physiology, is the work of Miller, Galanter, & Pribram (1960). Computer simulation models tend to represent the brain as an information-processing system with memory stores and alternative outputs or action programs. Some writers, in the more general cognitive tradition, emphasize particularly the active process of exploration and theory-building that is typical of humans (Kelly, 1955). The tendency to maintain and extend cognitive mastery is thought to be innate rather than acquired, and must be considered alongside the biological drives described in psychoanalytic, attachment, and behavioral theories (see Kreitler and Kreitler, 1972). It is important to note that the information processed includes, not only data derived from the perception of the external world, but also data from the bodily experience of the individual.

It is argued that a theory of this type is required to account for human thought and behavior; for although some forms of learning can be adequately expressed in terms of the forming, strengthening, and weakening of associations, as in simple learning theory, an adequate account of characteristically complex human learning requires concepts of organized mental representation (Neisser, 1967). Each individual develops hierarchical, interrelated mental structures or schemata to which new experience is assimilated, but which are also themselves open to modification by new experience. The understanding of this process owes much to work in the Piagetian tradition, which has also shown how the operations of the biologically immature brain are less complex than those of the fully mature one. The study of memory and the study of concept formation are, by this account, inseparable (Kleinmutz, 1967). Between the environmental event and the individual's response there is interposed an elaborated, historically determined process of selection, construction, and bias (Erdelyi, 1974); thus, the external event is never directly perceived but is necessarily perceived *as* something, for example, *as* a chair, or *as* a threatening person. The meaning accorded to such a percept is further related to, and integrated in terms of, the systematic construction of reality derived from the whole of earlier experience.

Individual differences in how these processes are carried out have been identified in the work on cognitive styles (Klein, 1970; Witkin, 1965). The response to events is, in turn, selected in terms of the anticipated implications of the event and the anticipated outcomes of the alternative plans for action from which the response is chosen. The choice of action is determined by the individual's need to support the integrity of, and carry out the intentions of, the self. The self is a mental construction of crucial importance to the understanding of human behavior. It is built up historically from the infant's development of body-awareness, and from his complex social interactions with others; included in this awareness is the consciousness of bodily states, indicative of emotion, which are themselves a part of the understanding of, but which are also experienced and understood in terms of, the personal meaning of the individual's experience (London & Nisbett, 1974; Schacter & Singer, 1962). Hence the individual's history determines his personal construction of himself and his world, but neither this history nor this structure, nor the processes of memory and thinking are necessarily or usually accessible to awareness; at any one time, only a fraction of the total memory store is implicated in a mental operation. Among the mental processes required in such a model must be included some with the function of preserving the cognitive processes themselves.

Psychoanalytic Theory

The relationship of this cognitive account to psychoanalysis is, at first sight, far from obvious. The *practice* of psychoanalysis, a personal relationship devoted to the teasing-out of the meanings of the patient's experiences, is not a scientific pursuit and may correctly be described as to do with meaning or as "hermeneutic" (Barratt, 1976; Home, 1966, Ricoeur, 1970; Slater,

1975). However, the essentially human pursuits of teaching, child-rearing, or politics, while also in no way scientific, are all open to scientific study, and psychoanalytic *theory* can reasonably claim to be a theory about human development, experience, and behavior. It is, however, a confused, poorly articulated, and inconsistent theory, as numerous critics have recognized (e.g., Farrell, 1964; Nagel, 1959; Popper, 1963; Slater, 1975).

The issues with which it is concerned can be expressed most clearly in cognitive terms, as follows:

1. What is the relation between a person's cognitive structure, or his personal construct system in Kelly's (1955) terms, and his behavior in, and experience of, the world?
2. How is this structure derived and, specifically, how far and in what ways does earlier experience, especially infantile and childhood experience, and especially experience not accessible to conscious recall or descriptions or expression in words, determine or limit the individual's construction of his world?
3. What procedures can help the therapist recognize and modify those constructions that are related to his patient's difficulties?

Psychoanalysis has failed to give clear, accessible answers to these questions. The early disputes over doctrine and the modes of training and control evolved in its institutions have inhibited clear and free discussion and have isolated it from the rest of psychology (Holzman, 1976). From the start there was an unfortunate confusion in the theory between the contents of minds and their processes. The models and metaphors of which the theory is made up bear traces of Freud's neurological background (Amacher, 1974; Burnham, 1974), the influence of 19th-century physical science, the use of the body metaphors current in everyday speech (Schafer, 1975), and a preoccupation with binary distinctions and simple models of opposing forces or entities endowed with quasi-human status (Freud, 1937; Grossman & Simon, 1969). In this respect, the theory stands as an example of man's theory-building capacity, but gives a poor account of the process of theory-building.

Discontent with the theory has been widespread within psychoanalysis, reflected in the past in its numerous ideological schisms and, latterly, in a willingness to accommodate new ideas which has not been matched by an ability to discard old ones. This process has allowed into the theory many contributions which are more consonant with the cognitive approach outlined above than with classical theory, a tendency shown particularly in the increasing concern with meaning and the decreasing concern with drives and instincts. Rycroft's (1970) statement that libido theory is a theory of meaning in disguise makes this point, but there seems to be no great hurry to cast off the disguise.

Many contributions to the theory, for example those of Sandler and his associates on the child's representational world (Sandler & Rosenblatt, 1962), on the unconscious peremptory urge (Sandler, 1974), and on the feeling of safety (Sandler, 1960), while seeming to offer quite major revisions of theory, do so deferentially, and without challenging any aspects of classical theory. The more general shifts in attention to conflict-free ego-functions (Rapaport, 1959), which are easily represented in cognitive terms (Loevinger, 1976), and the growth of object-relations theory, much of which can be well expressed in terms of mental representations, are important trends which have, nonetheless, been largely accommodated within the main body of traditional theory rather than led to its revision. Certain aspects of this theory will now be considered.

Infantile Experience

The psychoanalytic account of infantile development and its effect upon later life stages represented initially a major growth in understanding, but it has failed to adapt to the large volume of work done in other fields, notably observational studies in the ethological tradition as reviewed by Schaffer (1971), and even to work done within its own tradition (Mahler, Pine, & Bergman, 1975). One can recognize the contribution of psychoanalysis to this field without retaining the detailed account given in classical theory or in the Kleinian elaborations of it. The concept of the infantile amnesia, and Freud's belief in the possibility of contacting pure memory traces, have to be abandoned, for it is clear that memory always represents the later reconstructions of past constructions (Bartlett, 1954; Neisser, 1967). Freud's archaelogical metaphors are misleading; analyst and patient are construction engineers using old rubble, or authors rewriting old texts. That the reconstruction of early experience achieved in analysis may not be of actual events but represent rather later elaborations endowed with meanings derived from later experience is conceded on the basis of psychoanalytic material by Kris (1956) and is further illustrated by Kennedy (1971).

The importance of early infantile experience is best understood, not in terms of objects and instincts, but in terms of the elaborations of concepts and conceptual forms. The successive cognitive tasks of the infant, both as described by developmental psychologists working in the Piagetian tradition and those of central concern to psychoanalysts, which were mostly elaborated from the study of adults or older children rather than from observation, are both of importance. In the latter category, the recognition of body-boundaries and self–other discontinuity (see Kafka, 1971), the development of object-constancy (Edgcumbe & Burgner, 1973), the acquisition of cognitive control through play, and the separation and individuation processes described by Mahler et al. (1975) all represent the origins of subsequently elaborated schemata, and therefore provide the source or basis, more or less satisfactory, for all subsequent discriminations. The fact that so many of the descriptions *incorporated* in the *body* of psychoanalytic theory are based upon spatial body-imagery is just one example of the pervading influence of these early discriminations on the later creation of metaphors. Early experiences are clearly important, but their importance is not in the essentially irrecoverable content of memory, but in the persistence of, or regression to, early modes of thinking at later ages. We do not have to accept that babies have the terrifying time described in Kleinian theory to recognize that unresolved conceptual tasks from infancy may indeed determine the form, or formlessness, of fears or furies experienced later.

Primary Process Thinking

Freud's description of primary process thinking was original and important but became inextricably linked with his division of the mind into regions and with his simple opposition of the pleasure and reality principles. Primary process thinking is seen as typical of the unconscious system to which we have access in dreams, parapraxes, and psychotic thinking and is regarded as historically prior to, and more primitive than, secondary process thinking and as persisting more or less in this form throughout life. It is characterized by condensation, displacement, and symbolism, in which is found its relation to art, and by timelessness and impulsivity, by which it is linked with the supposed dominance of the pleasure principle in childhood. Noy (1969) argued that this definition was based upon a consideration of primary process thinking only as manifest in regressed states and suggested that there was evidence for an integrating function in primary process thought and for its continuing development and elaboration throughout life. Jung and later workers in the Freudian tradition, notably Winnicott (1971) and Milner (1955, 1969), have had a more positive view of primary process thinking than that enunciated by Freud. Many alternative therapies at the present time, some independent of psychoanalysis and some derived from it, encourage the exploration of this form of thinking through image and fantasy (Singer, 1974).

Cognitive psychologists have also been interested in different forms of thinking. Bartlett's (1954) distinction between thinking in terms of images and thinking in terms of words is clearly making a related distinction. Bartlett noted that the defining characteristic of images was that they were combined, not by juxtaposition in space and time, but on the basis of common emotions and interests, whereas what he called the thought-word method of thinking was the method of reason and inference. Neisser (1967) describes primary process thinking as omnipresent, and as comparable to the pre-attentive processes in perception, arguing that only when elaborated by some executive process does it become important. Paivio (1971) concludes that images and verbal memory commonly interact, and that images have a particularly important role in matching current impressions with what has been stored from the past.

It seems clear that the analytic technique developed by Freud facilitated access to primary process thinking, and that through the interpretation links were made with secondary process thinking. However, the varieties and forms of thinking and memory available to man are still the subject of considerable speculation and research, and the simple division of classical theory into two forms located in different systems, and derived from different developmental stages, provides an unsatisfactory model.

Defense Mechanisms and Conflict

For the dynamic therapist, the theory of ego-defense is of central importance. How far can the racy military metaphors used by Freud (1937) to describe the relationships between the superego, ego, and id be restated in cognitive terms? Such a restatement seems both possible and useful.

In cognitive terms, repression, denial, dissociation, isolation, and undoing represent examples of the selective perception and selective accommodation of perceptions to the whole structure of meaning of the individual's personal construct system. Reaction formation, reversal, and turning against the self, and sublimation, similarly represent particular examples of the selection of programs or plans of action. The editing of perceptions and the choosing of plans take place in relation to the individual's intentions and his predictions of their consequences; these consequences may well include expectations of punishment or harm, the need to preserve a sense of the self as being coherent, effective, and positively valued, and the need to preserve cognitive function. Plans elaborated to avoid adverse consequences may come to dominate behavior and thinking and prevent the testing-out of alternative plans. As Khan (1970) observes, it is often the patient's attempt at self-cure which is most difficult to resolve.

In a given situation, the actions or conditions believed to be necessary for the preservation of the self in the above terms may be falsely construed. This formulation is reflected in the form of group interpretation emphasized by Ezriel (1950, 1952) and paralleled in a different from by Whitaker and Lieberman (1964), in which the group's current behavior is noted, its avoided response identified, and the fantasied calamitous outcome of the avoided response explored.

These defense mechanisms, therefore, can be reformulated in terms of the predominance of certain restricted constructions of events, and of certain rigidly maintained plans for action, resulting in the exclusion of alternative interpretations and plans. The alternative unacted plans may remain "on store" and, because untested, unchanged. The defensive nature of this process lies in the need to avoid too much dissonance between conflicting views of the self and of the world. Experimental support for this cognitive formulation of defenses is found in the demonstration experimentally that those who use repression and denial, and show a marked distortion of perception under the influence of emotion, are characterized by marked field dependence (Witkin, 1965). A repertory grid study of neurotic subjects showed that cognitive complexity was reduced (possibly a related phenomenon) (Ryle & Breen, 1972). Much neurotic behavior can be explained in these terms, and in terms of the individual being trapped by the specific restricted perceptions he holds of possible behaviors and roles; such restricted views can often be usefully identified as false dichotomies and dilemmas. For example, women who construe femininity and achievement as polar opposites, or men who see masculinity and brutality as necessarily correlated, have no comfortable self-definition available.

The more primitive defenses described in object-relations theory as projection, projective identification, and splitting represent in cognitive terms confused boundaries between self and others, which could presumably stem from failures of conceptual development during the separation-individuation phase (see Blatt & Ritzler, 1974). This confusion may be accompanied by a restriction of the range of potential reciprocal role relationships that seem to be open to the individual. This was illustrated by a repertory grid case-study of a married couple in conjoint therapy (Ryle & Lipshitz, 1976). The collusive mechanism existing between the treated couple was described in psychoanalytic terms as projective identification, the husband keeping up his good spirits by "putting his bad feelings into his wife," who consequently remained depressed and ill until they separated. Grid evidence showed that this situation could be reformulated as follows. The husband could see the dyadic relationship only in terms of one being competent and active and caring, and the other being depressed. Given this view, the only way he could remain well himself was to cling to the competent role and be nasty enough to keep his wife in the depressed one.

The central role of conflict in psychoanalytic theory is accommodated in this cognitive account of the defenses, but not in terms of simple opposition between mental institutions. Perceptions are edited and behaviors are selected in ways taking account of drives and intentions and of the need to avoid too confusing and fragmented a view of the self and of the world. Neurosis can be seen as representing the predominance of the second of these over the first.

The Self

The psychoanalytic account of the ego balancing the pressures of the id, the superego, and external reality can be restated in terms of persons actively pursuing life-plans in terms of the (not always consciously) anticipated, and often conflicting, consequences of these plans to the self. With such an account, one can confine the terms used to the self, the other (which includes persons and external reality in general), and their mental representations, and replace the confusion generated by multiple terms (id, ego, superego, ego ideal, superego ideal, ideal self, self representation, object, object representation, person, self, other).

The self, however, remains an embarrassment to psychoanalytic writers. Kohut (1970), for example, wrote:

> It is best to confine ourselves to defining the self as an important content, a structure or configuration within the mental apparatus, i.e. self-representations which are located in the ego, the id, and the superego.

He went on to say he would not rule out its "acceptation" as "one of the centres of identifiable functions." This author's capacity for exemplifying the obscurity of psychoanalytic concepts is evident in his description of the origins of the narcissistic personality:

> The unexpected non-cooperation of this mirroring self creates a psychoeconomic imbalance which disrupts the ego's capacity to regulate the outpourings of the exhibitionist cathexis, and in consequence of its temporary paralysis the ego yields on the one hand to the pressure of the exhibitionist urge, and on the other hand tries desperately to stop the flow [Kohut, 1973].

In this area, a restatement in cognitive terms has been offered by Stolorow (1975), who suggests that, basically, narcissism as a normal process should be used to describe all those mental functions maintaining the structural cohesiveness, positive affective coloring, and temporal stability of the self-representation, i.e., a concept of the self as integrated, valued, and continuing. This writer suggests that pathological narcissism reflects the failure of these processes, with an overdependence on sources outside the self, rage and panic resulting from the failure of these resources. The characteristic transference patterns of borderline patients (Kernberg, 1974) can be described as manifestations of the cognitive problems referred to above in the discussion of primitive defense mechanisms, namely as representing the patient's impaired self–other discriminations and the expression of his limited range of reciprocal role relationships.

The clarification offered by a cognitive account of narcissism in place of a conventional psychoanalytic one is paralleled in respect of severe eating

disorders. Bruch (1973) notes that such patients, especially those with anorexia nervosa, represent personality disturbances similar in level to the
narcissistic disorders. In her experience, classical psychoanalytic formulations were not helpful in therapy. Patients required the opportunity to
correct their disturbances of body imagery, their inability to discriminate
between body sensations and affects, and their paralyzing sense of ineffec-
tiveness. The importance of body image distortion in anorexia has been
recently underlined by Russell (1977) and demonstrated in a repertory grid
study by Feldman (1975).

I have attempted to show, though necessarily very briefly, that some of
the central conceptions of psychoanalysis can be restated, with greater
clarity, in a language based on a model of cognitive processes. Peterfreund
and Schwartz (1971) have offered an excessively thoroughgoing reformulation of psychoanalysis on these lines, presenting a model of the mind as a
"feedback regulated information processing system," and claiming, rather
prematurely, a neurological justification for this. They suggest that the
focus should shift "away from psychological experience or behavior to the
larger world of information processes and their links to neurophysiology."
Such overstatements may have distracted attention from their argument.

Behavior Therapy and Its Theory

While many behaviorists still explain their actions and their results in
terms of relatively simple stimulus-response patterns, others, for example
Lazarus (1970, 1971) have expressed doubts as to the reality of this explanation of what they do. Bandura (1977a) has recently reviewed the developments and revisions of basic theory in the light of further experimental
work. He argues that there is a need for a revised account of the mechanisms involved in change brought about by behavioral techniques. The
research cited points to the limited effect on behavior of immediate consequences, except where the subject is aware of the link between the behavior and the consequences. Rewards, or other response consequences,
modify behavior largely through the subject's awareness, whereby what
have been assumed to be antecedent determinants are in fact interpreted
by the subject as predictive cues. Similarly, consequences, rather than
constituting simple rewards or punishments, are effective insofar as they
are means of informing subjects about what to do to gain benefit or avoid
punishment. Both learning and motivation are in this revised account seen
to depend primarily upon cognitive factors, and to understand and alter an
individual's behavior it is his cognitive processes that become the main
focus of attention. To this account, Bandura (1977b) adds a second range of

behaviors which are distinguished from those based on response outcome expectancies. These behaviors are those concerned with the individual's sense of efficacy, that is, with his belief that he can successfully execute behavior required to produce outcomes. In Bandura's view, it is the strengthening of this belief in self-efficacy that is the central component of all forms of psychotherapy. Singer (1974), reviewing work on imagery in psychotherapy, argues with great force for a cognitive (or, in his words, cognitive-affective) account of many behavioral techniques, such as so-called reciprocal inhibition, covert aversive therapy, covert conditioning, and implosive therapy. In this work, as in that of Bandura, the convergence between social learning theory and formulations derived from cognitive psychology are clearly very marked.

Discussion

A simple translation of a theory into a different language is of little interest, but where two major and apparently opposed theories can be stated in the same language the exercise becomes of more importance; and when this translation yields an account that is either more accessible or more adequate than the original forms, this importance is underlined. It has been argued in this paper that such a point has been reached, and that the concepts derived from cognitive psychology can provide such a common and clarifying account of both psychoanalytic and behavioral psychotherapies.

The adoption of a common language would aid communication between therapists using different approaches, and between therapists and experimental workers, and in time could lead to the more rational choice of treatment methods, whereby the form of intervention would be determined by the extent of the cognitive reconstruction required. Thus, the more the issue is one of relearning a more or less limited range of behaviors, the more likely are behavioral techniques to be appropriate; whereas the more the problem is one of reshaping and making more adequately complex a deficient conceptual organization or a deeply impaired sense of agency in the individual, the greater need for a method allowing slow change and working-through. It seems likely that the careful determination of goals and sub-goals for therapy, characteristic of the behaviorists, could be transferred with advantage to "dynamic" therapies, as characterizes the cognitive therapies of Beck (1976) and Raimy (1975).

The determination of the goals and sub-goals of "dynamic" therapy is a process integral with the early stages of treatment, in which the patient's problems are reconceptualized, traditionally in terms of what have been called the underlying dynamic processes. This reconceptualization has

often, in practice, been a somewhat loose amalgam of historical reconstructions and a recognition of recurrent familiar themes, for example
castration anxiety. In cognitive terms, the aim would be to identify these
processes in terms of their effect upon the subject's understanding of the
possibility of change. One would seek, primarily, to identify (1) aspects of
the self-construct relevant to the problem, (2) the ways in which the
possibilities of change are conceptualized in terms of limiting false dichotomies that prevent effective choice, or in terms of those predicted
outcomes of change which make it seem dangerous or unobtainable. The
definition of goals in these terms would often, but not necessarily, provide a focus for more active therapeutic methods than are traditional.
Where, however, the goal is to increase the individual's sense of being
effective in determining his life, or where the feared consequences of his
effectiveness are an incomplete, or unrealized, fantasy of harming others,
the treatment method may necessarily involve therapist inactivity and the
opportunity for slow change.

If all therapy has as its aim behavioral change and cognitive restructuring, whether the therapy itself focuses upon behavior or cognition, comparative research becomes more feasible. The goals of all psychotherapy
patients should be capable of definition in terms of those symptomatic (experiential), behavioral, and cognitive changes which are necessary to relieve
personal problems. From the research point of view, the assessment of
cognitive change presents the most problematic area. Further development
of repertory grid techniques, already used powerfully, if infrequently, in this
field (see, for example, Crisp & Fransella, 1972; Rowe, 1970; Ryle, 1975;
Ryle & Lunghi, 1969; Ryle & Lipshitz, 1975), and the elaboration of target
problem rating methods, focusing on cognitive as well as on behavioral
changes, should, however, prove feasible.

Summary

The account of mental processes emerging from the work of cognitive
psychologists is briefly reviewed, and aspects of the theoretical basis of the
work of psychoanalytic and behaviorist psychotherapists are considered in
the light of this. It is argued that in both traditions increasing attention is
being paid to cognitive processes. A restatement of psychoanalytic theory
in cognitive terms could free it from its present confusion of metaphors,
and an extension of behaviorist theory in this direction could free it from
reductionism. The advantages of the adoption of a common language, based
on the models of cognitive psychology, to theory, practice, and research
are briefly considered.

References

Amacher, P. The concept of the pleasure principle and infantile erogenous zones shaped by Freud's neurological education. *Psychoanalytic Quarterly*, 1974, *43*, 218–223.

Bandura, A. *Social learning theory*. Englewood Cliffs, N.J.: Prentice-Hall, 1977. (a)

Bandura, A. Self-efficacy—towards a unifying theory of behavioural change. *Psychological Review*, 1977, *84*, 191–215. (b)

Barratt, B. B. Freud's psychology as interpretation. In Shapiro (Ed.), *Psychoanalysis and contemporary science* (Vol. 5). New York: International University Press, 1976.

Bartlett, F. C. *Remembering—A study in Experimental and Social Psychology*. London: Cambridge University Press, 1954.

Beck, A. *Cognitive therapy and the emotional disorders*. New York: International University Press, 1976.

Blatt, S. J., & Ritzler, B. A. Thought disorder and boundary disturbance in psychosis. *Journal of Consulting and Clinical Psychology*, 1974, *42*, 370–381.

Bruch, H. *Eating disorders—Obesity, anorexia nervosa and the person within*. New York: Basic Books, 1973.

Burnham, J. S. The medical origins and cultural use of Freud's instinctual drive theory. *Psychoanalytic Quarterly*, 1974, *43*, 193–217.

Crisp, A. H., & Fransella, F. Conceptual changes during recovery from anorexia nervosa. *British Journal of Medical Psychology*, 1972, *45*, 395–405.

Edgcumbe, R., & Burgner, M. Some problems in the conceptualisation of early object relationships. *Psychoanalytic Study of the Child*, 1973, *27*, 283–333.

Erdelyi, M. H. A new look at the new look: Perceptual defence and vigilance. *Psychological Review*, 1974, *81*, 1–25.

Ezriel, H. A psychoanalytic approach to group treatment. *British Journal of Medical Psychology*, 1950, *23*, 59–74.

Ezriel, H. Notes on psychoanalytic group therapy: Interpretation and research. *Psychiatry*, 1952, *15*, 119–126.

Farrell, B. A. The status of psychoanalytic theory. *Inquiry*, 1964, *7*, 104–123.

Feldman, M. M. The body image and object relations: Exploration of a method using repertory grid techniques. *British Journal of Medical Psychology*, 1975, *48*, 317–332.

Freud, A. *The ego and the mechanisms of defence*. London: Hogarth Press, 1937.

Grossman, W. I., & Simon, B. Anthropomorphism—motive meaning and casuality in psychoanalytic theory. *Psychoanalytic Study of the Child*, 1969, *24*, 78–111.

Hebb, D. O. *The organization of behaviour*. New York: Wiley, 1949.

Holzman, P. S. The future of psychoanalysis and its institutes. *Psychoanalytic Quarterly*, 1976, *45*, 250–273.

Home, H. J. The concept of mind. *International Journal of Psychoanalysis*, 1966, *47*, 42–49.

Kafka, E. On the development of the experience of mental self, the bodily self, and self consciousness. *Psychoanalytic Study of the Child*, 1971, *26*, 217–240.

Kelly, G. A. *The psychology of personal constructs*. New York: Norton, 1955.

Kernberg, O. F. Further contributions to the treatment of narcissistic personalities. *International Journal of Psychoanalysis*, 1974, *55*, 215–240.

Kennedy, H. Problems in reconstruction in child analysis. *Psychoanalytic Study of the Child*, 1971, *26*, 386–402.

Khan, M. R. Towards an epistemology of cure. *British Journal of Medical Psychology*, 1970, *43*, 363–366.

Klein, G. S. *Perception, motives and personality*. New York: Knopf, 1970.

Kleinmutz, B. (Ed.). *Concepts and the structure of memory*. New York: Wiley, 1967.

Kohut, H. Moderator's remarks on a discussion of 'the self.' *International Journal of Psychoanalysis*, 1970, *51*, 176–181.

Kohut, H. Thoughts on narcissism and narcissistic rage. *Psychoanalytic Study of the Child*, 1973, *27*, 360–400.

Kreitler, H., & Kreitler, S. The model of cognitive orientation: Towards a theory of human behaviour. *British Journal of Psychology*, 1972, *63*, 9–30.

Kris, E. The recovery of childhood memories in psychoanalysis. *Psychoanalytic Study of the Child*, 1956, *11*, 54–88.

Lazarus, A. A. Behaviour therapy. *International Journal of Psychiatry*, 1970, *9*, 113.

Lazarus, A. A. *Behavior therapy and beyond*. New York: McGraw-Hill, 1971.

Loevinger, J. *Ego development: Conception and theories*. San Francisco: Jossey-Bass, 1976.

London, H., & Nisbett, R. E. (Eds.). *Cognitive alteration of feeling states*. Chicago: Aldine, 1974.

Mahler, M. S., Pine, F., & Bergman, A. *The psychological birth of the human infant*. London: Hutchinson, 1975.

Miller, G. A., Galanter, E., & Pribram, K. H. *Plans and the structure of behavior*. New York: Holt, 1960.

Milner, M. The role of illusion in symbol formation. In M. Klein, P. Harman, & R. E. Money-Kyrle (Eds.), *New direction in psychoanalysis*. London: Tavistock, 1955.

Milner, M. *The hands of the living God*. London: Hogarth Press, 1969.

Nagel, E. Freud and philosophy: An essay in interpretation. In S. Hook (Ed.), *Psychoanalysis, scientific method and philosophy*. New York: University Press, 1959.

Neisser, U. *Cognitive psychology*. New York: Appleton-Century-Crofts, 1967.

Noy, P. A revision of the psychoanalytic theory of the primary process. *International Journal of Psychoanalysis*, 1969, *50*, 155–178.

Paivio, A. *Imagery and verbal processes*. New York: Holt, Rinehart & Winston, 1971.

Peterfreund, E., & Schwartz, J. T. Information systems and psychoanalysis—an evolutionary biological approach to psychoanalytic theory. *Psychological Issues*, 1971, *7*, Monograph 25–26.

Popper, K. R. *Conjectures and refutations: The growth of scientific knowledge*. London: Routledge, 1963.

Raimy, V. *Misunderstandings of the self*. San Francisco: Jossey-Bass, 1975.

Rapaport, D. A historical survey of psychoanalytic ego psychology. *Psychological Issues*, 1959, *1*, 1–5.

Ricoeur, P. *Freud and philosophy: An essay on interpretation*. New Haven: Yale University Press, 1970.

Rowe, D. Poor prognosis in a case of depression as predicted by the repertory grid. *British Journal of Psychiatry*, 1970, *119*, 319–321.

Russell, G. M. The present status of anorexia nervosa. *Psychological Medicine*, 1977, *7*, 363–367.

Rycroft, C. Causes and meaning. In S. G. M. Lee & M. Hubert (Eds.), *Freud and psychology*. Harmondsworth: Penguin Books, 1970.

Ryle, A. *Frames and cages*. London: Sussex University Press, Chatto & Windus, 1975.

Ryle, A., & Lunghi, M. The measurement of relevant change after psychotherapy: Use of repertory grid testing. *British Journal of Psychiatry*, 1969, *115*, 1297–1304.

Ryle, A., & Breen, D. Some differences in the personal constructs of neurotic and normal subjects. *British Journal of Psychiatry*, 1972, *120*, 483–489.

Ryle, A., & Lipshitz, S. Recording change in marital therapy with the reconstruction grid. *British Journal of Medical Psychology*, 1975, *48*, 39–48.

Ryle, A., & Lipshitz, S. Repertory grid elucidation of a difficult conjoint therapy. *British Journal of Medical Psychology*, 1976, *49*, 281–285.

Sandler, J. The background of safety. *International Journal of Psychoanalysis*, 1960, *41*, 352–356.

Sandler, J. Psychological conflict and the structural model: Some clinical and theoretical implications. *International Journal of Psychoanalysis*, 1974, *55*, 53–62.

Sandler, J., & Rosenblatt, B. The concept of the representational world. *Psychoanalytic Study of the Child*, 1962, *17*, 128.

Schachter, S., & Singer, J. E. Cognitive, social and physiological determinants of emotional states. *Psychological Review*, 1962, *69*, 379–399.

Schafer, R. Psychoanalysis without psychodynamics. *International Journal of Psychoanalysis*, 1975, *56*, 41–55.

Schaffer, H. R. *The growth of human sociability*. Harmondsworth: Penguin Books, 1971.

Singer, J. L. *Imagery and day-dream methods in psychotherapy and behaviour modification*. New York: Academic Press, 1974.

Slater, E. The psychiatrist in search of a science: The depth psychologies. *British Journal of Psychiatry*, 1975, *126*, 205–224.

Sloane, R. B., Staples, F. R., Cristol, A. H., Yorkston, N. J., & Whipple, K. *Psychotherapy versus behavior therapy*. Cambridge: Harvard University Press, 1975.

Stolorow, R. D. Towards a functional definition of narcissism. *International Journal of Psychoanalysis*, 1975, *56*, 179–185.

Whitaker, D. S., & Lieberman, M. A. *Psychotherapy through the group process*. Chicago: Aldine, 1964.

Winnicott, D. W. *Playing and reality*. London: Tavistock, 1971.

Witkin, H. A. Psychological differentiation and forms of pathology. *Journal of Abnormal Psychology*, 1965, *70*, 317–336.

Chapter 24

Three Lacunae of Cognitive Therapy

Irwin G. Sarason

Cognitive behavior therapy emphasizes the interdependence of the overt and the covert and the need for persons to develop self-control over their lives (Goldfried, 1977; Mahoney, 1974; Meichenbaum, 1977). Clinicians who think along cognitive lines have sought to change behavior by changing specific thought patterns. For example, for some dental patients the cognitions requiring modification might be anticipations of pain recast as anticipations of no longer having a toothache, for highly text-anxious students it might be fear of flunking out at the end of the school year altered to planning how to study tonight, and for angry acter-outers it might be how to get back at their tormenters changed to focus on the undesirable consequences of acting out.

Progress in cognitive therapy in some areas has been so rapid that there has not been sufficient time to examine closely either several lacunae left by its uneven growth or complementary concepts in certain other areas. Three particularly important neglected topics turn out to have been major foci of psychoanalytic inquiry. They are (1) cognitions have histories, (2) cognitions have varying strengths and degrees of accessibility, and (3)

Preparation of this article was facilitated by a grant from the National Institute of Mental Health (MH 24823). I am indebted to the following colleagues, who thoughtfully reviewed earlier versions of the manuscript: Henry M. Levine, G. Alan Marlatt, Donald Meichenbaum, Steven L. Nielsen, Barbara R. Sarason, and Ronald E. Smith. I am also indebted to Eugene Goforth, who made one direct and many indirect contributions to the article.

Reprinted by permission of the author, Irwin G. Sarason, and the publisher from *Cognitive Therapy and Research*, 1979, 3, 223–235.

cognitions may interact with other cognitions. These areas of neglect require the attention of clinicians and researchers who are attracted to cognition–behavior linkages. Because some psychoanalysts recognize the importance of these topics does not imply that their treatment of them has been widely appreciated or productive. Indeed, there is a growing belief within psychoanalysis that too often the important role of cognitions as a precursor of maladaptive behavior is minimized by analysis in favor of preoccupations concerning emotions and hidden motivations (Arieti, 1977). The time seems ripe for a fresh attack on these neglected topics, and cognitive therapy researchers have the qualifications to carry it out.

Cognitive therapy has been concerned more with *how* to change cognitions than *why* the cognitions requiring change arose in the first place. While for some therapeutic purposes *why* questions may not be crucial, they are extremely important to a general understanding of the content of thoughts and the way in which that content influences behavior. Such an understanding might have enormous applicability in the *prevention* of maladaptive thought and behavior. An example from another field, epidemiology, perhaps best suggests the importance of this point. In 1848 outbreaks of cholera occurred in the city of London. One area that was particularly hard hit was the Golden Square district. This district was served by a common water pump in Broad Street. It was noticed that two groups of people in the district had relatively low incidences of cholera, workers in a brewery and inmates of an institution. The facts that the brewery workers drank beer while at work and the institution had its own well were clues that the Broad Street pump was implicated in the cholera outbreak. When the pump was dismantled, the epidemic in the Golden Square district was brought under control. Knowledge of how to curb the spread of cholera preceded identification of the microorganism that causes cholera. While identification of cholera's cause was not needed to curb its influence, only when the cause was identified could preventive measures be instituted on a widespread scale.

This example does not suggest that prior thoughts are causes in the same sense that *Vibrio choleral* causes cholera. It is offered to illustrate the need to identify antecedent conditions and the process by which personal and social problems come into existence. When this is accomplished, the scope of activities of scientists and clinicians is broadened, one result often being discovery of previously unanticipated contributions to human welfare. This paper raises several questions about the scope of cognition–behavior relationships and examines directions for future inquiry suggested by psychoanalysis.

Cognitions Have Histories

The exploration of cognitive history can extend over either the short or the long run. A short-run example is the person who worries about the lack of enthusiasm in a friend's greeting: "Is she angry with me?" "Did I insult her the last time we met?" While the environmental roots of these self-questions must not be ignored (there might actually have been an insult), as often as not the self-questions come from within. It might be a product of the person's system of personal constructs or fear of rejection by others. Kelly's (1955) personal construct and Ellis's (1962) rational-emotive therapies represent important steps toward recognizing the degree to which behavior is caused by classes of cognitions. However, Ellis, at least, has little interest in the genesis of these cognitions.

Cognitive histories can be quite complicated. The child therapy literature is replete with examples of satisfactory cognitive development in some areas but not in others. Yet the immature and incorrect assumptions of childhood about the self and the world may remain active even though chronological adulthood and maturity in many areas has been attained. The three-year-old child who in the home somaticized as a means of getting attention and affection may continue to do so in many social situations. By what mechanisms might the construals and self-directions of childhood continue to be influential in later life? More interchanges between cognitively oriented clinicians and personality development researchers might provide some answers to this type of question. The productive Piagetian study of cognitive development suggests the potential of such interchanges, as does the work of those interested in ethological approaches to personality (Bowlby, 1973). Lines of inquiry concerning the factors that give rise to specific streams of ideation and internal dialogue are currently being pursued.

Strength and Accessibility of Cognitions

Why are certain maladaptive thoughts so long-lived? Perhaps it is because these thoughts are associated with [such] high levels of arousal or activation, personal conflict and anxiety, that they go underground. The childhood cognition "I'll get sick, and she'll feel sorry for me and be nice to me" may remain a potent determiner of response long after the person would consciously reject such an immature chain of thoughts.

There is plenty of evidence that the residues of early experiences are like ashes in the fireplace, seemingly inert but actually smoldering. Anecdotes illustrating this point can be quite dramatic, particularly when a recovered thought leads to overt behavioral change. Such an example occurred in the life of a middle-aged man who became interested in netsuke, carved ivory appendages tied to cords worn around their kimonos by Japanese. This man became highly attracted to their intricate designs and how the netsuke were carved. Over a period of a few years he collected over 40 of them. This entailed going to specialized shops and attending auctions, both of which were time-consuming. Since he had not been a collector of oriental or any other objects earlier in life, he often wondered why in the world he was so taken with the netsuke.

One day when he was wondering about this, he happened to remember an event that occurred when he was a very little boy. His grandfather, who was in the delivery business, had asked the boy if he would like to come along as he made his rounds. The boy joyfully accepted the invitation. One stop made that day was at a store that had a display of very small Japanese dolls. The boy was attracted to one doll in particular and spent several minutes looking at it in the display case. The grandfather, noticing the boy's interest in the doll, offered to buy it for him, but the boy politely declined. When he got home he told his mother about the doll and asked her if they might go back to the store and buy it. Since the store was a considerable distance from their home, they did not go there until a few days later and then discovered that the doll had been sold. After remembering this event, which had taken place over 40 years earlier, the man lost all interest in adding to his netsuke collection. He kept the collection but neither purchased nor sought to purchase another piece. Years later another recollection came to his mind. It was that when he was a little boy, his mother often wore a kimono in the morning. He remembered clearly that the kimono's design consisted of a pattern of many small Japanese dolls.

This anecdote leads one to be curious, not only about the history of cognitions (for example, all the thoughts that directed the man's activities in collecting netsuke) but about the mechanisms by which thoughts live (perhaps in a dormant state) and die. Freud speculated about the motivations that keep thoughts alive and concluded that cathected libidinal energy played an important role. However, one need not accept all the complexities and circumlocutions of psychoanalysis in order to deal with the phenomena contained in the example. From a cognitive theorist's point of view it offers an interesting insight into the processes of human memory. The netsuke collector's experience suggests that experiences and habits of thought from different time periods are linked together in the memory system and that retrieval of these memories may change behavior even in an individual who is functioning at a well-integrated level. The anecdote raises a number of provocative questions. It is difficult to avoid wondering why the boy was attracted to the Japanese doll, why the middle-aged man collected netsuke, and why recovery of the memory of the childhood expe-

rience led to such a swift weakening of what seemed to be a highly preoc-
cupying interest and activity. One wonders also what stimulus evoked
recollection of the Japanese doll incident, whether its recall resulted in the
man viewing reinforcements differently, and how the recovered childhood
memory might have altered aspects of his internal dialogue.

Wachtel (1977) has pointed out that the residues of early experience
are not kept in a deep freeze. They influence the individual's further
experiences and encounters. It also seems likely that feedback-providing
events are capable of changing one's thinking enough so as to influence
access to past cognitions. Psychologists often think of feedback in terms of
information-providing experiences that incrementally influence behavior
and cognitions, such as one's self-concept and aspirations. Certain kinds of
feedback might also permit seemingly quantum jumps by which the individual gains access to previously forgotten thoughts. From a cognitive behavioral standpoint, it is necessary to specify the events and feedback that
provide such access.

Cognitive Processes

There are two paths to behavior change that may not only be noncompetitive
but actually are complementary. One is by way of recovering memories,
often accompanied by cognitive restructuring, that accentuate or inhibit
current behavior. In the example given, the recovered memory seemed to
inhibit or extinguish collection of netsuke. Insights, like the challenges to
ingrained ways of thinking with which rational-emotive therapists confront
their clients, may function as goads to behavior change. The other path, the
one typically followed by behavior therapists, leads to identification of maladaptive response patterns and application of specific response-alteration
procedures. Investigation is needed of the degree to which these paths
intersect and exert interactive effects on each other. For example, what
changes in thought and motivation result from elimination by means of
behavior therapy of a frustrating, time-consuming ritual? Might some
memories of past events be influenced by such a therapeutic success?

Cognitive psychologists study how probes (cues) activate an appropriate search set for retrieval of information from long-term memory. Their
experiments are usually conducted in the well-controlled psychology laboratory, but even that insulated sanctuary is not immune to such unwanted
influences as individual differences. Broadbent (1977) and Neisser (1976)
have both recently discussed the role of individual differences in *preattentive* processes, seemingly automatic features of information processing involved in the detection and analysis of information. Broadbent, for
example, has referred to factors other than those resulting from experi-

menter's instructions, which "may not always be reportable, and which nevertheless may cause attention to be caught by this stimulus rather than by that, in a way that is systematic rather than random" (1977, p. 110). Those things that subjects bring to the laboratory (attitudes, predilections, fears, information) exert influences over their performances and they may be as unaware of these influences as is the experimenter. An interesting possibility would be to approach this problem of repression and insight into its clinical problems from the standpoint of the factors that inhibit a person's ability to generate an appropriate probe needed to recover inaccessible memories. Defense mechanisms can be reformulated in terms of the predominance of certain rigid, limiting constructions of events and plans for action. It is perhaps because of the individual differences in these cognitive styles that Neisser (1976) has called for a widening of cognitive psychology's purview to include events of everyday life.

When one adds to individual differences in preattentive processes the idea of levels of information processing that virtually all cognitive psychologists feel called upon to deal with in some way, as well as other concepts such as rehearsal (which may take the form of internal dialogues) and imaginal processes (which play roles in dreams and daydreams as well as in visual perception experiments), it seems inescapable that what separates cognitive psychologists and psychoanalysts are different emphases concerning (1) the processes and mechanisms about which they conjecture and (2) the mental contents that are salient to them (Bower, 1978). The separation does not seem to be due to basic differences about whether mediating processes exist or if more than one level of mediation is needed. Neisser (1976) has observed how surprisingly contemporary Freud's theory about the unconscious seems to a cognitive psychologist and has pointed out the need to be aware that people don't just think about one thing at a time. More often than not, their thinking resembles more a juggling act with a lot going on all at once than a missile on its way to a particular target.

From a scientific standpoint, understanding the processes by which people think and solve interpersonal problems, as well as the determinants of the processes, is of equal importance to treating symptoms and the current (conscious) concerns of people. Study of these processes might contribute to therapeutic progress. Several types of data suggest the importance of the development of cognitions about ourselves and others. The work of Brown, Harris, and Copeland (1977) on depression is a case in point. These researchers compared depressed and nondepressed women with regard to vulnerability factors and found that depressed more often than nondepressed women had before 11 years of age lost their mothers through death or separation. The results of Brown et al. do not answer the question of the manner by which this vulnerability factor exerts its influence. From a cognitive standpoint, it seems important to obtain a clearer picture than we now

have of how losses—especially those experienced at an early age—are interpreted by survivors, how the pain of the losses is dealt with, and how
motivations and thoughts linked to the loss are perpetuated in one form or
another. These are questions about the development of internal dialogues at
various levels of accessibility. Some forms of behavior therapy (e.g., producing positive self-cognitions, programming socially reinforcing tasks into one's
schedule) are effective for some adult depressions, but the success should
not blind our curiosity about how ideas associated with early losses are not
just sloughed off but continue to exert an impact.

   Recent work in the area of child development influenced by ethological and Piagetian theories suggest the importance of finding out how particular developmental events are interpreted at the time they occur—and
later on. The evidence in the literature on attachment and separation suggests that the human infant comes into the world with some "prewired"
needs and capacities for social relationships with a caretaker. Fears about
loss, appropriate to a young child's level of cognitive development at the
loss of a separation from its mother, might well exert influences over
thought processes later in life (Bowlby, 1973). This might have been what
was going on with the netsuke collector, although unexplained by the
anecdote is why loss of the Japanese doll became translated into netsuke
collecting.

Cognitive Interactions

Thoughts do not retain an unspoiled pristine existence after they first pop
into our heads. They get mixed up with other thoughts, producing what
seem to be novel results. It was just this phenomenon that attracted Freud
to the study of free associations. However, it is not necessary to believe in
the libido theory in order to be interested in the associations that exist
among thoughts. Treatment of certain cases might not require extensive
free-association sessions, but the associations among ideas is a problem to
which cognitive psychologists and clinical researchers must be attracted. It
is possible that treatment of certain other cases could be accelerated by use
of some form of free association within the context of what Freud called
"talking therapy." The majority of cases that come to the attention of
behavior therapists involve relatively focalized problems in which the client
is troubled about something specific and desirous of a particular type of
behavior change. But there are many, many people whose psychological
problems are much more diffuse—often so diffuse that they cannot label a
specific class of their behavior or thought as being problematic. Behavior
therapists need to develop techniques useful in situations where the problem is not well defined.

The Reconstructive Approach to Cognitions

Cross-sectional and longitudinal studies of cognitive development constitute a very valuable source of knowledge about covert–overt behavior linkages. For the clinician, developmental research on changes in such concepts as self, others, and personal responsibility are of particular interest because they provide clues to information processing at various developmental levels. Another valuable source of knowledge is psychological reconstruction of the type that Freud and many other clinical workers have employed. Since clinicians see their clients only when a problem reaches intolerable levels, the reconstructive method is understandably very widely employed. The clinician usually weighs heavily the client's statement of the problem and relies on the client's self-reports in tracing its genesis.

Psychodynamic users of the reconstructive method have been relying less and less on libidinal explanations of just about everything. Equally important, but less well recognized, has been the conversion of psychoanalytic theory into something of a cognitive psychology. The most articulate exponent of this position was, perhaps, George Klein (1967), who, in discussing the nature of repression, spoke of clashes of peremptory ideas rather than systems of cathected and countercathected energy. Klein noted that repressed thoughts are relatively impervious to environmental influences but, nevertheless, still influence behavioral responses to environmental events. Increased recognition of the importance of cognitive processes is not surprising since psychoanalysts in their clinical work deal with the ideas presented by their patients and the historical roots and meanings of those ideas. For example, Bowlby (1973), in his discussion of school phobia or school refusal, emphasizes not the influence of libidinal impulses but the meaning for the child of not going to school. He points out that school refusal may indicate not that the child is afraid to go to school but rather that he or she is afraid to leave home (perhaps because of worries over leaving the mother home alone).

Klein (1976, p. 9) has referred to the "cognitive record of the experiences of sensuality," "meaning schemas," and peremptory ideas as information guides to future thought and action. A number of other writers have also written and done research on the perceptual and cognitive variables implicated in human motivations (Antrobus, 1970; Gardner, Holzman, Klein, Linton, & Spence, 1959; Ryle, 1978).

Even for the traditionalist, the events of psychotherapy are usually interpreted in terms of unconscious thoughts that are brought to the level of awareness and dealt with in some way. Insight, a goal of many psychotherapists, is interpretable as a concept that becomes available to a person for the first time. Insightful cognitions range from such statements as "I felt terribly rejected as a young child when my mother went to the hospital for an operation" to "When he didn't return my phone call, I figured he must be angry with me" to "A lot of times when I worry it's because I jumped to an unwarranted conclusion." Anxiety, transference, and a wide variety of the feelings and emotions expressed by clients are interpretable in terms of ideas that stimulate often complex chains of thoughts and physiological responses.

What distinguishes cognitions as dealt with by psychodynamic therapists is the belief that they are often related to past events that the client must struggle to be aware of and interpret and that motivations direct their expression. One goal of the psychoanalyst is completely congruent with the behavior therapist's interest in helping clients gain self-control over their lives. While insight for insight's sake may have some intrinsic intellectual interest, reconstructive therapists seek to foster their *use* by the patient. That is, the aim is for insights to become part of more adaptive self-regulation mechanisms. One patient in the course of psychotherapy acquired considerable insight into the intense competitive feelings he had toward his father from childhood onward. He came to see how this competitiveness toward older authority figures manifested itself in adulthood even though his father was no longer alive. His relationships at work improved when it became possible for him to anticipate his own need for confrontations and blowups with his employer. These anticipations served as a cue for a self-imposed "cooling off" period during which he thought about whether he was for some reason experiencing a transference reaction to the employer or a natural difference of opinion. While this strategy did not work every time, it was sufficiently reinforcing to strengthen his skill at regulating his behavior in a desired direction.

Much of what Freud and other psychoanalysts have written is either explicitly about cognitive processes or could be so construed. This statement appears in Freud's final formulation of anxiety: "Missing someone who is loved and longed for is the key to an understanding of anxiety" (1926/1959, pp. 136–137) In other words, thoughts about separation play an important role in the experience of anxiety. One of the distinctive features of the psychodynamic point of view is that persons react to their own ideas either overtly or covertly. The concept of defense might be interpreted as problem-solving efforts to cope with troubling or "dangerous" thoughts. One person might respond to a missed loved one by seeking out new social ties, while another might respond by means of a complex chain of thoughts. One way of characterizing defense mechanisms is to say that they involve cognitive restructuring, usually maladaptive, and distorted thought sequences relating to the self and to others.

The reconstructive approach may or may not be highly effective in achieving behavioral change. Clinicians oriented toward achieving personality reconstruction have many opportunities to make mistakes in exploring their client's cognitive histories. For immediate clinical purposes, here-and-now behavior therapy techniques might prove more efficacious in the sense that removing the Broad Street pump in Golden Square was effective despite lack of understanding of the mechanism by which it caused cholera. In addition, as Wachtel (1977) has pointed out, they may provide valuable here-and-now material in terms of which long-active cognitions can be more easily understood.

Cognitive therapists might profitably pursue the reconstructive approach, at least from a research standpoint. Doing so might contribute to broadening their clinical range, particularly with regard to the most debilitating disorders, the psychoses. For example, schizophrenics need help in making contact with the forgotten premises and construals upon which their bizarre behavior is based. Psychotically depressed persons are often so enmeshed in and preoccupied with their supersadness that they have lost contact with the cognitions that led to their sorrow. The success of somatic therapies (e.g., certain drugs) in reducing supersadness should not lead us to neglect the cognitions behind the supersadness (Beck, 1976). For the depressive, these cognitions often have to do with existential questions such as the meaning (or meaninglessness) of life. These questions grow out of cognitions in the form of expectations, hopes, construals, and perceived personal responsibilities. The personal significance of questions about the meaning of existence has often been better appreciated by poets than by psychologists. How many depressed people have had thoughts in the spirit of these lines from Shakespeare:

> Out, out, brief candle!
> Life's but a walking shadow; a poor player,
> That struts and frets his hour upon the stage,
> And then is heard no more: it is a tale
> Told by an idiot, full of sound and fury,
> Signifying nothing.

Freud saw his "talking therapy" as a naturally unfolding process in which free association played the key role. The outcomes of this process included recovered memories, insight, and cognitive reorganization. It is, of course, an empirical question which method is most facilitative in reconstructing paths of thought. Many of the interventions invented by behavior therapists are specifically aimed at reducing anxiety in problematic anxiety-loaded areas. If symptoms such as phobias and obsessive-compulsive rituals are linked to childhood construals of reality and self, anxiety-reducing techniques such as systematic desensitization might play a useful role in gaining access to memories of those construals. Since psychodynamically oriented clinicians believe that lowered anxiety and defensiveness levels aid the recall process, behavior therapy techniques might well speed up the process. However, regardless of its clinical value in cognitive reconstruction, the scientific contribution of specific anxiety-reducing and coping-enhancement techniques to our understanding of persons' remembrance of things past merits investigations.

Conclusions

It is too early to say what the outcome of the convergences discussed in this paper will be. But the convergences seem real and the contributions of the strange bedfellows described in this article can be identified. Psychoanalysis, with its emphasis on motivation and the levels at which mental life operates, and on the personality development of the individual, has provided a conceptual framework of the "whole person" through time. Cognitive psychology is at present largely devoid of motivational and developmental concepts, but the field seems to be moving toward recognition of these factors. What is clearly discernible in cognitive psychology is a sophisticated, albeit limited, treatment of levels of processing. Scientific rigor is for behavior therapy, as for cognitive psychology, a very powerful emphasis. Because of the fuzziness of much past psychodynamic theory, research, and practice, behavior therapy has stayed rather close to the observable data of maladaptive behavior. That this situation is changing is discernible from recent interest in internal dialogues, self-control of behavior, and cognitive restructuring.

Behavior therapists have had notable success in their efforts to eliminate specific symptoms and strengthen specific classes of adaptive behavior or thought. The vague, yet troubling, psychological problems that burden many people (e.g., a general feeling of dissatisfaction with one's social relationships and role in life) have yet to receive the systematic attention of behavior therapists. The therapeutic successes that have been attained should not detract attention from large questions about the relationships between present thoughts and behavior and past thoughts and behavior, or from that between past and current environmental events.

In extending the scientific and clinical scope of cognitive behavioral methods, certain areas of inquiry require special emphasis. One concerns the histories of our cognitions and the variables that shape them. A second concerns the need for some concept of motivation reflecting the fact that certain thoughts seem more energized and important than others. (Why did netsuke collecting play such an important role in the middle-aged man's life?) Psychodynamic theories, particularly psychoanalysis, can be interpreted as dealing with thoughts, their genesis, and the motivations and arousal linked to them, as well as the mechanisms by which they are expressed. Accepting orthodox Freudian ideology is not a prerequisite for approaching these topics. At the same time, attention should be given to ideas stemming from Freud's pioneering work in the areas of conscious and unconscious thought. To the extent that the past influences the present, we should take up the challenge of cognitive personality development.

This challenge is as important for the clinician as it is for the developmental researcher. The clinician is to a large degree at the mercy of the presentation given by the client or referral agent(s) in obtaining knowledge of the client's difficulty. The problem is particularly acute when the client is a child whose parents provide much of the presenting complaint and background information. In the case of a school phobia, mentioned earlier, does the child refuse to go to school because of fear of dangers there or at home? Surely the answer to such a question is of importance to the psychological growth of the child regardless of the success that specific behavior modification efforts might have in strengthening the response of going to school.

Do cognitive conflicts, unwitting misinterpretations of reality, and emotion-laden cognitions that we have forgotten contribute to the directions our lives take? Surely they do, as do the response contingencies that impinge on us throughout our lives. The time seems ripe for taking a broad enough perspective to encompass both processes.

Summary

This article has discussed three lacunae of cognitive therapy: investigations of cognitive histories, levels of cognitions' accessibility, and interactions among cognitions. The role of cognitions in psychotherapy is described and ways in which psychoanalysis and cognitive therapy complement each other are discussed. The growing concern of cognitive psychology with levels of processing and preattentive mechanisms is shown to resemble certain directions within psychodynamic theory. By viewing personality as an open system, influenced by experiential inputs throughout life, certain theoretical convergences become evident and lay the groundwork for future research directions.

References

Antrobus, J. S. (Ed.). *Cognition and affect*. Boston: Little, Brown, 1970.

Arieti, S. Cognitive components in human conflict and unconscious motivation. *Journal of the American Academy of Psychoanalysis*, 1977, 5, 5–16.

Beck, A. T. *Cognitive therapy and the emotional disorders*. New York: International Universities Press, 1976.

Bower, G. H. Contacts of cognitive psychology with social learning theory. *Cognitive Therapy and Research*, 1978, *2*, 123–146.

Bowlby, J. *Attachment and loss* (Vol. 2): *Separation*. New York: Basic Books, 1973.

Broadbent, D. E. The hidden preattentive processes. *American Psychologist*, 1977, *32*, 109–118.

Brown, G. W., Harris, T., & Copeland, J. R. Depression and loss. *British Journal of Psychiatry*, 1977, *130*, 1–18.

Ellis, A. *Reason and emotion in psychotherapy*. New York: Lyle Stuart, 1962.

Freud, S. *Inhibitions, symptoms, and anxiety*. Standard edition of *The Complete Psychological Works of Sigmund Freud* (Vol. 20). London: Hogarth Press, 1959. (Originally published, 1926.)

Gardner, R. W., Holzman, P. S., Klein, G. S., Linton, H., & Spence, D. P. Cognitive control: A study of individual consistencies in cognitive behavior. *Psychological Issues*, 1959, *1* (4).

Goldfried, M. R. The use of relaxation and cognitive relabeling as coping skills. In R. B. Stuart (Ed.), *Behavioral self management: Strategies, techniques and outcomes*. New York: Brunner/Mazel, 1977, pp. 82–116.

Kelly, G. A. *The psychology of personal constructs* (2 vols.). New York: Norton, 1955.

Klein, G. S. Peremptory ideation: Structure and force in motivated ideas. In R. B. Holt (Ed.), *Motives and thought: Psychoanalytic essays in honor of David Rapaport. Psychological Issues*, 1967, Monograph No. 18/19, p. 80–128.

Klein, G. S. *Psychoanalytic theory*. New York: International Universities Press, 1976.

Mahoney, M. H. *Cognition and behavior modification*. Cambridge, Mass.: Ballinger, 1974.

Meichenbaum, D. *Cognitive-behavior modification: An integrative approach*. New York: Plenum Press, 1977.

Neisser, U. *Cognition and reality*. San Francisco: W. H. Freeman, 1976.

Ryle, A. A common language for the psychotherapies? *British Journal of Psychiatry*, 1978, *132*, 585–594.

Wachtel, P. L. *Psychoanalysis and behavior therapy*. New York: Basic Books, 1977.

Chapter 25
Cognition and Experience

Marvin R. Goldfried

It has often been maintained that an understanding of the development, structure, and function of cognitive processes is ultimately based on the study of language (e.g., Staats, 1972, 1975). Language may function in various ways, whether it be as a means of labeling stimuli, of understanding one's associations to such labels, or of aiding an individual in overt action (Staats, 1975). Certainly, when one considers how very much the therapeutic enterprise is based on the interchange of language between therapist and client, it becomes strikingly evident that linguistic and communication analyses require far more attention than they have heretofore received in the behavior therapy literature.

Most of what has been discussed throughout this chapter is based on the assumption that an individual's internal dialogue or self-statements mediate emotional arousal. Although there exists some indirect empirical support for this premise, it is not at all unusual to encounter individuals within clinical settings who have great difficulty in describing the internal dialogue that may be mediating their upset in any given situation. Such observations may certainly call into question the validity of the assumption that cognitive variables are associated with emotional arousal. A more plausible interpretation, however, is that individuals often lack the ability to provide accurate introspective information on their cognitive processes (Nisbett & Wilson, 1977). It is of interest to note that psychoanalysts such as Kubie (1934) have suggested that people may be unable to report fully

Reprinted by permission of the author, Marvin R. Goldfried, and the publisher from Anxiety reduction through cognitive-behavioral intervention, in P. C. Kendall & S. D. Hollon (Eds.), *Cognitive-behavioral interventions: Theory, research, and procedures*. New York: Academic Press, 1979, pp. 141–146.

on their cognitions because of the well-learned associations between thoughts, emotions, and behavior.

Our knowledge of the complex interplay between cognition and overt behavior is certainly far from complete. However, if we ever hope to develop the field of cognitive behavior therapy, it is crucial that we have a more complete understanding of the interrelationship between cognition and experience. And although the study of language may provide us with useful information, it would be a mistake to assume that language and cognition can be equated. Menzel and Johnson (1976) have suggested that language and the communication process are reflective of basic cognitive structures that can be studied more directly. The section that follows describes some of the research in experimental cognitive psychology and offers some speculations that hopefully may point to potentially fruitful directions for future clinical and research efforts.

The Need for Experiential Referents

In attempting to understand the meaning of any given word or utterance, we need to know something about its referent. Much of what we encounter as miscommunication in everyday life can be traced to two or more individuals using the same words but intending different referents. This is clearly illustrated when another person attempts to teach you a physical skill. In learning to ski, for example, the instructor is forever directing the student to "bend the knees." Anyone who has ever struggled through the process of learning to ski will recall repeating such instructions covertly, bending one's knees, but having little success. After much practice, however, a day arrives when you bend the knees in just the right way, experience the sense of control, and then remark "Oh! Bend the *knees!*" Once having had a different and, in this case, more appropriate experience, the sentence takes on a completely different meaning.

A study by Bransford and Johnson (1972) has dramatically demonstrated how prior knowledge can provide the necessary experiential referent for language comprehension and recall. They presented subjects with a passage containing words having familiar lexical meanings. However, half of the subjects saw a picture offering an appropriate referent beforehand, whereas the remaining subjects did not have the opportunity to see the picture. The passage was as follows:

> If the balloons popped, the sound wouldn't be able to carry since everything would be too far away from the correct floor. A closed window would also prevent the sound from carrying, since most buildings tend to be well-insulated. Since the whole operation depends on a steady flow of electricity, a break in the

middle of the wire would also cause problems. Of course, the fellow could shout, but the human voice is not loud enough to carry that far. An additional problem is that a string could break on the instrument. Then there could be no accompaniment to the message. It is clear that the best situation would involve less distance. Then there would be fewer potential problems. With face to face contact, the least number of things could go wrong [p. 719].

After having seen this passage, it should come as no surprise to the reader that subjects not given the referent beforehand had greater diffi-culty in both comprehension and recall. Having had the opportunity to see the picture beforehand—the picture itself is reproduced as Figure 25.1, on page 372 of this volume—clearly made the task easier. And seeing the picture after having looked at the seemingly incomprehensible passage should provide the reader with a a rapid clarification of its meaning—as in the "bend the knees" example. This phenomenon is often seen clinically, when clients report sudden shifts or clarifications in belief systems, re-ferred to by Mahoney (1974) as the "cognitive click."

Repeating certain utterances under conditions when individuals "be-lieve" or "do not believe" what they are saying, or when the contrast between stating something one "understands" versus merely repeating words with no real comprehension, is strikingly similar to the differentia-tion between "emotional" and "intellectual" insight or understanding as described by psychoanalytic writers. Consistent with the illustrations noted, Dollard and Miller (1950) have suggested that emotional insight can be provided to clients only if they have the experiential referent for the labels offered by the therapist. They state:

> The patient himself must have the emotional experience and must cor-rectly label it. If the patient has only a collection of sentences not tied to emotional or instrumental responses, little immediate therapeutic effect may be anticipated, though some delayed effects may occasionally occur. If the patient is so frightened that he cannot listen, interpretation will have small effect. The therapist's interpretations must be timely, that is, must occur when the patient can listen and when the emotional response to be labeled is actu-ally occurring [pp. 304–305].

The examples cited provide instances in which the individual does not comprehend the utterance until exposed to the experiential referent (i.e., the feeling of bending one's knees in a given way, or visual exposure to the picture). However, there may be instances in which an individual has already encountered the relevant experience some time in the past, with the cognitive click occurring once that person is able to retrieve the event from long-term memory. In understanding the process in such cases, the distinction made between *episodic* and *semantic* memory is particularly relevant (Tulving, 1972). According to Tulving, episodic memory refers to the pool of relatively discreet or isolated past events that are not tied to any cognitive structure. Semantic memory, on the other hand, deals with more "meaningful" information, in the sense that the events are integrated or coded into a larger associative network. Because there are fewer associative cues to enable the individual to retrieve experiences stored in episodic memory, such events are less likely to be recalled and used as referents for comprehension. In such instances, one can explain the shift from an intellectual to an emotional understanding of an utterance as involving the retrieval of the needed referent from episodic memory, and its subsequent shift in "meaning" when it becomes integrated into the larger cognitive structure associated with [semantic] memory.

The clinical implications of such a conceptualization would suggest that the client needs to be provided with learning experiences prior to the use of language or labels that require such experiential referents for their meaning and comprehension. Or if such experiences have occurred in the past but are stored in episodic memory and are consequently not "being used" to gain a more accurate perception of current situations, steps may need to be taken to integrate such experiences into semantic memory in such a way that the existing conceptual categories become somewhat re-aligned. One wonders about the extent to which this latter guideline parallels what psychoanalysts have meant when they indicate that the therapist must be careful in the "timing" of interpretations, offering them only at the time when the patient appears ready to accept and to "understand" certain isolated and seemingly irrelevant past events.

Another study by Bransford and Johnson (1973) has shown how slight shifts in *context* can create striking changes in the meaning of an event. Consider the following passage:

> The man stood before the mirror and combed his hair. He checked his face carefully for any places he might have missed shaving and then put on the conservative tie he had decided to wear. At breakfast, he studied the newspaper carefully and, over coffee, discussed the possibility of buying a new washing machine with his wife. Then he made several phone calls. As he was leaving the house he thought about the fact that his children would probably want to go to that private camp again this summer. When the car didn't start, he got out, slammed the door and walked down to the bus stop in a very angry mood. Now he would be late [p. 415].

If the reader would now reconsider the passage, but this time adding "the *unemployed* man stood before the mirror . . . ," the meaning of the communication would, indeed, be different. As noted by Bransford and Johnson, change occurs not only in the understanding of what events took place but also in one's inferences about why they did. Consider now still a different meaning that emerges when the passage begins with "the *stock-broker* stood before the mirror. . . ."

The role of context in the communication of meaning has some very important clinical implications. The ability of the therapist to understand or to "empathize" with what a client described depends greatly on a shared pool of experiences that can provide the appropriate context within which the communication takes place. Baer and Stolz (1978) have dicussed the difficulty that *est* graduates have in describing the changes they have experienced to non-*est* friends. They suggest that the language used by *est* graduates to describe their changes has connotative meanings based on having gone through certain experiences (cf. bending the knees in a given way) and is not readily comprehended by those not having shared such experiences. Indeed, Baer and Stolz suggest that one of the main effects of *est* may be to provide the individual with a shift in epistemology, in that life events are now viewed within a different context.

Meaning and the Internal Dialogue

It has already been acknowledged that the clinical assessment of a client's "internal dialogue" is not as straightforward as it might seem. One reason why we may expect to have difficulty in assessing a person's cognitive processes by direct introspection is that we assume that the individual is reacting to specific and easily delineated stimuli. However, there are data to indicate that people react emotionally to classes of stimuli as well as to specific events (Proctor & Malloy, 1971; Staats, 1975). Inasmuch as those stimuli to which we frequently respond in real-life situations are indeed complex, our emotional reactions may be to only certain elements of this stimulus complex that in themselves can be part of a larger, and perhaps less obvious, conceptual class. Hence, we frequently speak of interpersonal events as reflecting "hidden agendas" or in some ways being "symbolic" of something else. Because referents (objects, persons, events) have a multitude of features, the meaning of any verbal or nonverbal communication can become clear only when we also know the broader context (e.g., past interpersonal events) in which it is being used (cf. Olson, 1970).

Despite clients' difficulties in reporting what they are "telling themselves" in any given situation, they frequently will acknowledge that they are behaving "as if" they are saying certain things to themselves. Perhaps our difficulties in assessing these cognitive mediators have been a function of our incorrect conceptualization of the nature of the "internal dialogue." Rather than assuming that an individual is emitting one or more coherent self-statements, it might be more appropriate to view such covert events as involving affective associations, comprising the *connotative meanings* assigned to events or objects (Osgood, Suci, & Tannenbaum, 1957). Indeed, one of the major characteristics of human memory is its associative nature; associations are involved both in the meaning assigned to concepts and in the retrieval of information (Bower, 1975).

As noted earlier, a procedure that has been found to be useful clinically in the implementation of systematic rational restructuring has involved the use of an associative task. Thus, instead of asking clients what they may be "saying to themselves" that contributes to their upset in given situations, the therapist assists clients in ferreting out the relevant cognitive mediators by having them complete such sentences as "Making a mistake in front of my friends would upset me because . . . ," or "If this other person disagrees with me that means. . . ." Clinical work with such a technique has been most fruitful in that it appears to help individuals to recognize more readily, and subsequently to reevaluate, the implicit meaning they assign to given situations in their lives. The similarity to Jung's early research (Jung, 1910) on the use of word associations to determine the idiosyncratically perceived significance of certain words is particularly striking. There is also a parallel to the clinical work of psychoanalysts, who have long recognized the need for gathering information on the associative meaning that individuals attribute to given events and people. Thus, Kubie (1952) has recommended the use of free-association techniques under standardized conditions for evaluating an individual's "thinking profile" and any changes resulting from therapeutic intervention.

An assessment instrument that may very well appeal to cognitive behavior therapists and psychoanalysts alike is the *semantic differential,* which is an associative scaling technique originally developed by Osgood et al. (1957) from a learning-theory base for the purpose of assessing connotative or affective meaning that people assign to objects, other individuals, or events. Although there have been occasional usages of the semantic differential to measure changes in meaning resulting from therapeutic intervention (e.g., Endler, 1961; Hekmat & Vanian, 1971), there nonetheless remains great potential for the use of such a procedure in placing interpersonal events of individuals in semantic space with regard to evaluation, potency, and activity. Alternatively, one may use *multidimensional scaling* methods. Such procedures not only have the potential for assessing semantic distance, but can also shed light on the characteristic features that individuals use in classifying things as being semantically similar (Rips, Shoben, & Smith, 1973). The ability to assess the connotative similarities and differences among problematic events and individuals in a client's life, noting how they compare with nonproblematic events and individuals, may very well provide us with the information required to effect therapeutic change. The implications for assessing dysfunctional marital interactions are particularly striking, as a way of evaluating how each partner perceives (or misperceives) the communication from one's spouse, and the relevant hidden agendas to which each may be responding.

Still another possible way of assessing semantic structure and the nature of faulty classificatory processes might make use of the methodology devised by Collins and Quillian (1969) for the measurement of category size. With this procedure, subjects are presented with a series of sentences in which specific objects are said to be part of more general classes of objects (e.g., "A canary is a bird," "A penguin is a bird," "An ostrich is a bird.") Depending on the number of similar features shared by the specific example and what the subject considers to be the prototype of the category (e.g., the "typical" bird), the reaction time in identifying these statements as being true will vary. As one might predict, "A canary is a bird" is more rapidly identified as being true than is "An ostrich is a bird." If modified for clinical use, such a procedure may prove to be helpful in assessing the cognitive structure of clients by having them classify specific problematic events (e.g., making a mistake, forgetting someone's name, being criticized) into more general anxiety-arousing semantic categories (e.g., Being an Unworthy Person).

Just as the meaning of a communication at times requires the differentiation of the intended referent from alternate referents that might conceivably be the object of the communication (Olson, 1970), so might such discrimination be helpful in facilitating change in cognitions, affect, and behavior. Perhaps one may more readily learn to ski if the instructor would take the time to point out to the novice the correct *and* incorrect ways of bending one's knees. In therapy, it might be more beneficial for us to assist clients in the appropriate use of labels that they apply to events, others, and themselves by pointing out the similarities and differences to other events or people to whom such labels might be applied. Thus, when a client employs the connotative label of "bad," it might be important to specify those other events or individuals that might also be labeled as being "bad," as well as those considered "good." Landau (1977), in describing how phobias may be understood within an information-processing model, has made some similar observations in pointing out how semantic structure associated with phobic objects may best be altered. He suggests that, at the same time the therapist is assisting a client to reassess the aversive characteristics of a phobic object (e.g., the dog's fangs), it might also be useful additionally to help the client to become more aware of the positive attributes involved (e.g., the handsome coat).

No doubt, there are numerous other procedures and principles from experimental cognitive psychology that can have important implications for assessment and for therapeutic intervention (see Bower, 1978; Lang, 1977). With the growing interest in cognitive variables among behavior therapists, further extrapolations are likely to be forthcoming. Inasmuch as concepts

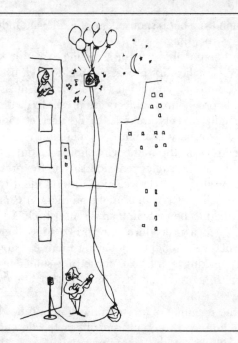

Figure 25.1.   Picture Used to Provide Appropriate Referent in the Bransford
and Johnson (1972) Study

from cognitive psychology are also currently being used by psychoanalytically oriented writers to explain various clinical phenomena (e.g., Horowitz, 1976), experimental cognitive psychology may very well offer us a
common language for bridging the gap between psychoanalytic and cognitive–behavioral approaches to intervention.

References

Baer, D. M., & Stolz, S. B. A description of the Erhard Seminars Training (est) in
      the terms of behavior analysis. Behaviorism, 1978, 6, 45–70.
Bower, G. H. Cognitive psychology: An introduction. In W. K. Estes (Ed.), Hand-
      book of learning and cognitive processes (Vol. 1). Introduction to concepts and
      issues. Hillsdale, N.J.: Lawrence Erlbaum Associates, 1975.
Bower, G. H. Contacts of cognitive psychology with social learning theory. Cogni-
      tive Therapy and Research, 1978, 2, 123–146.
Bransford, J. D., & Johnson, M. K. Contextual prerequisites for understanding:
      Some investigations of comprehension and recall. Journal of Verbal Learning
      and Verbal Behavior, 1972, 11, 717–726.
Bransford, J. D., & Johnson, M. K. Considerations of some problems of compre-

hension. In W. G. Chase (Ed.), *Visual information processing*. New York: Academic Press, 1973.

Collins, A. M., & Quillian, M. R. Retrieval time from semantic memory. *Journal of Verbal Learning and Verbal Behavior*, 1969, *8*, 240–247.

Dollard, J., & Miller, N. E. *Personality and psychotherapy*. New York: McGraw-Hill, 1950.

Endler, N. S. Changes in meaning during psychotherapy as measured by the semantic differential. *Journal of Counseling Psychology*, 1961, *8*, 105–111.

Hekmat, H., & Vanian, D. Behavior modification through covert semantic desensitization. *Journal of Consulting and Clinical Psychology*. 1971, *36*, 248–251.

Horowitz, M. J. *Stress response syndrome*. New York: Jason Aronson, 1976.

Jung, C. G. The association method. *American Journal of Psychology*, 1910, *21*, 219–269.

Kubie, L. S. Problems and technique of psychoanalytic validation and progress. In E. Pumpian-Mindlin (Ed.), *Psychoanalysis as science*. Stanford, Calif.: Stanford University Press, 1952.

Kubie, L. S. Relation of the conditioned reflex to psychoanalytic technic. *Archives of Neurology and Psychiatry*, 1934, *32*, 1137–1142.

Landau, R. J. A semantic-feature model of phobias. Unpublished manuscript, State University of New York at Stony Brook, 1977.

Lang, P. J. Imagery in therapy: An information processing analysis of fear. *Behavior Therapy*, 1977, *8*, 862–886.

Mahoney, M. J. *Cognition and behavior modification*. Cambridge: Ballinger, 1974.

Menzel, E. W., & Johnson, M. K. Communication and cognitive organization in humans and other animals. *Annals of the New York Academy of Sciences*, 1976, *280*, 131–142.

Nisbett, R. E., & Wilson, T. D. Telling more than we can know: Verbal reports on mental processes. *Psychological Review*, 1977, *84*, 231–259.

Olson, D. R. Language and thought: Aspects of a cognitive theory of semantics. *Psychological Review*, 1970, *77*, 257–273.

Osgood, C. E., Suci, G. J., & Tannenbaum, P. H. *The measurement of meaning*. Urbana, Ill.: University of Illinois Press, 1957.

Proctor, S., & Malloy, T. E. Cognitive control of conditioned emotional responses: An extension of behavior therapy to include the experimental psychology of cognition. *Behavior Therapy*, 1971, *2*, 294–306.

Rips, L. J., Shoben, E. J., & Smith, E. E. Semantic distance and the verification of semantic relations. *Journal of Verbal Learning and Verbal Behavior*, 1973, *12*, 1–20.

Staats, A. W. Language behavior therapy: A derivative of social behaviorism. *Behavior Therapy*, 1972, *3*, 165–192.

Staats, A. W. *Social behaviorism*. Homewood, Ill.: Dorsey Press, 1975.

Tulving, E. Episodic and semantic memory. In E. Tulving & W. Donaldson (Eds.), *Organization of memory*. New York: Academic Press, 1972.

Part IX
Epilogue

The final article offers an encapsulated summary of much of what has been presented throughout this book. Although the field of psychotherapy has been organized according to specific theoretical frameworks, this system seems to be breaking down, as therapists find that they are needing to look elsewhere in order to work with their patients/clients clinically. Just as patients'/clients' perceptions of the world change as a result of their corrective experiences, so has continued experience in the practice of psychotherapy caused clinicians to alter the paradigm that has typically guided their professional activities. Using clinical observations as a starting point, Goldfried maintains that rapprochement across orientations can come by looking for commonalities at a level of abstraction somewhere between the therapist's general theoretical orientation and the particular techniques that are used clinically. Although the guidelines for interacting with those of other orientations have typically been competitive in nature, attacks from outside the system of psychotherapy may very well provide the necessary impetus to engage in the kinds of collaborative efforts that are needed to advance the field.

Chapter 26

Toward the Delineation of Therapeutic Change Principles

Marvin R. Goldfried

It has been close to one hundred years since the practice of psychotherapy emerged as a recognized professional activity. Partly as a function of this unofficial anniversary, but more as the result of a growing zeitgeist in the field, the time is ripe for questioning how far we have come and how close we are to achieving a "consensus" (cf. Kuhn, 1970) within the professional community. The thesis developed in this article is that psychotherapy is currently in a state of infancy; anyone desiring therapy nowadays needs to decide which of more than 130 different approaches is likely to be most helpful (Parloff, 1976). It will be argued, however, that the time is rapidly approaching when more than ever before, we have the opportunity to advance the field in the direction of greater maturity.

Before developing this thesis, I might note that my original intent was to have this article published anonymously, but editorial policy prevented this from happening. The reason for wanting the article to appear anonymously was that all of us interested in the field of psychotherapy seem to have a tendency either to read or to ignore articles and books on the basis of our allegiance with the author's theoretical camp. We have all "taken up

The author is grateful to those colleagues and friends who offered their most valuable feedback and comments on an earlier version of this article and who generally provided support and encouragement to develop many of the ideas described in it.

sides" and have placed far too much emphasis on *who* is correct, not *what* is correct. I wanted to circumvent this tendency, as I believe the message has relevance to therapists of all orientations.

Much of what is included in this article is based on the writings of therapists from psychoanalytic, behavioral, and humanistic orientations. To let them speak for themselves, I have taken the liberty of quoting them liberally. My observation has been that there is a growing discontent among therapists within each orientation and that the need for rapprochement is becoming ever more appropriate. Although it may be possible to delineate commonalities across all theoretical persuasions, formidable pressures nonetheless exist that oppose such integration. Jerome Frank (1976) has astutely noted such barriers by suggesting that "features which are shared by all therapists have been relatively neglected, since little glory derives from showing that the particular method one has mastered with so much effort may be indistinguishable from other methods in its effects" (p. 74). The goal of this article is not to outline these shared features but to suggest what needs to be done to work toward integration.

Psychotherapy: Approaching a Crisis

In reviewing the history of various approaches to therapy, it becomes apparent that therapists have typically operated from within a given theoretical framework, often to the point of being completely blind to alternative conceptualizations and potentially effective intervention procedures. Considering the role schools of therapy have played in the development of the field, Raimy (1976) has observed that these schools "undoubtedly contributed to the enthusiasm and the competitive urge to drive therapists to develop their thinking and their techniques, but also imposed limited horizons which clamped their proponents into rigid molds" (p. 225).

Although examples of this are legion, a few may be offered to illustrate the point: Many of Freud's early attempts to introduce psychoanalytic insights and techniques into the profession were initially ignored, if not explicitly rejected, as they did not fit into the generally accepted theoretical framework at the time. Although procedures for progressive relaxation were originally described by Jacobson in 1929, it took nearly 30 years before the therapeutic potential was recognized. At the time it was introduced, it no doubt appeared superficial and mechanistic and did not "fit" with what was deemed to be necessary for effecting therapeutic change. Breger and McGaugh's (1965) criticism of behavior therapy for its exclusive reliance on classical and operant conditioning principles was initially rejected by behavior therapists, although the cogency of their critique is now being acknowledged indirectly by the rapid growth of cognitive behavior therapy. And though intervention procedures for the treatment of sexual dysfunctions were introduced into the literature in the 1950s (Seamans, 1956; Wolpe, 1958), their professional use was not fully explored until Masters and Johnson (1970) presented their suggestions for the direct treatment of sexual difficulties.

Despite our tendency to be suspicious of new ideas, we do eventually process novel information. Within the past several years, an interesting phenomenon seems to be emerging. There appears to be a slight, but clearly growing, trend toward questioning whether or not all the answers may be found within any given school of therapy (e.g., Appelbaum, 1975, 1979; Bergin & Strupp, 1972; Birk & Brinkley-Birk, 1974; Brady, 1968; Burton, 1976; Dewald, 1976; Egan, 1975; Feather & Rhoads, 1972; Ferster, 1974; Frank, 1976; Goldfried & Davison, 1976; Goldstein, 1976; Grinker, 1976; Haley, 1963; Horwitz, 1976; Lazarus, 1977; Lewis, 1972; London, 1972; Marmor, 1971; Martin, 1972; Raimy, 1975, 1976; Ricks, Wandersman, & Poppen, 1976; Segraves & Smith, 1976; Silverman, 1974; Wachtel, 1977). We seem to be entering a period of self-examination, with therapists beginning to ask themselves such questions as, Where does our approach fail? What are the limits of our paradigm? Do other approaches have something useful to offer? One gets the impression that therapists are starting to grow somewhat weary of a strict adherence to their theoretical orientation and are becoming more pragmatic. In recent surveys of clinical psychologists within the United States (Garfield & Kurtz, 1976; Kelly, Goldberg, Fiske, & Kilkowski, 1978), between 55 percent and 58 percent of those professionals contacted indicated that they did not adhere to any single orientation. This eclecticism may have evolved over a period of time or, in some instances, may reflect an integration of different orientations from the outset of their professional training (e.g., Birk, 1971).

Kuhn (1970) has observed that scientific revolutions are typically preceded by a period of "crisis," when well-accepted paradigms simply do not work as well as they did before. Such crises are reflected by the "proliferation of competing articulations, the willingness to try anything, the expression of explicit discontent, the recourse to philosophy and to debate over fundamentals" (p. 91). It appears that just as our patients/clients change their perceptions of the world as a result of corrective experiences, we, their therapists, are now becoming more willing to question our particular paradigm as a result of our own corrective experiences. In some cases this may occur because the therapist is successful with an intervention procedure typically associated with another theoretical orientation. In other instances, such changes appear to be the result of personal therapy with a therapist of a different persuasion.

One may argue that the tendency for therapists to look to other approaches for what they may have to offer is nothing new. Indeed, Fiedler

(1950) found some 30 years ago that greater similarity was to be found among experienced clinicians of different therapeutic schools than among beginning therapists of varying orientations. Presumably, with increased experience—both clinical and through living itself—more points of commonality emerge. These findings confirm what has frequently been observed among practicing clinicians, namely, that there exists a therapeutic "underground," which may never appear in the literature but which nonetheless reflects those informal, if not unspoken, clinical observations on what tends to work (Klein, Dittman, Parloff, & Gill, 1969; Wachtel, 1977). Although this underground may always have been there, we now seem to be at a point in time when clinicians are starting to acknowledge its existence more openly and are beginning to recognize the contributions from orientations other than their own.

Among psychoanalytically oriented therapists are several instances of this open acknowledgment that other theoretical orientations may have something valuable to contribute. For example, Dewald (1976) has stated that efforts need to be made toward rapprochement, suggesting that "the articulation of conceptual generalizations regarding the therapeutic process in different treatment modalities hopefully might initiate more objective and dispassionate comparison of similarities and differences" (p. 284). Silverman (1974) has similarly suggested that his psychoanalytic colleagues look toward nonanalytic intervention approaches, adding, "I am convinced that there is much psychoanalysts can learn from these other approaches that can make (unmodified) psychoanalytic treatment more effective" (p. 305). As the result of findings from the Menninger Foundation Psychotherapy Research Project, Horwitz (1974, 1976) has concluded that supportive therapeutic procedures, involving no uncovering, were just as effective as insight-oriented psychoanalytic therapy. Appelbaum (1979), a former colleague of Horwitz at Menninger, has argued that psychoanalytic therapy can learn much from the intervention procedures used by gestalt therapists. In one of his last papers, Alexander (1963) acknowledged the role of learning theory in the full understanding of the therapeutic process, prophesying "the beginnings of a most promising integration of psychoanalytic theory with learning theory, which may lead to unpredictable advances in the theory and practice of the psychotherapies" (p. 448). And in a recent scholarly evaluation of the clinical and theoretical links between psychoanalysis and behavior therapy, Wachtel (1977) has suggested how the two approaches to intervention may effectively be integrated.

Within behavior therapy one sees some similar self-examination and openness to the views of others. A survey recently conducted among leading behavior therapists, asking them to rate the degree to which they were satisfied with their current understanding of human behavior (Mahoney,

1979), revealed a most noteworthy finding. On the basis of a 7-point rating scale, it was found that the average rating was less than 2! One would certainly never have expected that from reading the behavioral literature. Lazarus (1977), one of the pioneers in the development of behavior therapy, has most recently stated his position as follows:

> I am opposed to the advancement of psychoanalysis, to the advancement of gestalt therapy, to the advancement of existential therapy, to the advancement of behavior therapy, or to the advancement of any delimited school of thought. I would like to see an advancement in psychological knowledge, an advancement in the understanding of human interaction, in the alleviation of suffering, in the know-how of therapeutic intervention [p. 553].

Davison (1978) and Thoresen (1973) have argued for the possible synthesis of behavioral and humanistic approaches to therapy. And Goldfried and Davison (1976) have appealed to their colleagues to seriously consider a rapprochement by suggesting,

> It is time for behavior therapists to stop regarding themselves as an outgroup and instead to enter into serious and hopefully mutually fruitful dialogues with their nonbehavioral colleagues. Just as we firmly believe that there is much that behavior therapy can say to clinicians of other orientations, we reject the assumption that the slate should be wiped clean and that therapeutic innovations should be—and even can be—completely novel [p. 15].

Even among those who are primarily Skinnerian in their behavioral emphasis, one sees efforts to draw on other orientations. Thus Ferster (1974) has argued that behavioral and psychodynamic approaches "are complementary rather than exclusive ways to uncover the actual events of psychopathology and the procedures of therapy" (p. 153). Another example can be found in Baer and Stolz's (1978) recent article in *Behaviorism* on the potential therapeutic effectiveness of *est*.

Among those who are primarily identified with a humanistic orientation, Landsman (1974) has emphasized some of the similarities between humanistic and behaviorally oriented intervention approaches, urging his colleagues to recognize the contribution that behavior therapy may have to offer. He suggests,

> If humanists are truly confident that they have much to offer then they ought to welcome what is being offered by the responsible behaviorists—attention to specifics, to details, careful quantification, modesty in claims, demonstrable results. And even beyond this we welcome its challenge, its role as stimulator to make the dreams of humanistic psychology more of the substance of reality, the spur to demonstrate our promises [p. 15].

Egan has modified his earlier reviews (Egan, 1970, 1973) of the interpersonal growth process by suggesting that there comes a time when the therapist must assist the client in acting differently in the real world (Egan, 1975). The therapist's goal then becomes "collaborating with the client in working out specific action programs; helping the client to act on his new understanding of himself; exploring with the client a wide variety of means for engaging in constructive behavioral change; giving support and direction to action programs" (Egan, 1975, p. 30). Egan goes on to suggest that a useful way of facilitating such direct action is to employ the procedures developed by behavior therapy. In a recent issue of the *Journal of Humanistic Psychology,* the editor acknowledged Lazarus's (1977) call for a rapprochement across various therapeutic orientations and urged the readers of the journal to be open to such attempts (Greening, 1978). It will be recalled that it was none other than Maslow (1966) who warned us against becoming too firmly entrenched within a given perspective, observing, "If the only tool you have is a hammer, [you tend] to treat everything as if it were a nail" (pp. 15–16).

Rapprochement Through Common Clinical Strategies

In considering how one might approach the task of looking for points of commonality among different orientations, it might be helpful to conceptualize the therapeutic enterprise as involving various levels of abstraction from what is directly observable. At the highest level of abstraction we have the *theoretical framework* to explain how and why change takes place, as well as an accompanying *philosophical stance* on the nature of human functioning. In the search for commonalities, it is unlikely that we can ever hope to reach common ground at either the theoretical or the philosophical level. Indeed, numerous differences can be found at this level within the psychoanalytic, behavioral, and humanistic orientations. At the lowest level of abstraction, we have the therapeutic *techniques* or clinical *procedures* that are actually employed during the intervention process. Although commonalities across approaches may be found in the realm of specific techniques (e.g., role playing, relaxation training), it is unlikely that such comparisons would reveal much more than trivial points of similarity. I would suggest, however, that the possibility of finding meaningful consensus exists at a level of abstraction somewhere between theory and technique which, for want of a better term, we might call *clinical strategies*. Were these strategies to have a clear empirical foundation, it might be more appropriate to call them *principles* of change. In essence, such strategies function as clinical heuristics that implicitly guide our efforts during the course of therapy. For illustrative purposes, I would like to offer as examples two such strategies that may very well be common to all theoretical orientations: (1) providing the patient/client with new, corrective experiences, and (2) offering the patient/client direct feedback.

Therapists of varying orientations have suggested that one of the essential ingredients of change in the clinical setting involves having the patient/client engage in new, corrective experiences (e.g., Gill, cited in Silverman, 1979; Grinker, 1976; Korchin, 1976; Marmor, 1976; Prochaska, 1979; Raimy, 1975; Rotter, 1954; Strupp, 1976; Thoresen & Coates, 1978). The role that new experiences play in the clinical change process was initially outlined in Alexander and French's (1946) description of the "corrective emotional experience," which suggested that concurrent life experiences could change patients even without their having had insight into the origins of their problems. Alexander and French emphasized the importance of encouraging their patients to engage in previously avoided actions in order to recognize that their fears and misconceptions about such activities were groundless. They even suggested giving homework assignments to patients so that they would act differently between sessions and facilitate such corrective experiences. In an attempt to justify their more liberal, if not seemingly radical, suggestion, they noted that "Freud himself came to the conclusion that in the treatment of some cases, phobias, for example, a time arrives when the analyst must encourage the patient to engage in those activities he avoided in the past" (Alexander & French, 1946, p. 39). The strategy was noted by Fenichel (1941), who made the following clinical observation:

> When a person is afraid but experiences a situation in which what was feared occurs without any harm resulting, he will not immediately trust the outcome of his new experience; however, the second time he will have a little less fear, the third time still less [p. 83].

In his analysis of how people change, Wheelis (1973) has suggested, "Personality change follows change in behavior. Since we are what we do, if we want to change what we are we must begin by changing what we do, must undertake a new mode of action" (p. 101). This observation has recently been confirmed by Horwitz's (1974, 1976) report of the Menninger Foundation Psychotherapy Research Project's finding that corrective experiences, provided to patients within the context of supportive therapy, resulted in as much long-lasting therapeutic change as did more traditional psychoanalytic psychotherapy.

In the case of behavior therapy, the same clinical strategy has been employed. Although behavior therapists have tended to place greater emphasis on the observable characteristics of the client's novel behavior patterns, rather than the more subjective experiences, they nonetheless en-

courage clients to do things in ways they have not tried before. Kanfer and
Phillips (1966) refer to this as the "instigation" aspect of behavior therapy,
the objective being to encourage the client to respond differently to various
life situations. Clients are taught new ways to deal with various situations
through role playing and are urged to try out these new behavior patterns
as homework assignments (Goldfried & Davison, 1976; Lazarus, 1971;
Wolpe, 1973). Although a variety of different behavior therapy procedures
have been used in reducing clients' fears and phobias, several behavior
therapists have suggested that the overriding clinical strategy involves having clients expose themselves to the feared situation (Agras, 1967; Bandura,
1969; Marks, 1969; Wilson & Davison, 1971). As stated by Bandura (1969),
"Extinction of avoidance behavior is achieved by repeated exposure to
subjectively threatening stimuli under conditions designed to ensure that
neither avoidance responses nor the anticipated adverse consequences occur" (p. 414). This conclusion is clearly consistent with Fenichel's clinical
observations quoted above.

Among humanistically oriented therapists, one sees a similar strong
emphasis on having clients experience change through concerted efforts to
behave differently. Thus Schutz (1973) has indicated that one of the ground
rules of encounter groups involves having clients take risks and attempt to
respond differently: "Whatever you are most afraid of is the thing it is most
valuable to do" (p. 425). A basic underpinning of gestalt therapy involves
the importance of learning through personal experience, going beyond the
mere discussion "about" these experiences (Fagan & Shepherd, 1970;
Polster & Polster, 1973). One of the ways of furthering this learning is
through *directed behavior,* the objective of which is to provide the client
with "the opportunity for relevant practice in behaviors he may be avoiding. Through his own discoveries in trying out these behaviors, he will
uncover aspects of himself which in their turn will generate further self-
discovery" (Polster & Polster, 1973, p. 252).

A second possible clinical strategy that may be common to all therapeutic approaches consists of *direct feedback,* whereby patients/clients are
helped to become more aware of what they are doing and not doing,
thinking and not thinking, and feeling and not feeling in various situations.
One of the first therapists to observe this phenomenon was Reich (1933/
1949), who made the following fortuitous observation:

> What is added in character-analysis is merely that we isolate the character trait
> and confront the patient with it repeatedly until he begins to look at it objec-
> tively and to experience it like a painful symptom; thus, the character trait
> begins to be experienced as a foreign body which the patient wants to get rid
> of. . . . Surprisingly, the process brings about a change—although only a tem-
> porary one—in the personality [p. 50].

Compare this observation with the more recent serendipitous finding by behavior therapists who, in an attempt to use self-monitoring procedures for assessment purposes, noted that their clients changed merely as a result of observing their own behavior. The typical conclusion reached by behavior therapists is that "when an individual begins paying unusually close attention to one aspect of his behavior, that behavior is likely to change even though no change may be intended or desired (McFall, 1970, p. 140). The similarity to the phenomenon that Reich unexpectedly uncovered is striking. In gestalt and encounter approaches to therapeutic change, considerable emphasis is placed on offering the client feedback, either from the therapist or from other group members. Bugental (1965) has suggested that providing feedback to the client is an essential component in enhancing personal awareness. And one of the procedural cornerstones of nondirective therapy (Rogers, 1951) has involved the therapists' attempts to reflect back to clients their thoughts and feelings.

No doubt there are other clinical strategies that may be common to psychoanalytic, behavioral, and humanistic approaches to therapy. I would like to emphasize, however, that my goal was not to outline all possible commonalities. Instead, it was to illustrate the level of abstraction on which we may need to focus in order to achieve such consensus.

Where Do We Go From Here?

In our attempt to study the effectiveness of our therapeutic procedures, we have expended far too much energy investigating techniques that may not be all that powerful clinically. Far too much time and talent have been spent on the detailed and parametric study of trivial issues. The more recent trend toward comparative therapy research, in which one orientation is pitted against another, similarly has its inherent limitations. To the extent that common elements indeed exist across all approaches to therapy, such a research strategy is likely to undermine any differential effectiveness. Further, if there are inert as well as effective procedures associated with each therapeutic approach studied, such comparative research would not seem to be the most efficient way of uncovering effective intervention procedures. As noted by Luborsky, Singer, and Luborsky (1975), "everybody has won and all must have prizes" (p. 1003).

On the other hand, it would be naive to conclude that the delineation of commonalities among different approaches to therapy will in itself result in consensus. A likely, although clearly unfortunate, reaction among some might be to conclude that "we're all doing the same thing" and to return complacently to their usual orientation and set of procedures. To be an eclectic is to have a marginal professional identity. By contrast, an identification with a school of therapy is likely to result in some very powerful economic, political, and social supports. After all, without a specific therapeutic orientation, how would we know what journals to subscribe to or which conventions to attend? Krasner (1978), in a candid analysis of the past and future in the behaviorism—humanism dialogue, commented on the factors that contribute to the continuation of varying schools of thought, noting,

> In effect, each new slogan and label takes on a full and happy life of its own. I write not as a disinterested historian of this game but rather as a participant-observer with as much guilt (or credit depending on your orientation) as anyone else in the controversy between behaviorism and humanism [p. 800].

The popularity of a therapy school is often a function of variables having nothing to do with the efficacy of its associated procedures. Among other things, it depends on the charisma, energy level, and longevity of the leader; the number of students trained and where they have been placed; and the spirit of the times. By contrast, there exist certain "timeless truths," consisting of common observations of how people change. These observations date back to early philosophers and are reflected in great works of literature. As suggested throughout this article, these observations have also been noted by most experienced and sensitive clinicians. *To the extent that clinicians of varying orientations are able to arrive at a common set of strategies, it is likely that what emerges will consist of robust phenomena, as they have managed to survive the distortions imposed by the therapists' varying theoretical biases.* Although it is clear that a systematic and more objective study of the therapeutic change process is needed to advance our body of knowledge, it would be a grievous error to ignore what has been unsystematically observed by many.

I do not mean to imply that these clinical observations will provide us with all the answers but, rather, that they can offer us an important supplement to, if not a starting point for, other research approaches. Basic research on the origin and maintenance of various psychological disorders is clearly needed as well. I would also like to emphasize that I am not arguing against theory per se, but rather against the very strong temptation to engage in premature speculation. We need to have a clearer consensus on the observable phenomena associated with change before we attempt to theorize about them.

It is presumptuous to expect that any one person will be able to outline a set of common clinical strategies. Inasmuch as there exists a gap between theory and practice, any individual from a given orientation can never really be knowledgeable about the therapeutic underground within other orientations. Moreover, the "I-have-the-answers—come-follow-me" message that would accompany any one person's attempt at integration may only serve to put off one's colleagues, or perhaps even end up in the establishment of yet another school of therapy! What is needed instead is a more cooperative effort. Unfortunately this is not easily achieved. The field of therapy—and certainly other disciplines as well—places too much emphasis on the ownership of ideas, such that we are unwilling to consider the merit of certain notions if they come from those we do not consider to be part of our reference group. Though it would be nice to find cooperative efforts naturally occurring among scientists, it is perhaps more realistic to expect their behavior to reflect the competitiveness inherent in our society at large. Noting how the scientist's early desire to forward a common goal often falls by the wayside, David and Brannon (1976) have observed that "many students are originally attracted to science by [the] image of non-competitive sharing, only to find a few years later that they are in a system not unlike the competitive world of business they once disdained" (p. 143).

It will be no easy task to get us to set aside our well-established, if not time-honored, practice of setting one approach against another and, instead, to work toward a rapprochement. What may be needed to get us to mobilize our cooperative efforts is *an attack from outside the system itself*. This clearly was the case during World War II, when scientists found themselves working cooperatively toward common goals. In the case of psychotherapy, there is a strong possibility that the attack from outside may come from questions associated with third-party payments. The pressure from governmental agencies and insurance companies—as well as the growing consumer movement—to have us demonstrate the efficacy of our intervention procedures may very well serve as the necessary impetus for the cooperative effort the field so sorely needs. In a stimulating and challenging account of policymakers' growing interest in the empirical foundations of psychotherapy, Parloff (1979) pointed out that

> members of our new audience are raising very pragmatic, prosaic, yet profound questions regarding the efficacy of the wide range of psychosocial interventions currently offered to the public. Clinicians and government officials are experiencing mounting pressures from such not easily disregarded sources as the courts, insurance companies, and national health insurance planners. Third-party payers—ultimately the public—are demanding crisp and informative answers to questions regarding the quality, quantity, durability, safety, and efficiency of psychosocial treatments provided to an ever-widening range of consumers and potential consumers [p. 297]

My fantasy is that one day we might be able to have a working conference directed toward the goal of developing the field of therapy, not toward the advancement of any given school of thought or of any one individual's career. Parenthetically, it might be noted that Rogers (1963) called for a similar dialogue and search for commonalities some years ago, but the zeitgeist may not have been as hospitable at that time. In the hypothetical conference I am suggesting, the participants would include practicing clinicians of varying theoretical persuasions who would be willing to sit down and outline intervention strategies. Such a dialogue would ultimately need to include the direct observation of what actually occurs during the therapeutic process. These clinicians would not be asked to give up their own particular orientation, but to take steps to work toward some consensus. In breaking set and looking for commonalities, we might even find ourselves more willing to acknowledge the unique contributions that other orientations have to offer. Also present at this conference would be individuals who have been involved in therapy research. Their task would be to guide the discussion in such a way that the strategies outlined can be operationalized and put to empirical test.

It is my hope that the resulting research would address itself to the parametric considerations associated with each potentially robust clinical strategy, as it is not likely that a given strategy would apply to all problems and under all circumstances. This point has been made time and again by therapists of varying persuasions: "*What* treatment, by *whom*, is most effective for *this* individual with *that* specific problem, and under *which* set of circumstances?" (Paul, 1967, p. 111); "The challenging question is not which technique is better than all others, but under what circumstances and for what conditions is the particular technique or particular kind of therapist more suitable than another" (Marmor, 1976, p. 8); and "What kinds of changes are affected by what kinds of techniques applied to what kinds of patients by what kinds of therapists under what kinds of conditions?" (Parloff, 1979, p. 303). Thus, if new, corrective experiences were seen as a common strategy, one would need to investigate the most effective tactic or technique for providing such experiences (e.g., individually, in groups, in imagination, via role playing, face to face), the number and nature of such experiences, the optimal level of emotional arousal needed for change to occur, and the extent to which the particular method of implementing the strategy interacts with other patient/client and therapist variables. On the topic of direct feedback, one might want to study the source of such feedback (e.g., therapist, self, peer, significant other) and how these specific procedures interact with other relevant variables.

Whatever merits there may be to what I have suggested, one needs to be realistic and, again, to recognize that this is by no means an easy path to pursue. Just as patients/clients often find it difficult to develop a new view of the world, so it is difficult for us to relinquish our theoretical paradigms. Kuhn (1970) has documented the reluctance of scientists to undergo a shift in paradigm, noting,

The source of resistance is the assurance that the older paradigm will ultimately solve all its problems, that nature can be shoved into the box the
paradigm provides. Inevitably, at times of revolution, that assurance seems
stubborn and pigheaded as indeed it sometimes becomes [pp. 151–152].

Happily, Kuhn goes on to observe,

Though some scientists, particularly the older and more experienced ones,
may resist indefinitely, most of them can be reached in one way or another.
Conversions will occur a few at a time until, after the last holdouts have died,
the whole profession will again be practicing under a single, but now different
paradigm [p. 152].

Clearly, we need to rewrite our textbooks on psychotherapy. In picking
up the textbook of the future, we should see in the table of contents *not* a
listing of School A, School B, and so on—perhaps ending with the author's
attempt at integration—but an outline of the various agreed-upon intervention principles, a specification of varying techniques for implementing each
principle, and an indication of the relative effectiveness of each of these
techniques together with their interaction with varying presenting problems
and individual differences among patients/clients and therapists. I sense that
the time is rapidly approaching when serious, if not painstaking, work on
gathering the necessary information for such a text can begin.

Summary

There is a growing discontent among therapists of varying orientations.
Psychoanalytic, behavioral, and humanistically oriented clinicians are starting to raise serious questions about the limits of their respective approaches and are becoming more open to contributions from other paradigms. This article documents this trend within the field, which resembles
a Kuhnian-type crisis, noting some of the political, economic, and social
forces apt to affect our likelihood of ever reaching a consensus within the
field and presenting an approach to the delineation and study of commonalities across various orientations.

References

Agras, W. S. Transfer during systematic desensitization therapy. *Behaviour Re-
    search and Therapy*, 1967, 5, 193–199.
Alexander, F. The dynamics of psychotherapy in light of learning theory. *American
    Journal of Psychiatry*, 1963, *120*, 440–448. [Reprinted in this volume.]
Alexander, F., & French, T. M. *Psychoanalytic therapy*. New York: Ronald, 1946.

Appelbaum, S. A. The idealization of insight. *International Journal of Psychoanalytic Psychotherapy*, 1975, *4*, 272–302.

Appelbaum, S. A. *Out in inner space: A psychoanalyst explores the new therapies.* Garden City, N.Y.: Anchor Books, 1979.

Baer, D. M., & Stolz, S. B. A description of the Erhard Seminars Training (*est*) in the terms of behavior analysis. *Behaviorism*, 1978, *6*, 45–70.

Bandura, A. *Principles of behavior modification.* New York: Holt, Rinehart & Winston, 1969.

Bergin, A. E., & Strupp, H. H. *Changing frontiers in the science of psychotherapy.* Chicago: Aldine-Atherton, 1972.

Birk, L. Personal communication, November 15, 1978.

Birk, L., & Brinkley-Birk, A. W. Psychoanalysis and behavior therapy. *American Journal of Psychiatry*, 1974, *131*, 499–510. [Reprinted in this volume.]

Brady, J. P. Psychotherapy by combined behavioral and dynamic approach. *Comprehensive Psychiatry*, 1968, *9*, 536–543. [Reprinted in this volume.]

Breger, L., & McGaugh, J. L. Critique and reformation of "learning theory" approaches to psychotherapy and neurosis. *Psychological Bulletin*, 1965, *63*, 338–358.

Bugental, J. F. T. *The search for authenticity.* New York: Holt, Rinehart & Winston, 1965.

Burton, A. (Ed.). *What makes behavior change possible?* New York: Brunner/Mazel, 1976.

David, D. S., & Brannon, R. (Eds.). *The forty-nine percent majority: The male sex role.* Reading, Mass.: Addison-Wesley, 1976.

Davison, G. C. *Theory and practice in behavior therapy: An unconsummated marriage* (Audio cassette). New York: BMA Audio Cassettes, 1978.

Dewald, P. A. Toward a general concept of the therapeutic process. *International Journal of Psychoanalytic Psychotherapy*, 1976, *5*, 283–299.

Egan, G. *Encounter: Group processes for interpersonal growth.* Monterey, Calif.: Brooks/Cole, 1970.

Egan, G. *Face to face: The small-group experience and interpersonal growth.* Monterey, Calif.: Brooks/Cole, 1973.

Egan, G. *The skilled helper.* Monterey, Calif.: Brooks/Cole, 1975.

Fagan, J., & Shepherd, I. L. (Eds.). *Gestalt therapy now.* Palo Alto, Calif.: Science and Behavior Books, 1970.

Feather, B. W., & Rhoads, J. M. Psychodynamic behavior therapy: Theory and rationale. *Archives of General Psychiatry*, 1972, *26*, 496–502.

Fenichel, O. *Problems of psychoanalytic technique.* Albany, N.Y.: Psychoanalytic Quarterly, 1941.

Ferster, C. B. The difference between behavioral and conventional psychology. *Journal of Nervous and Mental Disease*, 1974, *159*, 153–157.

Fiedler, F. E. A comparison of therapeutic relationships in psychoanalytic, nondirective and Adlerian therapy. *Journal of Consulting Psychology*, 1950, *14*, 436–445.

Frank, J. D. Restoration of morale and behavior change. In A. Burton (Ed.), *What makes behavior change possible?* New York: Brunner/Mazel, 1976.

Garfield, S. L., & Kurtz, R. Clinical psychologists in the 1970s. *American Psychologist*, 1976, *31*, 1–9.

Goldfried, M. R., & Davison, G. C. *Clinical behavior therapy*. New York: Holt, Rinehart & Winston, 1976.

Goldstein, A. Appropriate expression training: Humanistic behavior therapy. In A. Wandersman, P. J. Poppen, & D. F. Ricks (Eds.), *Humanism and behaviorism: Dialogue and growth*. Elmsford, N.Y.: Pergamon Press, 1976.

Greening, T. C. Commentary. *Journal of Humanistic Psychology*, 1978, *18*, 1–4.

Grinker, R. R., Sr. Discussion of Strupp's "Some Critical Comments on the Future of Psychoanalytic Therapy." *Bulletin of the Menninger Clinic*, 1976, *40*, 247–254. [Reprinted in this volume.]

Haley, J. *Strategies of psychotherapy*. New York: Grune & Stratton, 1963.

Horwitz, L. *Clinical prediction in psychotherapy*. New York: Aronson, 1974.

Horwitz, L. New perspectives for psychoanalytic psychotherapy. *Bulletin of the Menninger Clinic*, 1976, *40*, 263–271.

Jacobson, E. *Progressive relaxation*. Chicago: University of Chicago Press, 1929.

Kanfer, F. H., & Phillips, J. S. Behavior therapy: A panacea for all ills or a passing fancy? *Archives of General Psychiatry*, 1966, *15*, 114–128.

Kelly, E. L., Goldberg, L. R., Fiske, D. W., & Kilkowski, J. M. Twenty-five years later: A follow-up study of the graduate students in clinical psychology assessed in the VA selection research project. *American Psychologist*, 1978, *33*, 746–755.

Klein, M., Dittmann, A. T., Parloff, M. B., & Gill, M. M. Behavior therapy: Observations and reflections. *Journal of Consulting and Clinical Psychology*, 1969, *33*, 259–266.

Korchin, S. J. *Modern clinical psychology*. New York: Basic Books, 1976.

Krasner, L. The future and the past in the behaviorism–humanism dialogue. *American Psychologist*, 1978, *33*, 799–804.

Kuhn, T. S. *The structure of scientific revolutions* (2nd ed.). Chicago: University of Chicago Press, 1970.

Landsman, T. *Not an adversity but a welcome diversity*. Paper presented at the meeting of the American Psychological Association, New Orleans, La., August 1974. [Reprinted in this volume.]

Lazarus, A. A. *Behavior therapy and beyond*. New York: McGraw-Hill, 1971.

Lazarus, A. A. Has behavior therapy outlived its usefulness? *American Psychologist*, 1977, *32*, 550–554. [Reprinted in this volume.]

Lewis, W. C. *Why people change*. New York: Holt, Rinehart & Winston, 1972.

London, P. The end of ideology in behavior modification. *American Psychologist*, 1972, *27*, 913–920.

Luborsky, L., Singer, B., & Luborsky, L. Comparative studies of psychotherapies: Is it true that "everybody has won and all must have prizes"? *Archives of General Psychiatry*, 1975, *32*, 995–1008.

Mahoney, M. J. Cognitive and non-cognitive views in behavior modification. In P. O. Sjoden & S. Bates (Eds.), *Trends in behavior therapy*. New York: Plenum Press, 1979.

Marks, I. M. *Fears and phobias*. New York: Academic Press, 1969.

Marmor, J. Dynamic psychotherapy and behavior therapy: Are they irreconcilable? *Archives of General Psychiatry,* 1971, *24,* 22–28. [Reprinted in this volume.]

Marmor, J. Common operational factors in diverse approaches to behavior change. In A. Burton (Ed.), *What makes behavior change possible?* New York: Brunner/Mazel, 1976.

Martin, D. G. *Learning-based client-centered therapy.* Monterey, Calif.: Brooks/Cole, 1972.

Maslow, A. H. *The psychology of science: A reconnaissance.* New York: Harper & Row, 1966. [A selection reprinted in this volume.]

Masters, W. H., & Johnson, V. E. *Human sexual inadequacy.* Boston: Little, Brown, 1970.

McFall, R. M. Effects of self-monitoring on normal smoking behavior. *Journal of Consulting and Clinical Psychology,* 1970, *35,* 135–142.

Parloff, M. B. Shopping for the right therapy. *Saturday Review,* February 21, 1976, pp. 14–16.

Parloff, M. B. Can psychotherapy research guide the policymaker? A little knowledge may be a dangerous thing. *American Psychologist,* 1979, *34,* 296–306. [Reprinted in this volume.]

Paul, G. L. Strategy of outcome research in psychotherapy. *Journal of Consulting Psychology,* 1967, *31,* 109–119.

Polster, E., & Polster, M. *Gestalt therapy integrated.* New York: Brunner/Mazel, 1973.

Prochaska, J. O. *Systems of psychotherapy: A transtheoretical analysis.* Homewood, Ill.: Dorsey Press, 1979.

Raimy, V. *Misunderstandings of the self.* San Francisco: Jossey-Bass, 1975.

Raimy, V. Changing misconceptions as the therapeutic task. In A. Burton (Ed.), *What makes behavior change possible?* New York: Brunner/Mazel, 1976.

Reich, W. *Character analysis* (T. P. Wolfe, Trans.). New York: Orgone Institute Press, 1949. (Originally published, 1933.)

Ricks, D. F., Wandersman, A., & Poppen, P. J. Humanism and behaviorism: Toward new syntheses. In A. Wandersman, P. J. Poppen, & D. F. Ricks (Eds.), *Humanism and behaviorism: Dialogue and growth.* Elmsford, N.Y.: Pergamon Press, 1976. [Reprinted in this volume.]

Rogers, C. R. *Client-centered therapy.* Boston: Houghton Mifflin, 1951.

Rogers, C. R. Psychotherapy today or where do we go from here? *American Journal of Psychotherapy,* 1963, *17,* 5–15.

Rotter, J. B. *Social learning and clinical psychology.* Englewood Cliffs, N.J.: Prentice-Hall, 1954.

Schutz, W. C. Encounter. In R. Corsini (Ed.), *Current psychotherapies.* Itasca, Ill.: Peacock, 1973.

Seamans, J. H. Premature ejaculation: A new approach. *Southern Medical Journal,* 1956, *49,* 353–357.

Segraves, R. T., & Smith, R. C. Concurrent psychotherapy and behavior therapy. *Archives of General Psychiatry,* 1976, *33,* 256–263.

Silverman, L. H. Some psychoanalytic considerations of non-psychoanalytic therapies: On the possibility of integrating treatment approaches and related issues. *Psychotherapy: Theory, Research and Practice,* 1974, *11,* 298–305.

Silverman, L. H. The unconscious fantasy as therapeutic agent in psychoanalytic treatment. *Journal of the American Academy of Psychoanalysis,* 1979, *1,* 189–218.

Strupp, H. H. The nature of the therapeutic influence and its basic ingredients. In A. Burton (Ed.), *What makes behavior change possible?* New York: Brunner/Mazel, 1976.

Thoresen, C. E. Behavioral humanism. In C. E. Thoresen (Ed.), *Behavior modification in education.* Chicago: University of Chicago Press, 1973.

Thoresen, C. E., & Coates, T. J. What does it mean to be a behavior therapist? *Counseling Psychologist,* 1978, *7,* 3–21.

Wachtel, P. L. *Psychoanalysis and behavior therapy.* New York: Basic Books, 1977.

Wheelis, A. *How people change.* New York: Harper & Row, 1973.

Wilson, G. T., & Davison, G. C. Processes of fear reduction in systematic desensitization: Animal studies. *Psychological Bulletin,* 1971, *76,* 1–14.

Wolpe, J. *Psychotherapy by reciprocal inhibition.* Stanford, Calif.: Stanford University Press, 1958.

Wolpe, J. *The practice of behavior therapy* (2nd ed.). New York: Pergamon Press, 1973.

Subject Index

Abreaction, 116, 148, 286
Accountability, 26–28, 39, 41, 277, 279, 291–308, 387
Affect, 153, 158, 183, 202, 204, 234, 249; *see also* Emotion in therapy
Aggression, 254, 258
Alcoholics Anonymous, 298
Alcoholism, 298, 300
Anorexia nervosa, 346
Anxiety
  anticipatory, 212
  client/patient, 62, 181, 205, 208, 211–212, 241, 243, 249, 285, 301, 354, 360
  control of, 199, 361
  exposure to fearful stimuli, 240
  learning theory perspective, 9, 100
  relaxation responses, 198, 244
  separation, 300, 360
  treatment, 201, 213, 240, 257–258, 300, 324
  variable in research, 139
Assertiveness training, 229, 240, 254, 257
Assessment, 26, 109, 348, 370–371
Assimilation and accommodation, 36
Attitudes
  role in research, 357
  in therapy, 116–117, 181, 324
Autism, 299–300
Aversion therapy, 102, 197, 199–201, 347
Awareness, 8, 21, 158, 166, 168, 176–183, 186, 189, 221, 251–252, 346, 359–360, 384–385; *see also* Consciousness; Self-awareness

Behavior
  analysis of, 230, 238, 254
  change, 21, 162, 164, 174, 177–182, 188, 208, 213, 222–231, 240, 249, 348, 352, 355–356, 382, 385
  cognitions, role of, 18, 21, 37, 100, 162, 164, 174, 177–181, 229–230, 347–348, 356, 362–363, 385
Behavioral observation, 100, 220, 223–224, 234, 277, 362, 385
Behavioral responses, 75, 228
  maladaptive, 82, 84, 202, 223–224, 228–229, 234, 238, 242, 275, 353, 356
Behaviorism, characteristics of, 13, 97, 99, 101, 103, 247–256, 267, 270, 272, 276–277
Behavior rehearsal, *see* Role-playing
Behavior therapy
  contributions, 102–103, 261, 277, 295, 358, 362
  description, 22, 275–276
  emphases, 97, 213, 219, 221, 234, 238, 275–276, 383, 384
  goals of, 226, 229
  limitations, 12–13, 29–30, 98, 225, 254, 267–270
  principles of, 100, 204–205, 240
  scope of influence, 107
  target symptoms, 204, 223, 238, 241, 282, 299–300, 358
Bibliotherapy, 16
Bioenergetics, 286

Biofeedback, 107, 152, 166, 299
Brief psychotherapy, 89, 112, 115, 195, 217, 244–245, 284

Catharsis, 55, 57, 60, 137, 148, 204–205
Chemotherapy, 114, 204, 242, 244–245, 298–302, 321–322, 361
Clarification, 16, 116, 221, 227
Client-centered therapy, 35, 37, 275–276, 295
Cognitions, 352–363; *see also* Learning, cognitive
  change, 184, 187–189, 204, 230, 348, 352–353, 356–367
  cognitive processes, 35, 59, 74–75, 100–101, 103, 197, 205, 220, 248, 338–339, 346, 356, 359, 365, 369
  cognitive restructuring, 18, 227, 347–348, 356, 360–362, 370; *see also* Rational-emotive therapy
  cognitive styles, 339, 357, 371
  covert processes, 97, 101, 219–220, 233
  development in childhood, 255, 341–342
  distortions, 16, 20, 161–162, 167, 174, 179–180, 182, 187, 197, 202, 204, 218, 224–225, 228–229, 354, 360
  emphasis in therapy, 18, 20–21, 66, 161–162, 176–182, 187, 219, 248–249, 257
  implicit assumptions, 35, 221, 335
  symbolic processes, 100, 168, 197, 342
Cognitive psychology, *see* Experimental cognitive psychology
Communication
  and context, 369, 371
  in therapy, 187
  training, 23
Communications theory, 101
Conflict, 58–59, 66, 69, 81–82, 116, 147, 170, 194, 196–197, 207–209, 213, 218–219, 221, 228, 232, 242–243, 258, 344, 354, 363
  theory of psychosis, 115, 163, 238
Confrontation, 16, 167, 177, 182, 189, 276
Consciousness, 8, 21, 35, 54, 62, 65, 67, 72, 102, 145, 150–152, 164–166, 180, 200, 202, 217–220, 226, 257, 339–340, 363
Coping, 85, 151, 158, 160, 176, 178, 255, 258, 360
Corrective experiences, 10, 17, 22, 66–67, 74, 116–117, 137, 146, 153, 157–163, 164, 168–169, 175, 179–181, 186, 189, 202–204, 219, 314, 375, 379, 383–384, 388
Countertransference, 70–71, 73, 200, 210–211, 232
Cues, 62, 204, 257, 346, 356, 360, 368
Cultural aspects of psychological problems, 81–83

Defenses, 116, 197, 213, 344, 360
Denial, 117, 343–344
Depression, 24, 26, 227, 249, 257, 282, 298–299, 301, 357, 361
Desensitization, 139–140, 201, 225, 257–258, 299; *see also* Systematic desensitization
Displacement, 9, 239, 342
Dreams, 118, 168, 218–219, 234, 342, 357

Sibling rivalry, 69
Social learning theory, 98, 162, 181, 188, 248, 347
Social skills, 180, 212, 259, 298
Social support, 60
Socratic method, 61
Special treatment and rehabilitative training
    (START), 267–268, 272
Spontaneity, 251, 253, 257, 284
Spontaneous remission, 294–295, 300, 308, 332
Stress, 68–69, 81–84, 241–242, 258,
    288
    vulnerability to, 258
Sublimination, 6, 343
Suicide, 257, 268
Superego, 116, 147, 343, 345
Supportive therapy, 21, 116, 158, 185, 197, 240,
    302
Symptoms, 194–195, 201, 203–204, 213, 223, 238,
    241, 253–254, 263, 362
Systematic desensitization, 139–140, 157, 183,
    198, 212, 219, 223, 238, 242, 244–245, 299,
    361; *see also* Desensitization
Systems theory, 98, 201, 254–255, 257, 259, 262–
    263

Tension resolution, 59, 75–76, 204
Theory, role and function, 108
Token economies, 251
Transactional analysis, 177
Transference
    characteristics of, 203
    neurosis, 66, 116, 148, 158, 210, 219, 232
    in nonpsychodynamic therapies, 198–201, 216,
        231–232, 239, 345
    in psychodynamic therapy, 65, 67, 70, 72–73,
        108, 117–118, 148, 158, 163, 211, 228
    research, 73, 116, 260
    therapeutic utility, 68, 72, 149, 158, 163, 218,
        232
    therapist's understanding of, 71
Trauma, 68, 163, 171, 196, 213, 228

Unconsciousness, 8, 35, 54, 62–63, 65–66, 70, 72,
    116, 145, 150–151, 164, 180, 202, 207, 213, 217–
    220, 225, 229–233, 341–342, 357, 359, 363

Values, 78, 84, 158, 197–199, 224, 249

Working through, 18, 223, 276

Name Index

Wolf, M. M., 216, 220
Wolfe, B. E., 294, 297
Wolff, H. H., 241
Wolpe, J., 12–13, 88–89, 99–101, 113, 197–199,
    205, 220, 238–240, 244, 250, 253–254, 270,
    325, 379, 384
Wolpin, M., 136, 139
Woods, S. M., 3, 12, 20
Woodworth, R. S., 101
Woody, R. H., 3, 20

Yalom, I. D., 282, 287, 289
Yarrow, M. R., 82
Yorkston, N. J., 112, 216, 282, 295, 297, 337

Zener, K., 101
Zilboorg, G., 7
Zubin, J. A., 88, 322